ACQUIRING COUNSELING SKILLS

ACQUIRING COUNSELING SKILLS

INTEGRATING THEORY, MULTICULTURALISM, AND SELF-AWARENESS

Kathryn MacCluskie

Cleveland State University

Pearson/Merrill

Upper Saddle River, New Jersey
Columbus, Ohio

Library of Congress Cataloging-in-Publication Data
MacCluskie, Kathryn C.
  Acquiring counseling skills : integrating theory, multiculturalism, and self-awareness / Kathryn MacCluskie.
    p. cm.
  ISBN-13: 978-0-13-199133-0
  ISBN-10: 0-13-199133-7
 1. Counseling. 2. Counseling psychology. I. Title.
  BF636.6.M34 2010
  158'.3—dc22

                                              2008055874

Vice President and Editor in Chief: Jeffery W. Johnston
Acquisitions Editor: Meredith D. Fossel
Editorial Assistant: Nancy Holstein
Vice President, Director of Sales and Marketing: Quinn Perkson
Senior Marketing Manager: Darcy Betts Prybella
Marketing Coordinator: Brian Mounts
Senior Managing Editor: Pamela D. Bennett
Senior Project Manager: Mary M. Irvin
Senior Operations Supervisor: Matt Ottenweller
Senior Art Director: Diane Lorenzo
Cover Designer: Candace Rowley
Cover Art: SuperStock
Full-Service Project Management: Mohinder Singh/Aptara®, Inc.
Composition: Aptara®, Inc.
Printer/Binder: King Printing Co., Inc.
Cover Printer: King Printing Co., Inc.

This book was set in 10/12 Garamond by Aptara®, Inc. and was printed and bound by King Printing Co., Inc.
The cover was printed by King Printing Co., Inc.

Every effort has been made to provide accurate and current Internet information in this book. However, the Internet and information posted on it are constantly changing, so it is inevitable that some of the Internet addresses listed in this textbook will change.

Merrill
is an imprint of

www.pearsonhighered.com

4 5 6 7 8 9 10 V0CR 16 15 14 13
        ISBN-10:   0-13-199133-7
        ISBN-13: 978-0-13-199133-0

*This book is dedicated to the students whose aspirations
are to help and serve others.* Namaste.

ABOUT THE AUTHOR

 **Kathryn MacCluskie** is an Associate Professor of Counselor Education at Cleveland State University. She completed her undergraduate work and Masters in Rehabilitation Counseling at Edinboro University of Pennsylvania. Following several years working with youth in residential treatment, she earned an Ed.D. in Counseling Psychology from West Virginia University. Dr. MacCluskie served as the Drug and Alcohol Program Coordinator at Morgantown Federal Correctional Institution, and then worked as a therapist in a community mental health center. She joined the faculty at Cleveland State in 1994, and in addition to leading the Counselor Education section, also served as Chair of the Institutional Review Board for Human Subjects. Her professional interests lie in counseling student growth and development, and the interface between mental health and global sustainability.

PREFACE

This book's title identifies microskills, theory, multiculturalism, and self-awareness as themes of the text. Microskills, counseling theory, and multiculturalism comprise objective information. Yet, we know from learning theory that to a certain extent, learners' acquisition of new material is modulated by personal characteristics, including learning style and learning history. We also know that the extent to which a learner can assimilate new information is related to the personal meaning the learner imbues in the new information. If the learner finds the material to be personally relevant and can find ways to associate the new material with the knowledge and experiences that already exist in the memory network, integration and synthesis will be more efficiently and effectively achieved.

Each strand (theory, multiculturalism, and self-awareness) represents a domain of theoretical and applied knowledge. Many counseling programs offer entire courses devoted to each of those topics. Multiculturalism is a topic that is currently prominent, not only in the field of counseling, but in many other academic disciplines as well. Textbooks on multiculturalism and diversity in counseling often take the approach of reviewing the research findings about preferences and outcomes of counseling among particular groups of people. Although this information can be highly relevant, there is little in the way of practical information about how to understand and communicate about differences in values and worldviews among clients who differ from the counselor on key variables. Conceptualizing a client's characteristics, strengths, and challenges on the basis of his or her ethnicity or other variables of diversity is simultaneously necessary, yet also potentially minimizing and prescriptive. To assume that a client of a particular ethnic descent will require a particular counseling strategy is to neglect the characteristics that make that person an individual. Our field is lacking an approach that offers a template for understanding cultural differences.

Due to the lack of a research-based template for cross cultural interaction in counseling sessions, I selected a model with a high degree of relevance to counseling; the Hofstede model of cultural values. I chose to use it as the underpinning for the multicultural strand of the text because although in counseling there are multiple theoretical models for understanding cultures, Hofstede's model is firmly established *empirically*. The model of cultural values consists of five continua (axes) that comprise essential, universal features of all cultures. The anchor points of each axis are explicitly defined. These axes of values can be applied to enhance interpersonal understanding regardless of the cultural framework from which the viewer, and the observed, originate. As stated, the model arose out of a need for enhanced interpersonal communication in the business realm. Thus, it has obvious limitations when we attempt to apply it to a counseling context—namely, that the efficacy of the Hofstede model in counseling has never been investigated.

Nevertheless, there were many advantages of presenting such a versatile template of cultural differences. Those advantages are

- universal applicability due to the extensive empirical foundation for the model
- relative simplicity of the model
- removal of the need to have specific, particular information about cultural characteristics that is necessary in a prescriptive approach to cross-cultural counseling

From a teaching perspective, desiring to provide students with specific skills that can be used with versatility, the advantages significantly outweighed the disadvantage of lacking empirical evidence justifying use of the Hofstede model specifically in counseling. In the absence of any other template for cultural differences that had been researched specifically for counseling, the Hofstede model offers an acceptable compromise, at least until a better-suited template is articulated and empirically established. Although this model has not been validated for applicability to counseling, it nevertheless can provide a platform to stimulate critical thought for readers, opportunity for discussions in class, and offer pertinent insights into counseling diverse populations.

The self-awareness component of this text thus serves two purposes. One is to specifically draw upon the natural tendency readers will have to associate the objective material with their prior learning. The other purpose is to introduce and encourage self-reflection and introspection early in readers' training as mental health professionals.

CHAPTER STRUCTURE AND SEQUENCE

The decision about the best sequence for the chapters was a difficult one. Early versions of this draft placed the theories at the beginning of the book. From the perspective of conceptual development, it seemed advisable to present a thorough discussion of counseling theory prior to talking about how each microskill is applied within the context of a given theory framework. However, most students are very eager to begin practicing counseling skills, and the theories chapter is long and one of the most dense. The final choice was to move the theories to the latter section of the book and construct the chapter structure such that other than the microskills chapters, readings could be assigned in any sequence. Those instructors choosing to cover theories prior to the skill chapters should be able to do so without compromising the sense of continuity among the other chapters.

CHAPTER FEATURES

The beginning of every chapter includes bulleted items articulating the learning objectives for that chapter. Each chapter also provides questions for classroom discussion at the conclusion.

Personal Reflection items throughout the text directly ask readers to self-reflect. Instructors have the option of further capitalizing on the Personal Reflections by having students keep process journals, or by putting students into small discussion groups to share their thoughts about their personal reflections.

Each chapter also provides Author's Reflection components; these are anecdotes from the author's personal and professional experiences. There are several rationales for including this feature. One is to model for students the process of self-awareness and the integration of theoretical material with personal meaning. Another is to give the author an opportunity to share her voice with readers in an overt manner. Finally, the personal experiences serve to illustrate or emphasize particular points.

MICROSKILL CHAPTERS

The microskill chapters offer some unique components that are consistent throughout all six of the skills. The material in the skill chapters offers several things:

- An explanation of that microskill in the context of cultural variables, through the lens of the Hofstede model of cultural variability

- Information about how to access video examples of that skill actually being applied
- A discussion of the microskill in the context of three broad theoretical approaches
- A dialogue example of that microskill as it would be implemented with two clients, an adult named Carole and a boy named Derek, who are the case study clients throughout the text

(Note: I omitted a dialogue sequence in the client observation chapter because observation is, by definition, visual and does not easily lend itself to a dialogue transcription.) Each microskill chapter concludes with a dialogue with Carole or Derek that is intended to represent a progression of counseling sessions over a period of time. Then, Chapter 15 provides a culminating experience in which aspects of intakes, aspects of diversity, and aspects of counseling theory are all integrated in the development of treatment plans for each of the two clients.

MYHELPINGLAB VIDEO EXAMPLES

Numerous chapters indicate places where watching a video example can enrich readers' understanding of the skill or topic under discussion. These places are designated with an offset box labeled MyHelpingLab. MyHelpingLab is a companion website provided by the publisher that offers readers a variety of supplemental materials, including over 200 video clips of real counseling sessions. The video examples can be viewed by registering and then logging in to the website: www.myhelpinglab.com.

To give your students access to MyHelpingLab with this book for no additional charge, order package ISBN 0-13-508236-6. If your students purchase a used book without an access code, they can go to www.myhelpinglab.com to purchase access to this wonderful resource. Once registered, click on the link "Counseling and Psychotherapy." That will take you to a page with other links listed down the left side, one of which is "Video Lab." The counseling videos are organized by theoretical approach, and also are alternatively organized by course. You can access clips from the video lab either by course or by theoretical approach. For each spot in a chapter where you are directed to a video clip, the sequence of links you need to follow is specified.

'Please note that you might find it quite helpful to explore some of the other video examples in addition to the specific clips to which you were directed for this text. Many highly skilled therapists were recorded working with real clients with actual concerns. You may note significant differences in styles across different therapists, which can be enlightening to newcomers to this field.

ACKNOWLEDGMENTS

There are so many people whose support and help made it possible for me to complete this project. My editor, Meredith Fossel, has been phenomenal in her wisdom, guidance, encouragement, and professionalism. She helped me maintain a balance between seeing the big picture and managing the details to make it all come together into a coherent whole. Her expertise, wisdom, and understanding are what ultimately brought this project to fruition.

I would like to thank the reviewers of this text: Pamelia E. Brott, Virginia Tech; Scott E. Hall, University of Dayton; Ed Jacobs, West Virginia University; Bette Katsekas, University of Southern Maine; Debra Leggett, Indiana State University; Allen J. Ottens, Northern Illinois

University; Thomas Russo, University of Washington, River Falls and Walden University; and Robbie Jean Steward, Michigan State University. Several of these individuals spent a great deal of time considering and sharing feedback about how to make the project better. I am very grateful to them. Their suggestions significantly enhanced and strengthened the book.

Also, on a professional level, I am continually grateful to my students. They also read drafts and took their time to offer honest feedback. Beyond this particular book, in each course, they teach me at least as much if not more than I teach them.

In the personal realm, when one takes on such a big project, it necessarily involves one's partner, children, and other significant relationships. There are a finite number of minutes in a day, and writing a book often means choosing to spend time in front of the computer rather than with loved ones.

My husband David is my soul mate. He read (suffered through) multiple drafts and spent countless hours editing. He offered his insight, which has been and always will be invaluable to me. He has been so patient and willing to arrange his schedule to accommodate mine. There were countless evenings and weekends that he "fielded" the kids and the housework so I could write, and I appreciate that! His love and encouragement hold me up always; he truly is the wind beneath my wings.

The most diminutive (and so very precious) individuals who helped me get this project completed have been my sons, Davey and Alex. They pitched in on the housework and meal prep. To them, probably the biggest sacrifice was their ability to spontaneously express themselves, loudly and frequently, through their music. They were very conscientious about being quiet when my office door was shut. I often heard them say to their friends on the phone, "You can't come over, I have to come to your house 'cuz my mom's working on her book." They are probably the happiest of everyone that this book is done so that they can jam to their hearts' content and they no longer need to respectfully request a scheduled time for my undivided attention. Thanks, boys, for your patience—I love you so much!

BRIEF CONTENTS

Preface   *vii*

Chapter 1   Counseling Skills and You   1

Chapter 2   Multiculturalism and Diversity in Counseling   16

Chapter 3   The Microskills Model   40

Chapter 4   Attending Behaviors   51

Chapter 5   Client Observation   68

Chapter 6   Silence, Minimal Encouragers, Paraphrasing, and Summarizing   81

Chapter 7   Questioning   101

Chapter 8   Feeling Reflection   118

Chapter 9   Reflection of Meaning   140

Chapter 10   Confrontation   162

Chapter 11   Counseling Theories   181

Chapter 12   The Counseling Process   206

Chapter 13   Intake Interviews and Initial Assessment   224

Chapter 14   Empirically Supported Techniques and Common Psychotherapeutic Factors   244

Chapter 15   Integrated Case Conceptualization   262

Chapter 16   Self-Awareness and Self-Care   279

Appendix   *ACA Code of Ethics   293*

Reference List   313

Index   325

CONTENTS

Preface   vii

Chapter 1   Counseling Skills and You   1

Self-Awareness   2

*The Relationship Between Your Behavior
and How Others Respond to You   2*

The Impact of Life Experiences   3

Desire to Be of Service   4

The Role of Religion and Spirituality   4

Personal Pain as a Catalyst for Growth   5

Awareness of Cognitive Frames   5

Emotional Strengths and Liabilities   6

High and Low Self-Monitors   6

Sources of Satisfaction   7

Congruence   7

Participating in Personal Counseling   7

Resolution of Incongruence   8

Insight About Choices   8

Experience of the Power Differential   8

Resistance to Change   8

The Role of Theory in Counseling   9

Multiculturalism   10

Common Cultural Frames versus Stereotypes   10

Ethical Standards   11

*Chapter Summary   15   •   Questions for Class Discussion   15
•   Beginning Assignment   15*

**Chapter 2   Multiculturalism and Diversity
in Counseling   16**

Definitions of Terms   18

Culture   18

Multiculturalism   19

Diversity   19

Ethnocentrism   20

Historical Context of the Multicultural Movement   21

Immigration Policy in the United States   21

Multiculturalism in the Professions of Counseling and Psychology 22

Ecocultural Models of Human Functioning   24

Berry's Ecocultural Framework 24

Bronfenbrenner's Ecological Model 25

Sue and Sue's Model of Multiculturalism   26

Hofstede's Model of Cultural Differences   27

How Hofstede's Model Developed 28

Racial Identity Development and Acculturation 36

Implications of the Multicultural Material for Counseling Students 36

Chapter Summary 38 • Questions for Class Discussion 39

Chapter 3   The Microskills Model   40

Historical Context   41

Human Resource Development Model 42

Interpersonal Process Recall 42

The Microskills Model   43

Advantages of the Microskills Model 44

Limitations of the Microskills Model 46

Microskills in the Context of Counseling Process and Outcome 47

Extratherapeutic Factors 47

Client-Counselor Relationship 47

Hope 48

Therapeutic Technique 48

Other Considerations in Microskill Application   49

Cultural and Social Forces 49

Chapter Summary 49 • Questions for Class Discussion 50

Chapter 4   Attending Behaviors   51

Components of Attending   52

Eye Contact 53

Body Posture and Orientation   55

Open Posture 55

Leaning In 56

Room Arrangement 57

Chairs 59

Lighting   59

Verbal Behavior (Following the Client's Lead)   60

Multicultural Aspects of Attending   62

Attending in the Context of Three Theoretical Stances   63

Humanistic   63

Developmental   64

Cognitive-Behavioral   64
  Chapter Summary   66   •   Case Studies for Discussion   66
    •   Questions for Class Discussion   66

Chapter 5   Client Observation   68

The Role of Careful Observation   69

Four Observable Elements of Client Behavior   69

How Expectations Affect Our Perceptions   70

Nonverbal Behavior   70

Paraverbal Behavior   71

Verbal Behavior   72

*Congruence Among Nonverbal, Paraverbal,
  and Verbal Behaviors   75*

Silence   76

Client Observation in the Context of Three Theoretical Stances   77

Multicultural Aspects of Client Observation   77
  Chapter Summary   80   •   Questions for Class Discussion   80

**Chapter 6   Silence, Minimal Encouragers, Paraphrasing,
and Summarizing   81**

Silence   82

Multicultural Aspects of Silence   84

Silence in the Context of Three Theoretical Stances   84

Other Considerations in Silence   85

Minimal Encouragers   85

Intentional Withholding of Minimal Encouragers   86

Key Word Repetition and Restatement   87

Key Word Repetition   87

Restatement   87

Paraphrasing   88

Multicultural Aspects of Paraphrasing   91

Paraphrasing in the Context of Three Theoretical Stances   93

Summarizing   94

  Enumerating Possible Topics   95

  Beginning and Ending Sessions with Summaries   96

  Cultural Considerations in Summarizing   97

  Summarizing in the Context of Three Theoretical Approaches   97

  Chapter Summary   97   •   Questions for Class Discussion   98
      •   Case Studies for Discussion   98

Chapter 7   Questioning   101

Appropriate Use of Questions   101

  Open and Closed Questions   102

  Mechanical Aspects of Questioning   103

  Dialogue Examples of How to Achieve Specific Purposes   106

  Client Resistance   110

  Implied Problem Solution   111

  Imbalance of Power   111

  Cultural Considerations in Questioning   111

  Questioning in the Context of Three Theoretical Stances   112

  Chapter Summary   114   •   Questions for Class Discussion   114
      •   Case Studies for Discussion   114

Chapter 8   Feeling Reflection   118

Mechanical Aspects of Feeling Reflection   120

  Feeling Reflection Mechanics   121

  Accurate Feeling Reflection   124

Emotion Theory   126

  Universalist Model of Emotion   126

  Relativistic Model of Emotion   126

  Ekman's Neurocultural Theory of Emotion   127

  The Integration of Emotion Theory and Empathy   128

The Importance of Feelings   129

  Fear of Loss of Control   129

  Difficulty Verbalizing Emotional Experiences   130

  Complexity or Intensity of Ambivalent Feelings   130

Counselor Power and Responsibility   131

What Not to Do   131

Say, "You Shouldn't Feel That Way"   *131*

Ask, "Do You Feel _____?"   *132*

Ask, "What Did _____ Feel?"   *132*

Repeatedly Ask, "How Did That Feel?"   *133*

Confuse Thoughts and Feelings   *134*

Cultural Considerations in Feeling Reflection   134

Power Distance   *134*

Gender Roles   *134*

Affiliation   *135*

Uncertainty Avoidance   *135*

Feeling Reflection in the Context of Three Theoretical Stances   135

Humanistic   *135*

Developmental   *135*

Cognitive-Behavioral   *136*

Chapter Summary   *136*   •   Questions for Class Discussion   *136*   •   Case Studies for Discussion   *137*

Chapter 9   **Reflection of Meaning**   **140**

The Personal Nature of Meaning Making   141

Aspects of Individual Difference in Meaning Making   141

Spirituality   *142*

Level of Cognitive Functioning   *143*

Level of Emotional and Psychosocial Maturity   *144*

Trauma   *144*

Resilience   *147*

Cultural Considerations in Reflecting Meaning   147

Power Distance   *147*

Masculinity/Femininity   *147*

Affiliation   *149*

Uncertainty Avoidance   *150*

Reflecting Meaning in the Context of Three Theoretical Stances   151

Humanistic   *152*

Developmental   *153*

Cognitive-Behavioral   *155*

Chapter Summary   *158*   •   Questions for Class Discussion   *159*   •   Case Studies for Discussion   *159*

Chapter 10   Confrontation   162

Skill Definition: What, Why, and How   162

Why Counselors Use Confrontation   163

How to Effectively Confront a Client   164

Timing   165

Carrying Out the Confrontation   168

How You Respond to Your Client's Response   172

Immediacy   172

Cultural Considerations in Challenging   175

Power Distance   175

Gender Roles   175

Affiliation   176

Uncertainty Avoidance   176

Confrontation in the Context of Three Theoretical Stances   176

Humanistic   176

Developmental   177

Cognitive-Behavioral   177

Chapter Summary   177   •   Questions for Class Discussion   178
•   Case Studies for Discussion   178

Chapter 11   Counseling Theories   181

Introduction   181

The Relationship Between Theory and Microskills   182

Three Schools of Counseling and Therapy   183

Developmental Models   183

Adlerian Theory   185

Erikson's Psychosocial Development Theory   187

Attachment Theory   188

Humanistic Models   190

Client-Centered Counseling   190

Existentialism   193

Gestalt   194

Cognitive-Behavioral Models   196

Behavior Theory   197

Cognitive Theory   198

Cognitive-Behavioral Theory   199

Interplay of Multicultural Issues and Theories   201

Current Trends in Theory Development   202

*Integration of Traditional Theories with
Hofstede's Model   203*

Chapter Summary   203   •   Case Studies for Discussion   204
•   Questions for Class Discussion   205

Chapter 12   The Counseling Process   206

Introduction   206

Counseling Process and Counseling Outcome   206

Typical Stage of the Counseling Process   207

Process Across the Course of Counseling   210

Situational Factors That Influence Process   214

Self-Disclosure   219

Multicultural Considerations in Self-Disclosure   221

Chapter Summary   222   •   Questions for Class Discussion   223

Chapter 13   Intake Interviews and Initial Assessment   224

Assessment   225

Precipitating Events   226

Multicultural Considerations   226

Organic or Medical Conditions   226

Inconsistent Reports Between People   229

Personality Style and Typicality   229

Precipitants That Constitute Crises   230

Current Impairment   230

Subjective Distress   230

Impairment in Daily Functioning   231

Intake Interviews   232

Assessment of Suicide Risk   233

Assessment of Violence Risk   235

Threshold for Violence   237

Therapeutic Alliance   237

Diagnosis   237

DSM-IV-TR Multiaxial Diagnosis   238

The Sociopolitical Nature of Diagnosis   239

Errors in Clinical Judgment   240

Treatment Planning   242

Chapter Summary   242   •   Questions for Class Discussion   243

Chapter 14   **Empirically Supported Techniques and Common Psychotherapeutic Factors   244**

Empirically Supported Techniques   245

Historical Antecedents of the EST Movement   245

Strengths of the EST Approach to Treating Clients   247

Criticisms of the EST Approach   248

Common Psychotherapeutic Factors   250

Saul Rozenzweig   250

Hans Strupp   251

Strengths of the Common Factors Approach   254

Criticisms of the Common Factors Approach   255

Summary of ESTs and Common Factors   255

The Process of Change   256

Systematic Treatment Selection   256

The Readiness for Change Model   257

Recommendations for New Counselors   260

Chapter Summary   261   •   Questions for Class Discussion   261

Chapter 15   **Integrated Case Conceptualization   262**

The Case of Carole   263

Individual Assessment/Intake Information   263

Carole's Value Preferences (Hofstede's Cultural Axes)   265

Carole's Spheres of Influence in the Ecological Model   266

Diagnostic Impression and Readiness for Change   267

Treatment Plan   267

Carole's Treatment Plan   267

Potential Impediments to Successful Counseling   269

The Case of Derek   270

Individual Assessment/Intake Information   270

Derek's Family's Value Preferences (Hofstede's Cultural Axes)   272

Derek's Spheres of Influence in the Ecological Model   273

Diagnostic Impression and Readiness for Change   273

Treatment Plan   274

Derek's Treatment Plan   275

Potential Impediments to Successful Counseling   276

Chapter Summary   277   •   Questions for Class Discussion   278

Chapter 16   Self-Awareness and Self-Care   279

The Self-Awareness Strand   279

Professionalism   280

Ethics, Boundaries, and Impairment   281

Boundaries   281

Impairment and Self-Care   282

Developing and Implementing a Self-Care Plan   287

Chapter Summary   292   •   Questions for Class Discussion   292
•   Culminating Activity   292

Appendix   *ACA Code of Ethics   293*

Reference List   313

Index   325

CHAPTER 1

Counseling Skills and You

After studying this chapter, you should have a clear understanding of the following:

- The relationship among the three main themes of this text
- How each of those themes pertains to your development as a counselor
- The role of ethical standards in the counseling process
- Answers to commonly expressed student questions and concerns

This book is intended to assist your development as a professional helper. Over years of teaching and observing students learning how to implement and master counseling skills, it has become evident that ideally several components of learning should happen simultaneously. Those components are self-awareness, acquisition of technical skills, understanding of counseling theory, and understanding of how cultural variables interact with the three other components. Other authors who teach counseling and therapy skills (for example, Hill, Stahl, & Roffman, 2007) have similarly noted that instruction, modeling, practice, and feedback are all valuable components of good instruction for novice professional helpers.

The text is organized into sections that reflect the three components of self-awareness, skills, and counseling theory. This introductory chapter presents a broad explanation of the material that will comprise each of the three strands.

One specialty in the counseling profession is the realm of career development. You may be required to take a career development course as part of your graduate program. There are many theories and explanatory models for understanding how and why people make career choices. You likely have a fairly clear picture of how you have come to the decision to be a professional helper, even without knowing what those career development models are. However, if you do not, now would be a good time to do some soul-searching and get some perspective on your career choice. Make sure you are entering this profession for reasons that are consistent with your values and also consistent with your aspirations in terms of the lifestyle you intend to create for yourself. The word *lifestyle* used here refers not to income, but to the way you spend your time and the activities you do on a daily basis.

SELF-AWARENESS

Historically many prominent theorists in the field of counseling and psychology have identified self-awareness as an important trait of a helper. Recently, the importance of self-awareness has been most evident in multicultural and diversity issues. This emphasis arises out of the recognition that it can be difficult to differentiate the boundary between an observer and an observed person. It can often be challenging to objectively know the degree to which our perception of a person is influenced by our own history of life experiences, values, and beliefs. Each of us has a template of past experiences and values that affects our perception and our meaning making.

Because of that influence, students sometimes express concern and anxiety about how they will be able to remain completely neutral or accepting of every single client with whom they work. In reality, it is almost impossible to be neutral. Rather than expecting ourselves to be totally nonreactive, we should strive to be highly self-aware counselors. This self-awareness is a prerequisite to being able to consciously set aside our own preferences and reactions in favor of understanding and trying to take on the perspective of our client. The following section will identify specific aspects of self-awareness that affect your role as a counselor.

The Relationship Between Your Behavior and How Others Respond to You

When we first come into contact with another person, in virtually any setting, we respond primarily to the information that is provided by our senses. The immediately available information includes obvious aspects of the other person's appearance, ranging from clothing to posture, pleasant or offensive odors, voice tone, and subtle movement. The same will be true for the manner in which other people respond to you. Therefore, the clothes you wear, the cologne you wear, any other odors around your body related to your diet or hygiene, your personal grooming, and the manner in which you speak, will all contribute to other people perceiving you as carrying yourself in either a professional or an unprofessional manner. The perceptions other people have of you will have a direct bearing on how they interact with you. If you wish to be helpful to others or be a positive influence in their lives, one of the most basic aspects of working toward that goal is to consider the way you present yourself to other people.

In addition to the obvious physical aspects of how you present yourself, particular characteristics and attitudes may significantly contribute to your success as a mental health professional:

- Capacity for empathy
- Capacity for insight
- Level of self-awareness in interactions with peers and clients
- Ability to engage in self-reflection and personal and professional growth
- Willingness to explore personal issues related to the practice of counseling (countertransference issues)
- Openness and receptivity to feedback

- Ability to integrate feedback into subsequent practice counseling sessions
- Sufficient emotional stability to consistently attend to the needs of clients
- Ability to accurately assess own strengths and weaknesses
- Commitment to the profession

PERSONAL REFLECTION _____

As you read over the list of characteristics, what is your emotional reaction? Are these descriptors consistent with how you see yourself? Which ones are going to be the most challenging for you?

The Impact of Life Experiences

Throughout your life, you have been exposed to a wide variety of circumstances and events in your family, educational or professional experiences, peer and romantic relationships, and your physical and socioeconomic surroundings, to name a few. All of them have contributed to your becoming the person you are. It is important for you to have insight about how those life experiences have shaped the individual you are now. Some of those experiences will continue to exert influence throughout your life. Many theorists have researched and written about the course of human development and about the variety of aspects of human functioning in which development unfolds in a structured manner, often conceptualized as stages of development.

The insight you have and the sense you make of your life experiences are related in part to your stage of emotional development and self-perception. This statement should not be construed to imply that there is a right or wrong way to be, or a "proper" stage of development to achieve. It is simply an acknowledgment that stages of development affect the way we perceive the world and also the way we think of ourselves as fitting in the world. There are also factors related to our culture of origin and religious beliefs that can strongly influence our perceptions of where we fit in and how we make meaning of the world around us.

If in your training to be a mental health professional you have not taken the time or found the motivation to consider how your own beliefs and life events have shaped you, there is potential for you to cause damage to your clients. An applied example might elucidate this.

Case Example

Karen was the older of two children in her family of origin. Her father was an accountant who often worked long hours but was available to the family when he was not working. Her mother had a drinking problem that resulted in her being emotionally unavailable. Karen had the responsibility of doing all the household chores her mother neglected: cooking the meals for the family, doing the laundry, and looking after her younger sister. Karen went on to college and majored in psychology in an effort to better understand her mother's dysfunctional behavior. Karen became convinced that her father should have left her mother rather than "enabling" her drinking; that it would have been better for everyone involved if dad had just taken the girls and left. As Karen progressed in her training to become a counselor, she became more resentful of her mother's drinking and how it had affected the family. By the time Karen went on her counseling internship, she flatly advised her clients to get divorced and frequently told clients how harmful alcohol consumption was for everyone in the family, not just the drinker(s).

It is not hard to imagine how such an attitude could be detrimental or hurtful to a client, for example, one who was struggling but unable to take healthy action. Karen had the best intentions in her desire to save other people the heartache and emotional pain she had endured throughout her childhood and adolescence. But, by not dealing with her own difficulties, Karen inadvertently might cause damage to her clients.

Yalom and Leszcz (2005) discussed the "corrective recapitulation of early family dynamics" in their book, *The Theory and Practice of Group Psychotherapy.* Some of the clients with whom you work will have had families of origin in which there were pathogenic interactions. Pathogenic family dynamics may range from overt physical or sexual abuse to subtle verbal interactions that result in psychopathology, such as passive or continual low-level criticism. Perhaps you also had some unhealthy, unhelpful patterns of interaction in your own family of origin. There may be times when clients talk about issues or past experiences that bring to mind recollections of your own life events and interactions, or that result in your having a visceral emotional reaction because of prior experiences. You might be one of the first people in your client's life who has been able to engage with him or her in a manner that is completely accepting and nonjudgmental.

The likelihood of you being able to offer a nonjudgmental counseling relationship to your clients will be improved if you have self-identified and are aware of your own emotions, perceptions, and so on, caused by your personal history and triggered in the counseling relationship. Who you are as a person is likely to be an influential aspect of your client's counseling experience, every bit as important as the counseling strategies and techniques you use.

Desire to Be of Service

A number of prominent writers in the field of psychology have identified the drive for purpose and meaning as a central theme in human behavior. Examples include the existentialists Viktor Frankl and Rollo May, psychologists who explored the search for meaning. Offering one's efforts and service to others in need is, for some people, a very strong force in the career path they take. According to the existentialists, some individuals may find the process of offering service to others to be a means of meeting the internal need for meaning. In fact, interestingly, most of the jobs in the helping professions, such as child-care provider, teacher, community agency counselor, and school counselor, are not considered to be "hot," high-paying jobs, and yet many people continue to go into these fields. Their motivation for doing so is clearly something other than becoming affluent; some of those people might state that the knowledge and satisfaction of helping others compensates for the relatively lower pay of these occupations.

The Role of Religion and Spirituality

Perhaps your own spiritual or religious beliefs have helped shape your decision about your career path. Service to others has long been recognized as being of very high spiritual value in many faith traditions. People such as Mother Theresa and countless others offer examples of how, through their spiritual beliefs, they came to follow a path of service to others.

Personal Pain as a Catalyst for Growth

Past difficulties and your experience of pain may have resulted in your being "broken open." The Chinese character for "crisis" also means "opportunity." One potential result of an emotionally painful experience is personal growth.

Case Example

Aaron had been working as a sales representative for a medical supply company for a number of years, was married, and had no children. One day he came home from work to discover that his wife was involved in a relationship with another man and intended to leave Aaron. When his wife then moved out of the house and filed for divorce, Aaron was devastated. He became very depressed and eventually suicidal. Through the process of counseling, Aaron became aware of what had happened in his marriage that led to the divorce, and that actually he had been somewhat unhappy and unsatisfied in his marriage. He lived alone for the first time in his life and discovered that he really enjoyed cooking gourmet meals. He joined a gourmet cooking group, made new friends, and began traveling with his gourmet group.

PERSONAL REFLECTION

Think of an event in your life that was painful at the time, yet led to positive changes for you. What factors contributed to your ability to use the pain as a growth opportunity?

Awareness of Cognitive Frames

In Chapter 11, "Counseling Theories," we will talk about cognitive theory and, in that context, about the process of becoming aware of our thinking. This is a process referred to as *metacognition*, or thinking about how we think. This process is common among people training to become counselors and psychologists, but is probably much less common among the general public. In the context of training to be a counselor, you need to engage in metacognition. Your own cognitive style, style of learning, and ways of perceiving your environment are going to affect the way you learn and how you integrate the counseling skills and counseling theories that you will be taught.

It is possible that if, for example, you are an individual who is most comfortable with clearly distinct categories of black and white, you may experience some dissonance or discomfort when exploring different counseling theories. Using different theories for understanding a person requires fluidity in our thought processes. It may be difficult for you to take the perspective of your client, if you are focused on the idea that the client told you he or she did something you believe is wrong. Black and white thinking is, among other things, related to cognitive rigidity, in which a person resists alternative ways of thinking or defining a situation.

As a counselor it will be necessary for you to be able to see shades of gray; to realize that your own perception of a situation may be very different from your client's perception, and that *your perception is not the only right one*. The philosophical/psychological approach referred to as *phenomenology* is defined as the recognition that there is more than one reality, and that each person's perception is equally valid, regardless of whether or not we agree.

Emotional Strengths and Liabilities

Every person has strengths and weaknesses. In fact, most of us possess personal characteristics that could be a strength in one situation, but in another situation could be detrimental. For example, consider the personality characteristic of perseverance. Perseverance refers to sticking with an endeavor even when progress is not readily apparent, staying with something and seeing it through to the end, rather than giving up or admitting defeat. An example of persevering in a social situation would be to invite a couple for dinner. The couple decline the first invitation. A persevering individual would contact the couple again with another invitation for a different activity on another day. If these invitations were consistently refused, this could result in creating significant strain with that couple. On the other hand, it is possible that the couple simply did have conflicting plans, and by persisting, you might end up finding a date and activity when you could actually get together.

AUTHOR'S REFLECTION _____

When my children were small and would keep pestering me after they had been told "no," I humorously reminded my husband (and myself) that their persistence would be a strength as they grew up.

PERSONAL REFLECTION _____

What are one or two features of your personality or temperament about which people have commented? Imagine how in the context of counseling those features could be a strength, and also how they could be a liability.

High and Low Self-Monitors

In the specialty area of social psychology, the construct called *self-monitoring* refers to how closely we monitor the way people react to us and the extent to which we alter our behavior to elicit certain reactions from those around us. This construct is relevant in the context of counseling because you will be learning how to carefully observe your clients and to have a high degree of awareness of how your words and behavior are being received. When a person is a high self-monitor, he or she is very much in conscious control of what is being expressed, and he or she attempts to express thoughts and feelings in a way that will receive the approval of others. People who are high self-monitors are social chameleons. By the same token, though, high self-monitors are often very popular and get along with many people. For some people, the value of maintaining a friendship or collegial working relationship outweighs the value of being "right" or of expressing strong opinions or values about something.

On the other hand, people who are low self-monitors are more concerned with expressing thoughts and behaviors that are an accurate reflection of how they think and feel, regardless of how other people react or what reactions are engendered. As you might imagine, each of these two styles of self-monitoring offers advantages and disadvantages, and in reality, most people probably have some degree of both, depending on the situation. For example, some people might be more inclined to be high self-monitors at work and low self-monitors at home and with friends. If you are someone who tends toward being a low self-monitor, it may be necessary for you to modulate your speech and behavior somewhat when counseling your clients.

Sources of Satisfaction

Sometimes people go into helping professions because they really enjoy working with people and are fascinated by hearing about other people's lives. It can bring a great sense of satisfaction to help a person grow and to make changes that increase the person's enjoyment of life. It can also bring a tremendous sense of satisfaction and giving back to reach out to help other people after we ourselves have been helped. In addition, being social creatures, we all have some degree of wanting to be with other people.

PERSONAL REFLECTION _____

Take a piece of paper and jot down a list of the sources of joy in your life. When it is complete, take a look at how many of those sources involve interactions or relationships with other people. Would you characterize yourself as an outgoing or extroverted person? Someone who thrives in relationships with other people?

Congruence

Carl Rogers talked about congruence, which refers to an alignment between our head, our heart, and our gut. In the process of becoming a therapist, it is important to strive toward gaining congruence not only internally, but also in our lifestyles. If we are living in a manner that is not consistent with our values and beliefs, it will create internal dissonance that will make it quite difficult to assist clients with achieving congruence. Perhaps a concrete example will make this easier to understand. Consider a counseling student who is taking classes and preparing to do an internship. If that student is partying on the weekends, drinking heavily and staying out all night dancing, perhaps taking street drugs, it will be difficult for him or her to perform in a professional manner. It will also be extremely hard to help clients who are experiencing difficulties with substance abuse.

Of particular relevance in this case, it would be hypocritical for that student to counsel young adult clients about drinking on the weekend. If we are telling people to do one thing, yet are doing something else ourselves, we are being hypocritical. This hypocrisy can create internal dissonance and incongruence, which are impediments to being a sincere and effective counselor.

PERSONAL REFLECTION _____

What other possible examples of incongruence and congruence that could bear on the quality of your work can you think of?

PARTICIPATING IN PERSONAL COUNSELING

There are multiple reasons that personal counseling during your preparation to become a counselor could be advantageous to you. Some professional psychology training programs require students to engage in their own counseling. However, potential problems arise when someone is told he or she *must* participate in counseling; court-ordered therapy frequently does not work. Nevertheless, personal counseling can be a very valuable component of your preparation for the following reasons.

Resolution of Incongruence

A full discussion of the ways incongruence is detrimental to one's functioning is beyond the scope of our current discussion. However, the possible presence of incongruence is one of several reasons that participating in personal counseling could be of benefit to you. By investing your time in counseling, you could have the opportunity to resolve sources of dissonance and incongruence that cause you distress and might negatively impact your work as a counselor.

Insight About Choices

We talked at the beginning of this chapter about having self-awareness of how you came to pursue training as a counselor. It could be helpful to work toward that self-awareness through the process of participating in counseling. There are many reasons and sources of motivation that drive a person to become a professional helper, and it could be valuable for you to have considered and sincerely explored your own motivations.

Experience of the Power Differential

Yet another reason for personal counseling is for you to experience firsthand what it feels like to be in the role of a client, "sitting in *that* chair," so to speak. There is a power differential between counselor and client that cannot be fully realized or appreciated when one holds the position of power (as the therapist). Many students find it to be an extremely humbling experience to be a client. Having that experience can help to raise your awareness and respect for the extent to which the power differential can influence your relationships with your clients.

Resistance to Change

Besides the power differential, another nuance of the experience of being a client is to fully understand and appreciate how difficult it is to make personal changes, even when we absolutely want to do so. This phenomenon, referred to as *therapeutic resistance*, is a natural response that many people experience to some degree; it is the approach-avoidance conflict between wanting to move to a different (and hopefully healthier and more effective) way of acting and feeling, versus wanting to hang on to what is older and more familiar. Change is a process that many people approach with trepidation and ambivalent feelings. If you try to work with a client who has a high degree of ambivalence about changing, and you have not personally experienced that ambivalence yourself, it is much more likely that you will react toward that client with frustration or impatience, neither of which are particularly helpful responses.

It is this author's strong contention that a student can progress through a graduate program in counseling sticking just with the coursework, graduate, go on to work with clients, and probably do a perfectly acceptable job. However, it is not possible to be a stellar, phenomenal counselor or therapist without being a client at some point. Wilber (2001) observed that reading a map is not the same as driving on a road and becoming familiar with the territory. It is one thing to know a theory about parenting, or having a terminal illness, or trying to quit smoking. It is something entirely different to *be* a parent, someone who is dying, or who smokes and is trying to stop. You do not need to have had every disorder or problem in order to help your clients, but having had the experience of being a client yourself will greatly expand your awareness of your client's experience sitting in your office.

THE ROLE OF THEORY IN COUNSELING

Regardless of intended specialty or discipline, everyone who is in training to become a professional helper will have at least one course in helping theory. Some introductory helping skills texts do not have a section on theories, because it is too broad a topic to do it justice in an entry-level skills text. Practitioners need theories because it is our theory that drives our understanding and conceptualization of the client, the client's problem, and what strategies and techniques we might use to help the client grow and/or feel better. You will read more about theories when we get to Chapter 11, but the concept of theoretical models is introduced here so that you have a broad context in which to understand generally where we are going.

As you learn more about theories later in this text and in your education, you will find it fully apparent that your theoretical orientation has a great deal of bearing on your perception of a client. Consequently, it is important to be aware of your theoretical approach and to understand that you are making assumptions about how people develop and function. One of the challenges for new learners in the field of counseling is the recognition that there are many ways to conceptualize the same clinical observations. The counselor's own frame of reference, beliefs, and values will influence how he or she makes meaning of a client's problem.

An example might make this point more clear; this scenario might be similar to something you have observed yourself.

Case Example

The setting is a grocery store, in the cereal aisle. A harried mother who seems visibly stressed is pushing her 3-year-old child in a grocery cart as she is selecting some healthy cereal. The child is screaming and crying that she wants Fruit Loops. The mother reacts first by telling the child to quiet down, and when the child continues to scream, the mother becomes angry and then grabs a box of Fruit Loops and throws it in the grocery cart.

One counselor observing this interaction might be focused on the pattern of the child's behavior, which was rewarded in the form of getting the cereal for which she had been fussing. Another counselor might be focused on the mother's stress level and struggle to cope with the child's screaming, and the emotional needs that both the mother and child are experiencing in that moment. Yet another might focus on the mother's anger in response to the child's (inappropriate) request for a particular breakfast food. Any one of these conceptualizations of the tantrum problem could be considered appropriate. The professional training, theoretical inclinations, life experiences, values, and beliefs of the counselor will influence his or her perception of the child, the mother, and their interaction.

Your own professional training will be influenced by the theoretical orientation of the faculty members teaching the courses, as well as by your supervisors when you begin working with clients. Of most importance in this introductory chapter is your understanding of why we need to talk about theories at this stage of your training. When you begin learning and practicing the microskills, you will see that application of any given microskill will result in the focus of a counseling session going in a particular direction. Some microskill responses (interventions) will allow the focus of the counselor/client interaction to be entirely under the control of the client. Other microskill responses will overtly or covertly steer the focus in a direction that seems most relevant to you as the counselor. Even deciding about the extent to which you should guide and direct the focus of the discussion is an outcome of your theoretical orientation. A therapist who is person-centered will hardly ever lead, only follow where the client takes the discussion. In contrast, a Gestalt therapist will have very specific aspects of the client's presentation to which he or she will wish to direct the client's attention in the form of non-judgmentally observing the client's behavior.

MULTICULTURALISM

When authors talk about multiculturalism in a counseling context, they often are referring to the culturally based characteristics of the client and the counselor. As commonly done in introductory counseling books, we will be looking at those factors and considering how cultural factors influence the way a client responds to particular microskills. However, unique to this book is a consideration of how your own culturally based characteristics will influence how you experience and learn the curriculum material for this course, ranging from multiculturalism to theory to microskills.

Your own past and current experiences, both in and outside the classroom, will significantly affect the way you perceive the curriculum material your professor presents in this class. As an illustration, one of the assignments this author's students are given in a counseling skills class is to write a paper articulating their perceptions of the nature of humans, including their definition of mental and emotional health and illness, and the best way to offer help. In her paper, one student recently wrote the following preface to her philosophy statement: "I cannot ignore the fact that as a black woman, much of what I think and feel about human nature has been forged in my personal experiences with systemic racism and discrimination. Sad, but nonetheless very true, is the evidence that much of human nature is motivated by greed and power, and that is not likely to change any time soon." Clearly, her life experiences have been hugely different from this author's own life experiences as a white woman from an educated family with a life history of ample privileges and opportunities. For all of us, life experiences lead us to worldviews that significantly affect the way we conceptualize our clients' problems.

AUTHOR'S REFLECTION _____

In my family of origin, I had been taught to think through options and make "sensible" decisions. Consequently, as a beginning counselor, I found it frustrating and difficult to understand how clients would be unable to see they had choices, while they saw themselves as merely a continual victim of fate.

Developing not only an awareness of how another person's views differ from your own, but additionally a *sensitivity* to and tolerance of others' views, are important steps in acquiring multicultural competence.

Common Cultural Frames versus Stereotypes

A multitude of professional books and articles help readers to become familiar with various aspects of diverse cultural groups. One can find professional literature about working with clients who are Native American, African American, Asian American, and so on. There might be some job situations in which you find yourself working exclusively with one particular group, for example, working in a native village in Alaska, or in an agency or school specifically intended to serve a particular group.

Unless that is the case, you might find it challenging to learn all there is to know about the different types of ethnic and cultural groups that populate the United States. Often we learn a great deal about the culture common to the types of clients we work with regularly, and we learn a little bit about the cultures of clients who are members of groups with which we are unfamiliar. The problem is that when we make assumptions about a person based on group membership, we are stereotyping.

Stereotyping might be thought of as one means of reducing the complexity of our environment. Although stereotyping is often associated with prejudice, stereotypes and prejudice are not the same thing. It is possible to stereotype another person without intending to make a negative judgment about him or her. Once we come to the conclusion that a person is a certain way, we can basically conclude our thought process about that person, and thus avoid the cognitive dissonance of acquiring information that does not fit our existing belief system about that group of people. We can then shift our attention to something else in our environment. Because our environments continually bombard our senses with incoming information, our brains very efficiently develop mechanisms for reducing environmental complexity, and being able to place other people into preexisting categories with clear definitions and descriptions is one way to do that.

This is another example of a time and place where you as a counselor must have cognitive flexibility. Although some of the knowledge you have about a cultural group might apply to a given client, some of your knowledge may not be applicable. With flexibility you can then take in the additional information that contradicts your previously held expectations and beliefs. It gives you room to relate to each client as an individual person with his or her own idiosyncrasies.

ETHICAL STANDARDS

Most states now require that counselors hold a license in order to practice as a school or agency counselor. The licensure law in each state stipulates "scope of practice"; state laws spell out precisely what a counselor may (and therefore *may not*) do. In addition to the legal aspects of a counselor's professional activities, the American Counseling Association (ACA) has established a Code of Ethics, which is a set of guidelines articulating the standards of acceptable behavior for individuals in the profession.

The ACA Code of Ethics serves numerous purposes. These include identification of "best practices" among counseling professionals, providing guidelines for identifying a sound course of action to serve clients and also for choosing a course of action that best actualizes the values of the counseling profession. Readers are referred to Appendix A and encouraged to read the ethics code in its entirety.

In this text, space constraints allow for only a broad, general overview of the professional issues and behaviors covered by the ethics code. The principles of autonomy, nonmaleficence, beneficence, justice, and fidelity are philosophical tenets that comprise the structure of the code (Welfel, 1998). Following is a brief explanation of each of the five ethical principles and case examples that illustrate how ethical considerations intersect with other aspects of the counselor's work.

- *Autonomy* means respecting a client's right to decide for him- or herself the direction of his life. In a counseling context, it means an individual must have freedom to choose on many levels: *who* he or she sees for counseling, *how* the counseling will be conducted (treatment approaches and techniques), *what* the treatment goals will be, and *when* the counseling will be initiated and terminated.

Case Example

Jesse has entered counseling because he is depressed and trying to decide whether he should continue to major in pre-med or change his major to philosophy. His parents are pressuring him to remain in pre-med, because a bachelor's degree in philosophy will not make him very employable. There are several decisions to be made that will affect Jesse's treatment. One decision will be what the focus of counseling should be (possibilities include his depression, his career decision, his relationship with his parents). Jesse only wants to decide what to declare as his major, although the counselor believes that Jesse's relationship with his parents is at the root of the problem and that the parental relationship needs to be the focus. In the spirit of client autonomy, Jesse's preference to limit counseling to his decision about his major must take precedence over the counselor's opinion about what the goal should be.

- *Nonmaleficence* means doing no harm. This means that a practitioner must be careful not to use treatment techniques that have not been adequately researched, are harmful, or make a client's condition worse instead of better.

Case Example

Maria is a fourth grader being seen by her school counselor because of poor grades and a hostile attitude toward her teacher and peers. The school counselor recently heard in the news about a new type of counseling intervention in which children with problems similar to Maria's are aggressively confronted about the consequences of their behavior (called "No More Nonsense, Get Down to Business Counseling"). The technique has not yet been researched to determine how it affects children. Nevertheless, firmly scolding a child in a raised voice appears to the school counselor to be exactly what Maria needs. In this example, nonmaleficence means that the counselor has an ethical obligation to get much more information about the benefits, versus possible damage, of this new intervention before trying to use it in counseling Maria.

- *Beneficence* means that a counselor has the responsibility to the client and to the general public to do good. In a practical sense, it means having the intention to help as one's sole goal as the outcome of a counseling relationship.

Case Example

Ron is a mental health counselor in private practice who has been practicing for a number of years. Although he has not shared his most private, innermost values and goals with any of his previous coworkers or supervisors, Ron chose his career path mainly because he wanted to find an easy way to make "good money" and retire early. Sitting and letting someone else talk seemed much easier than trying to sell something. He likes the prestige of introducing himself as a therapist in private practice. Ron only accepts clients with the best health insurance coverage or those who have the financial means to pay the full fee themselves. When their benefits have been exhausted or they cannot make their co-payments, he suggests that they discontinue counseling or refers them to the local public agency. Ron does this because he has set certain financial income goals for himself if he is to reach his goal of retiring by the time he is 50. In this example, doing good is not Ron's primary motivation or intention for the work he is doing, and he is violating the Code of Ethics.

- *Justice* means treating everyone fairly. In the counseling context, it relates to not stereotyping and to offering one's professional services in a manner that is not discriminatory.

Case Example

Anna is a school counselor working with juniors and seniors in a high school. The district is in an area of the city that is economically middle to low income and ethnically diverse. The counselor who had been in Anna's position and then retired told Anna that it was easiest to just send all the students to the local community college since none of their students make it through college anyway. However, Anna felt a strong obligation to make sure that all her students had access and encouragement to consider all their options for post–high school training. She has spent several years accumulating catalogs for a wide variety of trade schools and 2- and 4-year colleges. She also has educated herself about scholarships and other forms of financial assistance for tuition. Anna's current short-term goal is to learn more about strategies for mentoring students whose families lack the resources to encourage them to pursue a profession.

- *Fidelity* involves being truthful and following through on one's promises. Loyalty is also a component of fidelity. It has to do with placing a client's needs or benefit ahead of our own, if circumstances require that we do that.

Case Example

Ramon is a counselor who has been working for several months with John, a client who has been making good progress in working on his social anxiety. One day, Ramon conducts an intake with a new client, and in the course of getting the background information, Ramon realizes that his new client is married to John's sister; he is John's brother-in-law. The new client is coming in to discuss marital problems with his wife (John's sister). Because this might create a conflict of interest, and John was a client first, Ramon is ethically obligated to refer the new client to another counselor at the agency.

There are eight sections of the ACA Code of Ethics:

Section A: The Counseling Relationship

Section B: Confidentiality, Privileged Communication, and Privacy

Section C: Professional Responsibility

Section D: Relationships with Other Professionals

Section E: Evaluation, Assessment, and Interpretation

Section F: Supervision, Training, and Teaching

Section G: Research and Publication

Section H: Resolving Ethical Issues

Many situations that arise in a professional counselor's work life will have a dimension that lies in the realm of ethics. Therefore, it is important to be aware that ethical standards will be a highly influential factor in your decision-making process in your work. This could include not only how you work with your clients, but also how you interact with and evaluate the work of your peers in the school or agency.

Common Beginner Questions and Concerns

- ***What if I can't help the person?***
  There are a couple of responses to this question. One scenario might be that you know what the client's presenting problem is, and you know that you have not been adequately trained to treat someone with that type of problem. It is unethical to counsel a person whose problem is not in your area of competence. In that case, you should take steps to get a list of other counselors in the area who do have the training and expertise to treat that problem.

  Another scenario might be that you have been working with a client for a period of time, but the client does not seem to be improving. When this happens, it is necessary to assess exactly why the client is not getting better. There are many reasons that a client might not respond positively to counseling, some of which may have little or no relation to your counseling efforts. In fact, extratherapeutic factors (factors that have nothing to do with counseling technique) have been found to be notably influential in both favorable and unfavorable counseling outcomes (Hubble, Duncan, & Miller, 1999).

  By the time you are actually working with clients on a practicum or internship, you will have some skills for evaluating a client's response to counseling. You also will have a supervisor who is qualified to help you learn how to determine why counseling is not helping and the way to proceed that will be in your client's best interest.

- ***What if I don't know what to do because I haven't had that problem?***
  It is not necessary to have personally had the same specific problem as your client in order to effectively help him or her. As you learn about the microskills and about using empirically supported treatment strategies, you will discover multiple ways to help another individual. Indeed, in the chapter about feeling reflection, you will see that it is not possible to have suffered every different kind of presenting problem your clients will have. Nevertheless, apart from specific details, you probably will have had some life experience that resulted in a similar emotional experience to that which your client is having. This shared emotional understanding becomes the gateway to empathizing with and validating your client's internal experience.

- ***What if I laugh accidentally?***
  Humor certainly has a place in counseling; it doesn't always have to be serious. However, laughing inappropriately at information your client has shared that is painful for him or her really could be hurtful to your client. By carefully listening and attending to what your client is sharing, you will be attuned to and maybe actually experience some of the feelings your client is expressing. It is quite unlikely that if you are empathizing with your client, you will laugh inappropriately. If it does happen, apologize sincerely and then spend some private time trying to understand what internal process led you to laugh.

- *What if I don't know what to say?*
  By the end of this text, you will have knowledge about a wide array of responses from which to choose. Although it may be hard to imagine at this moment, you will know not only what your choices are of what to say, but also what the likely outcome will be of each one of those choices.

Chapter Summary

This chapter offered you a preview, laying out the conceptual groundwork of what is to come. Besides being a text for a required course, it is an invitation for you to embark on a journey of self-discovery, learning, and skill acquisition. There will be a direct, linear relationship between the extent to which you invest in this process and the extent to which you benefit from it. As you open yourself to the processes of self-exploration and commitment to learning the objective material, you will benefit and grow.

Questions for Class Discussion

1. What parts of this chapter were consistent with what you expected to hear in this class?
2. What parts were a surprise and why?
3. What are some of your concerns about this learning process?

Beginning Assignment

Find a confederate, someone whom you know fairly well, and get his or her permission to record a 15- to 20-minute conversation, either audio or video. The topic should be an interaction or issue of concern to your "client." Your instruction for this tape is to listen, and then try to be as helpful as possible.

When you have completed the tape, set it aside and save it to listen to again at the end of the course.

CHAPTER 2

Multiculturalism and Diversity in Counseling

After studying this chapter, you should have a clear understanding of the following:

- How your own values and beliefs and other cultural characteristics may interact with your client's throughout the counseling process
- How other variables of diversity besides ethnicity will affect how you perceive your clients
- How other variables of diversity will influence your client's mental health
- The standards for being a multiculturally competent counselor
- How to use the Hofstede model of cultural variability for understanding value differences across cultures
- How level of acculturation in the United States affects people's self-perception

One recurrent theme throughout the chapter and this entire book is that self-awareness is one cornerstone of counseling skill acquisition. Thus, there will be opportunity for you to consider the concepts of cultural influence on development and mental health from two perspectives: your personal experiences and the universal experiences of all people. Additionally, exploring the issues related to cross-cultural counseling will help establish a conceptual context for application of the microskills and theories that will be presented later.

PERSONAL REFLECTION

On a sheet of paper jot down your own definitions of "culture," "multicultural," "diversity," and "ethnocentrism." Set them aside so you can refer back to them further on in this chapter.

In the last several decades there has been much criticism of the traditional Western counseling approaches, which are seen by many as making critical assumptions about human functioning that are not meaningful for some groups of people. The specifics of those criticisms will become clearer as this chapter unfolds. Multiculturalism is a theme in this text that will help you become acclimated to being continually aware of cultural variability as a factor in your interactions with clients. Mollen, Ridley, and Hill (2003) have said that multicultural counseling is one of the most central and critical constructs in contemporary psychology. Multiculturalism is so prominent a theme that it has been referred to as the fourth force (the first three being psychoanalysis, behaviorism, and humanism).

We will begin by considering some basic definitions and concepts that are central to an understanding of culturally sensitive counseling. We'll move from definitions to a very brief description of how multicultural focus has evolved over recent decades, and examine one current model for conceptualizing multiculturalism in counseling and psychology. One area of contemporary research in multiculturalism is Sue's work on racial microaggression; we will touch upon the controversies regarding that work as well.

We will then present a model for understanding cultural differences: Hofstede's model of cultural values across countries (2001). Hofstede's model is just one of many that could be used within the general construct of counseling and multiculturalism. It was chosen for this text because it is an empirically based model for understanding variations between cultures, derived from extensive research across 72 countries. This is a model that, because of its fluid structure, lends itself well to a comparison of culturally based values, beliefs, and preferences. As well, we will look at groups of people in the United States who have historically been oppressed and how some of those group characteristics might interface with the Hofstede model.

This in turn will lead us to consideration of how differences among clients might affect microskill use with a client. Cultural differences will have an influence on how a client perceives microskills you are using, and will also influence the effectiveness of your efforts to help a particular client. The subsequent chapters on microskills will use the Hofstede model as a basis for considering how effective each microskill might be in relation to the culturally based preferences of a given client.

There will be opportunities throughout this chapter for you to consider your own beliefs and feelings about working with clients who are different, for a variety of reasons, from yourself. It's very important that you take time to focus on where you are coming from in that regard. Your own characteristics and cultural background comprise the filters through which you will perceive and experience this information about multiculturalism.

Some readers have already completed a course in cultural and social foundations in counseling; for those people, this chapter will be a review of material with which they are already familiar. Other readers may be required to take a social and cultural issues course later in their studies. This chapter is not intended to replace the detail that would be covered in a course on multicultural issues in counseling. Rather, the intent of this chapter is to present an overview of definitions and concepts, as well as presenting a model for conceptualizing individual differences among people that will give readers some basic understanding of the concepts and issues.

One of the terms often encountered in professional literature about multicultural issues in counseling is *multicultural competence*. Competence and skill in multiculturalism is similar to competence in any other skill, such as riding a bicycle or cooking. There is a trajectory of development in each of these skill sets. As we explore the nature and scope of multicultural competence, the exploratory material is intended to establish a foundational understanding for readers.

PERSONAL REFLECTION

How old were you when you became aware that certain aspects of your family of origin differed from others around you? What feelings accompanied that awareness? How did your awareness evolve? Did you ever talk about your awareness of differences with anyone in your own family?

DEFINITIONS OF TERMS

Prior to moving into the content about cultural issues, it might be helpful for you to view a video example of one way cultural issues are addressed by a counselor in a counseling session. The following link is such an example.

———myhelpinglab —
Video Lab > By Course > Skills/Process/Techniques > Practical Issues: Ethical Dilemmas > Cultural Considerations in a Counseling Session
———

It makes sense to begin with some definitions of terms that will make these concepts explicit. The most important terms are *culture, multiculturalism,* and *diversity.* Following are the definitions to which you can compare your own definitions that you generated at the beginning of this chapter.

Culture

The concept of culture is multidisciplinary. The following definitions span numerous disciplines including linguistics, sociology, and anthropology. This heterogeneity is itself indicative of the extent to which culture is a component of our knowledge about humans. The Universal Declaration on Cultural Diversity (United Nations Educational, Scientific and Cultural Organization, 2001) states that

> Culture should be regarded as the set of distinctive spiritual, material, intellectual and emotional features of a society or a social group, and that it encompasses, in addition to art and literature, lifestyles, ways of living together, value systems, traditions and beliefs. (p. 2)

Another definition, offered by Miraglia, Law, and Collins (2006), is as follows:

> People *learn* culture. That, we suggest, is culture's essential feature. . . . Culture, as a body of learned behaviors common to a given human society, acts rather like a template (i.e., it has predictable form and content), shaping behavior and consciousness within a human society from generation to generation. So culture resides in all learned behavior *and* in some shaping template or consciousness prior to behavior as well (that is, a "cultural template" can be in place prior to the birth of an individual person). (p. 1)

Finally, Smith (2003) offered the following definition: "Culture is the combination of all the physical and behavioral aspects of a society. To study the people within a society, how they function, and what they value, gives the sociology student a more thorough understanding of society" (p.1).

There are a number of common threads across these definitions. One is that a group's *culture* is one of the things that make it look and sound different from other groups.

Language, nonverbal behaviors such as gestures, ways of organizing groups of people, types of food consumed, and types of products used and consumed, are all examples of features of society that vary among groups.

Another common thread across the definitions is that there is a relationship between a culture's spiritual or religious beliefs, subsequent values, and what the members of that culture define as acceptable behavior. It follows, then, that definitions of illness and health, including emotional disturbance and psychiatric disorders, are also culturally defined. Furthermore, methods for *treating* physical and emotional disorders are culturally defined as well. This is a concept to which we will return.

Multiculturalism

Multiculturalism refers to acknowledging and valuing many cultures within a society rather than just one mainstream culture. The concept of multiculturalism has gathered increasing exposure and momentum in part because of technology and the ease with which we now can see and learn about cultures around the globe.

AUTHOR'S REFLECTION _____

I remember in my early childhood looking at pictures of people from other parts of the world in *National Geographic* and being so fascinated by how others lived. Since that time (which my preteen sons refer to as the Dark Ages) there has been an astounding broadening in the accessibility of images and contact with people from other cultures, partially as a result of the Internet and other forms of technology such as satellite communication. This increased breadth of available information has resulted in more awareness about the importance of valuing other cultures in addition to our own.

An Internet search for a definition of multiculturalism yielded the following definition on a website that originates in Australia, entitled ReefEd, focusing on marine life and sustainable coral reefs: "*Multiculturalism:* Term used to describe many cultures and learning to get on with one another with mutual respect" (retrieved September 7, 2007 from http://www.reefed.edu.au/). This website is intended for K–12 learners. The fact that this definition appears on a marine biology website for children is one indication of the extent to which the idea of multiculturalism has permeated our thinking and awareness.

Emic and *etic* are concepts that originated in anthropology and are applicable in the context of multiculturalism in counseling. These two terms were derived from the words *phonemic* and *phonetic* by Kenneth Pike (as cited in Lett, 2006). Emic means understanding a culture from the inside, taking on the perspective of the insider—focusing on distinctions that are of relevance to individuals in a given cultural group, trying to perceive the world from the framework characteristic of a given culture. Etic, on the other hand, means understanding from the outside in, employing traditional, empirical scientific methods and objectively examining characteristics of a particular culture. Becoming thoroughly familiar with a culture requires knowledge that comes from both emic and etic perspectives.

Diversity

The word *diversity* refers to variety and differences on some essential variable. In the context of our discussion, it refers to characteristics or attributes of individuals that also can become the basis for group membership. Examples include gender, people who are over age 65 who are referred to as senior citizens, people who are gay or lesbian, people who are of a particular religion, people with a particular type of disability such as a hearing impairment or autism, and so on. These variables of diversity occur independently of ethnicity. The presence of particular variables of diversity can result in higher likelihood of preferential treatment, or discrimination, in particular cultures.

For example, in some cultures one's age can result in limited access to resources. The Gray Panthers are a group of senior citizens who advocate for fair treatment of people who are elderly. That organization was developed in part to advocate for people who were, because of their age, experiencing loss of jobs, reduction of income, and loss of contact with other people.

When *diversity* is used in the counseling literature, it may sometimes imply characteristics that may place an individual in a group that is a minority in comparison to the general population. Groups that are a minority are often in inferior positions in social strata, although not always. Individuals who are extremely wealthy are minorities, yet they do not experience the same type of discrimination, oppression, and disempowerment that might be experienced by members of other minority groups. Moreover, there are quasi-cultures that exist among particular groups of people who share a common characteristic. For example, among people who attend Alcoholics Anonymous meetings, there are clear norms and expectations for a person's behavior. There is a characteristic language that is used among members of that group. Similarly, there is an academic culture in higher education that may be more familiar to some readers than others as they begin graduate school.

Ethnocentrism

Ethnocentrism refers to the process by which a person evaluates another culture, using his or her own culture of origin as the basis for determining acceptability or desirability of a behavior.

AUTHOR'S REFLECTION _____

In my family of origin, appropriate table manners were rigidly expected at meal times. One person spoke at a time, no elbows were permitted on the table, chewing only happened when one's mouth was closed, and the fork was placed on the plate between bites. Being of Scottish, Welsh, and English descent, constraint, order, and emotional reserve were the rule. Thus, when visiting the family home of my college roommate I was astounded to observe this family of 10 siblings at the dinner table, all yelling over one another, lunging for second helpings. Besides the fact that it felt chaotic, I inappropriately made the judgment that my own table behavior was better because of my own upbringing, and thought that someone should teach them proper table manners. This was a demonstration of ethnocentrism on my part.

In this chapter and throughout the book, the term *multicultural* refers in the most inclusive manner possible to all variables of individual difference, which include racial heritage, ethnicity, gender, age, sexual orientation, ability and disability, and so on.

PERSONAL REFLECTION _____

Go back now to the definitions you jotted down at the beginning of this chapter. Compare them to the definitions offered above. What do you suppose are the reasons for any discrepancy between your own definitions and the definitions provided in the text?

With these definitions of terms now clarified, we can shift our focus to look at how the concept of multiculturalism has evolved in the United States, and more specifically, in the field of counseling.

HISTORICAL CONTEXT OF THE MULTICULTURAL MOVEMENT

Two aspects of history and current events warrant discussion here. One is the presence of multiculturalism in general in American society, and the other is the emergence of multiculturalism specifically in the disciplines of counseling and psychology. We'll begin with the broad level of recent history and contemporary events occurring nationally, and then move to a more specific focus on counseling.

Immigration Policy in the United States

The United States was founded as the result of Europeans landing here and claiming possession. Among the Native Americans there was cultural variability between tribes. When outsiders from other continents arrived and began interacting with Native Americans, there was cultural diversity. Diversity has continued to be one of the cornerstones of our national identity. It has always represented one significant feature of the nation's population, and the intention for the United States to be a "melting pot" is an institutionalized goal, evident in the mission statement of the U.S. Immigration Service (Congress of the United States, Congressional Budget Office, 2006). The U.S. Immigration Service has four goals:

1. Reuniting families who have members living in the United States
2. Meeting labor shortages by bringing in workers from other nations who have specific skills needed here
3. Providing a refuge for people who are being persecuted
4. Further enriching the nation's diversity by bringing in people from countries that have historically been underrepresented in this country

Despite this, as a nation we seem to have ambivalence about taking the steps to achieve those goals. For example, in the past several years there have been public demonstrations and public outcry on both sides of the argument about deporting people who are here without government permission. As recently as May 2006, there was extensive media coverage of the huge public protests about a congressional bill that would have made being in the United States illegally a felony offense.

In addition to the conflict and ambivalence at the level of governmental policy, many hate groups in this country promote racial supremacy, mostly white supremacy. These groups want to *eliminate* diversity.

Case Example

Mr. S., a greenskeeper at a golf course in South Carolina, was interviewed by a local television station because of vandalism to the golf course. On several occasions, vandals had spilled gasoline in the shape of swastikas on the grass and then lit them, so that the symbols were emblazoned on the ground.

Even among people who don't consider themselves to be racist, there nevertheless are subtle forms of oppression and discrimination that exert influence over the lives of people who are minorities for whatever reason, be it ethnicity, affectional orientation, or physical disability. Sue and Sue (2003) posit that working as a counselor and lacking multicultural competence is, itself, a form of cultural oppression.

PERSONAL REFLECTION

Do you agree with Sue and Sue's statement that lacking multicultural competence is a form of cultural oppression? Why or why not? What relationship exists between this level of agreement and the personal experiences you have had related to your own ethnicity?

Multiculturalism in the Professions of Counseling and Psychology

Several events have occurred in the fields of counseling and psychology that paralleled what was happening on a more global scale. One of the most notable happened in 1973, when the American Psychological Association held a meeting called the Vail Conference. At that conference, a resolution was established that it is unethical to provide services to culturally diverse clients if the counselor is not competent to provide those services.

Following the Vail Conference, counseling professionals published statements that further recognized and emphasized the model of multicultural counseling competence. For example, the Council for Accreditation of Counseling and Related Educational Programs (CACREP) established standards that specifically included standards for multicultural learning experiences in curricula for preservice and in-service training. A number of other articles and books (Atkinson, Morten, & Sue, 1989; Ponterotto & Casas, 1987) identified the critical importance of having a specific skill set to work with clients who are ethnically and culturally different from oneself.

Despite the Vail Conference resolution, it has been stated that psychology has been remiss in not fully appreciating the role of culture in many aspects of psychology (Christopher, 2006; Hoshmand, 2006; Leong & Ponterotto, 2003; Varenne, 2003). Neglect of acknowledging multiculturalism as a factor has been reflected in multiple ways, ranging from omissions in research to a lack of recognition about how culture shapes the values that are implicit in therapy process and outcome. So, while on one hand multicultural issues are considered to be one of the "hot topics" in counseling and psychology, a number of authors believe there is much more work to be done as far as infusing multiculturalism as a variable in counseling research, particularly research examining therapy outcome.

One of the biggest points of contention has been the lack of acknowledgment of the huge toll discrimination and oppression take on the recipients of the discrimination. The adage "Pull yourself up by your bootstraps" is an underlying assumption of several commonly used treatment approaches.

However, the ongoing disempowerment and subjugation that is experienced by people of low social status can take a tremendous toll on emotional and psychological health. For example, Trimble and Thurman (2002) discuss the cultural grief and trauma experienced by many Native Americans when their cultures were essentially lost to dominance by Europeans. This grief is the result of community trauma subsequent to European contact, a "wound to the soul of Native American people that is felt in agonizing proportions to this day" (Duran & Duran, 1995, as cited in Trimble & Thurman, 2002, p. 64).

RACIAL MICROAGGRESSION   It is the position of Sue et al. (2007) that racism and prejudice continue to be perpetrated in the United States by white people because racism is such an inherent component of our culture. They cite multiple examples of subtle expressions of prejudice that are continually present in human interactions. Sue et al. posit that microaggressions often happen unconsciously. They define three types of microaggression (p. 278):

1. ***Microinsult:*** Behavioral/verbal remarks or comments that convey rudeness and insensitivity and demean a person's racial heritage or identity.
2. ***Microassault:*** Explicit racial derogations characterized primarily by a violent verbal or nonverbal attack meant to hurt the intended victim through name-calling, avoidant behavior, or purposeful discriminatory actions.
3. ***Microinvalidations:*** Verbal comments or behaviors that exclude, negate, or nullify the psychological thoughts, feelings, or experiential reality of a person of color.

Sue et al. (2007) admonish that because microaggression is often unintentional and unconscious, there is elevated danger of white therapists continuing to perpetrate the aggression. This danger is compounded by virtue of the power imbalance between the counselor and the client. The remedy for this problem is to make a conscious, energetic effort to become aware of the possible ways microaggressions may appear in our counseling interactions. The following list provides specific examples of ways a counselor might demonstrate microaggression toward a client (Sue et al., 2007, p. 282):

- Assuming Asian Americans and Latino Americans are foreign-born
- Assigning a degree of intelligence to a person of color on the basis of his or her race
- Making statements indicating that a white person does not want to acknowledge race
- Presuming that a person of color is dangerous, criminal, or deviant on the basis of race
- Renouncing white racial biases
- Asserting that race does not play a role in career advancement or education
- Believing that the values and communication styles of the dominant/white culture are ideal
- Giving a white consumer preferential treatment over a person of color
- Displaying macro-level microaggressions, which are more apparent on a systemic level

CONTROVERSY ABOUT RACIAL MICROAGGRESSION   Sue et al.'s article elicited multiple comments from other authors who have criticized the paper for several reasons. Those subsequent comments are presented here because it is important for you to be fully informed as to the nature of the professional dialogue about this issue.

In the journal *American Psychologist*, where the Sue et al. article appeared, the Comment section featured reactions from multiple authors who provided counterpoints to Sue et al.'s microaggression propositions. One criticism, echoed by several authors (Harris, 2008; Schacht, 2008; Thomas, 2008), involves the inherent difficulty of establishing the objective reality of one's perceptions. For example, Thomas (2008) raised the question, "… doesn't everyone, regardless of race, occasionally experience verbal, behavioral, or environmental indignities?" (p. 274).

In a similar vein, Schacht (2008) observed that problematic interactions between therapists and clients are not limited to cross-racial dyads; microinteractions occur continually between any two people. He further pointed out that, "Each member of a therapeutic dyad acts and reacts, remembers and constructs, projects and internalizes, in a complex, cyclical, and recursive interpersonal and psychodynamic dance that defies simple reductive description or ascription of responsibility to one actor" (Schacht, 2008, p. 273). Thus, he emphasized that the client's actions and reactions are also critical aspects of the interaction. Assuming that both individuals are harboring unconscious hostility and aggression, then through their interaction *both* are perpetrators and *both* are victims.

PERSONAL REFLECTION

What is your gut-level reaction to this controversy? Have you witnessed or experienced microaggression in your own life? To what extent does each side of this controversy hold merit?

The focus of discussion will broaden now from racial differences to other variables of human diversity such as gender and mental health status. Some of your future clients will be dealing with problems that are the result of cultural differences and discrimination, factors over which they have little control. It's shortsighted to assume that someone *could* get an education or get a job, if they just tried hard enough. For some individuals this *may* be the case. On the other hand, it may not always be so. For a counselor who is not culturally sensitive, it may appear that a client has merely to set goals and work diligently toward attaining them, when in reality there are societal and institutional barriers that preclude goal attainment.

Case Example

Mr. T. was a 46-year-old man in counseling, receiving Social Security disability income because he had schizophrenia and could not maintain employment. He lived alone and rented an efficiency apartment in a large apartment building. The landlord was in Mr. T.'s apartment doing minor repairs and noticed some letters from Social Security lying on the table. When the landlord questioned Mr. T. and discovered Mr. T.'s diagnosis, he informed Mr. T. that he would need to move out of the building. Mr. T. willingly agreed, although he had nowhere else to go. Mr. T. did not know that he was being discriminated against until he shared the information with his counselor during a counseling session. The counselor then took steps to require the building management to comply with the Americans with Disabilities Act.

We'll continue in our exploration of multiculturalism as we turn now toward considering specific models of human functioning that incorporate cultural factors as essential components of the model.

ECOCULTURAL MODELS OF HUMAN FUNCTIONING

The topic of multiculturalism in psychology and counseling is an intersection point between the disciplines of anthropology and psychology. Many authors have contributed to the growth toward cultural awareness and multicultural competence. Two in particular whose thinking and writing about cultural issues have been influential are Berry and Bronfenbrenner.

Berry's Ecocultural Framework

Berry's Ecocultural Framework (Berry, 2003) holds that differences in people result from their attempts to accommodate and function within their environmental context, accommodation that occurs on an individual as well as group levels. Interestingly, these adaptations are subject to Darwinian principles: Some aspects of human behavior are universal, and yet environmental characteristics, such as weather and geographical features, influence many aspects of how a culture evolves. Some features of culture, such as methods for maintaining basic physical survival, i.e., shelter and staple food, are directly influenced by geographic area. Clearly, staple food, including ways of acquiring it and ways of consuming it, are radically different between a family who lives in the Arctic Circle and a family who lives on the equator. These regional differences in basic survival behavior in turn give rise to a multitude of rituals, customs, and norms that evolve within that group of people.

Bronfenbrenner's Ecological Model

Bronfenbrenner's work in child development resulted in the ecological model of human development. Bronfenbrenner (1979) defined human existence as a social experience. It is internal in terms of how we define ourselves, and external in terms of how we perceive and define other people. All social definitions, experiences, and perceptions occur in nested groups.

The smallest social groups and units begin with a dyad of people and expand to the family of origin and progressively broader circles of human social organization, moving out as far as government and social policy. This represents a holarchy (Wilber, 2001), in which each set of interactions exists on its own and simultaneously represents a part of a larger whole. This holarchic progression can be visualized as a series of concentric circles, with the smallest unit at the center being the individual (see Figure 2.1).

Relationships between the individual and others in the environment move progressively outward. These systems are referred to as the *microsystem level, mesosystem level, exosystem level,* and *macrosystem level.* Bronfenbrenner posited that human development

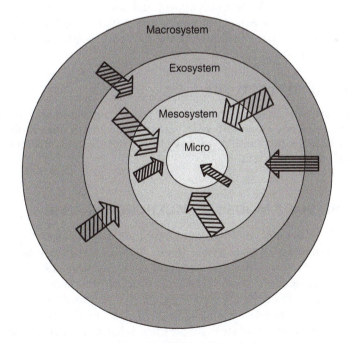

FIGURE 2.1 Bronfenbrenner's Ecological Model of Human Functioning.

must be understood contextually, taking into account the influences exerted upon an individual at every level of group of which a person is a member.

> ***Microsystem level:*** The microsystem is comprised of dyads and triads of an individual in face-to-face interaction with one or two others; this is the most proximal level of influence. These dyadic interactions occur between people in a household, friends, or teachers.

> ***Mesosystem level:*** The mesosystem is a web of many microsystem interactions, which consists of interconnections between the dyads and triads of the microsystem. An example would be a child's parents meeting for a conference with the teachers.

> ***Exosystem level:*** The exosystem is comprised of environments that have indirect influence on a person's internal experience, such as parents' place of employment, policies in a school, and local politics.

> ***Macrosystem level:*** The macrosystem is the broadest level of system that exerts influence on the individual. This includes a person's ethnicity, culture, social or political systems, belief systems, and lifestyle.

Terry (2005) noted that in a later refinement of his model, Bronfenbrenner emphasized that each individual is at the center of his or her microsystem, and that the expectations and demands on behavior in a dyadic interaction is where the cultural roles and cultural values are most intensely expressed. The nature of those interpersonal interactions comprises a significant component of how a person sees himself. Terry clarified that, "It is this interchange among internal and external systems that determines which environmental affordances will be perceived and activated . . . in accordance with the role 'expectations, evaluations, and obligations' . . . that define one's conceptual self" (p. 20). In other words, the force of cultural values that are exerted from the macrosystem, which is most distal to the individual, the whole way down the hierarchy to the proximal microsystem, all influence an individual's self-perception.

PERSONAL REFLECTION

Take a moment to diagram the circles of social connection and influence in which you find yourself right now, beginning with your most intimate relationship and moving outward. Consider how the relationship you have in each of those realms contributes to how you think about and define yourself.

SUE AND SUE'S MODEL OF MULTICULTURALISM

One article frequently cited as a landmark publication in establishing the concept of multicultural counseling competence is "Multicultural Counseling Competencies and Standards: A Call to the Profession," by Sue, Arrendondo, and McDavis (1992). It will be worth your while to read it. The authors pointed out that much of the cross-cultural research that had been conducted was based on erroneous premises that undermined the validity of the research itself. Multiculturalism was identified as a "fourth force" in the fields of counseling and psychology, and the idea was strongly presented that race, culture, and ethnicity are issues that pertain to everyone, not "just" people who hold minority status.

In that important article, Sue, Arrendondo, and McDavis offered a model for conceptualizing the multiple dimensions of multicultural competence. The essence of the model is that there are three realms of counselor training that should occur across three domains. The ability realms are beliefs and attitudes, knowledge, and skills. The three domains are counselor self-awareness, understanding the worldview of culturally different individuals, and developing appropriate strategies. Not everyone who writes about cross-cultural issues necessarily embraces that model; other authors have presented models that are complementary or somewhat divergent. Although we will not be exploring the implications and subtleties of those differences, or the particular steps for becoming fully multiculturally competent, these considerations need to be in your awareness as you begin developing your helping skills.

There have been research studies and other articles published pertaining to counseling issues and characteristics of several minority groups in the United States: Asian, Latino, African American, and Native American. One of the mitigating variables that will affect individual preferences as you work with each client will be the degree of acculturation and the stage of racial identity development at which your client is functioning. Following the presentation of the Hofstede model we will briefly look at acculturation and how it interacts with other client characteristics.

Case Example

Mr. P. was a 54-year-old man of African American descent. He was admitted as an inpatient in a psychiatric unit to be evaluated, assessing whether he would be a suitable candidate for an intensive outpatient treatment program for substance abuse. After several days of evaluation it was determined that he was not appropriate for the intensive outpatient group, and one of the staff counselors was given the task of telling Mr P. the program was not right for him. The counselor, Ms. D., was a 32-year-old woman of Asian descent who held a clinical counselor license. When Ms. D. informed Mr. P. that he would be referred to a different program, he stated, "When I first met you I thought you'd understand my problem because you're colored too. Now I see that you just want to keep your green card so you're going to do whatever the man tell you to do!"

What would be your first reaction to a client who made such a statement? What kinds of experiences might give rise to Mr. P.'s worldview? What would be the best response to his exclamation?

HOFSTEDE'S MODEL OF CULTURAL DIFFERENCES

The past several decades have seen an emergence of our own awareness of how traditional counseling approaches have been blind to cultural differences. Much has been written about the ethnocentrism inherent in the traditional theories of psychology and human development, and how traditional theoretical approaches contributed to oppression and to pathologizing human reactions among people whose characteristics placed them in an inferior status in society.

Tying this in with the Bronfenbrenner terminology, traditional Western psychology and counseling have neglected to consider the influence of the exosystems and macrosystems. As learners of counseling, the analogy to take from this introduction to multiculturalism is a simple one: A fish is not aware of being in water until it jumps out of the water into the atmosphere. So it is with culture. We become aware of our own culture when we have something to which we can compare it.

Case Example

Arman was a 13-year-old boy of Persian descent attending school in a predominantly white, middle-class suburban middle school. He was an only child, and his father had abandoned the family several years before. At the beginning of the school year, his mother had relocated to that suburb because publicly subsidized housing was available and his mother wanted him in a "good" school. Although Arman was gifted, within three to four months of beginning middle school his grades dropped from A's and B's to D's and F's. His appetite diminished significantly and he developed dark circles under his eyes. Arman's mother brought him to an agency where he was seen by a counseling intern; his mother listed as the main presenting concern "poor school performance." When Arman was alone with his counselor, he shared that the other students ignored him in the classroom, and on the schoolyard and in the lunchroom he was being consistently harassed by the other students. The counselor got the mother's permission to talk to Arman's teacher. Arman's teacher denied observing bullying, but also stated dismissively that she was "way too busy" to pay attend to the students' social patterns.

Generate a list of hypotheses that would account for Arman's symptoms. Was it the teacher's responsibility to manage the students' social behavior in her classroom? What responsibility did his mother have for managing these problems? What should the counselor have done in this instance?

Many textbooks that discuss counseling with people of racial minorities provide descriptions of characteristics of that culture. Research on counseling particular racial groups often generates specific directives and reported client preferences for a particular counseling approach. This is referred to as a *prescriptive approach* to counseling minorities. There are two problems with the prescriptive approach. First, there are many large groups of people who are culturally different; the United States is indeed a melting pot. Consequently it would be a very daunting task for a counselor to become fully multiculturally competent for every cultural minority group. The other big problem with the prescriptive approach is that it may lead one to make a broad generalization about members of a group and does not allow for nuances of individual variability.

Our field is in need of a model that allows therapists to honor individual differences in cultural values, while still maintaining an understanding of the general value differences characteristic of a culture. Such a model was discovered in a cross-cultural counseling text (Pedersen, Draguns, Lonner, & Trimble, 2002): Hofstede's model of cultural value differences. Despite the obvious limitation that the model was not created or tested specifically for use in counseling, it offers utility in the present context because it is empirically derived and is applicable across many situations and cultures.

How Hofstede's Model Developed

It may help readers to have some background about Hofstede to have a context within which to use and understand his model. Hofstede's academic background is organizational anthropology. After doing his doctoral work at Groning University in the Netherlands, he went on to establish and manage the Personnel Research Division at IBM. He also was a co-founder and director of the Institute for Research on Intercultural Cooperation in the Netherlands. The development of his model for understanding national values and beliefs is the result of longitudinal research that had an *n* of over 116,000 participants and spanned 72 countries! There is clearly an adequate sample size for him to have derived some conclusions and knowledge from the data set. To get a firsthand look at national scores from this data set, interested readers can go to the following website: http://stuwww.uvt.nl/~csmeets/. The data set is also available as an appendix in the book *Culture's Consequences* (Hofstede, 2001).

His model is presented as one means of understanding differences in thinking and in social action that may be observed across people from different nations. This is based on the assumption that values give rise to beliefs and consequently to behavior. Thus, differences in socially acceptable behaviors arise in part from differences in values across cultures. Hofstede posits that his model enables one to understand "five dimensions along which dominant value systems in more than 50 countries can be ordered and that affect human thinking, feeling, and acting, as well as organizations and institutions, in predictable ways" (2001, p. xix).

Our discussion of Hofstede's model is going to examine cultural values from an ecological perspective. This enables us to take into consideration the cultural values at the levels of the macrosystem and exosystem, and then how those values might manifest at the level of the microsystem. Here is where our work with clients in schools and agencies makes contact with these models.

One important caveat is that this five-axis model of national cultural variability is not one that has been empirically examined in the context of cross-cultural helping or counseling. It is not being proposed that readers should accept this model as a definitive method for engaging in cross-cultural therapy. However, where many publications talk in either general, philosophical terms about cross-cultural differences in therapy, or specifically about working with particular populations of individuals, this model provides a template for understanding both one's own value system, as well as the value system of one's clients, in a manner that is objective, nonjudgmental, and allows for application across a breadth of clients with a variety of cultural backgrounds.

One other aspect of this model that is particularly appealing is the use of axes, rather than categories, to describe characteristics. Professionals in the fields of counseling and psychology know that in understanding humans from the standpoint of personality, characteristics, and temperament, it can be quite useful (and behaviorally accurate) to think in terms of personality attributes as occurring on a continuum rather than as absolutes.

Any personality characteristic can be either a strength *or* a liability, depending on the context and particular circumstances in which that characteristic is appearing. As well, when we talk about characteristics and tendencies, we are not talking about something that is a fixed aspect of the person; we are talking about the probability that a person will act a certain way.

Personality characteristics and temperament are not "carved in stone"; while a certain behavior might have an extremely low probability of being exhibited by a person, the possibility always exists that the behavior *might* be exhibited given the right set of circumstances. An example might make this explanation more clear. Think of someone you know whom you would describe as selfish. It might be more accurate to describe that person as someone who sometimes demonstrates behaviors and thoughts that prioritize his or her own needs over the needs of others. Moreover, can you think of at least one instance in which he or she engaged in some action intended to meet someone else's needs or expectations? The point is that these categories or axes are continuums, and that human characteristics are fluid and, to a certain extent, unpredictable.

So it is for individuals with cultures similar to or different from our own. Although it might be highly likely that a person will demonstrate certain values and behaviors because of a particular cultural background, there are always individual differences within a group, and there are usually differences resulting from situational circumstances that result in behavioral variability within the same individual.

Let's turn now to the Hofstede model (Hofstede, 2001). Figure 2.2 offers a visual diagram of four of the five axes and the anchors that represent the two ends of each continuum. Please note that while the definitions of all five axes are presented in this introductory chapter, only the four axes on the diagram will be utilized in the subsequent skill chapters. The fifth axis of time orientation, as defined in the model, is one that would be heavily focused on treatment outcome. Because of that, the time orientation axis does not as easily lend itself to the counseling process in the same manner that the other axes do, and so it will not be presented as one of the cultural values in the subsequent microskill chapters.

The figure also lists the countries with the highest ranks with regard to each anchor of each continuum. These are listed merely as informative reference points.

1. *Power Distance:* This axis shows the extent to which less powerful members of a society accept that power is distributed unequally.

This axis accounts for how a particular culture addresses human inequality and power imbalance. At the macrosystem level, think about how the political structure of a nation might affect its members' perception of power distance. In a democratic country, in theory, any citizen has equal potential for acquiring political power. In addition, citizens have an opportunity to express opinions and exert some degree of influence over political decisions that are made in the form of laws and policies. In contrast, in autocratic or totalitarian societies, individuals in power can wield it over their constituents with little if any regard for what the citizens prefer. If one is not born into a ruling class, there is little hope of having influence or input into decisions or actions.

Hofstede refers to the work of a social psychologist, Mulder, whose research proved numerous hypotheses related to human power in relationships. Mulder (1973, 1977) defined power distance as the degree of inequality in power between a less powerful Individual (I) and a more powerful Other (O), in which I and O are members of the same social system.

Let's consider how this value would manifest at the level of the microsystem and mesosystem. In a family interaction among people in a low power distance culture, the parents may be more likely to run the family in a manner that is democratic, taking children's preferences into account. Children are not expected to care for their elders, and it is expected that they will be socially competent at a younger age. In contrast, in a high power distance culture, the parents are more likely to be seen as absolute authority; the adage "Children should be seen and not heard" reflects this view. Children in a high power distance culture are expected to take responsibility for taking care of their elders throughout the elders' lives.

These definitions of the two poles on the power distance axis suggest obvious influence on individual perceptions. Examples of such perceptions could include how a client

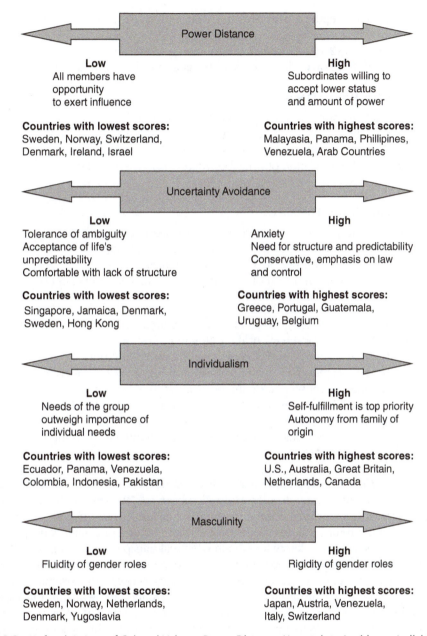

Power Distance

Low	**High**
All members have opportunity to exert influence	Subordinates willing to accept lower status and amount of power

Countries with lowest scores:
Sweden, Norway, Switzerland, Denmark, Ireland, Israel

Countries with highest scores:
Malayasia, Panama, Phillipines, Venezuela, Arab Countries

Uncertainty Avoidance

Low	**High**
Tolerance of ambiguity Acceptance of life's unpredictability Comfortable with lack of structure	Anxiety Need for structure and predictability Conservative, emphasis on law and control

Countries with lowest scores:
Singapore, Jamaica, Denmark, Sweden, Hong Kong

Countries with highest scores:
Greece, Portugal, Guatemala, Uruguay, Belgium

Individualism

Low	**High**
Needs of the group outweigh importance of individual needs	Self-fulfillment is top priority Autonomy from family of origin

Countries with lowest scores:
Ecuador, Panama, Venezuela, Colombia, Indonesia, Pakistan

Countries with highest scores:
U.S., Australia, Great Britain, Netherlands, Canada

Masculinity

Low	**High**
Fluidity of gender roles	Rigidity of gender roles

Countries with lowest scores:
Sweden, Norway, Netherlands, Denmark, Yugoslavia

Countries with highest scores:
Japan, Austria, Venezuela, Italy, Switzerland

FIGURE 2.2 Hofstede's Axes of Cultural Values: Power Distance, Uncertainty Avoidance, Individualism, Masculinity.

thinks about his or her responsibility as a parent, or as a child of elderly parents. The axis of power distance *also* carries implications for the counseling process in terms of how the client views the counselor and vice versa. For example, when the counselor is from a national culture, such as that of the United States, in which power distance may be somewhat lower than it is for a client who is from a high power distance culture, there may be discrepant perceptions between the counselor and the client as to how much control the client has over aspects of his or her life.

Draguns (2002) identified the following characteristics he hypothesized would correspond with the power distance axis (this is applicable for both the therapist and the client):

High Power Distance

- Likely to prefer a directive counseling approach
- Sees the counselor as authority figure and expert
- Concerned with conformity and social effectiveness
- Clear differentiation of roles between counselor and client
- Emphasis on counselor's credentials

Low Power Distance

- Likely to prefer a person-centered counseling approach
- Sees the counselor as a concerned, sensitive person
- Concerned with self-discovery and actualization
- Minimal differentiation of roles between counselor and client
- Emphasis on self-improvement

As you are working with a client and trying to ascertain his or her degree of power distance, ask yourself or the client the following questions:

○ To what extent does this person see me as an authority figure?
○ To what extent does this person seem to expect a formal counseling relationship?
○ To what extent will he or she be comfortable sharing in the goal-setting process?
○ What will be the best way to earn his or her respect? Is this someone who is impressed by credentials, or does he or she express a need to know me as a person?
○ How much personal information should I divulge to help the rapport and increase my trustworthiness?

2. *Uncertainty Avoidance:* This construct is based on the anxiety that individuals experience about future outcomes. Hofstede observed, "We are caught in a present that is just an infinitesimal borderline between past and future" (2001, p. 145). We are forced to accept the fact that the future is never the present. "Future" is an ephemeral concept that always eludes us; there is no way to know for certain what will transpire as time unfolds. When we are faced with excessive levels of uncertainty, we can experience extreme anxiety. Because of that, cultures have developed mechanisms that enable us to keep our existential anxiety at bay.

Those mechanisms take three forms: (1) technology, which in this case refers to a culture's human-made products (barometers, thermometers) that allow us to defend against the unpredictable events that occur in nature (e.g., tornadoes, hurricanes, earthquakes); (2) laws, which are arbitrary structures that define acceptable social behavior and therefore make human behavior within a given culture somewhat predictable; and (3) religion, which functions as revealed knowledge of the unknown. Religion is an avenue by which members of a culture can accept the unavoidable uncertainty not managed by technology or law.

At an individual level, the construct of uncertainty avoidance is associated with particular personality characteristics. A high degree of uncertainty avoidance is associated with authoritarianism, which is exemplified by black-and-white thinking, without shades of gray. Distinct differentiation is made between right and wrong, regardless of mitigating circumstances. People who exhibit a high degree of preference for authoritarianism tend to be intolerant of ambiguity, prefer clear black-and-white categories, are more rigid, and tend toward dogmatism, in which they create for themselves distinct categories. These same characteristics are reflected at the cultural level with rigid, harsh laws and clear behavioral expectations for acceptable and unacceptable behavior.

In contrast, cultures with a low degree of uncertainty avoidance tend not to place importance on rigid adherence to rules, are open to differences and risks, and generally demonstrate less anxiety among the general population.

Draguns (2002) suggested the following client characteristics that might correspond with high or low uncertainty avoidance:

High Uncertainty Avoidance

- Medical cause for problems is preferable explanation for emotional symptoms
- Structured behavioral techniques most appealing
- Likely to view certain treatment approaches as right or wrong in a black-and-white manner
- Most comfortable with a highly controlled and structured practice arrangement

Low Uncertainty Avoidance

- Emotional or psychological cause for problems is more likely explanation for emotional symptoms
- Unstructured, experiential therapy techniques most appealing
- Likely to view many treatment approaches as valid
- Comfortable with a loose, unstructured practice arrangement

To consider the degree of uncertainty avoidance, ask yourself the following questions:

- Is this a person who frequently experiences nervousness or worry?
- To what extent was that nervousness transmitted by significant people in his or her life?
- Does this person speak of physical symptoms in lieu of emotional symptoms?
- Does this person believe strongly that rules should *always* be followed *at all costs?*
- To what extent does he or she find interest or excitement in just sitting back and seeing how things unfold?
- Are schedules and timelines of great importance in this person's life?

3. *Individualism:* This axis focuses on the degree of affiliation and accountability an individual experiences among circles of people, such as nuclear family, extended family, tribe, local community. Draguns (2002) noted that the self is experienced as a separate entity in individualist cultures, whereas in collectivist cultures the self is experienced contextually. Individualism refers to the extent to which a person perceives him- or herself as separate from the family.

At the other end of this continuum is collectivism, which refers to the extent to which the needs of the group outweigh the needs of an individual, because it is assumed the best interest of the group *is* in the best interest of each individual member. There are differences across national cultures in the extent to which either of these anchors on the continuum is emphasized. For example, the United States tends to lean heavily toward individualism, whereas historically in China individualism was seen as a less mature, disciplined approach to decision making.

In a collectivistic culture, the group expects loyalty from each member. In exchange for loyalty, group members benefit from the protection and safety of the group. The value standards for the members of the group are different from those for nonmembers. There is strong emphasis on being part of the in-group.

The correlations between this axis of collectivism and the way these characteristics would pertain to counseling are hypothesized as follows (Draguns, 2002):

High Individualism (Low Collectivism)

- Seeking insight and self-understanding
- Seeking development of one's individuality
- Development of a sense of personal responsibility
- Likely to relate to the therapist as a parent figure, guiding and directing
- Emotional complaints likely to include guilt, alienation, loneliness

Low Individualism (High Collectivism)

- Seeking elimination or reduction of suffering
- Emotional complaints likely to include shame
- Relationship problems likely
- Seeking social integration
- Seeking acceptance of controls established and maintained by others
- Harmonious relationships of extreme importance
- Therapist likely to be seen as nurturing mother

As you work with a client and attempt to ascertain his or her inclination with regard to individualism, ask yourself the following:

- In major life decisions, to what extent did family or others' directives influence the client's choices?
- To what extent is he or she dependent on group membership as an aspect of self-definition?
- To what extent does he or she depend on the group membership for a sense of purpose in life?
- What are, in her or his mind, the ideal outcomes of a successful counseling experience?

Case Example

Mr. M. was a 28-year-old unmarried Caucasian male of German descent. His religious affiliation was Mennonite. He was seen by a counselor at the state prison, where Mr. M. was incarcerated for having incurred two convictions of driving under the influence of alcohol (DUIs). Mr. M. had been raised in a family who held strict Mennonite beliefs. Aspects of the religious belief system included strong emphasis on belonging to the group of worshippers, abstinence from alcohol, and individuals being responsible for making moral choices. Mr. M. began drinking when he got a job in a nearby town and some coworkers invited him to "happy hour." Mr. M. had never drunk alcohol before that. His drinking quickly became out of control, and shortly after he began going out with his coworkers he got his first DUI. When the pastor of the church and the other members found out about his DUI, he was shunned and informed that he was no longer welcome to worship at the church. This resulted in feelings of extreme guilt and alienation, which led to further drinking. By the time he had gotten his second DUI, no one from his Mennonite community wanted anything more to do with him, and in prison he also did not fit into any of the inmate cliques. Beyond his desire to overcome his addiction, his primary complaint to the prison counselor was that he just didn't fit anywhere; neither the inmates nor the church members wanted him to be part of their group. This alienation was a source of tremendous emotional pain for him.

Mr. M. likely had a high degree of uncertainty avoidance and a low degree of individualism. What would be appropriate topics or issues on which a counselor would need to focus?

4. *Masculinity and Femininity:* This axis refers to roles and responsibilities a culture associates with particular genders; specifically, the fluidity, or rigidity, of expectations for roles based on gender. Gender role socialization begins in the family of origin and is transmitted across generations by modeling as well as by direct instruction. In cultures that are on the masculine end of the continuum, gender roles are rigidly fixed, meaning that men are expected to be tough and aggressive, while women are expected to be passive and deferent. Cultures that fall more toward the feminine end of the continuum hold expectations of overlap in social roles between genders.

Gender roles may be fixed not only in terms of personality characteristics, but also in roles and responsibilities within that culture. Masculine cultures may have strict expectations about a female's role in the family as the one who bears children, takes care of the male and the children, and runs the household.

According to Draguns, the following characteristics might correspond with high and low degrees of masculinity/femininity:

High Masculinity (Low Femininity)

- Emphasis on responsibility, conformity, and adjustment to social norms
- Likely complaints of feeling guilty
- Less inclined to express feelings verbally
- Inclination to care for others (enabling)
- Focus on productivity
- Focus on competence

Low Masculinity (High Femininity)

- Emphasis on what's best for the individual person
- Valuing emotional expressiveness, creativity, and empathy
- Complaints of anxiety likely
- Focus on caretaking
- Focus on happiness and caring

In your counseling interaction and effort to ascertain where your client lies on this particular continuum, ask yourself the following questions:

- How competitive is this person?
- To what extent does this person express his or her feelings based on beliefs about gender (e.g., "Are you *kidding*? I didn't cry—boys don't cry!")?
- To what extent does this person see family roles and responsibilities tied to gender?
- To what extent is the "bottom line" the only thing that counts (i.e., outcome, as opposed to process)?

5. _Long- and Short-Term Orientation:_ This axis refers to the extent to which a culture programs its members to defer gratification of their material, social, and emotional needs. It was not initially identified in the IBM study, but emerged later in the data from a subsequent study of 23 countries that used the Chinese Value Survey. It would be remiss to discuss Hofstede's model without covering this factor. However, this axis is not going to be included in our subsequent discussions of the Hofstede model and microskills, because the construct as defined makes it difficult to apply to counseling issues with consistency. The primary feature of this axis is rooted in Confucian philosophy. At one end of the continuum is thriftiness and persistence, and at the other end, personal stability and honoring tradition. One of the main concepts in this realm is the idea of "filial piety," which refers to the Chinese value of honoring one's ancestors in one's present choices and behaviors.

PERSONAL REFLECTION

Looking back over the history of your extended family, how many generations have been U.S. citizens? Plot your own values and beliefs on each of these five axes. To what extent have your own beliefs evolved as an extension of your parents' or caregivers' beliefs? To what extent do you think their beliefs arose from the national cultures of the countries of origin of your ancestors?

Racial Identity Development and Acculturation

When two groups of people with distinct cultural characteristics come together, there is a process by which cultural features of one group are adopted and incorporated by the other group. This is the process of acculturation and racial identity development. Multiple models of racial identity development have appeared in the professional literature, although space constraints do not permit exploration of that topic. Nevertheless, acculturation pertains to our current discussion because it describes the process through which a person of minority status integrates and infuses cultural features of both groups. There are multiple models of minority identity development that clearly articulate phases of acculturation. As you work with your clients who are members of cultural minority groups, their stages of identity development and acculturation will be sources of significant individual differences.

Implications of the Multicultural Material for Counseling Students

Our brains continually receive a tremendous amount of data, entering our neurological system through all five senses. One cognitive strategy that our brains employ to reduce environmental complexity is to create categories, so that when new data comes in, we can place the information into a previously constructed category. In the case of stereotypes, research has indicated that when people must make a judgment about a situation and have been given ambiguous information about the individuals involved, they tend to rely on stereotyped information (Bodenhausen & Lichtenstein, 1987).

When we encounter other people, some of us make an immediate comparison, evaluating the ways in which we are the same and different from the other person. These comparisons are most likely to be based on those aspects of the other person that are readily observable: facial characteristics, gender, clothing, and physical attributes. Once we have that information, we may then go on to rely on stereotypes to make judgments about the person. Another study (Carter, Hall, Carney, & Rosip, 2006), found that some people are more inclined than others to stereotype. People with a greater tendency to stereotype have more rigid values concerning male and female gender roles, tend to be authoritarian in their preference for social structure, are less agreeable than others, and tend toward having black-and-white thinking.

The founder of person-centered therapy, Carl Rogers, enumerated core conditions that are necessary for growth and development. One of the core conditions is highly pertinent in this discussion about multiculturally competent counseling: the condition of empathy. Beyond Rogers's theory, an ethical component that pertains in this discussion is informed consent.

EMPATHY Empathy is a construct that you will come across often in your preparation to become a professional helper. The ability to empathize depends on one's ability to take on the perspective of another person. Perspective-taking is related to a construct referred to as *cognitive flexibility.* Spiro and Jehng (1990, p. 165) state: "By cognitive flexibility, we mean the ability to spontaneously restructure one's knowledge, in many ways, in adaptive response to radically changing situational demands." Being able to work effectively with a variety of clients or students depends to a certain extent on our ability to perceive a situation from another person's perspective.

It has been proposed that there are stages of social development related to perspective taking that begin in childhood, in which social reasoning becomes more sophisticated. Selman, Jaquette, and Lavin (1977) proposed four stages that progress from egocentric to subjective, to self-reflective, to third-person perspective. There is a certain level of social development that is necessary in order to see the value, or have the motivation, to attempt to see the world through another person's eyes.

In the context of cultural differences, it is critical that we have self-awareness of our own cultural template as well as awareness of how our clients' cultural templates might differ from our own. There needs to be a corresponding acknowledgment that what is true for us might not necessarily be the same truth for our client. Although aspects of individual differences can be expected as a result of visible differences between ourselves and another person, there will likely be other variables of difference that are not immediately apparent. The important point is not to assume that someone else will think, act, or feel as we do just because they look on the surface as though they are similar to us.

INFORMED CONSENT We will begin this discussion of informed consent and diversity with two applied examples of how beliefs and values could have substantial impact on the counseling process. One counseling student was doing his internship at an agency that was funded through a large religious organization. The agency did not have a religiously affiliated title; it was a title roughly similar to Mapleview Center for Human Development. The intern had a client, a 22-year-old woman who was unmarried and had just discovered she was pregnant. This client was very upset about her unplanned pregnancy, and she wanted to explore the full range of her options, from having the baby and raising it alone, through terminating the pregnancy by abortion.

She came to the agency hopeful that her counselor would be able to help her in the decision-making process about her pregnancy. The intern felt very strongly that he should not even use the word "abortion" with the client and also believed that if the client terminated the pregnancy, she would be committing a mortal sin. The intern was not willing or able to put his own religious values aside in his work with the client. He appropriately explained his predicament to the client and referred her to another agency that received public funding, so that she could work toward her counseling goals of exploring her options.

A school counselor had a seventh-grade boy referred to her by his teacher. The young man disclosed to the counselor that he was being picked on by other students because he had two mothers. The school counselor was very offended by the fact that the student's parents were lesbians, and she secretly believed it was fitting that the boy was being ostracized. Unfortunately, though, there were no other counselors in the area who could work with the young man, and so the counselor had to offer him counseling.

PERSONAL REFLECTION

What are your feelings about the dilemmas in which these counselors found themselves? What would you recommend to each of them? How do you suppose the services their clients received were affected?

The process of discussing aspects of treatment with a new client is referred to as *informed consent*. A good informed consent contains many elements, most of which we will not cover here. However, part of informed consent means explaining to a client the range of treatment options or full range of choices that are possibilities for the presenting problem. It also means making a full disclosure to clients if the counselor or agency is limited in how they can work with the client on the basis of religious or philosophical beliefs. For every client you see, you will need to make a decision about whether you will be able to impartially help the person reach a decision or if you are clearly skewed in a particular direction and intend to try to influence the client in that direction.

PERSONAL REFLECTION

Consider the aspects of life, lifestyle, religion, and spirituality that are most central in your life. Ask yourself if you subscribe to any of them so resolutely that there is absolutely no room for alternative beliefs or definitions. What are some ways those central tenets in your life may influence your work with your clients?

Chapter Summary

In this chapter we have covered ground that included counseling, anthropology, social psychology, and ethical issues. Multicultural competence, by definition, involves awareness of cultural similarities and differences, and willingness to honor the worldview of clients whose frameworks might be vastly different from your own.

The Sue, Arrendondo, and McDavis (1992) model of multicultural competence encompasses self-awareness, knowledge, and skills, components that are necessary for competence in general, as well as multiculturally. If you are going to work with clients whose cultures are unfamiliar to you, it will be important to the counseling process for you to become educated and knowledgeable about the cultural parameters of your client's community.

The chapter discussed two models that offer frameworks for conceptualizing the role of culture and community in individual differences, as well as specific ways that cultures differ on certain core value orientations. Bronfenbrenner's ecological model systematically articulates what some of us might take for granted as far as how multiple levels of our cultures affect our daily lives. Hofstede's model of cultural variability offers portability and applicability. Even if the cultural group with whom we are working was not represented in the data set of Hofstede's original research, the axes of cultural variability can nevertheless be used as a basis for understanding how a client's values differ from other cultural values. This is a template that will be used for considering advantages and disadvantages of each of the microskills we will cover in the chapters to come.

Finally, we looked in general at ways that your own value and belief system can affect the manner in which you work with your clients. One of the recurrent themes throughout the chapter was the importance of self-awareness and self-knowledge as a cornerstone for developing multicultural competence. Being willing to acknowledge and account for spheres of cultural influence beyond the individual that affect our clients' lives and emotional experiences represents a significant step toward being multiculturally aware.

Questions for Class Discussion

1. What is the relationship between your political beliefs and your thoughts about the multicultural competence standards?
2. How have your own family's cultural values affected your choice to become a professional counselor?
3. To what extent do you believe it is a counselor's responsibility to offer counseling in a manner consistent with a client's worldview?
4. What are examples of clients and worldviews with whom you absolutely could not work? Why would you be unable?

CHAPTER 3

The Microskills Model

After studying this chapter, you should have a clear understanding of the following:

- Understanding of the skill model used in this text
- Awareness of the history of how this model was developed
- Awareness of other models for learning counseling skills
- Understanding of where microskills fit in the overall process of counseling skill acquisition

The first chapter of this text presented the three-component approach of skills, theory, and multiculturalism with self-awareness comprising a common thread throughout. We turn now to the *skill* component of this text. *Skill,* as the term is used here, refers specifically to what you do while you are in the physical presence of your client. Other aspects of counseling also involve skill development, such as assessment, possibly diagnosis, consultation, and case conceptualization. The skills we focus on in this text are primarily those that would be used in a counseling intervention with a client.

If you have ever had the benefit of being in counseling yourself, with a counselor who was competent, perhaps you wondered about how he or she was able to master the broad range of skills that were components of the ability to be such a good helper. Learning the repertoire of helping skills isn't really much different or more difficult than learning any other complex skill. Consider, for example, the skill of learning how to play a musical instrument. A beginning student must learn a number of different kinds of skills and information. These include learning the names of musical notes, learning how to count a beat, learning how to read written music, and learning how to act upon the instrument to create sound. Listening to an accomplished musician play a piece of music, the listener is aware of the sound being emitted without conscious awareness of all the discrete components of learning and skill mastery that occurred prior to the piece of music being played. In counseling as well, there are a series of components that can each be mastered as discrete units and that, when combined, comprise a broader set of skills referred to as *counseling*.

As you develop the ability to perform each of these components with ease and comfort, your own style of helping will begin to emerge. Each individual's use of the counseling skills looks somewhat different from anyone else's. If 10 people each drew a picture of an apple, each composition would look different. It could be partly due to differing artistic ability among those 10 individuals, but it would also be partly due to the interplay between the drawing skills and the person engaging in the drawing.

This author's hope for each of you is that as you learn the skills you will be gentle and patient with yourself and allow yourself to integrate the skills into your natural style of interacting with others. Some students are highly critical of themselves and expect to be able to perform a skill perfectly the first time they try it. Being gentle with yourself means trying to maintain a realistic level of expectation about your ability. Students who have already been working in a helping capacity may hold higher expectations for themselves or already be familiar with this material. To the extent that you can, try to refrain from comparing yourself negatively to your instructor or your classmates; everyone is learning something, and we all have strengths and weaknesses.

HISTORICAL CONTEXT

When the microskills approach was first developed, behavioral theory and therapy were emerging in the field of psychology as scientifically respectable, viable options for treating clients with a variety of presenting concerns. At the time of behaviorism's emergence in the field of psychology, the cultural climate in the field consisted, in part, of a push to become a discipline as scientific and empirically "legitimate" as other hard sciences. Thus, the movement toward reducing behaviors and interactions to quantifiable, observable behavior became a major force in psychology.

It has been noted (Baker & Daniels, 1989) that prior to Carl Rogers's contributions, the field of counseling had not seen the development of systematic, intentionally focused models for training counseling students in specific skills. Rogers was responsible for directing the profession of counselor training toward a systematic method (Rogers, 1961). Other structured approaches emerged over the next several decades, including Carkuff's human resource training/human development model, Kagan's interpersonal process recall, and Ivey's microcounseling (also referred to as microskills) model. There are multiple other training approaches, but we will limit this discussion to a few of the most commonly cited training models.

The microskills model emerged in the late 1960s and early 1970s as an effective method for teaching counseling skills. The approach is based on theories of social learning and behavioral instruction. Since the development of the microskills model, there have been over 450 empirical studies that have supported a microskills model as an efficacious approach to skill development (Ivey & Ivey, 2007). This may be due, in part, to the strong emphasis on behavioral aspects of counseling skill acquisition; behavioral theory in general lends itself well to objective, quantitative research on its efficacy.

For those readers who are interested in learning more about the research on the microskills model, several excellent meta-analyses examine the effect size of results across many studies. One such meta-analysis is Baker, Daniels, and Greeley (1990) in which the authors compared Carkhuff's human resource training/human resource development model, Kagan's interpersonal process recall, and Ivey's microcounseling approaches. We will look briefly at the human resource development and interpersonal process recall models before moving on to focus in more detail on the microskills model.

Human Resource Development Model

Baker, Daniels, and Greeley (1990) noted that the human resource development model has been among the most commonly used approaches to training counselors. In Carkhuff's Human Resource Development (HRD) model, the supervisor creates and maintains the core conditions for change, making the learning process a parallel event to that which clients will experience in counseling. The philosophical and theoretical basis of this HRD approach is Rogerian. Thus, at the same time learners are developing skills, they themselves are experiencing what it feels like to be a recipient of intervention with a professional who has established core conditions for change, such as unconditional positive regard. The rationale behind this approach is that having the experience and seeing helping skills modeled is of greater value than simply having it explained didactically.

Carkhuff (1969) emphasized the importance of the trainer (supervisor) having a level of skill mastery far above the level of the trainees. He also observed, interestingly, that the training programs that were most effective in producing skilled trainees were those programs that systematically focused on facilitative and action-oriented domains, using a behavioral training approach.

Interpersonal Process Recall

Kagan's Interpersonal Process Recall (IPR) relies heavily on the learner's own process of discovery as a means of learning, rather than inundating students with a preponderance of didactic material. Kagan based his model on the premise that trainees often are inhibited from making appropriate counseling responses because of their own performance anxiety and concern about how the client is perceiving them (impression management). The IPR model relies heavily on videotaped counseling sessions. Students progress through several phases of training; at the beginning, they observe effective counselor responses and then practice them; then, students watch a videotaped statement from a client looking directly at the camera and must generate an effective response; and finally, the trainees conduct a session with a client and tape it for later review with the trainer. In the review of the session, the focus is not on the trainee's skills per se, but rather on the trainee sharing what he or she was thinking and feeling at various points during the session. These internal reactions become the primary vehicle for learning. The internal reactions provide a window for the instructor to better understand the trainee's internal process. If or when there are errors in the trainee's perceptions or thinking, the instructor can help correct them. This procedure also assists the student in the development of increased self-awareness. The process of tape review has been found to facilitate the trainee's recall of internal experiences after the fact.

Instructors of an introductory counseling skills course are faced with a decision about what model of skill development they will use, as well as how the course content will be organized. Some instructors, myself as an example, use an approach that incorporates teaching techniques and strategies from several models of counselor training. Each of the above approaches offers unique contributions to the teaching process, supporting an eclectic model of training that allows the strengths of each approach to be utilized.

THE MICROSKILLS MODEL

We turn now to the model for framing counseling behaviors that will be used in the remainder of this text. The essence of the microskills model is that therapeutic communication between a counselor and client is characterized by a number of specific, behaviorally identifiable strategies. Seasoned therapists engage in many of these microskills so frequently and comfortably that they are unaware of doing it. However, beginners sometimes find it awkward or uncomfortable to reduce their interactions to small, isolated components. Nevertheless, Ivey and his colleagues found that when complex helping behaviors were reduced to small behavioral components, students' ease of learning the skills increased. This process consists of the instructor describing a particular skill, modeling the desired behavior for the trainee, directing the trainee to practice the behavior, then offering feedback. The microskills model, as it is presented in Ivey and Ivey (2007), can be conceptualized as a pyramid, in which the most common and basic skill of attending behavior is at the base, and subsequent skills build upon one another until the higher order, more complex skills of confrontation and reflecting meaning comprise the top of the structure. The basic skills in the microskills model then are the foundation for applying more advanced skills through which specific theories are implemented.

As you progress through each of the levels of microskills, you will be using each of the microskill behaviors you have learned to that point as well as practicing the newest one. Students often report that at the beginning, they feel awkward engaging in attending skills, but by the time they have progressed to feeling reflection, they are attending extremely well and in fact are unaware of needing to think about the components of attending; they are simply doing it. Their descriptions reflect a process called *automaticity*. Automaticity has been identified as a learning process that occurs in identifiable stages (Bargh, 1992; Brown, 1989; Patterson, Rak, Chermonte, & Roper, 1992; Phillips & Hughes, 1988; Rak, MacCluskie, Toman, Patterson, & Culotta, 2003). It's likely that you, too, will experience the process of automaticity if you stick with the microskills approach throughout all the skill components.

Here is the list of skills that will be covered in this text:

1. Attending
2. Client observation
3. Minimal encouragers, paraphrasing, and summarizing
4. Questioning
5. Feeling reflection
6. Reflection of meaning
7. Supportive challenging

The skills at the beginning of the list are the ones most likely to be used by all counselors, regardless of their theoretical orientation, type of client, or setting. As the list progresses, the skills become more directive, and the likelihood of the skills being used universally among all therapists decreases. For example, attending behavior is an essential component of counseling intervention regardless of what the counselor's theoretical orientation may be. As well, regarding the skill of client observation, a counselor must carefully listen and observe the client's presentation in order to fully understand and appreciate the client's experience.

On the other hand, the more advanced microskills may be used more frequently by some therapists than by others, depending on the therapist's clientele, theory base, and

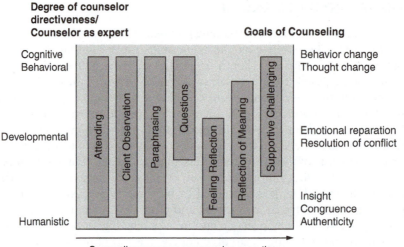

FIGURE 3.1   **Diagram of Microskills by Level of Directiveness and Goals for Each Theory Group**

personal style. For example, a counselor who works with clients who are court-ordered and chemically dependent might be likely to use supportive challenging. In contrast, a school counselor who works primarily with children who have been abused and neglected might be more likely to frequently use paraphrasing and feeling reflection.

Advantages of the Microskills Model

Chapter 11 offers a more detailed explanation of some theories commonly used in counseling. For our present discussion, I'll introduce the idea that various theories differ significantly in the degree of directiveness or influence the therapist exerts over the course and direction of the counseling. Microskills portrayed in Figure 3.1 as having shorter lines tend to be those that are more directive than others; these are the microskills that will have clearly identifiable influence on the course and direction of the focus of counseling.

With regard to directiveness, some counselors are very comfortable in the role of expert, with a clearly defined set of beliefs about the nature of human disturbance and what things need to happen for a client to feel better. Other counselors are more inclined to perceive themselves as coaches and collaborators, people who may be able to help other people to help themselves. These subtle differences in how a counselor defines his or her role has a not-so-subtle effect on how he or she implements particular microskills.

Many authors have hypothesized about why clinicians choose the particular theories that they do. Microskills can be conceptualized as discrete, free-standing behaviors that vary in the degree of directiveness imposed by the counselor. Directiveness in this context can be defined two ways. One definition is the extent to which the counselor directs the client's focus to a topic or to particular aspects of the client's material. The other definition of directiveness is the extent to which the counselor attempts to influence the client's thoughts, feelings, or behavior.

The nondirective approaches, primarily those that are humanistic or person-centered, focus exclusively on the material the client brings to the session and chooses to share with the counselor. The cognitive-behavioral approaches are quite directive, in that although the client is the one who takes the responsibility for defining the scope of the problem, the theoretical approach itself clearly defines the ultimate nature of the disturbance and also dictates a specific course of treatment. So, in your reading and practicing counseling skills, when you learn directive microskills and you make decisions about which part of the client's verbal and nonverbal material you are going to respond to first, those decisions will be based partly on your instinct, but should also be firmly grounded in the theories you are using to guide your conceptualization of what's wrong with the client and what needs to happen for him or her to grow.

There are a number of traditional theoretical approaches, three of which we will be using for illustration with applied microskill examples. We should also note here, though, that the movement in the field of counseling toward evidence-based treatment approaches is often integrative, meaning that these approaches incorporate numerous techniques that come from a number of different theory bases.

Here is something to think about. When you sit down to discuss someone's concerns, if you make a recommendation about what the person should do, your recommendation arises out of your assumption that you know more about what is wrong than the client does.

PERSONAL REFLECTION

Think of the advantages and disadvantages of giving a person advice about how to solve a problem. What personal examples can you think of in which you were told what to do to solve a problem? What influence do those personal examples have now on your view about how directive you should be?

Some theories and models of counseling emphasize the therapist as an expert consultant who guides and directs the material in the counseling session; other theories emphasize the client as the individual responsible for directing the focus and course of the session and the overall counseling process. It will be important for you to be aware of your own beliefs about this issue as you decide which microskills you will implement at any point in the counseling session.

An interesting study was conducted by Newman and Fuqua (1990) in which the researchers looked at 10 different microskills to see which of those microskills were preferred by 38 counseling students, some of whom were new to counselor education and some of whom were advanced students preparing to graduate. The researchers found stability of preferences among the students, with a higher degree of preference for the nondirective microskills.

Use of the more directive skills is something that commits the counseling process in a particular direction. Perhaps students are more comfortable not making that commitment.

AUTHOR'S REFLECTION

In my own work with clients, I have often found that my impression of a particular client and my perception of what was really wrong at the most basic level shifted over the course of several sessions. In other words, one's first impression of a client are not necessarily the same as the sense of the client that one will have after several meetings.

Recent years have seen increased accountability for mental health providers, particularly with regard to insurance companies, giving a diagnosis and generating a treatment plan within one or two sessions. This approach requires rapid assessment and intervention. That's good from the standpoint of reducing costs, but not from the standpoint of establishing a therapeutic alliance, which takes time, and also from the standpoint of carefully and deliberately taking time to actively listen to the client in a manner that fully accounts for and appreciates the whole client, including cultural template, past learning, systemic embeddedness, and so forth. The less directive microskills give helpers the opportunity to do this. As well, the microskills approach is advantageous in this regard because you will have a repertoire of skills that will also enable you to be directive and able to rapidly assess, if necessary, by intentionally implementing particular skills. This can be a significant asset in a school counseling session where the intervention may be brief and solution-focused.

Limitations of the Microskills Model

As with any unidimensional approach to a task, there are also limitations and weaknesses of the microskills model. One is that a behavioral approach that teaches technically correct counseling behavior does not necessarily also teach the intangible components of attitude and intention. Perhaps some of you have seen a physician who was outstanding in his or her technical skills, but who was cold and insensitive to your concerns as a patient. When we have a serious medical problem, we likely want to consult with a medical specialist who is expert in the area of the problem, and we will be more concerned with his or her ability to treat the problem than with his or her degree of compassion and empathy. In the case of counseling and therapy, however, our empathy is an integral aspect of what we offer our clients. Therefore, becoming proficient in the technical skills of counseling does notsensure that we will be able to establish relationships that are of benefit to our clients.

As well, empathy and compassion come from *within* ourselves, and while behaviors of a compassionate person can be observed and described, the individual's internal experience of *feeling* compassion is an aspect of that event that arises from within; it is not taught.

PERSONAL REFLECTION _____

Recall a time when a friend or family member agreed to do an activity with you even though inside, they didn't really want to. How could you tell they had some internal resistance? How did their resistance affect your experience of doing that activity?

Given the Personal Reflection described above, consider how, in your role as a counselor, your own ability to empathize, or conversely, your resistance or reluctance to engage with a client, might affect his or her perception of your technically correct counseling behavior.

One of the biggest drawbacks of teaching counseling using only the microskills approach is that the internal experience of a relationship between two individuals cannot be completely explained by describing the externally observable behaviors. That's because a huge part of a relationship is about what happens inside each person as he or she is interacting with the other. If we describe a musician's observable behavior, our description can't capture his or her immediate, internal experience of creating the music and using the instrument as a vehicle for expressing feelings or thoughts. Thus, while we can look at and learn how to exhibit certain behaviors, it will not approximate our internal experience of establishing a counseling relationship with another person who has come to us for help.

The experience of having genuine respect and concern for the other person and genuine desire to help another person in his or her suffering comes from one's heart. Humans are social beings, with a desire for connectedness and sharing of experience. The microskills are merely a vehicle for establishing the relationship with another. Each of us has our own ways of establishing relationships and being in relationships with other people, whether

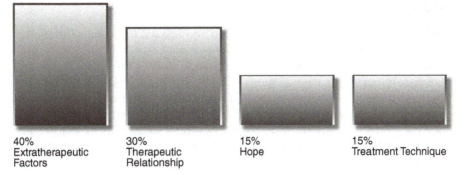

40%
Extratherapeutic
Factors

30%
Therapeutic
Relationship

15%
Hope

15%
Treatment Technique

FIGURE 3.2 **Proportion of Contribution to Treatment Outcome**

Source: Hubble, Duncan, & Miller, 1999. © American Psychological Association (APA).

those others are new acquaintances, clients, or family members. Those same styles of how you are in all your relationships will be a mediating factor in how you acquire and integrate the microskills for use with your clients.

Microskills in the Context of Counseling Process and Outcome

Hubble, Duncan, and Miller (1999) conducted a meta-analysis of many treatment outcome studies and then identified the factors that contribute to clients reporting favorable outcomes from counseling. They cited relative contributions of four major factors:

1. Client/extratherapeutic factors: 40% (these include client strengths, environmental support, i.e., support system, and some chance events)
2. Relationship between therapist and client: 30% (these include caring, empathy, warmth, encouragement of risk-taking)
3. Hope: 15%
4. Model or technique used by counselor: 15%

A bar graph of this information is presented in Figure 3.2. Looking at a visual representation makes the importance of the therapeutic relationship readily apparent. We'll talk about each of these contributors in more detail.

Extratherapeutic Factors

A multitude of things will happen in your clients' lives during the course of time you are working with them. Some are developmental events that happen in many people's lives (e.g., birth, relationship difficulties, retirement,), and others are events that are traumatic or unique to that individual. In either case, those events, as well as the client's support system or lack thereof, will exert a significant impact on the degree to which your counseling intervention is ultimately helpful.

Client-Counselor Relationship

The pioneering work on relationships that was conducted by Carl Rogers endures as a highly significant aspect of counseling outcome. Outcome research has indicated that the nature of the relationship between the counselor and client is significantly more influential than the actual intervention techniques that are used.

Hope

Seligman and colleagues have developed and refined the concept of learned helplessness (e.g., Maier, Seligman, & Solomon, 1969; Seligman, Maier, & Geer, 1968). The helplessness research was initially conducted as behavioral studies using laboratory animals that were repeatedly subjected to uncomfortable stimuli (electric shock to the bottom of a metal cage) with no option for escape. The researchers found that after a period of time in which no escape was possible, if the animals were presented with the option of climbing onto a platform to avoid the shock, they continued to stay on the metal floor. This phenomenon, referred to as *learned helplessness,* has been seen in people who are depressed.

The relevance of learned helplessness in the current discussion is that it is conceptually the opposite of hope. It is quite important for a person to believe there is some hope of getting better. Often, when a client first comes for counseling, he or she may be experiencing some degree of hopelessness. It is the counselor's job, in part, to help the client discover or develop some glimmer of hope that his or her suffering will at some point be transformed.

Snyder, Michael, and Cheavens (1999) explained that four things contribute to a client developing a sense of hope. Two of them, the counseling relationship and the very act of going to a professional's office, create a sense of beginning to overcoming the problem. The other two factors are the counselor's belief in the theory he or she is using (they refer to this as the *compelling myth*) and the associated treatment strategies (therapeutic ritual acts), which become avenues for overcoming the problem.

AUTHOR'S REFLECTION

In my own work with clients, I usually spent the first session gathering a wide breadth of background information as well as exploring the nature of the problem that brought the client to my office. Toward the conclusion of the session, I allowed time for the client to ask me questions. Frequently, the clients' questions were one or both of the following: (1) Do you know what is wrong with me? and (2) Is there a chance I can get (or feel) better? These questions illustrate their need for hope.

Therapeutic Technique

Therapists employ a variety of techniques, and extensive research has looked specifically at which approaches are most effective for particular problems or mental disorders. There are commonalities across all theories of helping that share the approach of helping a client prepare to take action. The focus of the content and specifics of how that preparation transpires are two of the essential features that differentiate theories. That content unique to theoretical approaches will be explored in more detail in Chapter 11. We will further explore similarities and differences between techniques in Chapter 14, which covers empirically supported treatment and common psychotherapeutic factors.

In the Hubble et al. (1999) meta-analysis, client extratherapeutic factors and relationship were by far the most influential contributors to a favorable counseling outcome. In additional, whatever other techniques the counselor is using, his or her efforts will clearly be well spent by identifying and enriching the client's strengths and by establishing the best therapeutic relationship possible with the client.

OTHER CONSIDERATIONS IN MICROSKILL APPLICATION

In discussion about counseling outcome and microskills within that context, we need to look briefly at other considerations that affect when and how microskills fit in with the bigger picture of the counseling process.

Cultural and Social Forces

Many individuals, not the least of whom is Allen Ivey, who pioneered the microskills model, have written about the need for understanding a client's difficulties both from his or her perspective and also within a social and cultural context. More specifically, Ivey emphasizes the need not only for individual counseling interventions, but also for help at the community level in the form of social advocacy for clients (Ivey & Collins, 2003). Discrimination, oppression, and prejudice are all aspects of interpersonal experience that occur at the societal level and yet manifest results on the level of the individual. This is consistent with Bronfenbrenner's ecological model of multiple levels of interaction that all simultaneously exert influence on each individual.

Besides the fact that it may be important for a counselor to intervene at the level of social impediments and barriers to a client's healthy functioning, there will be events occurring outside the realm of the counseling interaction that nevertheless will significantly influence the favorable or ineffective result of the counseling experience. This became evident as an outcome of the Hubble, Duncan, and Miller (1999) meta-analysis.

We have talked about the relationship between theory and microskills. Another variable beyond the theoretical orientation of the therapist, which will affect the extent and frequency of usage of any microskill, is the stage of counseling: initiation and relationship development, problem definition, action, or termination. In the early stages of counseling, many counselors are likely inclined toward the nondirective microskills, whereas in the later stages, some therapists could be more likely to implement supportive challenging and questioning, which tend to be more directive.

Finally, the role of cultural template, values, and general worldview will also influence the likelihood that certain microskills will be used. This results from two sources: the cultural template of the counselor, and the cultural template of the client. Your own life experiences and background may prove to be influential in the microskills with which you are most comfortable. Likewise, your client's background may have a significant impact on how he or she perceives microskills you attempt to implement in a counseling session.

Chapter Summary

This chapter provided a conceptual framework for understanding where and how the skill component fits in with the overall approach of the text. Instructors of a counseling skills course have many options for how to present and teach the basic helping skills; microskills are just one approach.

In the microskills model, there are multiple discrete, identifiable behaviors, which will often have a predictable result when you implement them in a session. The subsequent skills chapters will provide you with systematic steps and examples of each skill. Making a choice about which skills to use when, and developing a rationale for the use of the skill, will occur over time.

Early in the chapter, we looked briefly at the Interpersonal Process Recall model and the Human Resource Development model. Elements of each of those approaches can be used even within the microskills approach. One of the most salient contributions is to consider the HRD model's basic tenet that trainee feedback should occur in conditions of unconditional positive regard. In other words, as you are participating in learning these skills, including offering feedback to your peers, remember that your feedback to others will be most helpful if it is behaviorally descriptive and does not judge the counselor trainee as a person. From the IPR model, be aware that as you and your peers are practicing these skills, it might be helpful to share with your peers what your thought process and emotional reactions were in the role of counselor.

Questions for Class Discussion

1. What are the ideal conditions under which you can learn? Discuss with your classmates a difficult skill you mastered and the sequence of steps you took in order to master it. What are the implications of that sequence in your current efforts to learn counseling skills?
2. What are some specific barriers that might arise as you attempt to acquire these skills? What ideas do you have about how to work around those barriers, or possibly use them as strengths?
3. On a scale of 1 to 10, with 10 being expert and 1 being complete beginner, what number rating would you give yourself at this point in the course? What number is your goal for the end of the course? How can your peers best help you reach that competence goal?

CHAPTER 4

Attending Behaviors

After studying this chapter, you should have a clear understanding of the following:

- The specific behavioral components of attending
- The purpose and value of competent attending
- A clear mental picture of what not to do
- Awareness of the interaction between cultural characteristics and attending

Up to this point our focus has been upon laying the groundwork for the context in which you will learn, practice, and apply each of the microskills. We begin with the most basic of all the microskills, attending. Attending can be defined as fully engaging in the listening process as a client is communicating with you. You will communicate your full engagement through a number of verbal and nonverbal behaviors. Those behaviors are the focus of this chapter.

Referring back to Figure 3.1 on page 44, note that attending is a microskill used by all counselors, regardless of their theoretical orientation and regardless of the stage of the counseling process in which a given counseling session is occurring. Attending is equally important in a last session as it is in the first. There has been research on the effect of attending on the process of a counseling session. One such example was a study conducted by Fretz, Corn, Tuemmler, and Bellet (1979) in which they found that regardless of counselor gender, clients rated them as more attractive and more facilitative when counselors exhibited a high degree of eye contact, forward lean, and a direct body orientation.

Perhaps to a novice this seems like a "no-brainer," that is, the importance of paying attention to a client is so obvious that it does not seem necessary to even talk about it. However, you might find that, particularly as your skill acquisition process unfolds and the other skills are introduced, it becomes more difficult to remember all the different components of the various skills. It makes sense to begin with something relatively easy and to become comfortable with it early in your learning process before moving to more sophisticated counseling skills.

PERSONAL REFLECTION _____

Take a moment to recall a recent conversation you had with someone in which you were not listening or were only listening with "one ear." What was distracting you that precluded your listening?

Here is what one student wrote in her journal about not being heard:

Case Example

"Not only was J. my friend, he was my resident advisor, so I really expected him to be able to listen well and help me with my problem. (It's funny . . . I no longer remember what this problem was, but I certainly remember his unhelpfulness.) Instead of listening and really participating in my dilemma, J. kept his back to me most of the time. He was having a conversation on his computer, and occasionally when I lapsed into silence, he would nod to show that I should continue or say, "I'm listening," or, if he thought I had finished a thought, he would take a break from his conversation to turn towards me (finally) and reply to what I had said. But even when he replied, there would be gaping pauses between when I had stopped speaking and when he picked up the conversation. I felt like I was being such a burden on him, distracting him from what I thought must be a very important conversation. But more than that, I felt frustration and anger. If this were a bad time, I would rather he told me that than do a poor job of listening. It made me and my problems feel infinitely small and unimportant." (emphasis added) Hester T., 9/6/06

A book related to attending that you may find helpful is *The Lost Art of Listening* (Nichols, 1995). Although this book is not specifically about counseling skills, it is a very helpful piece of writing that is not particularly technical. The book's emphasis is on raising our awareness of the many times and ways that we do not listen to other people around us. Many students find this reading to be quite eye-opening.

COMPONENTS OF ATTENDING

myhelpinglab —

Video Lab > By Course > Skills/Process/Techniques > Module 1: Engagement >

⇒ **Focusing on Presenting Concerns**

⇒ **Empathy as a Foundation**

Prior to reading further about attending, take a few moments to view the example of attending on the MyHelpingLab website. The sequence of links to find the recommended video clip is explained above. Attending behavior is really about listening with your whole being. The microskills model offers us a means of breaking up the common verb *listen* into all of its component parts. Those parts are eye contact, body posture/orientation, following the client's verbal content, and voice/paralinguistics. Another aspect of the counseling environment, your office, or the place where you are interacting with your client, will also be touched upon in this discussion. We will take each of these components in turn and examine them in detail.

Eye Contact

There is a large volume of literature on gaze and eye movement during interpersonal interaction (Harrigan, 2005). In the disciplines of communication, social psychology, and anthropology, systematic research on eye contact has been underway since the 1960s. One early finding that has been consistently replicated is that there are differences in patterns of eye contact as a function of ethnicity and cultural context (LaFrance & Mayo, 1976; McCarthy, 2005; Sue & Sue, 2003). Other findings are that a moderate amount of gaze is preferred by most people rather than avoiding eye contact (Kleinke, 1986), and that one cue people use in deciding whether to continue a conversation is the degree of the listener's eye contact (Kendon & Ferber, 1971).

PERSONAL REFLECTION _____

Think about what you were taught about eye gaze in your family of origin. When you were being disciplined, were you expected to look away or look the adult in the eye? How did that affect your belief about how you look at someone in authority now? What about the way you now use your eyes when you gaze at people who are your peers or who have less authority or social status than your? How will that affect the way you gaze at your clients?

One of the first studies that specifically investigated gaze was conducted by Kendon (1967), who proposed that there are three different purposes for gaze: monitoring (to get information about how another person is behaving), regulation (modulating the interactive flow of a conversation), and expression (communicating to another our feelings and attitudes). Harrigan (2005) noted that "our gaze patterns provide information regarding our attention, interest, and possible motivations and intentions" (p. 172).

Aspects of gaze such as frequency and length of direct eye contact are somewhat determined culturally. Most important is the idea that the diagnostic significance with which we, as counselors, interpret our client's eye contact arises from our own cultural background (Sue & Sue, 2003). Several authors of texts on counseling skills (e.g., Ivey & Ivey, 2007; Young, 2005) caution against making assumptions about the meaning of a client's eye contact pattern without information about the cultural context of the client. Logically, then, it's important to recognize that *your own* perceptions and expectations about gaze are determined by your own culture. Webbink (1986) noted that eye language is created and used in specific cultural contexts, which make its rules or usage and its meaning unique to those cultures. She further observed that generally speaking, in middle-class North American culture direct eye contact is considered to be a form of respect.

Perhaps some readers are familiar with the phrase, "Look me in the eye and tell me the truth." The origin of this directive probably comes from the belief that people generally have a harder time lying when they are maintaining direct eye contact. A common saying in the English language is that "the eyes are the windows of the soul." It will be valuable for you to communicate your listening posture by looking the client in the eye as he or she is talking, and to maintain eye contact when you are speaking. Remember, though, it is not a staring contest. A gaze held for too long it can become uncomfortable.

A study done by Sharpley and Sagris (1995) examined whether eye contact increases counselor-client rapport. They compared the incidence of counselor eye contact to the degree of rapport as experienced by the client. The authors found that the level of counselor-client intimacy was enhanced by eye contact, and that a high level of rapport was further enhanced by eye contact. However, they cautioned counseling students about the power of eye contact; using a high degree of eye contact while a client is feeling anxiety or apprehension about the counselor's reaction can be detrimental to the counseling process. In other words, when a client is disclosing content about which he or she expects to be negatively judged by the counselor, intense eye contact from the counselor could actually be more harmful than beneficial to the counseling. In contrast, when a client is self-examining some difficult material or making a commitment to some change in the working phase of the session, direct eye contact with the counselor can be experienced as an additional source of support from the counselor.

Another study examined eye contact and its relationship to other social psychological variables (Knackstedt & Kleinke, 1991). The authors concluded that people in Western society are evaluated more favorably by others when they maintain a high degree of eye contact if the interaction is nonthreatening. More specifically, the interviewer is more likely to be perceived as more potent (e.g., strong, ambitious, assertive, dominant, competent, independent) and as more mature and efficient.

When a speaker maintains eye contact with the listener, an assumption of believability is more likely (Young, 2005). American males have been found to perceive other males as more potent as the duration of eye contact increased (Brooks, Church, & Fraser, 1986). Additionally, Droney and Brooks (1993) found that viewers watching videotaped interviews rated interviewees as having higher self-esteem when the interviewees held prolonged direct eye contact with the interviewer.

Try to take note of whether your client is holding your gaze or tending to look away. If the client is often averting his or her gaze, your eye contact may be too intense. Consider also the possibility of cultural variables influencing the eye interaction.

MULTICULTURAL ASPECTS OF EYE CONTACT IN COUNSELING   We will move our focus now to consider two of Hofstede's (2001) axes of cultural variability and how they might manifest in patterns of eye contact.

Power Distance.   In a culture with a high degree of power distance, we might expect to see an attitude of deference to authority. A counseling session is an interaction in which the counselor holds a degree of power over the interaction. Therefore, high power distance could result in a high degree of eye contact in those cultures where respectful behavior is defined by maintaining direct gaze. Contrasting that scenario is one in which the client's culture of origin defines deferent behavior as averting one's gaze.

Masculinity.   Among cultures that are heavily masculine, that is, with rigidly prescribed gender roles, we might expect a male to be more assertive in his eye contact than a female, who by cultural definition would be expected to be more passive.

The axes of affiliation and uncertainty avoidance might play less of a role than the other two axes in influencing patterns of eye contact. Keep in mind that when we talk about how these cultural axes influence a counseling session, we are talking about two facets: the client's comfort level with the behaviors you are exhibiting, and your own comfort level with the behaviors you are exhibiting. In addition to these cultural variables, there could be other reasons that either you or the client is uncomfortable with the gaze pattern.

PERSONAL REFLECTION

Think of a time when it was hard for you to look someone in the eye as you were talking. What were you feeling and thinking as you turned your eyes away from the other person?

The purpose of that personal reflection is to help you recognize that you may not know the reasons a person might not be holding eye contact with you; it's important not to assume you know the reason unless he or she has told you. The context of your discussion may hold some clues for you, but until you have been directly told about the internal experience of your client, your observations can only support possible hypotheses.

BODY POSTURE AND ORIENTATION

In 1970 a pop psychology book entitled *Body Language* was published. In it the author, Julius Fast, introduced to the general public the science of kinesics, the study of nonverbal communication. It was one of the first popular books on the market that offered readers a systematic means of "reading" another person's communication in his or her nonverbal behavior.

We continually give and receive messages with our words and also with our bodies. In the context of microskills we need to be aware of what messages we are *sending* to the client (attending behavior) and what messages we are *receiving* from the client (client observation). In this discussion we are focusing only on what messages you are sending to your client. We will consider client observation and the messages the client is sending in Chapter 5, "Client Observation."

Open Posture

The client, sitting and facing you, will be most aware of what you are doing with your upper body. This includes your head, face, shoulders, arms, and torso. Your leg positioning will probably be less influential. As you consider the upper body parts just mentioned, think about how the client's ability to see them will be impeded if there is a physical object such as a desk or table between you and him or her.

To feel free to disclose information, a person needs to feel that you are open to what he or she has to say. You can communicate this openness nonverbally by having an open upper body posture. This includes having your arms down at your sides, resting on your legs, or folded on your lap and not across your torso. It's best to have your hands empty and still. If you can do so comfortably, you might consider mirroring your client's posture and limb positioning. This is referred to as *postural congruence* or *mirroring*. Some authors (Maurer & Tindall, 1983) have found that clients rated the counselor as significantly more empathic when the counselor mirrored the client's arm and leg positions and that mirroring may be a component in the development of helping relationships (Solley, 1988).

Other research on postural congruence has been conducted in the field of social psychology. Maxwell and Cook (1985) found that in pairs (dyads), people who sat in similar chairs and thus had similar postures tended to judge the other person as liking them more; in other words, congruence in postures had a significant effect on judging liking. Although we need to be careful not to jump to conclusions about the extent to which these findings are equally valid in therapeutic relationship development, there is some basis for considering them as offering additional information about how we might enhance our relationships with our clients.

The decision about whether to take notes while your client is talking is a personal preference; there are advantages and disadvantages to note taking. On a day when you are working with many people, it may be necessary for you to take notes in order to keep track of the details of your clients' cases. As well, your employment situation might require that you record client information as part of a first session. If you will be taking notes during the first meeting, try to be aware of what you are doing with your hands when you are not writing. For example, you might find yourself clicking a retractable ballpoint pen in and out, doodling, or otherwise fidgeting with your pen. If you do this excessively while in session, your client might interpret your behavior as indicating boredom, distraction, or impatience, even if that was not the message you intended to send. Your torso should be oriented toward the client. Your head as well should be facing the client. It is okay to lean a little bit forward in your seat, but be careful not to lean in too far.

A classroom example of a situation that happened highlights how a counselor's posture can affect the client's experience. One school counseling intern had been frustrated because she had a teenage boy as a client who was very shy and reluctant to talk in their counseling sessions. She videotaped a session in the hope that she could get suggestions from her classmates and the professor (this author) on how to draw him out. When the videotape was shown in class, she was amazed to see that the more she asked him questions to which he gave one-word answers, the more she leaned forward in her chair. The more she leaned forward, the more he slumped and moved further back into the corner of his own chair. Within 10 minutes of the counseling session, she was actually perched on the edge of her chair, lunged forward into the common space between them, while he had pulled back into the corner of the chair as far as he could go.

One of the most significant aspects of that video was that until the counseling intern watched it, she had no awareness of her own eagerness and leaning and, most importantly, how it was affecting her client's behavior. It is possible to have too much of a good thing: Eagerness on the counselor's part might be perceived by the client as forwardness or even aggression.

Leaning in

The person who did the pioneering work on how humans use space in different cultures was an anthropologist, Edward T. Hall. In 1966, Hall published *The Hidden Dimension,* in which he presented the theory of proxemics, which proposes that human perceptions of interpersonal space are culturally determined. Hall's research found successive realms of interpersonal distance; the actual physical measurements of those realms vary by culture. The realms he categorized were intimate space, social and consultative space, and public space. Related to these realms is a psychological construct called *subjective distance*, which refers to an individual's internal experience of an objective interpersonal distance.

Ford and Maloney (1982) researched subjective distance and hypothesized that the way we feel about a person influences the way we perceive both their size and our physical distance from them. They found that, consistent with prior research, the less we like a person, the more likely we are to perceive their physical size as larger. To paraphrase, when we are in the presence of someone we do not like, we are more likely to experience the physical distance between ourselves and them as smaller than it really is and more likely to perceive the person as physically larger than they really are.

These findings pertain to the current discussion about proximity in counseling by illustrating the importance of maintaining a respectful distance from the client, particularly in the beginning stages of the counseling process when it is more likely that the client may be feeling intimidated or threatened about seeing a counselor. This leads to the next component of the discussion: how your office is arranged.

Room Arrangement

Lawson (2001) talked about how we use space to communicate with other people:

> Architecture organizes and structures space for us, and its interiors and the objects enclosing and inhabiting its rooms can facilitate or inhibit our activities by the way they use this language. Because this language is not heard or seen directly, and certainly not written down, it gets little attention in a formal sense. . . . Perhaps we tend only to notice this language when it is in some way abused. (p. 6)

In the context of office arrangement and furnishings, there is minimal empirical evidence about the effect these variables have on treatment outcome. However, one aspect of use of office space and treatment that has been researched is the reported preferences of clients who were exposed to a variety of furniture arrangements in a series of counseling sessions. Haase and DiMattia (1970) noted that clients prefer to interact with their counselors across the corner of a desk, rather than having a piece of furniture between them. Other knowledge bases such as architectural design and interior design acknowledge ways in which a room's furnishings and arrangement affect the inhabitants' emotional experience of being in that environment. Three reasons readily come to mind as to why an awareness of your office arrangement and furnishings should be a consideration in a discussion of relationship building in counseling.

AESTHETICISM   Merriam-Webster defines *aesthetics* as "having a pleasing appearance or effect." Aestheticism is a subscale on a personality assessment, the NEO-PI-R (Costa & McCrae, 1995). On the NEO-PI-R, the aestheticism subscale attempts to measure the importance or value a person places on physical beauty. In the context of the present discussion, the aestheticism factor refers to creating a physical space for counseling that features objects of comfort and beauty to promote a sense of comfort for your clients. For example, if a counselor is working primarily with small children, it might be aesthetically pleasing to the children to have developmentally appropriate artwork hanging on the walls at a level easily viewed by children. Consider the furniture size and wall adornments in a typical kindergarten classroom.

The concept of aestheticism becomes more ambiguous in working with adults, because perception of beauty and comfort is a personal and subjective experience. Nevertheless, there are aspects of furniture choice and furniture placement, as well as artwork and objects of interest, that can be conducive to a sense of physical comfort. Besides the fact that having a pleasant office arrangement might be beneficial for your therapeutic relationships, it could also be beneficial for your own wellness and self-care in your professional role.

GROUNDING OBJECTS   The helping professions have potential to be careers in which practitioners experience burnout, meaning that their energy and ability to help becomes completely expended. Self-care for mental health professionals is of utmost importance. One means by which we can do that is to have objects in our offices that help us to maintain some "grounding," that is, conscious awareness of other aspects of our lives that help us maintain emotional balance or are a source of joy. For example, for a person whose main source of emotional centeredness comes from spending time at the ocean, perhaps a shell that was acquired on a trip to the beach could be of value sitting on the corner of the desk. Often people have portraits of family members, close friends, pets, or favorite images in their office. Paying attention to how you furnish your office can be a form of self-care.

TRANSPARENCY When we walk into a person's home, carefully observing the rooms can give us some information about who that person is; his or her preferences, values, and sources of comfort. The same can be true for clients walking into your office. What you have hanging on the walls, the books on your bookshelf, the objects you may have placed around the room, will all be sources of information for your clients about who you are as a person. Knowing this can help you to make choices about the extent to which you reveal to your clients who you are.

For reasons mentioned above, it is advisable to arrange your furniture so that there are no physical barriers between yourself and the client. If you do have a need for furniture between your two chairs, it should be as low as possible, such as a coffee table. The removal of physical barriers can have an impact on the client's perception (either conscious or subconscious) that there are no barriers, physical or otherwise, between you.

Sometimes, sitting directly in front of another person with no barriers might feel a bit threatening or overwhelming to a client. For that reason, placing chairs at an oblique angle to each other may be ideal. This arrangement is consistent with the findings from the Haase and DiMattia study on furniture placement. View several selections from the following MyHelpingLab files, watching specifically for the seating arrangements. Note that on some videos the counselors are sitting off to one or the other side, while in other videos the counselor is directly in front of the client. Two video clips feature children; one is the Adlerian Play example, and the other is Person-Centered. Note that in Adlerian Play, the counselor is sitting on the floor with a small child. In the Person-Centered example, a table is used to enable the child to create expressive artwork.

myhelpinglab

Video Lab > By Theoretical Approach >

⇒ **Existential-Humanistic > Clip A**

⇒ **Experiential > Clip A**

⇒ **Adlerian Play > Clip A**

⇒ **Person-Centered > Clip A**

PERSONAL REFLECTION

Think of a time when you had to meet on important business with someone who holds a position of authority. This might have been getting called to your school principal's office, seeing a banker about a financial matter, or maybe meeting with an attorney. How big was the person's desk? Did you sit across the desk from him or her? How did that distance affect your perception of being in that office?

Note that in some situations, establishing power, authority, and distance are intended on the part of the person in authority. Similarly, at some formal presentations, there is no intention of creating a private, trusting, atmosphere.

In a study completed in 1987, Darby and Judson examined gender of student, gender of professor, and office arrangement, and the relationship of those variables to students' perceptions of how much control they had during an interaction with the professor. The office arrangements compared in the experiment were "desk between" the faculty member and student, and "desk beside" the faculty member and student. The "desk between" condition was assumed to equate with a higher degree of faculty control. The researchers found, not surprisingly, that students rated the less-faculty-controlled offices more favorably than the faculty-controlled offices, and that male students were most likely to rate negatively the male faculty, faculty-controlled environments.

In the case of counseling, you will be trying to create a welcoming atmosphere or ambience. There are a number of ways you can communicate your willingness to listen by the way you arrange and furnish the environment in which you will be listening. Depending on your theoretical orientation, there may be a varying degree of importance you place upon trying to arrange an office in which the power differential and distance between yourself and your client is reduced as much as possible. A table or desk placed between you and the client creates a physical barrier that can also become a metaphor for an emotional barrier between yourself and the client. In a school counseling setting or in a situation in which the counselor is doing artwork or playing a game with a client, sometimes a table is necessary. When that is the case, sitting either alongside the child or on an adjacent edge at 45 degrees may mitigate the negative impact of the barrier between you and the student.

Chairs

The seating in your office will be the main avenue through which your awareness of proxemics can be applied. If you have positioned the chairs too close together, it may feel like a violation of personal space to the client. If they are too far apart, there may be a sense of distance or remoteness that can inhibit relationship development. Each of you will need to experiment with chair placement to find the distance that feels right. It is also perfectly fine, and perhaps advisable, to ask your clients if the chair placement is comfortable for them, and if not, give your client permission to identify what position would be most comfortable and then move the chairs accordingly. Obviously, if you have heavy furniture, this could be a bit of a problem, but most likely if the chairs aren't quite right for a person it will be because they are either a bit too close or too far. It might be beneficial to make the effort to inquire about your client's preferences.

Lighting

Real estate books about how to sell a home often mention turning on as many lights as possible in every room. That is because lighting is an environmental variable that affects our perception of a room, although we are often not aware of the lighting unless it is problematic, either too dark or glaring. Nevertheless, the light source and light level contribute significantly to our physical experience; this may be due to the fact that many of us are visual beings, and light has so much influence on the visual information we are processing. Visual artists are aware of this; use of light is a topic discussed when an artist's work is described. Similarly, photographers and film directors pay careful attention to lighting as they create their compositions.

Interestingly, virtually no professional literature or research has evaluated lighting conditions as a variable of client comfort or therapeutic benefit. As a side note, there is evidence that light can have an effect on our mood, as evidenced by the *DSM-IV-TR*, which allows for a seasonal pattern of clinical depression for which one treatment is light therapy (Glickman, Byrne, Pineda, Hauck, & Brainard, 2006; Martiny, Lunde, Unden, Dam, & Bech, 2005; Putilov & Danilenko, 2005).

For some people, overhead lighting may be distracting. In a professional setting such as a school or office, fluorescent lights are sometimes glaring, and at times might even be a source of stress. Fluorescent overhead lights often hum, which can cause headaches or contribute to a sense of tension. Additionally, the light given off by overhead lights can be harsh.

AUTHOR'S REFLECTION

In my own work with clients, I try to use natural light (open curtains on the window) if possible, and indirect lights in the form of a desk lamp, end table lamps, or floor lamps.

If you are fortunate enough to have a window that lets in light from outside, be careful if your office may be visible from the outside; you need to be aware of confidentiality and privacy concerns. However, even if you need to keep your blinds drawn, you can use Venetian or mini blinds that can be adjusted to let in natural light while still offering privacy.

Use of natural and indirect lights tends to create an atmosphere less businesslike and more conducive to reflection and disclosure. Obviously the room needs to be lit, and not so dim that it is hard to read a piece of paper or to see the other person's face. Also, some people have visual impairments that require a certain level of light in order to see optimally.

Verbal Behavior (Following the Client's Lead)

PERSONAL REFLECTION

Recall one or two of the stories that were told to you as a child. Perhaps there was one that was a source of comfort for you. Think of another that was a source of pain or used as a means of scolding or shaming you. Consider how those stories have influenced your own life story—either by being an important thread, or by representing something you intentionally reject or choose to change for yourself.

There are a number of counseling approaches in which storytelling plays a central role. One example is narrative therapy (White & Epston, 1989), in which the focus of the work is on the stories or narratives people create to define themselves or their lives. Even if the theoretical approach you use does not involve narrative therapy, it will nevertheless be important for you to give the client the opportunity to tell you her or his story. Other academic disciplines, such as cultural anthropology, emphasize oral histories as a rich and important source of data in learning about cultures.

Every single person has a story. *Almost* everyone has the need at some time to tell his or her story and be heard. Your very first undertaking, as you sit down with a client for the first time, is to truly listen to the story that is unique to him or her. Besides an infinite number of circumstances and events they will share, there are as many different styles of storytelling as there are individuals. One general style is to share a great number of details, while other people tend to speak in vague generalities as they share information. Some individuals use metaphors to explain their experiences, which can further enrich your understanding of their internal landscape.

Later on, as the counseling relationship progresses, you will need to make some choices about the theoretical frameworks with which you are conceptualizing your client's issues and goals. However, in the early stages of relationship building, it will be more valuable to put aside your thoughts about the theories you are going to use and instead focus your attention mostly on the person sitting before you.

When you respond verbally your responses should be pertinent to whatever the client is disclosing with you; in other words, "verbally tracking" the client. As a metaphor, imagine the client walking through the woods and establishing a path through light underbrush. Your goal is merely to follow that track, not to try to veer the client toward another path. It is okay to inquire about the path, or the way the client is walking, or how he or she made the choice to take that particular course, but your queries and observations should all pertain to that path. As the client veers from one direction and heads another way, you should follow without comment. Make a mental note if there are many direction changes, but continue to follow.

PARALINGUISTICS   The term *paralinguistics* (sometimes termed *paraverbals*) refers to the way spoken material is expressed vocally. This includes rate of speech, voice tone, volume, and inflection. Paralinguistics convey a huge amount of information about the message being expressed. A further discussion of using paralinguistics in client observation will be presented in Chapter 5. Our present emphasis is on your *own* use of paralinguistics to communicate counseling conditions that will facilitate the counseling process.

Surprisingly little research has looked at the therapist's paralinguistics as a contributing factor in counseling effectiveness. Nevertheless, my own clinical experience has suggested that paralinguistics are very important components of building relationships, because they are the mechanical conveyers of the verbal content. Beatty (1980) observed that voice cues are significant sources of information because they are unavoidable in a communicative interaction. There has been some research suggesting that nonverbal cues, including paralinguistics, may be a more reliable indicator than verbal cues of the emotional state of the speaker (Rothman & Nowicki, 2004). It would seem to follow that your own stance toward your client will be as evident in your paralinguistics as it will be in all the other aspects of your nonverbal behavior that we have already covered.

In conceptualizing our paralinguistics as a metaphor, if we have a fine piece of crystal we wish to mail as a gift to someone far away, we will package it with great care, using bubble wrap, foam, and possibly two layers of boxes with foam in between. Packing the crystal carelessly will result in its arriving at the recipient in pieces. Paralinguistics are basically the packaging in which we send our verbal messages that deserve the same amount, if not more, attention as the content of our message.

PERSONAL REFLECTION _____

Think for a moment about how the voice would sound if someone close to you said, in a worried way, "Where have you been? I was so worried!" Now think about how the voice would sound if the speaker angrily said, "Where have you been? I was worried!" What kinds of feelings and reaction would each of those voice tones elicit in you?

There are several aspects of paralinguistics.

RATE OF SPEECH   Rate of speech varies from person to person. There are regional differences; sometimes people who have lived in a particular geographic area may demonstrate some mannerisms in speech, such as rate of speaking. Ask some of your coworkers, friends, and family members if they think you speak too rapidly at times, and if so, when.

VOICE TONE   Voice tone refers to the pitch of your voice. Higher pitch requires increased muscle tension in your throat, similar to a guitar string. Anxiety and anger can be associated with muscle tension. In a relaxed state, the muscles throughout our bodies, including our vocal cords, tend to be looser. This results in a vocal pitch that may be a tone or two lower than the pitch we use in day-to-day conversation. Use of a lower vocal pitch as you make statements or pose questions to your client may be conducive to your client giving you a more reflective, less superficial response.

VOLUME   Some people talk more loudly than others. In addition to things that can be happening internally (emotions such as sadness or anger), voice volume may be determined by environmental variables such as background noise or social expectations. In a counseling session, intentionally altering the volume of your voice may affect the client's experience. When asking a question or making an observation about something the client has said, posing your message in a voice that is slightly softer, in addition to being at a lower pitch, will be most conducive to the client directing his or her attention inward to self-reflect.

INFLECTION   Inflection enables us to do a couple of things. One is that we differentiate between a statement and a question by our use of inflection. When asking a question, we typically raise our voice pitch on the last word or two of the query. If someone asks us a question and does not raise their voice at the end it may sound strange, perhaps even robotic. Another way inflection is used is to vocally underline or highlight particular words we wish to emphasize. Sometimes vocal underlining is done because there is a relevant detail or piece of information that is critical to the speaker for the listener to understand. Other times vocal underlining happens without our conscious awareness, and the word being emphasized is reflective of a higher level of emotional energy.

Admittedly, some of these paralinguistics are aspects of speech over which we have little control. For example, certain nasal or sinus conditions can affect the nasal quality of our voice; if we are congested, have a cold, or a permanent sinus condition, we might sound nasal to other people. The relevant points to hold in your awareness are the aspects of your paralinguistics over which you definitely have volitional control.

MULTICULTURAL ASPECTS OF ATTENDING

Four multicultural axes were presented in Chapter 2 that will be the focus of cultural consideration throughout the microskills:

1. Power distance
2. Individualism versus collectivism
3. Masculinity versus femininity
4. Uncertainty avoidance

Earlier in this chapter we discussed those axes in the context of eye contact. Now we will examine the other aspects of attending: body posture and leaning in, physical aspects of the counseling environment, and paralinguistics. Among these aspects of attending, particularly in the early stages of helping, the cultural axis most relevant is probably power distance and the client's expectation about the level of directiveness the counselor will demonstrate.

For a client with a cultural frame of a high power distance, there might be an expectation that the counselor is the expert who will treat the client and/or her or his problem, and that the counselor will be in total control of that process. In this case, the client might be expecting the counselor to structure or define the discussion topics. A therapist who is simply following the client's speaking could provoke discomfort for such a client.

On the other hand, a client with a cultural frame of low power distance might be more comfortable with the idea of counseling being a collaborative venture in which the counselor and client together embark on the treatment process.

Consider the manner in which you are going to relate to the client with regard to this continuum of "learned expert" at one end and "collaborative coach" at the other. Think about how you see your role as a helper with your clients. Bear in mind that the way your office is arranged will either reinforce or contradict what you are communicating to your client with your other nonverbal and verbal messages. From the standpoint of congruence between verbal and nonverbal messages, your office environment should reflect your own stance.

ATTENDING IN THE CONTEXT OF THREE THEORETICAL STANCES

In keeping with the three thematic strands of this text, having discussed attending from a multicultural perspective, we need also to consider the role of attending from each of three broad theoretical perspectives presented in Chapter 11.

Humanistic

In the humanistic tradition, attending is of the utmost importance. When Rogers (1961) enumerated the conditions necessary for therapeutic change and identified the first three as congruence, empathy, and unconditional positive regard, he implied a complete engagement with the client and his or her emotional experience in the present moment. Furthermore, it is in part a function of the counselor's attending to the client that a therapeutic alliance is established. In humanism, which deemphasizes specific treatment techniques, the therapeutic alliance *is* the treatment. Thus, attending lies at the heart of this approach to helping.

Here is a dialogue example of attending in a first counseling session as it might sound with a humanistic counselor:

COUNSELOR: I'm glad you were able to make it. What brings you in today?

MYRON: I'm really stressed about a promotion I'm trying to get at work. When I went for my annual checkup last month, the doc said my blood pressure was too high and that I should do something to relax. When we talked more about it, he suggested I come to see you; he said you're really good. So I finally decided to schedule an appointment.

COUNSELOR: Well, you mentioned several things that sound like they are keys. One is the work promotion, another is your need to relax, and another is your blood pressure. Where do you think would be the best place to start?

MYRON: Let me tell you about this awful boss I have and how I get headaches trying to do everything he gives me to do. . . .

Developmental

The developmental theories also view attending as critical to the therapeutic process. Their conceptualization of the role attending plays, however, has a somewhat different slant than that of a humanistic counselor. Developmental theories see present behavior as reenactment of earlier conflicts and relationship patterns, and as an attempt to resolve those conflicts. Some developmental therapists specifically seek to elicit a relationship between the counselor and client that basically reenacts the client's relationship with a parent or other figure. Other developmental therapists watch the relationship unfold and conceptualize the relationship with the counselor as a microcosm of how the client constructs relationships across multiple aspects of his or her life (Yalom & Leszcz, 2005). Consequently, by attending appropriately and with proper boundaries in the professional relationship, the counselor has the opportunity to observe and learn about how the client functions in many relationships.

Here is an example of attending dialogue in a first counseling session from a developmental perspective:

COUNSELOR: I'm glad you were able to make it. What brings you in today?

MYRON: I'm really stressed about a promotion I'm trying to get at work. When I went for my annual checkup last month, the doc said my blood pressure was too high and that I should do something to relax. When we talked more about it, he suggested I come to see you; he said you're really good. So I finally decided to schedule an appointment.

COUNSELOR: In order for me to fully understand your problem, I'd like to get more information from you about this whole situation. Let's start with your job. What do you do for a living?

MYRON: I'm a drill press operator in a tool and die shop.

COUNSELOR: Tell me more about your job, like how long you've been doing it and how satisfied you are with the work.

MYRON: I've been a drill press operator for my whole life. I guess it's okay, I mean I haven't ever done anything else and it pays pretty good. Lately our shop has been getting contracts from this one manufacturer that expects the work to be done yesterday. I don't get a lunch break and they're giving me lots of overtime. And I've been trying to get bumped up to floor supervisor because it pays $5.00 more an hour. But that's not going so good.

Cognitive-Behavioral

Behavioral and cognitive-behavioral therapists take an active, directive role in counseling. Cognitive-behavioral theorists, such as Aaron Beck, saw the therapeutic alliance as necessary, but not sufficient. Consequently, while some aspects of attending, such as open posture and paralinguistics, are important in developing a working relationship, a cognitive-behavioral therapist is much more likely than a nonbehaviorist to verbally track the client less and lead the session more. A cognitive-behavioral therapist may have a more specific agenda for a particular counseling session and be more active in guiding the conversation in particular directions to get the specific information needed to help the client attain his or her treatment goals.

Here is a sample dialogue from a cognitive-behavioral first session:

COUNSELOR: I'm glad you were able to make it. What brings you in today?

MYRON: I'm really stressed about a promotion I'm trying to get at work. When I went for my annual checkup last month, the doc said my blood pressure was too high and that I should do something to relax. When we talked more about it, he suggested I come to see you; he said you're really good. So I finally decided to schedule an appointment.

COUNSELOR: What we're going to do today is that I'm going to get a lot more background information from you about the nature of your struggles, and then we'll talk about possible ways I can help you as well as a possible game plan for how we'll do this work together. Does that sound okay?

MYRON: I guess so. I've never seen a shrink before.

COUNSELOR: Okay. Let's start with you telling me more about your stress and the promotion.

Table 4.1 offers you another set of dialogue comparisons that illustrate differences in attending depending on the counselor's theoretical orientation. These examples are segments from a counseling session in a later stage of relationship development. The client and counselor have already seen each other for several sessions.

As you compare the responses from each of the three theoretical approaches, in what way do you see the content differing? Which of them, if any, would feel most natural for you to use in your own counseling interactions?

TABLE 4.1   Attending Responses from Three Theoretical Stances

This client is a 15-year-old girl seeing the school counselor for friend issues.

Maggie: I'm so stressed out about this Homecoming dance, I don't know what to do! I have an appointment to get my nails done and my hair, too, this evening, but now I have to go shopping for new shoes too, and there isn't enough time to get it all done! On top of that, Abby and Morgan are texting each other all the time and keep making excuses instead of figuring out how we'll meet up to go to the dance. I think they're trying to ditch me.

Humanistic	Developmental	Cognitive
Intent would be to explore this client's sense of rejection from her friends and also the stress and pressure of needing to prepare for the dance.	Focus might be on the importance of "looking good" and what the significance is, in terms of how she sees herself. Might also be concerned about the friends' perceived rejection and how that fits with her self-perception.	Focus would be on what she is thinking and feeling about the dance and about her friends that results in her feeling stressed and rejected. Might be looking for errors in her self-talk and coping cognitions and behaviors that could help reduce her stress.
It sounds like you have a huge amount going on.	Tell me about this thing with Abby and Morgan. What gives you the sense they intend to ditch you?	What are you doing to cope with all this stress?

Chapter Summary

This chapter presented attending, the first of the microskills covered by this book. We started by talking about eye contact, with the intent of raising your awareness of gaze in a communicative interaction with another person. Myriad variables within the counselor and the client may influence the pattern of gaze during a counseling session. Some of those variables arise from the cultural contexts of the counselor and the client.

We next considered other aspects of your physical presence with your client. Orienting your body toward your client and sitting with an open posture by not folding your arms across your torso will communicate openness to your client. This message may have a subtle effect on your client's experience of you, even if he or she is not consciously aware of how you are sitting. Besides to orienting yourself toward the client, leaning in slightly toward the client also can communicate interest and concern for him or her.

In addition to your physical presence with the client, we also examined aspects of the physical environment of the office or room in which you are counseling. Although there is not a great deal of literature about aspects of an office such as furniture placement, a few studies and my own clinical experience have suggested that mindful use of desks and tables, availability of comfortable chairs, and the type of lighting may be conducive to establishing rapport with clients. There is additional justification for a comfortable office in the context of self-care for you as a counselor, an aspect of professional life that should not be overlooked as a possible contributor to your longevity as a mental health professional.

The next aspect of attending we looked at was verbal behavior, consisting of following your client's lead rather than introducing new topic directions, and paralinguistics. Paralinguistics refer to aspects of your nonverbal behavior that are conveyed through speech but are completely separate from the verbal content. Aspects of paralinguistics we discussed included voice tone, volume, and inflection. Although paralinguistics in a spoken communication may be consistent or inconsistent with the spoken words, the important consideration in this discussion of attending is that you are aware of the paralinguistics you are using as you communicate with your client.

In the concluding sections we considered, as we will in all the skills chapters, how attending might manifest differently across the five axes of cultural differences and how attending might be used differently by therapists from different theoretical orientations.

Case Studies for Discussion

At the conclusion of the subsequent microskill chapters there will be a sequence of dialogue from the same two clients: Carole and Derek. In this chapter, the first of the microskills you are learning, the main purpose of including these client descriptions is to introduce these two individuals to you. Because much of attending is nonverbal in nature, it is difficult to present a meaningful description of dialogue. So here you will simply meet these people and learn about their life situations. Each additional microskill chapter presents dialogue that reflects the counselor demonstrating the skill covered in that chapter.

Questions for Class Discussion

1. Do you consider yourself to be a good listener? At times in the past that you were not a good listener, what got in your way?

2. How does your self-awareness and knowledge about your own cultural profile and the axes of culture-based values affect your thinking about each of these clients?

3. Think of some examples of times when it would be most appropriate *not* to attend to something a client is saying.

CASE DESCRIPTION—ADULT CLIENT

(Carole's case is being presented and considered in the context of a community agency counseling environment.)

Carole is a 37-year-old biracial woman of Caucasian and African American descent. She has been married for 8 years and has two children, ages 7 and 5. Her husband is a 43-year-old Caucasian man who is employed at a local automobile factory. Carole graduated from high school and has been employed periodically in unskilled labor jobs, but never for more than about a year at a time. She stopped working when she got married; her husband made it clear that her job was to tend to the house and have children. She is a homemaker and, while she loves her children dearly, she finds herself feeling very sad and lonely when the children are in school and her husband is at work. Her 7-year-old is in second grade while the 5-year-old attends an all-day kindergarten. Carole has been referred to counseling by her family physician due to her tearfulness, insomnia, and significant weight gain for which the doctor can find no physical cause.

CASE DESCRIPTION—CHILD CLIENT

(Derek's case is being presented in the context of a school counseling relationship in which you are seeing him in your role as a school counselor. If you are intending to work as a community agency counselor, consider how your work with him would differ from the way the case is presented here.)

Derek is a 9-year-old boy of Latino descent who has been exhibiting significant behavior problems in school and has been referred to you, the school counselor, for help. Since the beginning of the school year, he has been aggressive in the lunchroom, taking other students' food, and has been suspended for fighting on the playground. His grades are C's, D's, and F's, and he frequently does not turn in or complete his homework.

Regarding his home life, Derek is being raised by his maternal grandmother; Derek's biological mother lives directly across the street from them. His mother has retained custody of Derek's four younger siblings. His father is in prison in Puerto Rico. Derek's mother sent him to live with his grandmother because his behavior was so disruptive in the household that his mother felt she could not control him. Derek's disruptive behavior at home was primarily characterized by disobeying rules, staying out on the street at night past his curfew, hanging around the neighborhood with older boys who often are in legal trouble, and yelling when he doesn't get what he wants.

CHAPTER 5

Client Observation

After studying this chapter, you should have a clear understanding of the following:

- The aspects of client behavior that are important to note
- The rationales for careful client observation
- The importance of trying to refrain from judgment or interpretation of your client's behavior
- How conscientious observation can augment the counseling process

As we move forward from attending behavior toward increasingly complex skills, we arrive at the skill of client observation. In mastering the skill of attending, you will be able to transition your attention from self-consciousness or worrying about what you will say next toward focusing on client observation. This chapter emphasizes learning how to notice the vast range of things your client is doing and saying that can be sources of information about him or her. In the chapter on attending we looked at the behavioral elements of visual, verbal, vocal, and body orientation as components of fully attending to a speaker. In the context of attending, the emphasis was on the behaviors you, as the counselor, should be exhibiting that are conducive to effective listening.

Client observation, as the name of the skill implies, is about noticing obvious and subtle behaviors that your client is demonstrating. Those same components of visual, verbal, vocal, and body movement are client behaviors to which you will pay attention, because they will be sources of information and communication from your client to you. Keep in mind that behavior in all of these categories can be at least partially the outcome of cultural origin and custom.

As you observe behavior being exhibited by the client, remember that your impression and sense of him or her is only a hypothesis, not an absolute, and then continue to observe and determine the degree of accuracy of your hypotheses. This will be an ongoing process in which your hypothesis and impression of him or her may refine, deepen, and evolve over time as you observe more and more.

The term *confirmatory bias* refers to a researcher disregarding data that do not support his or her hypothesis. There is ample evidence of a general human tendency to see in another person or situation what we expect to see. Be careful not to enter your counseling interactions with an expectation that your client will be a certain way; make a conscious effort to refrain from confirmatory bias in your observations.

THE ROLE OF CAREFUL OBSERVATION

Why is client observation important? There are a number of questions we hope to answer as we observe our client's behavior. Here are some of them:

- Does there appear to be situationally appropriate affect (emotion) for the content about which he or she is speaking?
- What is the content of the presenting problem? Is the precipitating event the result of trauma, is it developmentally typical, or is it some other kind of situational precipitant?
- How easily is the client able to engage with a stranger (you) and communicate?
- What is the client's mental status?
- What are the ways in which his or her cultural template interacts with the problem and with the assets?

Answers to these questions will help us develop a comprehensive and accurate understanding of the presenting problem. This also will help us establish rapport with our client.

FOUR OBSERVABLE ELEMENTS OF CLIENT BEHAVIOR

Video Lab > By Course > Skills/Process/Techniques > Module 2: Establishing the Therapeutic Relationship >

⇒ **Encouraging Clients to "Listen to Their Center"**

⇒ **Examples of Active Listening**

Many aspects of human behavior can be observed. As we move into the material about observing your client, it may be helpful for you to first view a short video segment on the MyHelpingLab website. Follow the links specified above to watch the recommended video clip related to client observation. To a certain extent, the behavioral aspects of other people that are most salient to you will be the result of your own values and beliefs, and also will be related to your theoretical orientation. We will be covering four aspects of your client's behavior that will be readily available for you to observe. They may not all be equally important for every single client. Unfortunately, though, it's hard to know that before you are fully familiar with a person. There is danger of making a judgment or arriving at a conclusion about a client too soon; a premature conclusion on your part could result in an inaccurate diagnosis, which would be doing a great disservice to your client.

AUTHOR'S REFLECTION

When I'm working with a client, I conceptualize the initial assessment process as one in which I am mentally putting together pieces of a jigsaw puzzle. Different aspects of the client sitting with me represent puzzle pieces, and I try to be careful not to come to any conclusions about what the final image will be before I have carefully and thoroughly examined each component. Most importantly, each puzzle piece may have different relevance in the context of the whole picture.

How Expectations Affect Our Perceptions

The phenomenon of confirmatory bias was introduced earlier. Perhaps one of the most compelling research projects investigating confirmatory bias was a study conducted in the early 1970s (Rosenhan, 1973). In this project, eight confederates who were "sane" people checked themselves into psychiatric wards in different hospitals on the east and west coasts of the United States, complaining of hearing voices. As soon as the confederates were admitted to the hospital, they immediately stopped complaining of any abnormal symptoms and attempted to interact the way they normally would with other patients and staff. Nevertheless, seven of the eight were subsequently diagnosed as schizophrenic.

One major conclusion of the Rosenhan study was that hospital wards create an environment in which behavior is easily misunderstood. However, these results were also consistent with the findings in the cognitive literature, namely, that we tend to see what we expect to see and to disregard any data that contradict our beliefs. That is why it is important to try not to have preconceived ideas about a client, and to enter a counseling relationship completely open to observing and taking in *all* the available data about the person without jumping to conclusions or making judgments.

Following are detailed explanations of categories of easily observable behavior:

- Nonverbal behavior
- Paraverbal behavior
- Verbal behavior
- Congruence among nonverbal, paraverbal, and verbal behavior

Nonverbal Behavior

FACIAL EXPRESSION   One of the physical aspects of your client that is most visually available to you is his or her facial expression. The facial expressiveness people exhibit as they process feelings and share information varies from person to person. Some people (you may know someone like this) display very little variation in their facial expression throughout the day and across situations. These people are sometimes described as "stoic" or perhaps "flat." Other people have many different expressions, and what they are feeling (or sometimes thinking) may be immediately obvious. This a characteristic is referred to as "wearing your heart on your sleeve," meaning that one's emotional experiencing is so evident on one's face that it is public information.

It has been recognized for many years that there are six facial expressions of emotion that can be universally identified by other people, regardless of the cultural background of the observer or the person expressing the emotion. Those six emotions are surprise, anger, disgust, happiness, sadness, and fear (Ekman & Friesen, 1971; Ekman, Sorenson, & Friesen, 1969).

Think about all the different types of facial expressions you have observed in your conversations with others. Of course, the external situations associated with those emotions may vary considerably across cultures, but the emotions themselves do not. This is a concept to which we will return in the next chapter when we explore reflection of feeling.

PERSONAL REFLECTION _____

How do you know when someone you are talking to is about to cry? Get a mental picture of someone who recently began to cry as he or she was talking to you. In your mind, think of three facial cues.

The indicators you thought of may have included eyes filling with tears, reddening around the nose area, reddening around the mouth, lips quivering, tightening or muscle tension around the mouth, eyes looking down, a furrowed brow, or a facial grimace. As your client is talking, look at her or his face and try to get a sense of the emotions being expressed there.

BODY MOVEMENT   Note which parts of your client's body are moving and those that are still. Is there excessive fidgeting with the hands? Shuffling of the feet? Moving around in the chair? Picking at the fingers? Or is he or she sitting completely still? Note the posture and the placement on the chair. It's possible that the person's body size doesn't work well with the physical structure of the chair, that is, someone with short legs and circulatory problems may have no choice but to perch on the edge of the chair so that his or her feet don't go to sleep. Alternatively, perching on the edge of the chair could reflect anxiety, wanting to get up and walk out, or back pain. Slumping in the chair could indicate depression, defeat, anger or defiance, or trying to shrink away from contact with you.

Note also if there are particular topics of conversation in which the client's behavior and body movement changes. A change in body movement could suggest some agitation, excitement, or some other form of emotional energy around the topic. Conversely, becoming very still could suggest that the topic is a source of reduced energy, which could be either comfort, relaxation, or perhaps helplessness or despair.

Paraverbal Behavior

Paraverbals are also referred to as *paralinguistics*. Listen to the *way* he or she is speaking. If you listen carefully you'll find that particular words are spoken with more emphasis in volume or pitch. These are words that, for your client, reflect heightened emotional energy for some reason. This process is called is *verbal underlining*. When we move on to discuss minimal encouragers and reflection of feeling, you will find the skill of noting verbal underlining to be of particular value, because identifying the verbally underlined words is a main avenue toward identifying and processing emotional energy.

There may be some topics or aspects of a topic in which the volume, rate, or pitch of the person's voice changes in quality. This, again, may indicate emotionally laden content. For example, when someone is excited, the voice tone may become louder or the rate of speech may increase. These same qualities may also be evident when someone is excited. Determining the exact nature of the emotional energy will be a point of exploration and reflection for you and the client; this exploration will be further covered in the subsequent chapter. For now, just practice noticing it.

Another caveat, very relevant in this section about paraverbals, is a research finding noted by Scherer, Banse, and Wallbot (2001) regarding vocal expression of emotion across cultures. It has been found that when a speaker and listener are of similar cultural background, the listener is often able to accurately infer the emotions being expressed by the speaker. In contrast, when the cultural backgrounds of the speaker and listener are dissimilar, the listener is frequently inaccurate in his or her inferences about the emotions being expressed through the voice. Know, then, that if your client happens to be culturally dissimilar to yourself, you may experience a reduced ability to accurately interpret the person's implied emotions. Although personal style varies tremendously, many individuals do not express their feelings by overtly saying, "I feel ____." Instead, their emotions are expressed indirectly through paraverbal and nonverbal behavior.

Verbal Behavior

CONTENT OF THE VERBALIZATION   Observing a client's verbal behavior is probably what many novice counselors think of when they think about counseling. Listening to the client's story carefully (the "verbal tracking" discussed in Chapter 4, Attending Behaviors) falls into this category. Novice counselors often are concerned about getting every little detail of a client's story. However, beyond the content of the story itself, there are several aspects of the client's story that can be of benefit to note. These are dimensions of the story that extend beyond the obvious, overt content. For example, consider the following client statement:

> CLIENT: I want to talk to you about my friend. She always tells me about compliments her boss gives her about her work. She just told me the other day about a great e-mail she got, praising her for a project she finished. When she does that, I feel like I have to talk about all the good things I do on *my* job.

In response to this statement, a beginning counselor might want to ask the client about where she works, how long the two have been friends, how long this has been a problem, or why her friend does that. A more experienced counselor, who is focusing mainly on observing the client, might simply note internally that the client seems to take personally comments her friend might simply be making in passing, and wonder about the internal processes happening for the client that result in her feeling that she needs to defend the quality of her own work.

Just as noteworthy in observing client verbal behavior is what the client is *not* saying. For example, a client may enter a counseling session and talk excessively about other people in his or her life, without talking about her own concerns or feelings. Does there seem to be an excessive amount of focus on him or herself, or on other people? Again, these are simply qualities of the client's presentation to note. These qualities may have some relevance when the time arrives to generate hypotheses and a treatment plan.

A variety of factors could account for any particular style of verbal behavior. For example, in the case of a client who talks exclusively about other people rather than him or herself, perhaps that individual comes from a family of origin in which the benefit of the collective group is of more importance than the individual family members. Or perhaps the client tends to keep attention focused outward in an attempt to avoid being aware of her own emotional discomfort. On the other hand, maybe the client is simply someone whose attention is generally focused more outwardly than inward. There is no implication of value or judgment on any of these possibilities; we are simply consciously noting them to return to in future observation and/or exploration with the client.

JUDGING SITUATIONAL APPROPRIATENESS   A variety of emotional and mental disorders can result in a person having impairment in his or her ability to behave in socially appropriate ways. From the standpoint of your client's mental status, you will be observing whether the words, content, and apparent emotional reaction to his or her presenting story are situationally appropriate. The term *situationally appropriate* encompasses the degree of intimacy of the content, whether the story is consistent with what would be typical for many people at the chronological age and developmental stage of your client, and whether the associated affective (emotional) reaction to the content seems to be a typical response, that is, whether it is the same kind of response we would expect from anyone else with a similar cultural background telling the same story.

Making a decision about whether aspects of a client's presentation are situationally appropriate is a judgment call on the part of the counselor. Caution is necessary partially because as the counselor you will be the holder of the power. Arriving at the conclusion that a client's behavior is situationally inappropriate can potentially have negative implications for the client. As the holder of authority and power in the counseling relationship, you also carry the responsibility of making the estimation of situational appropriateness with as much fairness and objectivity as possible.

Your judgment about whether the client's emotional reaction and verbal content is situationally appropriate will be based on at least two factors. One of those factors will be your own belief system about the particular topic. Here is a place where your own values and beliefs might be in conflict with those of your client's. The other factor will be an internal comparison that you make between your specific client and your knowledge about most other people with some of the same general characteristics (e.g., stage of development, chronological age, gender).

Here, you need to be aware of your own internalized normative sample that comprises the basis for your comparison; make sure you have a large enough sample size of different people in order to make an accurate comparison. We'll take each of the above three criteria for determining situational appropriateness and explore them in more detail.

INTIMACY OF CONTENT   It often takes time before a person feels comfortable disclosing personal information of a sensitive nature (examples would be sexual behavior, illegal behavior, or private details of feelings about a personal situation). The level of disclosure considered to be appropriate in a given conversation is partially culturally determined; some people are reluctant to share anything intensely personal with someone outside the family circle, or with anyone at all. Judging whether the degree of intimacy of disclosure is appropriate should be based on several criteria. One of those criteria is your own beliefs and knowledge about the client's cultural framework.

It is to be expected that the intimacy of disclosure a client makes will increase as trust develops over time and the counseling relationship deepens. However, it may be clinically significant if the level of disclosure, particularly at the beginning of counseling, is giving you details of a nature that most people would withhold from a conversation with an acquaintance. For example, it often happens in counseling that a clinician may ask a client a question during a first session, which the client denies, only to admit in later sessions that he or she was not completely honest when the counselor asked the question. This is often the case if the client believes that telling the truth will result in the counselor having a poor impression of the client.

Another variable to consider in level of disclosure is the nature of the presenting problem or the reason for referral. If the client is coming to the appointment seeing you as the "expert," he or she may be more inclined to come forth with intimate details he or she wouldn't share with someone else.

AUTHOR'S REFLECTION _____

I once worked at a mental health center in an extremely rural area. I saw a middle-aged female client, "Brenda," who was referred to me by her family doctor for "nerve problems." When I asked Brenda about her understanding of why the doctor sent her to me, she shared that she was having "plumbing problems in her privates" and offered to show me what her physical problem was. As we talked more about her symptoms, it became clear that the client thought I was a gynecological specialist, and the nature of her disclosure to me was because of her misperception about my specialty area. In this case, Brenda's seemingly inappropriate verbal behavior of offering to show me her "privates" happened because of a lack of communication between the physician and Brenda about referring her to me, and a subsequent lack of understanding on Brenda's part.

Excessive self-disclosure or inappropriate verbal behavior can indicate a number of things, including clients' misperception about counseling and your role as a counselor, or possibly the presence of traits and/or psychiatric conditions within the client. In any case, inappropriate verbalizations are worth noting.

DEVELOPMENTAL APPROPRIATENESS   You also need to make an assessment of whether the client's concerns are developmentally typical for most individuals at that stage of development. Again, developmental expectations may vary from culture to culture, and so if the client's cultural background is one with which you are unfamiliar, it is most important to simply note the developmental context without conceptualizing it as disordered or even atypical.

As an illustration of whether a presenting concern is developmentally typical, consider a client who is expressing anger because his parents will not let him use the family car to go out with friends one weekend. If the age of the client is between 16 and maybe 20, this would be a typical issue. On the other hand, if the client is 42, it is a *developmentally atypical* concern.

Another case example of a developmentally atypical concern would be a 9-year-old boy seen for counseling by this author, whose parents were divorcing. There were many concerns and issues in the family, but the boy's focus, and the main source of his discomfort, was his worry about his mother's financial status and ability to make the mortgage payment. While some degree of concern about the family's money isn't necessarily too unusual for a child of 9, having detailed information about specific bills such as the mortgage payment is a level of involvement in family financial business that *is* unusual for a 9-year-old.

Developmental typicality is an important observation because it carries implications about other possible issues or concerns that may be influencing the problem, for example, the health of the boundaries in the family system. In the above case, the boy's mother was talking to him about her financial worries and asking for his advice, which was causing the child significant emotional distress. Expecting financial advice from the child was clearly unreasonable on the mother's part.

CONGRUENCE BETWEEN CONTENT AND AFFECT   Here is another place where careful observation will yield information about your client's mental status. Gross misalignment between content and affect can indicate significant impairment in functioning. An example of misalignment would be a person laughing hysterically when telling you about the death of a beloved pet. Of course, there are a multitude of examples of severe mismatches. A woman who had recently gotten married shared with a friend that she had just found out she was pregnant, and although she and her husband had been trying to conceive a child, upon telling the friend she was pregnant, she broke into sobs and talked about how sick and unhappy she was. In this case, there were physiological and hormonal changes that contributed to her emotional instability.

Congruence Among Nonverbal, Paraverbal, and Verbal Behaviors

PERSONAL REFLECTION _____

Have you ever been traveling in an unfamiliar area and stopped to ask for directions? Sometimes the person giving directions is not a clear communicator; other times the person is a good communicator but gives wrong information. In asking directions, you assumed that the person would be a good communicator with accurate information. What was the outcome when your assumptions were wrong?

The term *congruence* in the context of this section means that the emotions that are being expressed verbally and nonverbally are aligned with and reflective of the client's internal experience. This section began with the Personal Reflection above because making an accurate assessment about the congruence among nonverbal, paraverbal, and verbal behavior presupposes that your perception of the person's nonverbal and paraverbal communication is accurate.

When you try to gauge the congruence among a person's verbal, nonverbal, and paraverbal content, your judgment depends on the accuracy of your perceptions of their behavior, that is, whether what you are perceiving is in fact what they are demonstrating. For example, a client might be talking about a new job and relocation, exhibiting a great deal of fidgeting and agitation while talking about all the arrangements that need to be made. His voice might be somewhat loud and his speech pressured. One therapist could interpret this agitation as being a reflection of the client's anxiety, while another counselor might interpret it as excitement and anticipation. Yet another therapist might mistakenly perceive anger because of the apparent emotional arousal. In contrast to congruence, when a person demonstrates *incongruence*, it may indicate that the person is experiencing ambivalence or conflicting emotions about the topic. Another term for incongruence is *mixed message*.

PERSONAL REFLECTION _____

Think of a time someone told you something that you did not believe, perhaps a salesperson, a coworker, or a personal acquaintance. As you recall that memory and recall what was being said, try to identify which parts of the communication told you that the person was not to be believed. What was source of the incongruence that you sensed?

AUTHOR'S REFLECTION _____

When I decide someone is not trustworthy, I make that decision because I have detected incongruence or inconsistency (a mismatch) among his or her words, the paraverbals with which the words are spoken, and his or her nonverbal behavior.

This is probably a concept to which you've been exposed before, typified by a saying common in 12-step meetings such as Alcoholics Anonymous: "It's not enough to talk the talk, you have to walk the walk." Another common saying is, "Talk is cheap," meaning that it's easy for us to *say* we think or feel something, but the true evidence of our beliefs and feelings lies in the behavior we exhibit. Likewise, in client observation, you may note discrepancies between the words being said and the nonverbals or paraverbals.

An example might be a client vehemently exclaiming, "That's just fine for him to do that—it doesn't bother me at all!" with a furrowed brow and loud voice. This author once asked a female client whether she was looking forward to her upcoming wedding, which she had been excitedly planning and telling me about for several months. As she was verbalizing, "Oh, yes, it's going to be great!" she was moving her head back and forth in a shake, nonverbally indicating her answer was no. She appeared to have no conscious awareness that her gesture was saying no.

Nonverbal and paraverbal behaviors may carry as much as 85% of the meaning in a spoken message (Ivey & Ivey, 2007). Moreover, as demonstrated in the example above, it is relatively easy to choose our words carefully and to use words that are not truthful. Yet, it is far more difficult to exhibit paraverbal and nonverbal behavior over an extended period of time that communicates something other than how we really feel about someone or something. We are often unaware of what our nonverbal behavior communicates, particularly to an astute observer who is looking at us carefully as we speak and act.

Again, in the use of the client observation microskill, your only job at this point is to mentally note the discrepancy and tuck it away in your memory bank. If you are jotting down notes following your session, noting some of the behaviors you've observed in session can help you in future sessions to recall incongruencies. There is no need at this point to do anything other than to hone your observation skills and begin to raise your conscious awareness of discrepancies.

When you note the incongruence, it may be helpful to you (and ultimately to the client) to do more observation to ascertain the nature of the inconsistency. There are a number of possible explanations for verbal/nonverbal inconsistency. One explanation would be that the client may be intentionally withholding information from you for a variety of reasons. These reasons could include embarrassment, resentment, guilt, or some other feeling he or she is unwilling to share with you. Another explanation could be that your client may be unaware or underaware of some of the conflicted feelings because they are socially unacceptable. An example of this would be a mother angrily talking about the degree to which her children depend on her, yet when asked directly, reporting that she loves being a full-time, stay-at-home mother, denying her resentment. She may be suppressing those feelings of resentment because she believes a "good mother" should not have those feelings.

Silence

One other aspect of client behavior that may be relevant to note is silence. Many students who are novices are uncomfortable when silence occurs during a role play or counseling session.

PERSONAL REFLECTION _____

Are you a person who feels most comfortable when there is some kind of noise? What is it about quiet that makes you uncomfortable? Do you also feel the need to fill silences when you are with other people, or are there some people with whom you can be together not talking and feel comfortable?

In a counseling session, just as in any other conversation, there may be times when silence elapses. In a verbal interchange, silence may occur when one person has asked a question and the listener is considering what to say before offering a response. In general, aspects of verbal interaction such as *response latency*, which is the lag between when one person finishes talking and the next person begins to talk, are defined in part by culture and in part by colloquialism (local idiosyncracies). Within one general cultural group there may be regional differences not only in how people pronounce words, but also in other aspects of their speech production, including the lag between two people's verbal contributions to a conversation. The response latency your client demonstrates will be yet another aspect of her or his presentation worth noting. We'll talk later about what to do with that observational information after it has been acquired.

CLIENT OBSERVATION IN THE CONTEXT OF THREE THEORETICAL STANCES

One recurrent theme throughout this chapter has been the emphasis on noting behaviors and characteristics of the client's presentation while refraining from drawing conclusions about the behavior. One of the major determinants of the meaning, significance, and conclusions you draw about your client's behavior will be the result of the theoretical orientation to which you subscribe. From the standpoint of any theory, be it developmental, humanistic, or cognitive-behavioral, the client's relationship with you provides a window through which to view how the client generally functions in relationships.

The client's view of you as an authority figure, for example, will likely result in him or her relating to you in the same way he or she reacts to other authority figures, such as work supervisors, church clergy, and so on. A therapist whose orientation is primarily developmental will be looking primarily at earlier stages of the client's development and how he or she related early in life with key caregiving people. That therapist will be most attuned to the content of what the client is saying, and what that message indicates about his or her level of development. A therapist whose orientation is person-centered and existential will be looking primarily for congruence and awareness of his or her own emotional experiencing, whereas a cognitive-behavioral counselor will be listening for content that suggests particular patterns of thinking and behavior and analyzing how those patterns are related to the nature of the client's strengths and complaints.

Multicultural Aspects of Client Observation

Likewise, the client's attitude about counseling and reaction to you as a counselor or person in a role of authority will be partially an outcome of his or her cultural template. One of your main objectives in client observation, particularly early in the relationship development, is to ascertain the person's cultural context as well as ways the cultural template contributes to your overall conceptualization of his or her concerns.

As we consider Hofstede's axes of cultural variability in the context of client observation, keep in mind that there are multiple ways of exploring and understanding a client's preferences or characteristics. A host of data sources will be available to you, beginning with the immediately obvious information regarding how he or she is interacting with you in the counseling session. In addition, you may be able to observe your client interact with other family members or people of significance, if those individuals accompany your client. As well, the content of the client's stories and statements may also offer some clues about these five axes. After you have generated some hypotheses about your client's values in each of the five categories, perhaps the easiest way to affirm the accuracy of your guesses is to ask the client outright whether your hunches are right.

We will explore four of the five axes, excluding long- and short-term orientation, and take a look at the kinds of statements and behaviors that would be typical of people with high or low degrees of each of these characteristics. If these applied examples cause you any confusion, return to Chapter 2 to review the more detailed explanations of Hofstede's axes.

POWER DISTANCE   This is the axis that deals with the extent to which members of a culture accept and expect that there will be a power differential between those in authority and subordinates. Note that this differential between people in power and their subordinates may be as comfortable for the subordinates as it is for the people who hold the power. In other words, try your best to refrain from making the judgment that your own values on any given axis are the preferred, "normal," or "healthy" ways to be. Here is an example of an interchange between a high power distance client and a low power distance counselor:

> COUNSELOR: Mr. Gonzalez, it sounds to me as though your family's financial worries are happening in part because you are being underpaid at your job. Is there any hope for you of getting a raise or a promotion any time soon?
>
> CLIENT: My team leader has made it very clear that we are never to ask when we might be considered for promotion.
>
> COUNSELOR: But why wouldn't you want to know the timeline and your supervisor's criteria, so you can work toward that?
>
> CLIENT: It is *extremely* disrespectful to question the leader! They make their own judgments about these things and our job is to simply do our job and wait.

The above dialogue illustrates not only a client's statements that reflect a value of high power distance, but also how an insensitive counselor's lack of awareness of cultural differences between herself and the client could create tension or a lack of therapeutic rapport between herself and her client. Her questions imply that the client *should* be taking action, which clearly, from the client's perspective, would be impudent and ill-advised. On the other hand, the possibility also exists that this client is being oppressed or discriminated against in the workplace, and that the supervisor is intentionally taking advantage of the client's deference to authority.

MASCULINITY   Recall that this axis is concerned with two things: the way a culture distributes roles and jobs across both genders, and also the extent to which there is fluidity of values and behaviors in general across both genders. In other words, a culture with low masculinity would be accepting and supportive of androgynous values and noverbal behaviors. Characteristics typically defined as "masculine" are assertiveness and competitiveness. "Feminine" characteristics in the context of this axis are cooperativeness, modesty, and caring. In a culture with low masculinity, it would be more acceptable for men to show emotional vulnerability and to cry, for example. In a culture with high masculinity, in contrast, the gender roles are extremely clear with regard to who does which tasks, as well as which expressed emotions and behaviors are acceptable from each gender. Following is an example of a statement that might be made by a client who has low masculinity and high fluidity of gender roles in her family.

> CLIENT: When my husband lost his job it was clear that we would have to rely on my income. I was the one with the good health insurance anyway, so

it made sense for me to keep my job. I was so relieved that he offered to do the grocery shopping! Now it's at the point where we've basically switched and he's doing the Mr. Mom thing. It's working out really well for all of us and I'm so glad he enjoys being a dad. Now he gets to help out in the kindergarten room with Joey and can take David to soccer practice too.

AFFILIATION   This is the axis defined by the extent to which a culture defines allegiance to the collective as an important aspect of a person's behavior. High affiliation societies expect that an individual's actions should always be considered in a group context, as opposed to an individual context. The United States generally has an extremely high degree of individualism. Thus, as a national culture, there is little expectation that any one person has much responsibility to the community. Please note that this statement is based specifically on Hofstede's data about national profiles on the five axes of cultural differences. Although the United States as a nation has a high degree of individuality, many people belong to subgroups of the culture; within those subgroups there may in fact be a high degree of collectivism. Can you think of groups to which you or people you know belong, in which there is an expectation that the interests of the group will outweigh the importance of individuals' needs?

There are other cultures in which, on a national level, the needs of the group are seen as far outweighing the needs of any one individual. In those cultures, people make life choices and decisions not on the basis of what they personally would prefer (as is often the case in the United States), but instead on the basis of what is best for their family or community, which in turn will be best for the nation. Here is an example of a statement that might be typical of someone with a low degree of individualism:

CLIENT: I've been working at the bakery for as long as I can remember. From the time I could walk my parents gave me work to do, carrying bags of sugar, cleaning out the cases, and eventually running the mixers. We have recipes that have been handed down through many generations, and it's just always been expected that our family are the ones that do all the baked goods. Our family has catered every wedding and funeral in our neighborhood for so many years, I don't think there was ever a time that we didn't! My great-grandparents carried these recipes over in the boat from the old country.

COUNSELOR: Do you like baking breads and pastries?

CLIENT: What else do I know? It's all I've ever done.

UNCERTAINTY AVOIDANCE   This axis has to do with a person's preference for structure and, to some extent, seems related to autonomy. People in cultures with low uncertainty avoidance are comfortable with ambiguity and unstructured situations. These are cultures in which multiple viewpoints or values are allowed or even encouraged. On the other hand, people from cultures with high uncertainty avoidance live in societies where there are very clear, explicit rules about "right" and "wrong" and rigid guidelines about acceptable behavior. High uncertainty avoidance may arise in part, from anxiety and fear of loss of control. Uncertainty avoidance, according to Hofstede, is very much related to one's philosophical approach to life in general, which may be a by-product of one's religious or spiritual beliefs. A religious or spiritual belief system that holds that there is only one absolute truth is one that would be high on the uncertainty avoidance axis.

CLIENT: I follow the rules because the rules are what keeps the order around here. Everyone else should follow the rules too. It's when you get troublemakers like John sneaking around breaking the rules and looking for the loopholes that everything gets messed up. There never should have been any loopholes in the first place! But he'll have his punishment soon enough and then we'll be able to get back to business.

Chapter Summary

In this chapter we considered aspects of your client's behaviors that you will have opportunity to observe. There are a multitude of behaviors that can be noted and, when placed in the context of *all* the behaviors and the cultural template, may provide a fairly accurate and comprehensive picture of your client and his or her concerns.

Perhaps the most consistent theme throughout this chapter has been the need for the counselor to refrain from judgment or interpretation of those behaviors. Ironically, you may find the skill of client observation to be quite easy, and yet find it extremely challenging *not* to judge that client. Additionally, many of us gravitate to and value whatever is most familiar. Thus, it is easy to look at someone whose values and behaviors are different from our own and see them as "abnormal" or unhealthy. Sometimes those behaviors will be unhealthy; other times, they will simply be different from your own. In several of the following chapters we will cover the topic of judging and diagnosing in greater detail.

Questions for Class Discussion

1. Ask your role play "client" a series of true/false questions and see if you can discern when he or she is lying.
2. Discuss a time when you misinterpreted someone else's behavior. In retrospect, what was the cause for your misinterpretation?
3. Consider your own values and beliefs that could interfere with your ability to objectively observe another person. Discuss with your classmates client characteristics in each of the following categories and ways those characteristics could be barriers for your observation:
   a. Sexual identity and sexual orientation
   b. Religion
   c. Age
   d. Dietary preferences (e.g., vegetarian)
   e. Personal history (e.g., clients who have a history of perpetrating domestic violence or other illegal behavior)

CHAPTER 6

Silence, Minimal Encouragers, Paraphrasing, and Summarizing

After studying this chapter, you should have a clear understanding of the following:

- Awareness of the components of minimal encouragers (including key word repetition and restatement), paraphrase, and summary
- Awareness of what impact these microskills exert upon the counseling process
- Understanding of the purposes served by effective paraphrasing and summarizing

Up to this point in our coverage of the microskills, our focus has been on nonverbal skills counselors use; attending mindfully and carefully observing the client. Our focus is about to shift to counselors' spoken responses that facilitate further depth and development of the conversation with the client. The next several microskills focus on verbal contributions you can offer in the interchange that will influence and direct the focus of your interaction with your client.

This chapter will cover a range of verbal responses that can be conceptualized as occupying a continuum ranging from a small amount of verbal expression, that is, silently attending, to single-syllable utterances, words, phrases, and at the other end of the continuum, an entire paragraph. The unifying theme of this continuum is some type of output from you that provides the client with a reflection of what he or she said. This chapter will be organized by type of counselor output. Each section will begin with a definition of the skill, followed by a general discussion about advantages and disadvantages, and dialogue examples.

Two introductory things need to be stated about aspects of this chapter. First, a word about silence. It appears here because it plays a role in all the spoken microskills; in each case there is a time for talking and a time for silence. Considering intentional use of silence as an aspect of each microskill, we'll be looking at times when the counselor can actually be *more* effective not speaking. Silence is included in this chapter because it represents one type of counselor response that can result in the client's continued verbalization and elaboration on a particular theme or topic.

The other preliminary explanation that will help your understanding of the following material is the differentiation among client content, client affect, and counseling process.

Being able to differentiate among these three things will help you to have a more precise understanding of what the client is expressing, and also what is happening between the two of you in the counseling relationship. *Client content* refers to his or her story, meaning the topics and issues he or she is bringing to the session. As the story is being told, he or she will have associated feelings and internal emotional experiences in the context of the story. This is *client affect*. Finally, *process* refers to what is happening in the present moment between you and your client. This includes both the complex relational interactions occurring in the here and now, as well as the stages of counseling over the entire experience, from intake to termination. The material covered in this chapter is concerned only with client content. Although the client's emotions in the dialogue examples may be clear to you, the skills in this unit focus only on the client content for now.

SILENCE

Early in their professional training, counseling students may do "practice sessions" in role plays with other students. They go on to work with real clients under close supervision on practica and internships. Novice counseling students are often surprised to discover that they are not necessarily expected to fill every available minute of client interaction with speech. Many students expect that since "counseling" means "talking to someone in a helpful way," it means they will be talking the whole time. There are some therapists, namely psychoanalysts, who may have an entire session with a client without uttering a word. Although that particular type of therapy comes from a specific theoretical approach and does not represent the type of counseling you are being taught in a textbook such as this one, the point is that silence is a legitimate counseling response. There are going to be times in your sessions when it will be best for you to say nothing and let the client process and work with the material internally.

PERSONAL REFLECTION _____

How comfortable are you with silence in your daily life? Are you the kind of person who keeps the radio or television on at all times to have the background noise? On a 1–10 scale, with 10 being completely comfortable, how easy/comfortable is it for you to be in the physical presence of another person and not talk?

If your own level of comfort with silence is low, you may find it beneficial to do some self-exploration to understand yourself as fully as possible. What is it that keeps you from silence? Or, what is it about silence that is uncomfortable for you when you are alone? If you find silence intolerable when you are alone, you may find it exceedingly difficult to permit silence to elapse when you are with a client.

If you *are* comfortable with silence in other situations but don't think you would be comfortable in silence with a client, again ask yourself where your discomfort comes from. When posed this question, the two most common responses my students give are that they are afraid the client will perceive them as incompetent, or that as counselors they believe they should have all the answers and solutions for their clients. Both of these reasons are erroneous. In the first case, regarding a client perceiving them as incompetent, it is far more likely that the counselor will appear to be incompetent if he or she is talking without giving thought ahead of time to what should be said or where the conversation should go. In the second case, while the client might want the counselor to fix the problem, it is not necessarily the *counselor's* job to solve the client's problems. It is the client's responsibility, and the counselor's role is to assist the client in finding the internal and external resources to resolve the difficulty. It would be an unimaginable feat to solve a client's problems without the client's participation; it just is not possible.

We turn now to an exploration of ways silence can be an extremely effective tool in therapy. Silence can occur in a counseling session under a number of different circumstances:

1. The client has made a statement and it is the counselor's turn to talk.
2. The counselor has asked a question and the client doesn't answer.
3. The counselor has made a paraphrase or summary that doesn't require a response from the client.

When students worry about looking "incompetent," they may be envisioning the first bulleted example: The client has said something, finished the sentence, and it is the counselor's turn to say something. Students frequently worry about figuring out what to say next. Silence under this circumstance isn't necessarily therapeutic for the client, although depending on the topic of conversation, if the counselor refrains from saying anything, the client may continue with additional material or may change the subject. If this circumstance arises and it's your turn, it's fine to take a few seconds to gather your thoughts and formulate an appropriate response before beginning to talk.

In the case of the second bulleted item, asking a question, we will go into more detail about how to handle this in the chapter on questioning. However, know that if you ask a question and don't get an immediate response, it could be for several reasons. Beginner counselors might second guess themselves and assume that they asked a poor question or that the client is not responding appropriately. When you have made a paraphrase or summary that doesn't necessarily require a response from the client, try letting the silence transpire for a little while. Give your client a bit of time to sit with your paraphrase and see whether he or she will expand or develop the theme further.

Your client's silence might be the result of his or her internally processing some feelings or thoughts. Many people are unable to internally process and talk at the same time. Thus, if a client is silent and you jump in too quickly with another paraphrase or question, you may interrupt the internal process and inadvertently undermine the counseling process. If you have made a good paraphrase or summary, the client might need time to explore that content internally; remember that the whole intent of the paraphrase or summary is to reflect the client's content back to him or her.

How long should a period of silence go on? If the client is searching for an answer to a question you have asked, or you are waiting for some other response to something you have said, such as a key word repetition, carefully observe the client's nonverbal behavior. A silence of less than 10 seconds might be too brief for the client to sufficiently process his or her response. On the other hand, a silence of 2 minutes could be excessively long, unless the client is specifically doing some activity the counselor is directing, such as internal imagery or writing something. Different clients require different amounts of silence to engage in their internal processing. By watching their nonverbals you will have some behavior cues as to when you should intervene and break the silence if they are not spontaneously responding to you.

Some of the most important work your clients will do in a counseling session will occur during the silences. Realizations and insights come most easily when we turn our attention inward, listening to what is happening *inside*. After becoming aware of our thoughts and feelings, we can put them into words to share with others and experience the empathy that comes when we express ourselves and are truly heard.

Multicultural Aspects of Silence

POWER DISTANCE   This is the axis that deals with the extent to which members of a culture accept and expect that there will be a power differential between those in authority and subordinates.

A client from a culture with high power distance may be deferential toward the counselor, who represents a person in authority. In that case, the client may wait expectantly for the counselor to break a silence to direct the session, and permitting a long silence to elapse might create tension.

MASCULINITY   Recall that this axis is concerned with two things: the way a culture distributes roles and jobs across both genders, and also the extent to which there is fluidity of values and behaviors in general across both genders. In other words, a culture with low masculinity would be accepting and supportive of androgynous values and nonverbal behaviors. In a culture with high masculinity, the gender roles are extremely clear with regard to who does which tasks, as well as which expressed emotions and behaviors are acceptable from each gender.

In a counselor/client dyad where the client is from a culture with high masculinity (a male client working with a female counselor or a female client working with a male counselor), the client may expect that the male of the dyad will be the person in control of the session. These expectations could affect the way silence transpires in the session.

AFFILIATION   This is the axis defined by the extent to which a person's culture defines allegiance to the collective as an important aspect of behavior. High affiliation societies expect that an individual's actions are considered in a group context, as opposed to an individual context. This particular axis doesn't seem to have much bearing on silence.

UNCERTAINTY AVOIDANCE   This axis has to do with a person's preference for structure and, to some extent, seems related to autonomy. People in cultures with low uncertainty avoidance are comfortable with ambiguity and unstructured situations. Societies with high uncertainty avoidance have clear, explicit rules about right and wrong and rigid guidelines about acceptable behavior.

For individuals from cultures with a high level of uncertainty avoidance, ambiguity is uncomfortable. It stands to reason, then, that lapses of silence could be uncomfortable, if the client holds rigid expectations and role definitions for the counselor and client.

Silence in the Context of Three Theoretical Stances

HUMANISTIC   From the person-centered, humanistic perspective, there are a number of possible reasons that a client may be silent. The simplest and most obvious explanation is that the client may not have any emotional energy to move in the direction the conversation is headed. This could be lack of interest or simply lack of concern about a topic. Another possible explanation for client silence could be discomfort with a topic, yet an inability to assertively change the subject or tell the counselor it is uncomfortable. Related to this, the client might be intentionally avoiding discussing a topic with you. Finally, there could be some kind of emotional block that prohibits emotions from being expressed or from the client even being able to consciously acknowledge them.

A counselor's choice to allow silence to elapse, from this theoretical stance, reflects permitting the client to have control of the counseling session. Additionally, the discussion about permitting the client to introspect and develop insight, presented in the preceding section, emanates from a client-centered position.

DEVELOPMENTAL   Some developmental counselors might view client silence as indication of dynamic resistance or denial. In this case, the silence would be evidence of psychic blocking, meaning that the basis of a conflict or some of the emotions the client is experiencing are too threatening to other aspects of the self and so are pushed away from consciousness.

COGNITIVE-BEHAVIORAL   There may be frequent incidents of silence in a cognitive-behavioral counseling session for a couple of reasons. The counselor may ask a client to identify his or her self-talk about a particular topic or issue, requiring the client to go on an internal search to articulate the self-talk. Another circumstance would be if the counselor is doing guided imagery with the client and is pausing between directive statements as part of the relaxation and imagery.

Other Considerations in Silence

Despite our concern about providing for clients the best care we can, we also need to temper our consciousness with a caution about not overinterpreting. Sometimes people don't talk because there just isn't anything to say. A topic has been exhausted and there is no more material. Additionally, some people are naturally more extroverted and talkative than others. Some of your clients are going to be people who characteristically don't talk much. Be careful not to conclude that the person has major emotional blockage or is walking around feeling uncomfortable when some of the quietness is simply his or her temperament.

AUTHOR'S REFLECTION _____

A dear friend of mine was an English literature major before going on to become a psychoanalytic psychologist. This friend often interprets others' behavior, including artists' intended messages and metacommunication in literature and works of art. In keeping with his artistic interests, he once went to an art exhibit and selected a lithograph to buy, which was entitled *Dog in Ann Arbor*. Always wanting to hear about the underlying meaning, my friend dreamily asked the artist, "Tell me the story of this lithograph. What does it *mean*?" The artist stared at my friend for a moment and mumbled, "Well, I live in Ann Arbor, and I have a dog." This is a good example of trying to interpret something that has no underlying meaning, just the obvious one.

We move now from the nonverbal skill of silence into the realm of verbal responses. One caveat necessary to emphasize is that the paraverbals used when delivering any of these verbal responses are highly influential in how the responses are perceived. When you are using a minimal encourager, for example, if your voice tone is loud, you speak quickly, or your vocal style is clipped, the same utterance that could be invitational could instead end up sounding sarcastic or even aggressive. I'm not going to belabor this point any further, but need to mention, as we have in other chapters, that appropriate paraverbals are an essential component of these verbal microskills.

MINIMAL ENCOURAGERS

A *minimal encourager* is defined as a slight verbal response. Think for a moment about how you let someone know you are listening. As we reviewed when talking about attending, there are a variety of ways that we nonverbally communicate to someone that we are listening. For example, when we are talking on the telephone and are deprived the visual input usually available during in-person contact, we must provide *verbal* cues to the other person. The smallest unit of verbal feedback you can offer a speaker to indicate your attentiveness is the minimal encourager. There are many minimal encouragers. Take a moment and brainstorm all the different minimal encouragers you use or that have been used on you. Here is a list of possibilities:

Okay

Uh-huh

Um-hmm

Right

Yes

Huh

Oh

Chances are that you say these, or some variant of them, with frequency. The good thing about minimal encouragers is that if they aren't used too much, they don't get in the way and essentially serve the purpose of communicating to the other person that you are agreeable to their continued speaking.

Following is a counseling dialogue example of minimal encouragers:

DAVID: My band camp experience was really good. I liked my roommate a lot, we played cards and shared snacks, and we both got to meet the other one's friends.

COUNSELOR: Um-hmmm.

DAVID: But the one thing I didn't like was my conductor. He was often sarcastic and sort of mean to some of the kids.

COUNSELOR: Oh.

DAVID: Yeah, he was pretty much a jerk all week.

COUNSELOR: Hmm.

Note that if you continue to use minimal encouragers, the client will, as the name implies, be encouraged to follow his or her stream of thought about the topic of discussion.

Intentional Withholding of Minimal Encouragers

If you think that the direction of the conversation is not productive or that the focus needs to be elsewhere, an alternative way you can use minimal encouragers to gently guide the focus is to *withhold* them. This is a subtle and somewhat passive way of directing a conversation.

Withholding your minimal encouragers is likely to result in one of three outcomes. Those clients who are highly attuned to how others are responding to them will take your subtle hint and slow down or stop talking. If this is the outcome, the client may gradually move toward closing the topic and then direct his or her attention to you to see where you want the focus to go. This is most likely to occur if your client is a high self-monitor. The client may also gradually begin to move toward another topic. Note that when these conversational effects occur, they are so subtle that the client might not even be consciously aware that it is happening.

The disadvantage of using this withholding technique is that the client may experience you as not listening. Particularly when the counseling relationship is in an early stage, this could be detrimental to your developing rapport with the person. People who are low self-monitors will be so absorbed in their stories that they will not notice your lack of encouragement and will likely need to have more direction from you if the topic or focus is to change.

KEY WORD REPETITION AND RESTATEMENT

Besides minimal encouragers, the technique of key word repetition is a minimally invasive counselor response that can influence directionality of the focus. Restatement similarly can elicit emotional content or create conditions for a more careful exploration of something the client has shared.

Key Word Repetition

A *key word repetition* consists of the counselor selecting a single word that the client has verbally underlined, and then repeating that word. The counselor's repetition can be in statement form, meaning that the vocal inflection does not change throughout the articulation of the word. Key word repetition can also be expressed as a question, which is a more overt communication that the counselor wants the client to expand on a particular topic. Following is a dialogue example of key word repetition.

CLIENT: So all in all, it just didn't go that well. Considering all the preparation I put into this trip, it really was a pretty big disappointment. I won't be doing a trip like that again any time soon. What a huge pain in the neck!

COUNSELOR: A disappointment.

CLIENT: Well, yeah. Here I thought my sister would appreciate all the effort I put into traveling and instead she complained constantly. On top of that, I was sick from drinking the water, my hotel room was uncomfortable, and I got madder and madder at her over the week.

COUNSELOR: Madder?

CLIENT: I started out the week being a little annoyed, then every day got worse. . . .

By selecting the key words, which in this example did happen to be feeling words, the counselor is able to direct the client's focus toward her internal experience, which was a source of discomfort. Had the counselor not done those key word repetitions, the client's spontaneous conversation might have gone in numerous other directions, such as the location of the vacation or the details of her illness. These topics, in this case, would not have been as helpful to the client because at the moment, most of her emotional energy lies in the strained relationship with her sister.

Restatement

A *restatement* is similar to a key word repetition, but rather than selecting one word, the counselor repeats back to the client a longer phrase or complete repetition of what he or she said. The outcome of a restatement is similar to key word repetition, but the restatement is an even more overt counselor communication. Here is the same dialogue clip as above, but using restatement rather than key words.

> CLIENT: So all in all, it just didn't go that well. Considering all the preparation I put into this trip, it really was a pretty big disappointment. I won't be doing a trip like that again any time soon. What a huge pain in the neck!
>
> COUNSELOR: It didn't go that well.
>
> CLIENT: Well, yeah. Here I thought my sister would appreciate all the effort I put into traveling and instead she complained constantly. On top of that, I was sick from drinking the water, my hotel room was uncomfortable, and I got madder and madder at her over the week.
>
> COUNSELOR: You got madder and madder over the week.
>
> CLIENT: Ugh! Let me *tell* you about that! . . .

One word of caution about key word repetition and restatement. It is possible to overuse both of these, and if you do overuse them, your client may feel some frustration with you. Sometimes in conversation people use restatement as a way of tuning out because they are not adding their own input to the interaction. Therefore, key word repetitions and restatements should be used judiciously and interspersed with other forms of dialogue.

PARAPHRASING

myhelpinglab

Video Lab > By Course > Skills/Process/Techniques >
⇒ Module 3: Diagnostic Assessment > Reviewing Intake Information with Clients
⇒ Module 7: Psychodynamic Intervention > Directive Clarifying and Summarizing

We move now to one of the microskills that comprises the heart of active listening. Paraphrases are fun! One great thing about paraphrasing is that you can practice them all the time. Whereas with minimal encouragers it's possible to mumble, "Uh-huh" every time another speaker pauses, while tuning out and thinking about something completely different, it isn't possible to do that while paraphrasing. That's because you have to really be listening, and processing in your head, the content of what the speaker is disclosing. For that reason, paraphrasing can be quite an effective way of having a true verbal interchange with another person while communicating your attentiveness. As with many of these microskills, though, there is a point of diminishing return, meaning that it is possible to paraphrase too much, which can end up defeating the purpose.

Paraphrases focus on *content*, as opposed to the emotional message or affective undercurrent. Focusing on the emotional message is the realm of reflecting feelings. Indeed, when we explore feeling reflection, we will be using some of the same basic techniques we are learning now. It is being mentioned here mainly so readers can differentiate conceptually between a paraphrase and a feeling reflection.

First we will learn the verbal structure for a basic paraphrase, and then you will have a couple of different dialogue examples. Included in the examples will be samples of inappropriate paraphrases, along with an explanation of why they are inappropriate.

Various authors suggest slightly different formats for a proper paraphrase. Poorman (2003) identified four components of a paraphrase: (1) Recall the message, (2) identify the *essential* content, (3) translate the content into the counselor's words, and (4) check out, that is, receive verification from the client as to accuracy. The accuracy verification from the client will come from the client's verbal acknowledgement of what you said. There also will be a variety of nonverbal indications that you are either on target or off base. Young (2005), on the other hand, identifies only two steps: (1) listening carefully to the client's story, and (2) feeding back to the client a condensed, nonjudgmental restatement of the facts and thoughts.

For beginners, the following steps are recommended:

1. Initiate with a recognition that this is *your perception* of what he or she is saying.
2. Identify the essence of his or her message (only the content).
3. Verify your accuracy—make sure you give the client room to disagree with you or correct you if the message you heard was not accurate.

Paraphrase examples

I think I _____ (e.g., perceive, hear, see, sense) that _____ (the situation). Did I hear you right?

OR

It sounds like you're saying that _____, no?

OR

I want to make sure I have this. You're telling me the situation is that _____, right?

Now let's take a client situation and problem statement and I will provide two alternative appropriate and one inappropriate examples of paraphrase responses.

CLIENT: My father has been gone for close to a year now. I think it's a long time for Mom to still be moping around the house. She's actually started whining. I've suggested that she resume her yoga classes and do some other things too . . . going out to lunch with her friends, like she did before he died, but she always has an excuse for why she can't do whatever it is I suggest. I don't know what else to do for her. And I don't know what it is she wants from me, either.

Appropriate paraphrase #1: It sounds to me like you experience your mom as being mopey and even whiny, but when you make suggestions she usually has a "yes, but" response for you. Am I hearing you right?

Appropriate paraphrase #2: It looks to me like your mom is still grieving your father's death and she doesn't seem to be finding your suggestions helpful. Do you see it that way?

Inappropriate paraphrase: Your father died a while ago and before he died, your mom was a pretty busy person. Is that right?

Appropriate paraphrase examples 1 and 2 are effective because they capture the essential elements of the client's content: The mother had a higher level of functioning before the father's death, she now seems to be still very full of grief, and she is not responding favorably to the client's suggestions about how to feel better. The inappropriate paraphrase is ineffective because it misses two essential elements of the client's message; one, about the mother's grieving, and the other, about the mother's lack of initiative to change her behavior.

What differentiates a good paraphrase from a poor one? Several variables can make the difference between a paraphrase that completely achieves your intention and one that falls short of the goal. Let's consider what some of those characteristics are. A good paraphrase:

- Is age appropriate
- Parallels the client's level of cognitive complexity
- Incorporates the client's key words

The first thing an effective paraphrases needs to be is *age appropriate*. Children, particularly *younger* children, tend to respond more favorably to paraphrases that are concrete. Here is an example of an 8-year-old child's statement, followed by a counselor paraphrase that is appropriately concrete and one that is overly abstract.

> CLIENT: Today in class Mitchell kept kicking my chair even though I told him at the beginning of the day that I didn't want him bugging me anymore. I figured since I told him at morning line up that he'd cut it out, but he just kept right on doing it all day and I messed up my spelling test because of it.
>
> *Appropriate paraphrase:* You told Mitchell in the morning not to kick your chair, but he went ahead and did it anyway. And you messed up a spelling test because of that.
>
> *Inappropriate paraphrase:* You tried to anticipate problems and behaved proactively by asking Mitchell not to bug you, but he persisted, which resulted in you failing your spelling test.

Although the *content* of the inappropriate paraphrase is correct, it is worded in a way that makes it too abstract for a child of 8 to fully grasp and perceive as empathic. In the case of the appropriate paraphrase, however, the restatement is more concrete and likely to result in the child feeling heard by the counselor.

The next component of a good paraphrase is a matched, parallel level of complexity. As a graduate student, you may find yourself using technical language or jargon without realizing that your clients might not be able to understand you. If possible, use language form and sentence structure that are roughly parallel to that of your client. A client who is highly educated may use different language than a person who has not graduated from high school. Here is an example of a client statement with appropriate and inappropriate paraphrases:

> CLIENT: My daughter Brenda's boyfriend said he don't want to date her no more. I told her good riddance to him—he's a no-good piece of crap! And tell him to bring back that dang power washer too. . . . I work way too hard for him to be walking off with my stuff.
>
> *Appropriate paraphrase:* You were glad the boyfriend broke up with her—good riddance. And he still has some of your stuff you most definitely want back!
>
> *Inappropriate paraphrase:* Your daughter's boyfriend was an imposition on you and your daughter. On top of that he was somewhat manipulative and you suspect that his motives were materially focused.

The first paraphrase is appropriate because the counselor kept the statements somewhat concrete and straightforward. The second paraphrase is inappropriate because, while the counselor's interpretations are likely to be correct, the client may wonder what in the world the counselor is saying. This will not result in the client feeling heard or experiencing empathy from the counselor.

Finally we come to the last item on the list of suggested techniques for enhancing your paraphrasing effectiveness: incorporating some of the client's words. Using some of the client's words in the paraphrase, particularly the key words that have been vocally underlined, will help to maximize your client's sense of being heard. However, if you continually repeat everything the client says, you will sound like a tape recorder. This can have the opposite of the intended effect and result in the client feeling as though you are *not* listening. Glance back over the examples above and note how, in the examples of appropriate paraphrases, the counselor chose particular key words to integrate into the paraphrase.

Multicultural Aspects of Paraphrasing

Following a brief review of the definition of each of Hofstede's axes of cultural variability, and we will then examine more specifically how each of those might affect use of paraphrasing. Considering the definition of a paraphrase, it seems that the use of a paraphrase in and of itself wouldn't necessarily change as a function of the client's cultural background. Instead, the way that use of paraphrases will be affected by cultural variability is in the content of what the client is sharing and what elements the counselor is choosing to paraphrase. In other words, the actual content that a client is sharing is going to be in part the result of the cultural template, and so the essential elements that are most pertinent for the paraphrase will also shift.

POWER DISTANCE   This is the axis that deals with the extent to which members of a culture accept and expect that there will be a power differential between those in authority and subordinates. Here is an example of a paraphrase for a client whose culture has a high power distance:

CLIENT: I find myself not looking forward to the committee meetings after the church service. There are parishioners there who do not share my views about how we should be volunteering and trying to raise money. We have people right here in our own diocese that are starving and need our help. Yet the priest has already made the assignments for who will chair each volunteer group and I was not chosen. So now I just do what is assigned, but my heart is not in it like it should be.

COUNSELOR PARAPHRASE: Okay, I want to make sure I'm hearing you. The priest has assigned leaders for the volunteer groups. You were not chosen as a leader, and you disagree with the leader's decision about how to raise money and who should receive the help, and so you don't feel very committed to the cause. Am I getting it?

This example is reflective of high power distance. Although the client is unhappy with the direction of the committee activities, there is an implied resignation about just accepting the circumstances, because they were established by the priest, a person with authority.

MASCULINITY   Recall that this axis is concerned with two things: the way a culture distributes roles and jobs across both genders, and also the extent to which there is fluidity of values and behaviors in general across both genders. In other words, a culture with low masculinity would be accepting and supportive of androgynous values and nonverbal behaviors. In a culture with high masculinity, the gender roles are extremely clear with regard to who does which tasks, as well as which expressed emotions and behaviors are acceptable from each gender. For illustration, let's consider a client whose mother died and whose father is moping around the house, not eating or sleeping very well.

CLIENT:	Since Mother passed on last year, my father just sits around the house all day. I was over there last week and all the food in the refrigerator was spoiled. I can't imagine what he is eating. I told him, "Pop, you need to get back down to the club to play poker," and he says, "Yeah, yeah, yeah." Mother was going downhill for such a long time, I'd think he'd be relieved not to have to take care of her, since he complained all the time about the money he had to spend on the nursing care and the housekeeper. It's time for him to move on already, find a good woman to cook his meals and keep his laundry clean.
COUNSELOR PARAPHRASE:	From your perspective, it seems like your father should be done grieving by now, especially since your mother was ill for a while before she died. You believe it would be much better for your father to find a new wife who can take care of his needs around the house. Is that right?

AFFILIATION   This is the axis defined by the extent to which a person's culture defines allegiance to the collective as an important aspect of a person's behavior. High affiliation societies expect that an individual will consider his or her actions in a group context, as opposed to an individual context. Level of affiliation to one's family or other group of origin (e.g., community groups) may be one of the more obvious sources of cultural variability between you and your clients. Here is a dialogue example and paraphrase for a client with low affiliation/high individualism.

CLIENT:	I decided to take the transfer to the East Coast since there's a lot more chance of promotion once I get there. The main thing I need to do here is make sure I've signed the forms turning over legal guardianship for all my mother's care to my sister. She's not happy about that since she travels a lot, but it will be much easier for her to manage Mother's affairs than for me, since I'll be so far away now.
COUNSELOR PARAPHRASE:	Taking care of the details for your mother's care has been one of your main concerns, and although your sister is somewhat unwilling, you think it would be best for her to take over.

UNCERTAINTY AVOIDANCE   This axis has to do with a person's preference for structure and, to some extent, seems related to autonomy. People in cultures with low uncertainty avoidance are comfortable with ambiguity and unstructured situations. Cultures with high uncertainty avoidance have clear, explicit rules about right and wrong and rigid guidelines about acceptable behavior. Here is an example of a paraphrase with a client from a culture with a low degree of uncertainty avoidance.

CLIENT: I saw in the paper this morning that our neighbor, John Smith, has been found guilty of several counts of federal tax evasion and other crimes related to his money management. I was completely shocked when I heard that John had committed such a crime. But knowing him as well as I thought I did, I just have to believe that there were extremely extenuating circumstances, and I just hope the judge takes that into account when it's time to sentence him.

COUNSELOR PARAPHRASE: John's behavior came as a surprise to you, and you suspect there were aspects of the situation that gave John no choice other than to break the law.

PERSONAL REFLECTION

As you read the sample client dialogues above, were there some client statements that "pushed a button" for you, that is, triggered some kind of internal emotional response? What was the nature of your emotional response? What was it about the client statement that triggered your response?

If the nature of your emotional response was recognition or familiarity, the process of feeling and expressing empathy to that client will be easier. On the other hand, if your emotional response was bewilderment, distaste, or frustration coming out of strong disagreement, it may be hard for you to formulate a paraphrase that is neutral and nonjudgmental. When this is the case, you will have to make a conscious effort to draw on your ability to separate the content of your client's story from his or her entitlement to his or her worldview, even though you disagree.

Paraphrasing in the Context of Three Theoretical Stances

The intention behind a paraphrase may vary as an outcome of the therapist's theoretical stance. Each of the three broad theoretical orientations conceptualize different counseling goals. We'll consider how the use of a paraphrase could take the counseling toward different counselor goals.

HUMANISTIC   In the humanistic, person-centered realm, the client's experience of your empathic understanding is a central treatment goal. Thus, paraphrasing is one of the key techniques of the person-centered approach. A skillful paraphrase can significantly help the client's sense of your empathic understanding. Besides the client's experience of your empathy for him or her, there also is the chance that by hearing his or her words repeated back, the client will have a different sense of what is being said. The paraphrase is essentially a content reflection back to the client. When we see our reflection in the mirror, we have the chance to observe how we appear to others. Likewise with a verbal reflection; sometimes when we hear our words repeated by another person, we have a chance to experience ourselves from a slightly different perspective, which may result in insight and self-understanding we did not previously have.

DEVELOPMENTAL   From a developmental perspective, the main purpose of paraphrasing is to deepen the therapeutic rapport and ensure that the lines of communication are open. The process of restatement is an opportunity to ensure that the message communicated by the client is in fact the message received by the counselor.

COGNITIVE-BEHAVIORAL   A cognitive-behavioral therapist will definitely use paraphrasing, but with a far different intended goal. For the cognitive-behavioral counselor, the goal of paraphrasing is to clarify the client's statement. A cognitive-behavioral counselor will be listening in particular for several specific aspects of the client's presentation. These aspects include:

- The client's cognitive distortions and erroneous thought patterns
- A sequence of events with the emphasis on the trigger, the behavior, and the outcome

Here we conclude our exploration of paraphrasing. We looked at multiple aspects of paraphrasing, including the elements of a good one, ways to enhance one, what to avoid, and the relationship between paraphrasing and cultural template as well as relationship and theoretical orientation.

SUMMARIZING

We turn now to the last of the skills that are geared just toward reflecting client content. As was mentioned at the beginning of this chapter, if we think about a continuum of counselor "air-time," with silence at one end, summarizing would fall at the other end. A summary is similar in nature to a paraphrase, except that paraphrases are typically a sentence or two whereas a summary more closely resembles a paragraph.

A summary in a counseling session is very similar to a summary in a written document. It serves to distill extensive client content down to about a paragraph's worth of focused information, and it may conclude with whatever conclusions have been reached as an outcome of those main points.

Following an example of a counselor appropriately implementing a summary, we will talk about the ways and times that a summary can be helpful. Because a summary ties together themes over a longer expanse of a conversation, it is necessary in this example to give a more elaborate dialogue sequence. Here is a continuation of the dialogue example from the 8-year-old boy, Alex, used above.

CLIENT: Today in class Mitchell kept kicking my chair even though I told him at the beginning of the day that I didn't want him bugging me anymore. I figured since I told him at morning line up that he'd cut it out, but he just kept right on doing it all day and I messed up my spelling test because of it.

COUNSELOR: You told Mitchell in the morning not to kick your chair, but he went ahead and did it anyway. And you messed up a spelling test because of it.

CLIENT: Yes! And that's not fair. That kid has been a pain in my backside since kindergarten. And none of the teachers do a thing about it. He just bugs and bugs and bugs and I can't stand it! I wish he'd just go to another school.

COUNSELOR: I can see you have reached the end of your rope; your fists are clenched and you have a big scowl on your face.

CLIENT: Oh yeah! And I want to just beat him up. I could do it, too, you know! I have my purple belt in Tae Kwon Do and I could put a hurt on him big time. But if I do that the teacher will say, "Oh, poor little Mitchell," and I'll be the one to get in trouble just like every other time. I can't stand it!

COUNSELOR: You are seriously thinking about going after Mitchell and hurting him, but you know that you'd just end up in bigger trouble.

CLIENT: Yep. And I'll be grounded for the D I got on the spelling test. I just don't get it. I studied and studied at home and when I practiced those words I got them all right.

COUNSELOR: Okay, Alex, let me just review what we've been talking about here. You've mentioned several things you're upset about. Mitchell has been a pest to you for a very long time. The latest thing is he kicked your chair and made it hard for you to do well on the spelling test. On top of that, Mitchell seems to be the one that the teacher is worried about, and you think that even if you did beat him up, which you would like to, Mitchell would come out of it okay and you'd be in big trouble. Then you also mentioned that your grades don't really show the amount of work you put into studying for the spelling test. Is that a decent sum up of what you've told me this morning?

First, let's talk about the elements of the summary. Like the paraphrase, while the client's words are not repeated verbatim, there is definitely a similar tone. The essential content of the client's words are reflected in the summary. The counselor is making no attempt to ask questions, interpret Mitchell's behavior, or suggest a solution. Those are microskills that we will look at later, but a summary is merely intended to be a reflection of the client's material.

How does one know when to use a summary as opposed to a paraphrase? There are a number of different circumstances in a counseling interaction that would indicate a summary might be in order. Those circumstances include:

1. After a client has enumerated a number of concerns or possible topics
2. Beginning a session with a recap of what was discussed in a prior session
3. At the conclusion of a session as a means of reiterating what was discussed

Enumerating Possible Topics

In the case of the example above with Alex, he was expressing not only anger, but also a desire to pick a fight with another student. From a counseling process point of view, that means that the client has some emotional energy for looking at solutions to the problem. Clearly, assaulting the other student is not a good choice, yet an effective counselor will refrain from simply saying, "Oh, Alex, you can't do that!" and instead will guide the client toward considering multiple alternative solutions, of which assaulting Mitchell is one. Obviously it isn't the best one, but it *is* one of the choices. So, at the point that the client is expressing ideation about taking a particular action, the focus of the session is going to move from telling the story to what's going to be done about it now. This represents a focus shift, and it can be helpful in managing the counseling process to punctuate the focus shift with a summary. This ensures that the message and content *you* perceive as central is consistent with what the *client* considers to be the central theme.

Another indicator that the time is right for a paraphrase, in the dialogue example above, is the topic shift that occurred. The client moved from his frustration about Mitchell to his frustration about his spelling grade not reflecting the amount of studying he did. A client will often identify multiple issues or concerns without necessarily differentiating, in his or her own mind, the complete list of issues. A summary can let you help the client see these issues as possibly being separate concerns, with separate solutions.

Beginning and Ending Sessions with Summaries

When you have a specific agenda or set of issues on which you are working with a client, summarizing the previous session can be an effective way of setting the stage for the current session. Note that you can use the summary as a counselor-generated or client-generated contribution to the conversation. Following is an example of how a summary might be used to open a subsequent counseling session with the youngster, Alex, above:

COUNSELOR: Alex, I'm so glad you came to see me today. Last time we talked, we spent a lot of time talking about what a hard time you've had with Mitchell and also with your studying. I think that at the end of last session you had decided you would ask Alicia, the peer conflict helper for your room, and your teacher, Mrs. Clark, for a meeting with all of you and Mitchell. I want to hear about the studying issue too, but I'd like to start with the peer conflict issue first. Let's start there—tell me what has happened since I last saw you.

This type of summary sets the stage for the current session and also creates a sense of continuity from one meeting to the next. Another way a counselor summary can be used is as a covert indication to the client that it is time to begin winding down the session and discussing any kind of action plan that will occur between that meeting and the next one.

You also have the option of soliciting a summary from the client. A disadvantage of having your client summarize is that when you turn over the responsibility for that task, the client may not be as succinct or focused in his or her summary.

There are several advantages, however, of requesting the client to summarize. For one thing, it can be enlightening to you as the counselor to ask the client to summarize the highlights of the session. You might find that what the client perceived or took from the session is quite different from what you thought he or she perceived.

AUTHOR'S REFLECTION

In a final termination session with a young man, I asked, "As you look back over our process of working together, how would you best summarize what we worked on?" That question focuses the client toward a response that is a summary. After a moment of silence in which he reflected on our work together, he replied, "Well, doc, what did it was the day I came in here and you told me to $#@* or get off the pot. That really made me get my act together!" I was quite surprised to hear this, especially because (1) I don't use profanity in counseling sessions, and (2) I was unaware of being as directive as the client obviously perceived me to be.

What you think are the main points or the most impactful aspects of a session might not match what your client thinks. Summaries are one means of comparing your perceptions with your client's to examine where, if any, differences lie.

Cultural Considerations in Summarizing

The axes of cultural templates bear a similar relationship to summarizing as they do to paraphrasing. Because a summary is a more extensive version of a paraphrase, the same considerations come into play.

Summarizing in the Context of Three Theoretical Approaches

Summaries definitely play a role in the three theory realms. As in other cases, while a summary might look similar regardless of the theory base, each theory indicates the use of summarizing with a unique intention. A summary could be used by a counselor employing any one of the three theoretical stances discussed in this textbook. Let's take a moment to consider the intended counseling goals from the three approaches and see how effective summarizing would facilitate attainment of the goals.

HUMANISTIC   Because the person-centered humanistic approach is highly reflective, with emphasis on client content and client emotional processing, summarizing will play a central role in a counseling interaction. Indeed, along with paraphrasing and other reflective statements (reflection of feeling and reflection of meaning), this is the essence of person-centered intervention.

DEVELOPMENTAL   A counselor working from a developmental stance will be summarizing with an emphasis on those aspects of the client's concerns that represent stages or phases of development. For example, the adult client whose mother requires nursing care is experiencing a developmental crisis that is a relatively common concern for middle-aged adults in U.S. culture. A summary from a developmental counselor might focus on the transition involved in dealing with an aging parent.

Other developmentalists might be interested in exploring the history of the relationship between the client and his mother, and might offer a summary that more heavily emphasized the aspects of the client having responsibility for mother's care. There might also be dynamics around the past relationship between the client and his mother, and the extent to which he felt that his mother took care of him when he was the dependent individual in the dyad.

COGNITIVE-BEHAVIORAL   A cognitive-behavioral counselor would use summaries as a means of making the cycle of reinforcement clear to the client. This would be a summary of the essence of the cognitive-behavioral counseling session. It might consist of summarizing the cycle of antecedent, behavior, and consequences, and the cycle of antecedent, erroneous thought process, maladaptive behavior, and resultant outcome in the client's life that the client and counselor have jointly analyzed.

Chapter Summary

This chapter has covered the range of possible counselor interventions that begin with no response, that is, silence, and end with extensive counselor talk in the form of summarizing relevant aspects of the counseling interaction.

Permitting silence to transpire during counseling has distinct benefits, but it needs to be under the proper circumstances if it is to be effective. When it is the counselor's turn to talk, it is acceptable to permit some amount of silence to elapse, either to see what the client does with the silence, or to give yourself an opportunity to gather your thoughts and decide where to go next. However, note that in some combinations of cultural differences, silence may create tension or discomfort rather than being helpful.

Minimal encouragers are a way of saying "I'm listening" without interrupting the client's flow of conversation. They are best used when the client is in the middle of a story and pauses briefly to take a breath. Key word repetition and restatement are excellent ways of sharpening focus on a particular topic while using minimal "air time," but they must be used parsimoniously to retain their effectiveness.

Paraphrases focus on distilling the essential elements of the client's content and reflecting it back to him or her. A paraphrase is a more involved, invested form of communicating to your client, "I'm listening." A good paraphrase uses some of the counselor's words and some of the client's key words, acknowledges that it is the counselor's perception of what the client said, and allows room for the client to correct the counselor if the counselor's perception is not consistent with the client's intended message.

Summarizing goes beyond communicating that you are listening and is a way of either sharpening the focus on a particular topic or transitioning into or out of a counseling session or onto a completely different topic. Summarizing can be especially helpful in generating a sense of continuity from one counseling session to the next.

Questions for Class Discussion

1. What are your reactions to the chapter material about silence and its role in a counseling session? Discuss with your classmates.
2. Practice paraphrasing in a small group.
3. Share with your classmates some experiences you have had with someone using minimal encouragers excessively with you. How did you discern whether the person was really listening?
4. Practice summarizing in a small group.

Case Studies for Discussion

In Chapter 4, you were introduced to two clients, Carole and Derek. This is the first chapter that lends itself to a meaningful presentation of how the microskill is used in the context of a client/counselor dialogue. I will reiterate the background information on each of them to refresh your memory.

ADULT

Carole is a 37-year-old biracial woman of Caucasian and African American descent. She has been married for 8 years and has two children, ages 7 and 5. Her husband is a 43-year-old Caucasian man who is employed at a local automobile factory. Carole graduated from high school and has been employed periodically in unskilled labor jobs, but never for more than about a year at a time. She stopped working when she got married; her husband made it clear that her job was to tend to the house and have children. She is a homemaker and, while she loves her children dearly, she finds herself feeling very sad and lonely when the children are in school and her husband is at work. Her 7-year-old is in second grade while the 5-year-old attends an all-day kindergarten. Carole has been referred to counseling by her family physician due to her tearfulness, insomnia, and significant weight gain for which the doctor can find no physical cause.

COUNSELOR:	Why don't we start, Carole, with you describing for me what's been going on recently that you ended up coming here to see me today?
CAROLE:	Well, I haven't been able to sleep for a long time. I wake up in the middle of the night and just lie there worrying. I stopped drinking coffee several months ago because I read where caffeine was bad for your sleeping.
COUNSELOR:	Your insomnia isn't new; sounds like you were concerned enough about it several months ago to quit caffeine.
CAROLE:	The worst time for me is at about 3:00 in the morning. I wake up feeling so upset and lonely even though my husband is right there. I just don't know what to do.
COUNSELOR:	It sounds like the early morning awakening is especially distressing and leaving you wondering how to handle this problem.
CAROLE:	The other thing is, by the time the kids and John get up in the morning I feel all squirrely, like I didn't sleep at all. Then I'm trying to make their breakfasts and get their lunches packed and it all seems overwhelming. I stand there in the kitchen looking around and can't get myself organized to get their things ready.
COUNSELOR:	You are so fatigued and upset you can't think straight, especially in the mornings.
CAROLE:	After I get the kids to school and John leaves for work, I come home and sit. There's all this work piled up around me. Laundry, dishes, yard work, and I don't want to do any of it. I'm tired of being the pack mule and the workhorse in the house. I love them, but I'm just so darned tired. And there's no help for me, I just have to do it. John comes home exhausted and expects a square meal on the table in a clean house. That's not really too much to expect considering how hard he works all day.
COUNSELOR:	You can understand what he expects and it doesn't seem unreasonable, yet you also feel like you're carrying a heavy load.

Questions for Discussion about Carole's Case Study

1. What is your initial reaction to Carole's dilemma?
2. To what extent do you believe Carole's depression is the result of her environment?
3. What additional information about her would you like to obtain and why?

CHILD

Derek is a 9-year-old boy of Latino descent who has been exhibiting significant behavior problems in school and has been referred to you, the school counselor, for help. Since the beginning of the school year, he has been aggressive in the lunchroom, taking other students' food, and has been suspended for fighting on the playground. His grades are C's, D's, and F's, and he frequently does not turn in or complete his homework.

Regarding his home life, Derek is being raised by his maternal grandmother; Derek's biological mother lives directly across the street from them. His mother has retained custody of Derek's four younger siblings. His father is in prison in Puerto Rico. Derek's mother sent him to live with his grandmother because his behavior was so disruptive in the household that his mother felt she could not control him. Derek's disruptive behavior at home was primarily characterized by disobeying rules, staying out on the street at night past his curfew, hanging around the neighborhood with older boys who often are in legal trouble, and yelling when he doesn't get what he wants.

COUNSELOR:	Derek, I was hoping we could use this first time together to get to know each other a little bit. Tell me about what kinds of things you like to do for fun.
DEREK:	I like Yu Gi Oh. I'm the best kid in my class when I duel. No one can beat me. And . . . let's see . . . I do real good on my skateboard. I can slide, grind down rails, jump curbs. I'm out there on my skateboard every day.
COUNSELOR:	Skateboarding is a real skill you've developed.
DEREK:	We watch lots of movies too. I just watched this one movie we got from the library, *Komodo*, about these huge Komodo dragons that attacked all the people on this island and the people got dragged all over the place and these dragons were unbeatable. It was so cool!
COUNSELOR:	You like Komodo dragons, sounds like.
DEREK:	Oh yeah. They rock. Grandma came home and saw that movie and it was *so funny!* She was so scared! She said if one of those Komodos came into her house she'd take a frying pan to its head.
COUNSELOR:	Your grandma sure isn't going to wait around for the animal catcher!
DEREK:	I could do that too, but if that were me I'd just run away. I'm a really fast runner; no way that old Komodo could catch me!
COUNSELOR:	Sounds like you've given this some thought.
DEREK:	It could happen. . . . I have a few friends that come over but mostly I just hook up with my homies out on the street. There's always kids around so I just go out the front door with my board and there are lots of guys to hang with.
COUNSELOR:	So let's see; you like skateboarding, watching movies, Komodo dragons, and spending time with your friends.

Questions for Discussion about Derek's Case Study

1. What aspects of Derek's verbalization do you think the counselor inappropriately neglected?

2. In what direction would you have steered the discussion?

3. How engageable does Derek seem? What behaviors does he exhibit that are the basis for your answer?

CHAPTER 7

Questioning

After studying this chapter, you should have a clear understanding of the following:

- The difference in outcome between open and closed questions
- The occasions in a session when questioning is appropriate
- The advantages and disadvantages of asking questions

In Chapter 6 you learned about silence, paraphrasing, and summarizing, with the recognition that paraphrasing and summarizing represent higher levels of counselor directiveness than the earlier microskills. The present chapter on questioning takes us further into the realm of counselor directiveness; the questions you ask, if you ask any, will most definitely steer the focus of your interaction with your client in a particular direction.

One recurrent theme throughout this text is that your theoretical orientation influences not only your conceptualization of what is causing a person's disturbance, but also your belief about the path most likely to lead the person to growth and/or reduction of discomfort. Thus, as we now move into questioning, the role of theory becomes even more pertinent than it has been in the previous microskills.

APPROPRIATE USE OF QUESTIONS

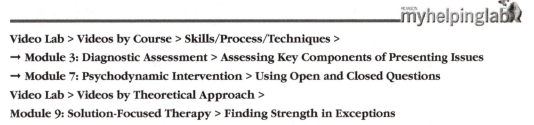

Video Lab > Videos by Course > Skills/Process/Techniques >
→ Module 3: Diagnostic Assessment > Assessing Key Components of Presenting Issues
→ Module 7: Psychodynamic Intervention > Using Open and Closed Questions
Video Lab > Videos by Theoretical Approach >
Module 9: Solution-Focused Therapy > Finding Strength in Exceptions

Questions must be used with mindfulness, for a number of reasons. It is quite important that when you use questioning in a counseling session, you do so with a clear and specific intent, rather than relying on questions as an easy way to keep your client talking. Keeping your client talking for the sake of filling silence is not the best use of your time together, and in fact can be detrimental.

Thus, of all the microskills, in questioning it is perhaps the most important that you have a clear idea of your purpose in mind before you actually use the skill; you need to be cognizant of your intention *before* you ask a question. Skilled counselors use questions to serve a variety of purposes. Some of those purposes include:

1. Conducting an intake or assessment
2. Beginning a counseling session
3. Clarifying a client's statement
4. Determining the accuracy of your perception or getting more information to enhance your understanding
5. Sharpening the counseling focus in a particular way (e.g., on content or on affect)

Our first step will be to look at the specific mechanics of asking a question. The subsequent discussion is organized around each of the listed purposes. Each discussion section will provide dialogue examples of how that purpose is accomplished. Before turning to the cross-cultural and cross-theoretical interactions with questions, a few general considerations need to be explored.

Open and Closed Questions

One of the common ways that questions are categorized is *open* versus *closed*. An open question is one that will likely result in a person answering with a lengthy response. The answer to an open question is usually not one that can be given in a single word. In contrast, closed questions seek a specific response, often one that can be offered in a single word or two. Novice counselors may erroneously assume that in a counseling session, open questions are always better than closed questions. This is not necessarily true; in some circumstances closed questions are preferable. An example would be when a counselor needs to solicit a particular bit of information from the client.

Open questions begin with the following words:

How

What

When

Where

Who

Why

Closed questions begin with words such as:

Is

Are

Do

Did

Could

Would

Have

Generally speaking, open questions will result in the client continuing to talk and giving you more material, some of which may be pertinent to the counseling focus, and some of which may not. Among the open-ended question stems, "what" questions are likely to result in a person giving facts and details, whereas "how" questions are more likely to yield process or sequence information (Ivey & Ivey, 2007). For example, "What happened?" will be answered with a factual recounting of an incident; "What was the movie about?" will result in a summary of the movie plot. In contrast, "How did that situation come about?" or "How was the movie?" will be answered with responses that are more process oriented, that is, describing how the situation unfolded and what the feelings and internal experiences were.

Mechanical Aspects of Questioning

Regardless of whether a counselor's questions are open or closed, asking questions is directive, because the client's response will take the focus of discussion in a particular direction. One basic choice you will make as you ask questions will be whether you wish to place the focus on the *content* of the client's story, or on the client's subjective experience about the story, which is a *process*-oriented direction.

PERSONAL REFLECTION _____

In conversation with others, what is your general style of asking questions? How did that style develop? Where does it come from? Some students want every detail in order to maximally understand the speaker's situation, while others ask questions about particular solutions that seem appropriate for the circumstance. Do you fit one or both of those categories?

The actual wording of your question is your overt message to the client. Also present and affecting the interaction will be the covert message of the question; the covert message is communicated in part by the paraverbals and in part by the focus of the question. As you have noticed, the paraverbal aspect of the interaction between you and your client has been a recurrent topic of discussion. That emphasis on paraverbals continues in this present discussion of how to ask effective questions. Your voice tone and the mechanics with which you speak will make all the difference between a respectful, thoughtful, thought-provoking inquiry and an interrogation.

PERSONAL REFLECTION _____

Have you ever had a person ask you two or more questions in the same breath? Take a moment to recall that experience and your subsequent reaction. How did those multiple questions affect your interaction with that individual?

Avoiding an ambiance of interrogation can be accomplished if you do two things. First, ask *only one question* at a time. One common error is that in our eagerness to help, we ask more than one question at a time. Keep in mind that if a client feels interrogated there will be less likelihood of a shared process of exploration and change, which is the whole purpose of your work with your client. One good question is far better than three mediocre questions asked in rapid succession. Here is an example of an ineffective series:

KAITLYN: I'm so glad to be back here to see you. My visit with my sister was okay, I guess, but it's a relief to be back home and coming for counseling.

COUNSELOR: So the trip wasn't good? What was the problem? You seem upset. Did she say something that upset you?

This counselor response could leave the client feeling bewildered or overwhelmed by which question to answer first, even though it seems pretty clear that the counselor is asking these questions out of genuine concern for Kaitlyn. Take a moment to think about what you want to ask, and then word your question *briefly* in a way the client will be able to answer you. After you've asked the question, stop talking, sit back, and wait. If your question is one that provokes introspection, your client may not be able to immediately produce a response. This is where your comfort with silence will come into play. Here is an example of a better question in response to the client's statement:

KAITLYN: I'm so glad to be back here to see you. My visit with my sister was okay, I guess, but it's a relief to be back home and coming for counseling.

COUNSELOR: I get the sense your visit wasn't perfect. In what way were you not pleased with it?

The second thing you can do to minimize an "inquisition" is to take time to respond to the client's response to a question before asking another one. After using your attending skills to attune yourself to the answer to your inquiry, take the time to either paraphrase or otherwise acknowledge the answer, before asking another question. This will slow down the process and minimize a pattern of rapid-fire questions. Asking just one question and then responding to the client's response with a paraphrase, before asking another question, will enhance your client's sense that you are truly listening to what he or she is telling you. I'll continue the dialogue example with Kaitlyn from right above.

KAITLYN: She was busy with friends the whole time. I don't think we went out for lunch or dinner even once all weekend without a whole bunch of her friends coming along, and they drank the entire time and got really loud. She never asked me anything about my life or my new job or anything!

COUNSELOR: It sounds like she was too busy with friends to focus on you even though you haven't had any chance yet to tell her about all the changes happening in your life. Did I hear you correctly?

THE FISHING ANALOGY   One of the ways I conceptualize the questioning process is like fishing. You can either cast a net or drop a line; a dropped line may or may not result in catching a single fish, whereas a widely cast net will catch a variety of fish as well as other creatures.

Sometimes when novice counselors begin working with clients, they are so conscientious and concerned about being helpful that their counseling sessions consist mainly of directly focused questions that get one discrete piece of information. Then, as the question and answer conversational pattern becomes established, it becomes unclear what direction or focus would be best for the client, and the client becomes accustomed to the counselor setting the agenda and direction.

In some cases, the circumstances of the client's referral for counseling might be such that it is appropriate for the counselor to be structuring the interaction. For example, if a client has been referred to a mental health clinic for an anger management counseling program, the counselor may need to ask a specific set of questions. On the other hand, especially in work with children who are expecting the adult to be "in charge," the child will just wait for the counselor to determine the direction of the conversation.

Ineffective Use of Direct Questions (Fishing)   Here is a dialogue example of a string of inappropriate direct questions:

COUNSELOR:	Lisa, I'm so glad you came to see me today. So how are things going in your classroom?
LISA:	Pretty good, I guess.
COUNSELOR:	That's great! What were your grades on your last report card?
LISA:	I had an A in math, a B in language arts, a B in social studies, and C's in art and gym.
COUNSELOR:	Well done! And how about your behavior grades?
LISA:	I had S's for satisfactory on everything.
COUNSELOR:	Excellent! Are things going pretty well with your friends?
LISA:	Some of them.
COUNSELOR:	Are you still going to the movies and doing the MySpace thing a lot?
LISA:	I guess.

So far, the counselor has been the individual directing the focus, and although her questions have been answered, she still has no information as to why Lisa has asked to see her.

Particularly if a client has had no prior experience with counseling, he or she may feel comfortable deferring to the authority of the counselor. Some people may have expectations that counseling will be like going to any other doctor. In Western medicine, when we go to a physician, we expect the physician to ask questions we will answer before the doctor then gives us a diagnosis and recommendation for how to treat our problem. In those interactions, the doctor is the person responsible for doing the asking, thinking, diagnosing, and treating.

It is possible, if you are working with someone who has never before been a client, that he or she will hold similar expectations about the counseling process. So, if you lapse into a pattern of interaction like the one above, you become the one doing the work, meaning that you are thinking, reasoning, processing, and the client's role will only be to receive your mental efforts. Ideally, the client should be making at least the same degree of mental and emotional effort in the interaction as you are. I refer to this as the client "working," and a general guideline is that you as the counselor should strive never to work harder than your client. In the dialogue example above, the counselor is definitely working harder than the client.

Here is another dialogue example using the same client, but with the counselor placing the onus of work responsibility on the client:

COUNSELOR:	I'm so glad to see you today, Lisa! What's been going on that you asked to see me?
LISA:	I'm really upset about Mary's birthday party. All the other girls are invited except me and they're being mean to me, too.
COUNSELOR:	I want to hear more about this birthday party invitation thing. What happened?
LISA:	Well, . . .

By asking these two open-ended, yet focused questions, the counselor got right to the heart of Lisa's concerns and reason for requesting counseling. This gave Lisa the opportunity to establish some control over the interaction, and also saved considerable effort on the counselor's part.

Something else important to recognize is that the metamessage in these focused, open-ended questions is that this is the client's work to do, not the counselor's. If the counselor had been asking a whole string of closed questions, and then at the end said, "You know, this is your counseling session and you'll be the one working toward the solution," the spoken message would not match the counselor's behavior. This would constitute a mismatch between the counselor's words and actions, which would create dissonance for the client. The client could become distrustful of the counselor because of the misalignment between the counselor's words and behaviors.

THE PROBLEM WITH "WHY?"   "Why" questions are particularly tempting for those of us who are psychologically minded and want to understand a person's underlying motives. However, when we ask a why question, it puts the other person in the position of needing to provide a reason. What we're essentially doing is requiring a justification. "Why are you angry at your husband?" is asking a woman the reason for her anger. Asking why is a question that is likely to be useful for the counselor but will have limited, if any, benefit for the client.

Asking why subtly carries a covert implication that we as counselors are in a position to judge whether the woman is entitled to her anger. This implication is clearer with another example of a commonly asked question: "Why did you do that?"

Asking a child why may result in a literal, concrete response. I was once working with a boy who had run away from the treatment center where I worked. When the police picked him up, he gave them his correct name but his incorrect birth date. After he returned to the treatment center, I asked him why he had given his wrong birth date, and he replied, "That's my alias!" While this was true, that in his mind the incorrect birth date was his disguise, it didn't help me understand his motivation for lying. It would have been more effective for me to comment on his behavior by saying, "I saw in the police report that you gave them a wrong date of birth. What was going on for you that you decided to do that?"

If you ask an adult why he or she did something or feels a certain way, the most likely outcome is either some type of justification or a defensive reply of "I don't know." This might be the truth, too—perhaps the person really *doesn't* know why he or she did something or has a particular feeling. Asking why in the manner described can be detrimental to your efforts to establish and maintain a therapeutic alliance. For that reason, I often encourage novice counselors to studiously avoid using "why" when they use questions.

Dialogue Examples of How to Achieve Specific Purposes

At the beginning of the chapter I listed numerous purposes that can be served by the judicious use of questions. Now we will return to that list and I will give you some dialogue examples of how questions could be used to accomplish each purpose.

    1. *Conducting an intake or assessment*—When a client is seen for a first session, it is necessary for the counselor to gather information. Depending on the setting (school, agency, clinic), the degree of comprehensiveness of background information will vary. Note that Chapter 13 of this text is devoted almost entirely to doing intakes, so we won't go into great detail here about the breadth of information that might be gathered in a first session.

What *is* relevant to discuss here is that even in a first session, when you don't know a person very well, a couple of well-phrased questions interspersed with other microskills will be more conducive to relationship development than a lengthy series of questions. Here is an example of a good opening that uses one well-phrased question.

COUNSELOR: Let's start by talking about what's been going on with you that led you to schedule this appointment with me today.

CLIENT: Well, I just found out my wife is going to move out of the house and she is filing for divorce.

COUNSELOR: You just got this information about your wife leaving you. Tell me about what parts of this I can help you with.

Here is another example of a gentle, open-ended question that helpers often use to begin a counseling session.

COUNSELOR: It's very nice to meet you, Mrs. Smith. How can I help you?

2. *Beginning a counseling session*—A common way that novice interns begin a counseling session with a client they've been seeing is to ask, "What's been going on lately?" Here's an example of how an interaction might transpire when you initiate a counseling session this way:

COUNSELOR: Hi, Roberto, what's been going on?

ROBERTO: Well, let's see. The motor on my car has been making a funny noise, so I took it to my brother-in-law who has a garage over on the west side. Turns out it's something with the timing chain and the air intake valve, and I'm going over there this weekend so we can work on it.

This type of opening question is fine if you wish to hear the client recount what has happened in his or her life in the recent past. Sometimes that is what you are hoping for, but the disadvantage is that it may takes the focus of discussion in a direction that doesn't really pertain to the client's main issue.

Alternatively, you can begin the session with a question that immediately focuses the client's attention in a relevant direction. Consider the following example:

COUNSELOR: Roberto, the last time we met, we were focusing on some things you could try doing to help you parent your daughter and not give in to her when she argues with you. Were you able to try any of them?

ROBERTO: Yes.

COUNSELOR: Tell me about that.

ROBERTO: Okay. You know how you said I could try giving her to the count of 3 to follow my direction? Well . . .

3. *Clarifying a client's statement*—Sometimes a client will say something that is confusing to you, or that will seem to have ambiguous meaning. Where a paraphrase could be helpful, sometimes it just is easier and makes more sense to ask a question that clarifies what the client is trying to communicate.

CLIENT: So there we were walking around at the mall, and all of a sudden Karen turned to me and said, "Cut it out right now or I'll just leave you here and drive home by myself!" and then she walked away. I ended up taking the bus home.

COUNSELOR: Do you mean she really *did* just leave you at the mall?

CLIENT: No, she didn't leave. But I got tired of her nastiness so *I* left.

4. *Determining the accuracy of your perception or getting more information to enhance your understanding*—This is essentially the same thing we talked about in the previous chapter in which you paraphrase and then do a checkout to verify that you correctly understand what the client is communicating. A question can be used the same way. Let's take the same dialogue example right above and add a question that could help you understand better.

CLIENT: So there we were walking around at the mall, and all of a sudden Karen turned to me and said, "Cut it out right now or I'll just leave you here and drive home by myself!" and then she walked away. I ended up taking the bus home.

COUNSELOR: Do you mean she really *did* just leave you at the mall?

CLIENT: No, she didn't leave. But I got tired of her nastiness so *I* left.

COUNSELOR: So basically, she got mad at you, but you were already mad at her, and so you just took matters into your own hands and left and rode the bus home? Am I getting it?

5. *Sharpening the counseling focus in a particular way (e.g., on content or on process)*—In the dialogue example above, the clarifying questions up to this point have focused on the *content* of the client's concerns: the details of the story. The questions sharpened the focus on the sequence of events. That same discussion about the client's concerns would go in a completely different direction if the counselor chose to ask questions that emphasized the process rather than the content. Here is an example of how that might unfold:

CLIENT: So there we were walking around at the mall, and all of a sudden Karen turned to me and said, "Cut it out right now or I'll just leave you here and drive home by myself!" and then she walked away. I ended up taking the bus home.

COUNSELOR: How did that feel when Karen said that to you?

CLIENT: Oh, who cares? What kind of a friend is she anyway if she'd just leave me like that?

COUNSELOR: It sounds to me like you're asking yourself whether you really have a friendship with someone who would threaten to strand you at the mall. I can understand that. Let's talk about how you think a "good friendship" might look different from this one. Could that be helpful?

Table 7.1 provides a more detailed example of a sequence of questions, some of which are key word repetitions. Table 7.1 also includes an explanation of the counselor's thought process as he or she decides how to direct the questions.

TABLE 7.1   Dialogue Example of a Sequence of Questioning

Holly is a Caucasian married woman of 39 who is seeking counseling for depression. The following sequence is taken from her third meeting with her counselor.

	Verbalization	Type of Question	Counselor's Thought Process
Counselor	Holly, in our last session we were discussing your overall stress level and the relationship between your stress and your feelings of depression. **What thoughts have you had about that since then?**	**Open-ended question**	The last session seemed unfocused and I need to work a bit harder to get down to the bottom line about what's going on for her.
Client	I've had a lot of thoughts. I guess it's time for me to be completely honest about everything. So you're sure everything I say here you will keep completely secret, right?		
Counselor	As long as you don't disclose that you intend to hurt yourself or someone else.		
Client	Oh no, no, nothing like that. But it is really private and the only person who knows everything is my best friend. Okay, here it goes. I've been seeing another man for quite a while now. . . .		
Counselor	First, let me say that I can appreciate how hard it was for you to take the risk to share that information with me. I'd like to hear as much as you're willing to tell, about this relationship. **What part is the most important to you that I hear and understand?**	**Open-ended question**	What is her motivation to engage in that behavior?
Client	I told you before about Bill's [her husband] drinking. I just can't stand it and I can't stand him. If it wasn't for my son I'd be so far gone out of there. But how can I leave them? We're still paying off the medical bills for the fertility specialist. We worked so hard to have this baby and I thought that once we were a family that Bill would change. But I've finally accepted how wrong I was. Jeremy is so kind and loving and I can't believe I have to go through the rest of my life without him.		
Counselor	Sounds like the prospect of living without Jeremy leaves you feeling hopeless and depressed. . . .	Feeling reflection	I need more information in order to help her process feelings and to work on elucidating our counseling goals.
	I'd like to know more about the details of your relationship with Jeremy. **When did you meet?**	**Closed-ended question**	*(continued)*

TABLE 7.1   Dialogue Example of a Sequence of Questioning (*Continued*)

	Verbalization	Type of Question	Counselor's Thought Process
Client	We work together. I've known him for 12 years. It started when I was having such a hard time with the fertility drugs, and Jeremy and I would eat lunch together every day. He was so caring and concerned about me—way more than Bill has ever been—and one thing led to another.		
Counselor	**How long ago was that?**	**Closed-ended question**	I wonder if this a long-standing relationship or a brief fling?
Client	It's been about 6 years now.		
Counselor	**Does Jeremy share your views and feelings about the hopelessness of the situation with this relationship?**	**Closed-ended question**	I want to establish a context for understanding the status of her extramarital relationship
Client	Oh, not at all. He wants to marry me and he's been patient so far, but he really thinks I should leave Bill so that Jeremy and I can live our lives together. But Jeremy doesn't have children and he doesn't understand how hard it is.		This gives me much more information about the nature of the conflict; this conflict stems primarily from her ambivalence about where her responsibility lies. I need to find out more about the nature of her ambivalent feelings.

These dialogue examples make clear the difference between effective and ineffective questioning technique, and also the ways that questions can be used appropriately. A couple of other general considerations pertaining to questioning bear mention before we move on to look at cross-cultural and cross-theoretical applications of questioning. Those considerations are client resistance, implied solutions, and imbalance of power.

Client Resistance

Sometimes people are reluctant to share information. Asking questions can exacerbate the difficulty.

AUTHOR'S REFLECTION

I worked with an adolescent girl who was rebellious and angry with her parents, although she had a decent relationship with me. She came to a session one day having had a nasty fight with her mother. I suspected that my teenage client's version of the story had omitted some details about things the girl had said and done that contributed to the fight. In that situation, after she had gone through her story, I first responded to her feelings of frustration and resentment toward her mother. Then I paused, and in a soft, slow voice said, "Okay, Tiana, what parts of the story are you *not* telling me?" At that point she burst into tears and went into much greater detail about some things she had done and said.

Use of the phrase, "What are you not telling me?" gives a person implicit permission to admit to the information that he or she is reluctant to share. The client may say, "Nothing, I've said it all," and if that happens the person is either telling the truth or establishing a boundary that you need to honor. In other words, if your client denies any omitted material, accept the denial and move on.

Implied Problem Solution

One other thing about which you need to be very careful is to refrain from asking questions implying that some problem-solving strategy should have been used. For example, during class in student role plays, a pretend client might say something like, "I've been really upset about the way my mother-in-law is interfering with my decisions about how to discipline my children." A novice counselor often replies by asking, "Have you talked to her about it?" This question implies that she *should* have spoken to the mother-in-law. While talking to the mother-in-law is one option for how to cope with the problem, there are a number of other solutions, and some clients may be more comfortable with less direct problem solutions than to talk to the offending individual. Additionally, the client's cultural template might be such that a direct communication about the problem is not acceptable behavior. Rather than asking about a specific problem-solving strategy, you're better off asking, "What have you tried to do about this?"

Imbalance of Power

The counseling relationship inherently has an imbalance of power between the client and counselor. By virtue of being the one sought out for professional services, the counselor is the holder of the power. There is potential for abuse of that power in any number of ways, and counselors must be aware of this potential in order to avoid causing damage to the client. When someone asks a question, there is the expectation of a response, which automatically puts the question asker in a position of having some control over the respondent. The respondent can refuse to answer, which reestablishes him or her as having the control. Therefore you must be cautious not to inadvertently misuse your power. Also, some populations of people have historically been disempowered (for example, women, gays and lesbians, and people in other minority groups). It is especially important for you to be mindful not to wield a disproportionate amount of the power in your interaction with your clients (Poorman, 2003).

Cultural Considerations in Questioning

POWER DISTANCE   This is the axis that deals with the extent to which members of a culture accept and expect that there will be a power differential between those in authority and subordinates. With regard to questioning, this axis is likely to be manifested in a couple of ways. One is that, for clients who come from cultures that have a high degree of power distance, there will be a greater likelihood of them seeing you as expert and expecting a diagnosis and prescription (i.e., recommendation about what to do to get better). Conversely, if a client comes from a culture that has a low degree of power distance, he or she may be more inclined to ask you questions too, or possibly to be more comfortable taking on a role as the creator of his or her counseling process.

GENDER ROLES   Recall that this axis is concerned with two things: the way a culture distributes roles and jobs across both genders, and also the extent to which there is fluidity of values and behaviors in general across both genders. In other words, a culture with low masculinity would be accepting and supportive of androgynous values and nonverbal behaviors. In a culture with high masculinity, the gender roles are extremely clear with regard to who does which tasks, as well as which expressed emotions and behaviors are acceptable from each gender. Clients from cultures with high masculinity may have some discomfort with female therapists in general, especially when the therapist is in a position of power as occurs in questioning.

AFFILIATION   This is the axis defined by the extent to which a person's culture regards allegiance to the collective as an important aspect of a person's behavior. High affiliation societies expect that an individual's actions be considered in a group context, as opposed to an individual context.

Once you become aware of the extent to which a person's affiliative status is individualistic or collectivistic, you will be in a better position to ask your questions in a manner that will support exploration of the issue from that group context. For example, if a client said, "Next year I have to decide whether I want to major in biology or chemistry," the counselor's question for a person who is highly individualistic might be something like, "What do you see as the advantages and disadvantages of that choice?" For a person who is highly collectivistic, on the other hand, the question might be, "What are your family's views on this choice?"

UNCERTAINTY AVOIDANCE   This axis has to do with a person's preference for structure and, to some extent, seems related to autonomy. People in cultures with low uncertainty avoidance are comfortable with ambiguity and unstructured situations. People from cultures with high uncertainty avoidance live in societies where there are very clear, explicit rules about "right" and "wrong" and rigid guidelines about acceptable behavior.

It is not clear that this variable would directly influence or affect the types of questions or how the questions might be asked.

Questioning in the Context of Three Theoretical Stances

Table 7.2 gives dialogue examples that illustrate differences in questions across theories. The initial client statement is the same in all three columns, and then as the theory differentiations become apparent in the counselor's questions, the client dialogue diverges too.

The following sections give a more detailed explanation of the intentions that would be typical of a therapist with this orientation.

HUMANISTIC   The majority of the humanistic theories see the client as the expert on him or herself. Thus, therapists who are primarily humanistically oriented are disinclined to use questioning with any frequency. When questioning is used, the emphasis is likely to be most heavily focused on process and feelings, as opposed to details or content. A humanistic counselor would help a client articulate for her or himself what his or her questions are.

DEVELOPMENTAL   For some therapists who are developmentally oriented, questions could play a larger role in the counseling process than they do for a humanistic therapist. Especially if the counselor is seeking to increase a client's awareness of the developmental tasks associated with a presenting problem, the questioning process is one that could be used in moderation.

TABLE 7.2 Comparison of Questions and Possible Client Responses from Different Theoretical Approaches

	Humanistic	Developmental	Cognitive-Behavioral
	Emphasis on process and feelings	Increasing awareness of developmental tasks he or she is facing	Specific material and information to identify a focus for treatment
Kaitlyn	I'm so glad to be back here to see you. My visit with my sister was okay, I guess, but it's a relief to be back home and coming for counseling.	I'm so glad to be back here to see you. My visit with my sister was okay, I guess, but it's a relief to be back home and coming for counseling.	I'm so glad to be back here to see you. My visit with my sister was okay, I guess, but it's a relief to be back home and coming for counseling.
Counselor	A relief? Tell me more.	I get the sense it really wasn't okay. Can you tell me about it?	In what way is it a relief?
Kaitlyn	Well, it was so hard. There were all her other friends around the whole time. Marcy and I didn't have any time alone together, and on top of that she didn't ask even once about how my new job was going.	Well, it was so hard. There were all her other friends around the whole time. Marcy and I didn't have any time alone together, and on top of that she didn't ask even once about how my new job was going.	Well, it was so hard. There were all her other friends around the whole time. Marcy and I didn't have any time alone together, and on top of that she didn't ask even once about how my new job was going.
Counselor	As I listen to you talk I get a sense the whole week was both rushed and crowded. Is that how it felt?	You really miss her, don't you?	I'm especially interested in your depression and what you did to manage that while you were on your trip. Did you keep track of your depression intensity over those three days?
Kaitlyn	Yes. Like there wasn't room in her life for me.	Yes! And even though I was there this weekend it didn't help. I'm so homesick since our Mom died and Marcy acted like she doesn't miss me at all!	I didn't actually write it down, but I can tell you exactly. I was not depressed the day I arrived and each day got worse and worse.
Counselor	Displaced?	Sounds like Marcy is sort of your emotional anchor as far as your family of origin. Is that your experience?	Okay, tell me about what was happening that made it progressively worse as the visit went on.

COGNITIVE-BEHAVIORAL In this theoretical orientation the process of questioning is most likely to occur. The reason is that in the cognitive-behavioral approach, the counseling process is considerably more directive than it is in either of the other two theory groups. A cognitive-behavioral counselor is looking for specific material and information from the client in order to design and implement a counseling intervention that is consistent with cognitive-behavioral theory.

Chapter Summary

In this chapter we looked at multiple purposes that can be served by asking questions. At the same time, however, we emphasized that significant damage to the counseling relationship can be done if the questions are not worded and delivered properly. Additionally, there is an inherent power imbalance in a counseling relationship, and misuse of questioning can contribute to an exacerbation of that imbalance.

There was discussion about the difference between open and closed questions. Each type of question carries a high likelihood of receiving a particular kind of response; open questions tend to elicit expanded verbalizations, whereas closed questions can be answered in a word or two.

We further identified several specific strategies that will minimize the potential damage caused by excessive or inappropriate questioning. Those strategies include being aware of your paraverbals and asking your questions in a soft, slow manner; asking only one question at a time and then paraphrasing or reflecting the client's response before asking another; avoiding asking "why?" questions.

Questions for Class Discussion

1. How did the material in this chapter fit with what you've previously thought about questioning in counseling?
2. What do you see as the main disadvantages of keeping questions to a minimum?
3. To what extent do you associate asking clients questions with being in an "expert" role? How does this relate to your self-expectation about your responsibility and role as a professional counselor?

Case Studies for Discussion

ADULT

Carole is a 37-year-old biracial woman of Caucasian and African American descent. She has been married for 8 years and has two children, ages 7 and 5. Her husband is a 43-year-old Caucasian man who is employed at a local automobile factory. Carole graduated from high school and has been employed periodically in unskilled labor jobs, but never for more than about a year at a time. She stopped working when she got married; her husband made it clear that her job was to tend to the house and have children. She is a homemaker and, while she loves her children dearly, she finds herself feeling very sad and lonely when the children are in school and her husband is at work. Her 7-year-old is in second grade while the 5-year-old attends an all-day kindergarten. Carole has been referred to counseling by her family physician due to her tearfulness, insomnia, and significant weight gain for which the doctor can find no physical cause.

> COUNSELOR: Carole, the last time you were here, we talked a lot about your background and the symptoms that have been bothering you the most. I think we left off with you saying that you'd like some time to ponder what you wanted to work on in counseling. How about if we start there?

CAROLE: I think I've been walking around the house feeling sorry for myself because everyone has a life except me. They all leave every day to go do their things and the only thing I can do is clean up and do laundry. I need to find something to do with myself.

COUNSELOR: You've come to the conclusion that you're having a hard time because everyone else has things to do during the day while you're left at home doing housework. You'd like to figure out something to do that would bring you some satisfaction.

CAROLE: Yes, that's it.

COUNSELOR: That certainly sounds like a reasonable goal. What kind of a thing do you think would help?

CAROLE: Well, I don't know exactly. I think I might like to try to find a job, but then I think about how hard it will be to get a work schedule I can do with picking up the children from school, taking them to dance and soccer practice, and all the errands. Then I get sad again because it just seems like I'm not going to be able to get a job out of the house until after the kids finish school and leave home.

COUNSELOR: So, let me get this straight. It sounds like after you think about getting a job, you then go on to think about all the reasons getting a job wouldn't work, and you talk yourself out of it before even applying, and then you are sad and discouraged.

CAROLE: On top of that, my husband tells me I have no business looking outside the house for a job. He is more than capable of supporting our family and for me to get a job is a disgrace to him as a provider. In fact, he forbade me from getting work outside our house.

COUNSELOR: He has instructed you to stop looking and feels that it would reflect badly on him as a husband and father for you to have a job.

CAROLE: You got it. So I'm completely stuck. To be honest, the main thing I thought this week is that there is no point in counseling. Nothing can be done. But you seemed like a nice person so I figured I'd come back one more time to explain why counseling won't help me.

COUNSELOR: From where you sit, you can't imagine a solution to your dilemma, that you seem to be completely stuck.

Silence

CAROLE: So there's nothing for us to do here, right?

COUNSELOR: I can see why it would look that way to you. Of course it's completely your decision about whether to come for counseling. The other thing I want to say, though, is that even when a situation cannot be changed, people sometimes find it helpful just to be able to talk about it with someone who is not involved. Some of my clients have said they felt better by having the chance to get their feelings out, and this is a safe place to do that. It's also possible that we could find some solutions that you don't see right now. Since you're already here for your appointment, I suggest we spend some more time now exploring your feelings of sadness and stuckness, and then at the end of the session you can decide whether you'd like to reschedule, or just be finished with counseling and not return. Does that sound okay?

Questions for Discussion about Carole's Case Study

1. Would you have asked more questions of Carole than the counselor did in this example? If so, what other questions would you have asked?
2. Of the three theoretical approaches, which do you believe lends the most utility to understanding Carole's concerns, and why?
3. What is your sense of where Carole's values could best be described with regard to individualism and uncertainty avoidance?

CHILD

Derek is a 9-year-old boy of Latino descent who has been exhibiting significant behavior problems in school and has been referred to you, the school counselor, for help. Since the beginning of the school year, he has been aggressive in the lunchroom, taking other students' food, and has been suspended for fighting on the playground. His grades are C's, D's, and F's, and he frequently does not turn in or complete his homework.

Regarding his home life, Derek is being raised by his maternal grandmother; Derek's biological mother lives directly across the street. His mother has retained custody of Derek's four younger siblings. His father is in prison in Puerto Rico. Derek's mother sent him to live with his grandmother because his behavior was so disruptive in the household that his mother felt she could not control him. Derek's disruptive behavior at home was primarily characterized by disobeying rules, staying out on the street at night past his curfew, hanging around the neighborhood with older boys who often are in legal trouble, and yelling when he doesn't get what he wants.

COUNSELOR:	Derek, it's nice to see you today. Last time you were here we talked about what kinds of things you like to do and I enjoyed getting to know you. Today I was hoping we might start by talking about your understanding of why Grandma and your teacher thought it was a good idea for you and me to talk.
Silence	
COUNSELOR:	What questions do you have for me?
DEREK:	None. I thought you just wanted to talk to me that one time so I don't know why I got called down here again. Am I in trouble?
COUNSELOR:	Well, sometimes when kids come here, no one has explained too much about why they are coming, and it seems to me like understanding is a good place to start. I also hoped we might continue to get to know each other a little bit more. Do you like to play Uno?
DEREK:	I guess.
COUNSELOR:	It just so happens I have an Uno deck in this drawer. Let's play. (Counselor shuffles cards and the game starts.)

The rest of this dialogue occurs *during* the Uno game.

COUNSELOR: Wow, you're pretty good at this. Who do you usually play Uno with?

DEREK: Sometimes we play at school when there is inside recess.

COUNSELOR: Tell me some more about school. What goes on at recess?

DEREK: My recess is in Block B, which is from 12:15 to 12:40. We go outside if it isn't raining. I can go the whole way across the ladder on the new jungle gym with my hands. I'm working on doing pull-ups.

COUNSELOR: Sounds like you are focusing on being in good shape. Pull-ups are really hard; you have to have a lot of muscle strength in your arms. How's that going for you?

DEREK: I can pull myself up to about my nose.

COUNSELOR: That's way better than I can do! Keep working at it and I'll bet you'll be getting the whole way up pretty soon. Describe for me a typical school day for you.

DEREK: Okay. I get there and we line up and go into the classroom. We have math first, then language arts. Then we go to lunch, then recess. After recess I have gym class or art or music, and at the end of the day we do science.

COUNSELOR: Which of those is your favorite?

DEREK: I don't like any of it except recess and gym.

COUNSELOR: School isn't enjoyable for you.

DEREK: The teachers yell at us all day. I hate sitting there. It's boring. I can't wait till I'm old enough to drop out.

COUNSELOR: That's really a drag having to go and sit all day when you don't find anything interesting.

DEREK: Yeah.

Silence

COUNSELOR: Well, how about some of the things that you *do* like to do outside of school? Tell me about some of them.

Questions for Discussion about Derek's Case Study

1. What aspects of each of the three theoretical approaches seem most relevant to Derek's issues?

2. As you review the various questioning techniques and client responses from Table 7.2, which resonate most strongly with you?

3. Are there specific areas where you would hone in with additional questions? Why?

4. Discuss the cultural value aspects of Derek's extended family system and how they are influencing his life situation and current emotional experiencing.

CHAPTER 8

Feeling Reflection

After studying this chapter, you should have a clear understanding of the following:

- The components of an effective feeling reflection
- The purpose of reflecting feelings
- The ability to identify when a feeling reflection would be an effective response

A feeling reflection is a counselor statement that extracts and mirrors the emotional elements of the client's communication. Feeling reflection is one of the microskills that most clearly differentiates counseling from other types of conversation or interactions between people.

In this chapter, several related terms will be used that we first need to clarify; that is, the difference among *feeling, emotion,* and *affect.* This is a somewhat challenging proposition, and there are many ways various authors have defined these constructs. In general, when a counselor or mental health professional refers to a client's *affect,* he or she is talking about the client's *displayed emotion;* the observation of feeling in another person (such as the client). On the other hand, *emotions* and *feelings* refer to one's *internal, subjective experience* of emotional arousal, including the physiological experience, the physical, and the nonphysical aspects of having a particular emotion.

PERSONAL REFLECTION

What are some of the ways you would describe feeling "sad"? Try to identify at least two descriptors that reflect your physical experience of sadness, your mental experience of sadness, and your emotional experience of sadness. Now try to do the same for "relaxed" or "joy."

Ivey and Ivey (2007) noted that typical social conversations tend to ignore feelings or affective content unless the speaker's affect is strikingly overt. An example of overt affect would be a person discussing with another person how angry he or she was about an incident, in which the disclosure focused specifically on the anger. In general, avoidance of disclosure about feelings in a social interaction is one of our cultural norms.

Even though we don't talk about them very much, however, our emotional experiences are a hugely significant aspect of being alive. Our emotions are one of the ways that we are internally aware of existing as human beings. What's more, our feelings are often the force that prompts us to make changes in our thoughts and behaviors. A number of authors of counseling skills texts (e.g., Cavanaugh, 1982; Ivey & Ivey, 2007; Poorman, 2003; Seligman, 2004; Young, 2005) have noted that feelings are catalysts for growth. Countless others who have preceded them, including some of the most well-known figures in the field of psychology, such as Freud and Rogers, have postulated similarly that emotional processing is a central component of growth and development.

It follows, then, that when we suppress or repress our experience of emotions, growth does *not* occur, and in some cases, problems will emerge as a result of our internalized affect. For example, some people use a strategy of truncating, or cutting off, awareness of painful feelings when the emotional pain becomes too intense. However, while truncating does eliminate some discomfort for a while, it prevents the pain from serving the function of motivating the person to make necessary changes. Physical pain sometimes serves a similar purpose. That is, pain can be a signal from our bodies to do something different, such as shifting our sitting position when there is reduced circulation to the feet, or removing a hand from a hot stove burner. Similarly, if we don't have emotional pain, we don't have feedback that we need to do something different, for example, ending an unhealthy relationship.

Another cost when we truncate our feelings in order to restrict the range of intensity as a strategy for coping with emotional uncomfortableness, is that the restriction will also influence our ability to experience intensity of positive or pleasant feelings as well. In other words, if we intentionally cope with intense emotional pain by restricting our range of feeling, we also restrict our ability to feel intense emotional pleasure such as joy.

Recently, Western medicine has recognized that our emotions play a significant role in our physical well-being. Emotions constitute a psychosomatic component to many physical symptoms and problems including migraine headaches, high blood pressure, ulcers, and other gastrointestinal disorders. Although these physical conditions are often caused by many factors that are not related to anything psychological, stress or other emotional difficulties can definitely contribute to intensification or exacerbation of symptoms.

Many of the clients who come to see you may be trying to cope with feelings that are causing them discomfort. The discomfort might be because the feelings themselves are painful, or it may be that the feelings are causing secondary symptoms. For example, a parent whose last adult child just moved away might come in talking about loss and sadness. Or that parent might complain of insomnia and irritability, and problems getting along with her husband. Even when a client is struggling with what appears to be a straightforward cognitive decision, such as which college to attend, emotions will be involved in the decision process that are contributing to the struggle. One of your main tasks as a counselor will be to help your clients identify and fully acknowledge their feelings. In the college decision example above, feeling identification would be one aspect of the decision-making process.

AUTHOR'S REFLECTION

My graduate training was heavily cognitive-behavioral. That model was a good fit for me, being a pragmatic and no-nonsense, get-down-to-business type of person at that time. As a novice therapist, I attempted to deemphasize the client's experience of feelings, choosing instead to focus on the individual's self-talk and behaviors that seemed to be creating and perpetuating the uncomfortable feelings. Through my own personal work as a client, though, I discovered that my tendency to avoid focusing on feelings with clients paralleled my tendency to avoid uncomfortable feelings in my own life. As I became more comfortable with experiencing and processing suppressed emotions, I became better able to sit still with people in pain, and to work more patiently with clients on experiencing their emotions.

PERSONAL REFLECTION

How comfortable are you when you are interacting with another person who is clearly exhibiting one of the following emotions: happiness, surprise, anger, fear, disgust, contempt, or sadness? What is the connection for you between observing those feelings in another person and your ability to express those same feelings yourself?

This chapter will give you the basic format and mechanics for doing a feeling reflection. Following, there will be a general discussion about emotional theory and emotional functioning in people, and a call for you to explore and consider your own emotional functioning. In order to develop the skill to process feelings with clients, the helper must be comfortable with his or her own emotional functioning.

MECHANICAL ASPECTS OF FEELING REFLECTION

myhelpinglab

Video Lab > By Course > Skills/Process/Techniques > Establishing a Therapeutic Relationship > Challenging Clients to Think About Feelings

The sequence of links above will enable you to view a counselor helping a client to access and explore feelings. It may be helpful to take a moment to watch it prior to reading further about feeling reflection. When a person is speaking about almost anything, several levels of communication are co-occurring. One level is the content, which is the overt message. The content is typically communicated through the choice of words. In the chapter on paraphrasing, you learned how to respond to the content of another person's message in a manner that is active yet unobtrusive.

Yet another level of communication is implied and covert. This more subtle communication occurs through other means such as shifts in paraverbals and shifts in other nonverbal behaviors. In Chapter 5 we covered client observation and talked about the importance of being carefully attuned to many pieces of data, distinct from the spoken words, embedded in the individual's communication. One of the reasons it is so important to attentively observe is that observation gives you a clue about the person's emotional experiencing in that moment. Sometimes a person will be fully aware of his or her feelings in the moment, while other times the awareness will only be partial, or it may be completely absent. There are a number of possible reasons that we are sometimes underaware of our emotions, which will be discussed later in the chapter.

What does a feeling reflection sound like when you use one in conversation? Feeling reflection statements are similar to paraphrases, except that whereas a paraphrase rewords the content, a feeling reflection identifies the affect being communicated in a client's message. As you have read in every other skill chapter, your paraverbals while reflecting feelings are of paramount importance! The tone of your voice, rate of your speech, and volume of your speech should match the client's feelings you are attempting to reflect.

Feeling Reflection Mechanics

The steps of a feeling reflection are as follows:

1. Entry qualifier

Looks like you're feeling . . .

I hear you expressing . . .

If I were in that situation, I might feel . . .

It feels to me as though you are experiencing . . .

2. Feeling identification

Properly identifying a person's feelings requires a good feeling word vocabulary. There are two aspects of emotions, both of which are important to accuracy of identification. One is the general category of the feeling itself, and the other is to choose a word that correctly corresponds with the intensity level. The point of getting the intensity level right is that even when you are in the right general feeling category, if the word you choose is mismatched in intensity, the client will experience it as inaccuracy in your empathy. This will require that you develop an extensive feeling vocabulary and get comfortable using a range of feeling words that cover different intensity levels.

You can get excellent lists of feeling words from a number of sources, such as Young (2005) or Poorman (2003). Table 8.1 provides a list of feelings that are experienced when a person's needs are satisfied, and Table 8.2 is a list of feelings we may have when our needs are not satisfied. These lists are presented with permission from the Nonviolent Communication website at http://www.cnvc.org/feelings.htm.

3. Accuracy check

Am I hearing you?

Did I get that?

Does that fit for you?

If you have been working with a client for several sessions, you may have sufficient rapport that you can just try waiting silently after you've made the feeling identification, rather than doing an overt accuracy check. Using silence in this manner could be particularly effective if the client is somewhat unaware of the feeling.

The purpose of this step is to provide the individual the opportunity to consider whether your feeling word choice is an accurate depiction of her or his internal experience. By allowing the client room to correct any misperceptions you have, you give the person an occasion to put the internal emotional experience into words. Note also that for some individuals, there may be a lapse of silence as he or she moves attention inward to consider the fit between the feelings you've observed and the internal experience, or as he or she permits the feeling to bubble up into full awareness. In the event that the person *does* correct or refine the feeling word you used, there still can be benefit; the process of verbalizing one's emotional experience to another person, in and of itself, can be therapeutic for many people.

Here are two examples of appropriate feeling reflections:

Example 1

CLIENT: I made dinner reservations for me and Bob to go out on our anniversary. Then he called and said he had to stay late at the office to work

TABLE 8.1   Feelings That Are Experienced When One's Needs Are Satisfied

Affectionate	Confident	Engaged	Excited	Exhilarated	Joyful
Compassionate	Empowered	Absorbed	Amazed	Blissful	Amused
Friendly	Open	Alert	Animated	Ecstatic	Delighted
Loving	Proud	Curious	Ardent	Elated	Glad
Open hearted	Safe	Engrossed	Aroused	Enthralled	Happy
Sympathetic	Secure	Enchanted	Astonished	Exuberant	Jubilant
Tender		Entranced	Dazzled	Radiant	Pleased
Warm		Fascinated	Eager		Tickled
		Interested	Energetic		
		Intrigued	Enthusiastic		
		Involved	Giddy		
		Spellbound	Invigorated		
		Stimulated	Lively		
			Passionate		
			Surprised		
			Vibrant		

Peaceful	Inspired	Grateful	Hopeful	Refreshed
Calm	Amazed	Appreciative	Expectant	Enlivened
Clear headed	Awed	Moved	Encouraged	Rejuvenated
Comfortable	Wonder	Thankful	Optimistic	Renewed
Centered		Touched		Rested
Content				Restored
Equanimity				Revived
Fulfilled				
Mellow				
Quiet				
Relaxed				
Relieved				
Satisfied				
Serene				
Still				
Tranquil				
Trusting				

on his presentation for tomorrow and that we'd have to reschedule dinner! I couldn't believe work was that much more important to him than spending time with me on our anniversary. (Gazing down, clasping hands) So instead I made myself a peanut butter and jelly sandwich and watched reruns on TV.

COUNSELOR: It sounds as though his phone call and postponement left you feeling hurt and very alone. Am I hearing you?

TABLE 8.2   Feelings When Needs Are Not Satisfied

Afraid	Annoyed	Angry	Aversion	Confused
Apprehensive	Aggravated	Enraged	Animosity	Ambivalent
Dread	Dismayed	Furious	Appalled	Baffled
Foreboding	Disgruntled	Incensed	Contempt	Bewildered
Frightened	Displeased	Indignant	Disgusted	Dazed
Mistrustful	Exasperated	Irate	Dislike	Hesitant
Panicked	Frustrated	Livid	Hate	Lost
Petrified	Impatient	Outraged	Horrified	Mystified
Scared	Irritated	Resentful	Hostile	Perplexed
Suspicious	Irked		Repulsed	Puzzled
Terrified				Torn
Wary				
Worried				

Disconnected	Disquiet	Embarrassed	Fatigue	Pain
Alienated	Agitated	Ashamed	Beat	Agony
Aloof	Alarmed	Chagrined	Burned out	Anguished
Apathetic	Discombobulated	Flustered	Depleted	Bereaved
Bored	Disconcerted	Guilty	Exhausted	Devastated
Cold	Disturbed	Mortified	Lethargic	Grief
Detached	Perturbed	Self-conscious	Listless	Heartbroken
Distant	Rattled		Sleepy	Hurt
Distracted	Restless		Tired	Lonely
Indifferent	Shocked		Weary	Miserable
Numb	Startled		Worn out	Regretful
Removed	Surprised			Remorseful
Uninterested	Troubled			
Withdrawn	Turbulent			
	Turmoil			
	Uncomfortable			
	Uneasy			
	Unnerved			
	Unsettled			
	Upset			

Sad	Tense	Vulnerable	Yearning
Depressed	Anxious	Fragile	Envious
Dejected	Cranky	Guarded	Jealous
Despairing	Distressed	Helpless	Longing
Despondent	Distraught	Insecure	Nostalgic
Disappointed	Edgy	Leery	Pining
Discouraged	Fidgety	Reserved	Wistful
Disheartened	Frazzled	Sensitive	
Forlorn	Irritable	Shaky	
Gloomy	Jittery		
Heavy hearted	Nervous		
Hopeless	Overwhelmed		
Melancholy	Restless		
Unhappy	Stressed out		
Wretched			

Reprinted with permission. © 2005 by Center for Nonviolent Communication. Website: www.cnvc.org, email: cnvc@cnvc.org

Example 2

CLIENT: Two days ago I got my test scores in the mail and guess what? They were high enough for me to be in the Advanced Placement track! Now I get to take algebra and biology a year ahead of some of the other kids.

COUNSELOR: I can hear that you are pretty excited about taking some new subjects, and proud, too, that you did so well on the test! Did I get that right?

Accurate Feeling Identification

One of the reasons feeling identification can be a challenging skill to master is that we seldom experience one pure, basic emotion. The process of understanding complex combinations of feelings is similar in some ways to observing and understanding primary colors, secondary colors, and tertiary colors. When you look around at your immediate environment right now you can probably pick out some objects that are purely one of the three primary colors of red, blue, or yellow. However, there are many more objects in your environment that are comprised of combinations of primary colors; these are secondary colors including green, purple, and orange, as well as tertiary colors that are actually a blend of all three primary colors in varying amounts. Emotions are similar; people often experience more than one feeling at a time, perhaps with more frequency than they have just one pure emotion for any significant length of time.

PERSONAL REFLECTION _____

Think about a time in your life when a major change was occurring; maybe taking your first class in graduate school, or possibly a relocation. Did you have more than one feeling about that change? Did those feelings seem to be contrary to one another? Were you able to fully acknowledge *all* of them?

Adding to the complexity of emotional functioning is the fact that in the course of a day, multiple situations occur, about which we may have a range of feelings. For many people the process of daily living brings a constant ebb and flow of feelings. There is individual variability in how often and how intensely we react to situations in our day-to-day lives. Some of it depends on individual temperament and how reactive we are in general, and some of it depends on the style of our internal dialogue.

The ability to skillfully reflect a client's feelings depends on more than the technical, verbal mechanics. It also requires a counselor's skill in accurately assessing, through careful client observation, multiple aspects of feelings. One or more of these aspects may need to be a focus for exploration. Seligman (2001, p. 203) offered a helpful set of dimensions on which a client's emotions can be understood by the counselor, experienced by the client, and discussed in session:

- Emotional, physical, or a combination
- Overt, covert, or a combination
- Positive, negative, or neutral
- In or out of awareness
- Of varying levels of intensity
- Appropriate or inappropriate to context and stimulus
- Congruent or incongruent
- Helpful or harmful

When a therapist uses the term *processing feelings*, he or she is likely referencing focusing with a client on feelings with an emphasis on at least one of the above dimensions. We will take a moment to explore in more detail the types of information and client experience you might work on in each of the eight bulleted areas.

EMOTIONAL, PHYSICAL, OR A COMBINATION   There are questions in this regard that you may ask yourself and also ask the client. In what way is the client experiencing the emotion? Is he or she aware of the feeling itself? If not, is he or she aware of particular physical sensations associated with the circumstance or topic? You might be able to use a behavioral observation of a client's nonverbal behavior to help him or her access awareness of how the emotion is manifesting physically.

OVERT, COVERT, OR A COMBINATION   To what extent is the client openly expressing the feeling(s)? Does he or she have a need to keep the feelings suppressed or hidden from awareness or the awareness of others? How does the overt or covert nature of the feelings affect the client?

POSITIVE, NEGATIVE, OR NEUTRAL   Does the client perceive the feelings as positive, negative, or with no valence either way? To what extent does the positivity or negativity of the experience affect the client?

IN OR OUT OF AWARENESS   To what extent is the client aware of his or her feelings? If you observe nonverbal or paraverbal behavior that is inconsistent with the verbal content and suggests particular feelings, you may want to gently identify the feelings you believe you are observing. However, as will be discussed in Chapter 10, "Confrontation," if the client denies experiencing what you have reflected, it is not necessarily a good idea to pursue that avenue of discussion. Other variables need to be assessed to decide whether to proceed with trying to bring the feelings into the client's awareness.

VARYING LEVELS OF INTENSITY   How intensely is the client experiencing the feelings? One way to fully explore this is to use a scaling question, in which you identify two anchors of a scale and have the client assign a number rating to his or her level of the feeling. A scaling question would be phrased as follows: "If we were to give your anger (or whatever the emotion is) a number on a scale of 1 to 10, with 1 being a tiny amount of it and 10 being such an intense amount that you are consumed with it, what number would you give it right now?"

APPROPRIATE OR INAPPROPRIATE TO CONTEXT AND STIMULUS   Given what you know about the client's cultural background, are the emotions contextually appropriate?

CONGRUENT OR INCONGRUENT   Are the felt emotions and corresponding physical sensations consistent with one another?

HELPFUL OR HARMFUL   Considering the impact that the feelings are having upon the client, does there seem to be any benefit, or harm, that is occurring because of the feeling? For example, is the client experiencing guilt that is having a secondary, negative impact on other aspects of his or her life?

The preceding information about aspects of emotional functioning can serve as a segue. We now shall transition away from the mechanics of feeling reflections to look in more detail at emotion theory. Exploring emotion theory will provide you with a broadened conceptual frame with which you can understand and facilitate your client's growth.

EMOTION THEORY

There is a massive body of research and theoretical literature in psychology, cultural anthropology, and communication about emotion. We couldn't possibly cover in this text all the theories and research pertaining to emotion and affect. Before moving into this section it is necessary to offer the following caveat.

Please be aware that this presentation of emotion theory is not intended to represent all the different theory and research streams in this topic area. The theory line that will be presented was chosen based upon general recognition of construct validity in the professional literature. This model of emotional theory also offers easy applicability and accessibility of integration with the microskills model and Hofstede's cultural axes model.

Across some of the emotion research is frequent reference to landmark research conducted by Ekman, who is considered to be one of the most prominent contributors to the body of knowledge about emotions and emotional expression (Matsumoto, 2004). Seven basic emotions have been found to occur in all humans. It was Ekman's early research efforts that created the foundation for this finding. Those seven universal emotions are happiness, surprise, fear, anger, disgust, contempt, and sadness (Keltner, Ekman, Gonzaga, & Beer, 2001).

Historically there have been several competing theories about emotional functioning and expression. Burgoon, Buller, and Woodall (1996) provided a concise overview of three schools of thought about emotions. In all three lines of theory, data have been generated that support the tenets of the theory. The categories of emotion theory are universalist, relativist, and neurocultural.

Universalist Model of Emotion

Some emotion theorists, such as Darwin, Allport, Tomkins, and Izard, have taken a *universalist* position, meaning that they saw experience and expression of emotions as being consistent across cultures, as well as across generations and even across species (Keltner et al., 2001). The cross-cultural studies conducted by numerous researchers have yielded results suggesting that there is some universality of emotions and facial expression of emotions.

Equally relevant have been studies that compared people's *interpretation* of facial expression when the observers are from different cultures. Much of the cross-cultural facial recognition of emotion research has been criticized for a variety of reasons related to methodology. Nevertheless, there seems to be a substantial body of evidence that there is cross-cultural similarity in both facial expression of feelings and observers' interpretation of those facial expressions.

Relativistic Model of Emotion

In contrast to the universalist model, other theorists, such as Mead, Birdwhistell, and Gordon, have taken a *relativist* stance, positing that emotional expression is culture-specific. According to this view, people learn which emotions go with each expression in the same way they learn language (which is clearly culture-specific). These theorists view culture as the prime determinant of how our emotions are experienced and communicated to others. Some studies have found significant cultural differences in how emotions are expressed.

One of the biggest differences that has been observed across people of different cultures has been the *meaning* people ascribe to facial expressions. That is, while certain basic facial expressions are consistent cross-culturally, the reason or meaning that an observer might ascribe to another person's emotion and facial expression varies significantly across cultures (Keltner et al., 2001).

Ekman's Neurocultural Theory of Emotion

Another theory integrates the universalist and relativist views of emotional expression: Ekman's neurocultural theory of emotion. This theory fits closely with what I have observed in my own clinical work with clients. It is essentially a synthesis of the universalist and relativist positions; the crux of neurocultural emotion theory is that emotional expression is not purely universal or purely culturally defined, it is both. There is currently some very interesting research being conducted by Dr. Charles Raison at Emory University about the relationship among thoughts, behavior, and emotion. This relationship encompasses both positive emotion and its effect of bolstering our resistance to stress, as well as negative emotion and the relationship to physical pain. Interested readers can view Dr. Raison explaining his findings at the following web site: http://whsc.emory.edu/multimedia_mindmood.cfm.

Neurocultural theory holds that emotional expression is wired into the structure of our brains. However, our respective cultures prescribe specific rules for how expression of those emotions will manifest. In other words, all humans experience a range of those seven basic emotions, although each of us may experience a huge range of unique combinations. Whereas the fundamental emotional experience is the same across all people, the environmental events that precipitate certain emotions vary significantly across cultures. Also, the *meaning* we attach to particular feelings varies significantly across cultures.

When an individual experiences some type of emotional arousal, two events happen internally. In the presence of an emotional stimulus, the brain evaluates the significance of that stimulus and on the basis of that evaluation produces responses appropriate to the meaning of the stimulus (Ledoux, 1994). Ledoux differentiates between Type I and Type II responses. Type I responses are elicited and immediate; examples are freezing behavior and fearful facial expressions in the presence of impending danger. Type II responses are the more typical kinds of emotional processes you will observe and be working with among your clients; these are responses that are unique to individuals and involve judgments and predictions about the immediate situation and the applicability of past experiences to the situation (p. 271).

In other words, there is the affective reaction, the emotional reaction, and the meaning a person makes about the situation *and* about the feeling. In the next chapter, we will focus on reflection of meaning. As a brief aside, note that the cognitive component of the cognitive-behavioral model is basically a process of learning and understanding how one's cognitive appraisal affects one's experience of emotion.

Recent meta-analyses of emotion research have indicated that when an observer is attempting to accurately identify emotion expressed by another person, there is an "in-group advantage" (Elfenbein & Ambady, 2003). The in-group advantage means that people from the same culture are more accurate than people from another culture when observing and trying to correctly recognize emotions being expressed by another person. This seems obvious from a commonsense point of view; if we have been raised in a cultural environment closely similar to our clients', we will be more readily able to identify their emotions and empathize with their experiences. This does not mean that if a client is dissimilar you will be unable to accurately identify and reflect the expressed emotions; it just means that you will be at somewhat of a disadvantage in comparison to another counselor with a cultural template more similar to that of the client. Moreover, it means that you need to be cognizant of assuming you are accurately perceiving the client's expression.

Basically, when you are doing a good feeling reflection, it should help the individual to give voice to his or her emotional experience, and raise the person's self-awareness about what the emotional experience is. Ultimately, after we also learn about reflection of meaning, use of these reflections will help your clients put their feelings into a cognitive and/or situational context that enables them to make meaning of the emotional experience. It will also give them a sense of being kept company through that experience by another person who is concerned about them (you). This is the essence of empathy.

The Integration of Emotion Theory and Empathy

How does an understanding of emotion theory help you to develop your skills in feeling reflection and to be empathic? It can happen in two ways. For one thing, it will assist in your self-understanding of your own emotional experiences. Second, it will assist you in understanding your clients as they work with you through their own emotional experiencing during your counseling sessions. Elfenbein and Ambady (2003, p. 162) have observed that "people tend to interpret another person's behavior in terms of what they would have intended if they had used the same expression." By having the understanding afforded with these models of emotion, you will reduce the likelihood that, in your attempts to reflect feelings with your clients, you project your own cultural template onto them and possibly reduce your ability to accurately empathize. In order to empathize, we have to know our own emotional and cognitive perspective, while simultaneously perceiving what another person perceives (Poorman, 2003).

Certain types of settings in which you are providing counseling may result in your working almost exclusively with clients who are highly similar to yourself. It's more likely, though, that you will have a number of clients whose cultural templates are quite different from your own. Novice counselors, conscientious and concerned about doing the best work they can, often worry about not being able to "relate to" the stories clients share, which are the contexts from which the clients' feelings arise. Feelings and emotions, as they are expressed or implied, will always happen in the context of some story or narrative a client is sharing with you. Beginner counselors sometimes become immersed in questioning a client to obtain a multitude of details about the story, mistakenly thinking that by having more details they will be better able to understand the client's feelings.

The good news, however, is that an infinite variety of life circumstances and situations can occur for all of us. It would be virtually impossible to be knowledgeable about different types of problems and life situations that might occur in order to understand the associated feelings. It is a more efficient, realistic, and effective tactic to listen carefully as your client shares the story, simultaneously observing the nonverbal and paraverbal behaviors carefully, and then making the best educated guess you can about the feelings that are being expressed covertly.

Transcending the cultural templates we have been talking about in general, within any given culture there are individual differences in temperament and comfort level with emotional experiencing. Even if you are working with a client whose cultural background would be conducive to broad, open expressions of emotion, that particular individual may prefer less intensity of emotional experience or less intensity of emotional expression.

People's comfort level with emotional expression tends to be higher among others with whom they have intimate relationships; there is more of a tendency to suppress or modulate our expression of emotion among strangers or people who are only acquaintances. We all control our emotional reactions with a high degree of frequency (Averill, 1994); it is an essential component of maintaining social order (Levenson, 1994). As we become more comfortable with another person and trust deepens over time, it becomes easier to more honestly share our emotional experiences. To be transparent and let another person witness our emotional pain and emotional struggles is to permit ourselves to be vulnerable.

Opening oneself to vulnerability in a trusting way occurs in other species too. Any of you who have had experiences with dogs has probably had a dog roll on its back so you could rub his belly. This is a behavior that communicates trust; one swift blow from a predator or aggressor while the dog is on his back could be fatal. Sharing our feelings with another person carries, for some of us, a similar type of vulnerability. Someone who wanted to could easily hurt us emotionally by holding and misusing the information we have shared.

Thus, it is an honor when a person trusts us enough to safely disclose his or her innermost feelings, especially because some of those feelings may be a source of shame, embarrassment, or guilt, or might incur judgment by others. It means that we have been successful at communicating our unconditional positive regard and creating a safe space. It correspondingly places a responsibility on us to be able to respond to our clients' disclosures in a manner that accepts, without judging, what the person is sharing.

THE IMPORTANCE OF FEELINGS

We all have basic needs for emotional awareness and processing, as we established early in this chapter. Sometimes people come for counseling because there is such an overwhelming degree of an emotional experience that they are partially or completely immobilized by their feelings. At other times there is a notable lack of emotional expression about situations that for most people would elicit observable affect.

For example, this author once had a client who came for counseling because of problems he was having getting along with his boss at work. During that first session he mentioned that his father had died six months prior. As the man described his father's illness and painful, difficult death due to pancreatic cancer, his voice tone was monotone and there was absence of expression on his face. He stated in a flat, matter-of-fact voice, "Yes, it was a horrible experience and I feel so awful about the way Dad suffered." This is a life experience and spoken statement that would seem to lend themselves to emotional expression of grief and sadness. The lack of affect could be the result of one of several processes for this client.

At the beginning of this chapter we mentioned that there are a number of reasons that could account for a person being unaware or underaware of feelings. We turn now to consider some possible reasons a client may suppress emotions.

Fear of Loss of Control

Sometimes when our loss or grief is profound, the feelings may be so intense that we simply cannot cope and we emotionally shut down, similar to a surge protector that protects a computer from power surges. One of the initial reactions to trauma is shock, and another is denial. When the magnitude of our loss is too big to comprehend, we retreat from it out of fear that the loss will take over; that we will completely lose control of our lives, or of ourselves.

Other times, the fear of losing control has more to do with what will happen in our day-to-day lives if we honestly express our feelings. The cost of being honest with ourselves and with others about our true feelings can be high. For example, a person who is struggling with accepting his or her homosexuality may experience great fear (founded in reality, sometimes) about how other people will react to him or her as a person who is gay or lesbian. This particular fear has been so overwhelming for some people, especially teens and young adults, that they have chosen to take their own lives rather than face the judgment, disdain, and disappointment they anticipate receiving from others.

Yet another aspect of fear of losing control might be a more basic fear of expressing feelings in general. In the film *The Accidental Tourist*, an excellent depiction of emotional suppression in families, several adult siblings live together and clearly care deeply for one another, yet their ability to express their emotions is extremely limited. There is an associated fear of loss of control that is evident in the structured, organized way they live, as exemplified by a variety of idiosyncrasies such as alphabetizing the items in their pantry.

Difficulty Verbalizing Emotional Experiences

Some people are highly aware of the emotions they feel yet lack the verbal ability to express them. This could be the result of a limited feeling word vocabulary, or lack of learning how to express oneself in one's family of origin. A school counseling intern was counseling (on videotape) a 15-year-old boy who was quite withdrawn and looked very depressed. For session after session, the intern would ask excellent open-ended questions, offer feeling reflections, and yet the boy struggled unsuccessfully to put his feelings and experiencing into words. Finally, one day he said, "Mrs. Metcalf, I just can't explain to you what it feels like inside. Would it be okay if I played it for you on the piano?" The intern and the boy went to the school auditorium and she audiotaped him playing a rendition of Samuel Barber's *Adagio for Strings* that was so heartfelt every other intern listening to the tape was in tears themselves. It couldn't possibly have been any clearer; there was no question in any listener's mind or heart what this young man was feeling.

Complexity or Intensity of Ambivalent Feelings

As we discussed earlier, feelings are often combined and complicated. Sometimes a person's ambivalence is too uncomfortable or is not possible for the person to understand, and so he or she pushes it out of awareness.

Less commonly than the above dynamic, you may work with clients who have been neglected or abused physically, sexually, or emotionally. Physical and sexual abuse always carry a component of emotional abuse; emotional abuse is not necessarily physical or sexual but can result in significant disruption of development nonetheless.

When abuse or neglect occurs, the perpetrator is frequently a caretaker or person who has some position of authority, and the victim is often someone who is somehow dependent on the perpetrator. This creates a relational dynamic in which the victim experiences intense, extreme, ambivalent feelings. The ambivalence can result in disintegration of aspects of the self and can manifest as a splitting off that is dissociative. This dissociation serves an important emotional purpose for the individual in the abusive situation. However, even after the victim is no longer in contact with the perpetrator, the splitting and dissociation may continue.

COUNSELOR POWER AND RESPONSIBILITY

The above section covered a number of possible reasons for clients to be unaware under-aware of their own feelings. All of them are necessary for you to understand, because you will have clients who are exhibiting emotional suppression for these reasons. Their emotional suppression is serving, for each of them, an important purpose. Because you as the counselor are in a position of power in the therapeutic relationship, your clients will have varying degrees of willingness to meet your expectations. You must be careful not to try to strip them of their coping strategies of reducing emotional awareness before they have developed the tools and the strength to fully acknowledge and experience their feelings.

If you push too hard to get at emotional expression before the client is ready and able to engage in that process, he or she may try to comply with you but feel imposed upon, violated, or threatened. In fact, Poorman (2003) noted that insensitive or poorly timed feeling reflections might have the paradoxical effect of forcing the client to push feelings even further away from his or her awareness.

Clearly your good judgment and common sense will be required. If you make a feeling reflection about an emotion that seems fairly evident to you, but the client denies it, he or she may not be ready to acknowledge to him or herself that the feeling exists. Forcing the issue will only result in a heightened feeling of risk and threat for the client. If your client is emotionally fragile, and you insist on feeling focus before he or she is ready, you might actually do damage.

At this point, you might be wondering how in the world you will know when to push and when not to. The short answer is that if you do a feeling reflection of a feeling that seems obvious to you and the client denies that feeling, in your own mind note the discrepancy, but outwardly let it go. Continue the session while carefully observing and gathering more data, and try to get a sense of why the client is denying feelings you suspect are present for him or her.

WHAT NOT TO DO

Our discussion leads us now to some common errors that well-meaning beginners often make. These are some of the mistakes that can occur when a therapist means to be helpful but falls short; things you shouldn't do if you wish to make an effective feeling reflection.

Say, "You Shouldn't Feel That Way"

As you are listening to someone explain his or her feelings and the context in which those feelings have occurred, the emotions might seem to you like an inappropriate or incorrect interpretation of the context. Here is a dialogue example of a counselor invalidating a client's feelings:

CLIENT: One thing I need to tell you about is the problem I had with my neighbors over the weekend. They were grilling outside and they had some friends over who drove loud motorcycles. When I was in the yard working on my garden a couple of the guys started catcalling me and I felt so uncomfortable. I decided to just go hide in my house; I was afraid of what they might do to me and embarrassed that they would think I'm the kind of person that would want them to be whistling and yelling suggestive things at me.

COUNSELOR: You shouldn't be embarrassed. For one thing you were in your own yard minding your own business, and for another thing it's not *your* fault they whistled at you.

Even when the person's feelings seem irrational or don't make sense to you, refrain from saying, "Oh, don't feel that way." The fact is, the person *does* feel that way, and he or she is fully entitled to those feelings. Although the feelings may seem irrational or unfounded to you, and you believe it would be in the client's best interest *not* to have them, there are other ways to help process, integrate, or diminish the feelings. In addition, your client may already be telling himself he shouldn't feel a certain way, and your saying it too will be less than therapeutic. This statement actually discounts the validity of the client's emotional experience. Feelings just are, and they need to be given voice and acknowledgment.

Here is a more appropriate feeling reflection in response to the above client statement:

COUNSELOR: When the bikers started whistling and catcalling at you, you felt afraid and embarrassed, and you coped with it by returning to the safety of your house. Am I hearing you correctly?

From here, then, there are a couple of different directions you might choose to direct the focus.

Ask, "Do You Feel _____?"

Novice counselors are sometimes fearful of making a mistake when they help a client with feeling identification, and so rather than taking a chance on reflecting a feeling inaccurately, they ask a closed question about a particular emotion. Here is an example:

CLIENT: This morning I got on the school bus and everyone was staring at me. I walked back down the aisle and no one would let me sit with them, so I had to sit in the yucky last seat no one else wants, and there's a lot of gum all around there, and the window didn't open.

COUNSELOR: Did you feel mad?

In the preceding chapter about questioning, we talked about "fishing expeditions." This dialogue is an excellent example of a failed fishing expedition. The counselor asked a closed question, and on top of that the feeling reflection identified in the question was inaccurate. Here is a better feeling reflection in response to the client's statement:

COUNSELOR: Sounds like that was uncomfortable and lonely. It sounds also like you felt sort of unwanted. Is that it?

Ask, "What Did _____ Feel?"

Sometimes we get so caught up in the story that we want to know more about the other people and their behavior, and in that process we forget who our client is. Here is an example of how inappropriate focus of a feeling reflection might transpire in a counseling session:

CLIENT: I came home from work and the first thing Ken said to me was, "Where in the heck have you been? Dinner's been ready for the last half hour and now the chicken casserole is *completely ruined!*"

COUNSELOR: Hmm. Sounds like he was really mad.

CLIENT: Oh, yeah. Then he said, "Next time you can make dinner. Forget about me *ever* doing this for *you* again!"

COUNSELOR: Sounds like he was very frustrated with you. Had you been late like this before? Is that why he was so mad?

This is a line of feeling reflections and questions that have little to do with the client. Although it might be interesting conjecture for the counselor, these reflections and questions do not directly pertain to the client's counseling process; they are all focusing on Ken's process. It would be more beneficial to the client to understand her own emotional process and experience, and then to put it in the context of the interaction with her husband. Here is a sequence more appropriately client focused:

CLIENT: I came home from work and the first thing Ken said to me was, "Where in the heck have you been? Dinner's been ready for the last half hour and now the chicken casserole is *completely ruined*!"

COUNSELOR: I can see by your tears and hear in your voice that this was *very* painful for you when Ken said that.

CLIENT: Well, yes it was. I was late because I worked overtime to earn extra money for our vacation next month. He knew where I was. It's like it doesn't matter that I'm working so hard, it's just a big deal that I wasn't home when *he* thought I should be.

COUNSELOR: It's *so frustrating* when your efforts to make money aren't acknowledged by Ken. I hear resentment in your voice, too, maybe because to you Ken's reaction seemed selfish?

Repeatedly Ask, "How Did That Feel?"

Using this question is the open-question equivalent of "Did you feel ____?" It's okay to ask what something felt like occasionally if you really don't have a sense of the client's feelings. Sometimes, though, inexperienced counselors get into a rut. They ask this question continually, mistakenly thinking that prompting clients to verbalize for themselves what they are feeling is better than reflecting to the client what they perceive the client is feeling. Here's an example:

CLIENT: I took Fluffy to the vet last week and found out that she has a blood condition that can't be treated.

COUNSELOR: How did that feel?

CLIENT: Horrible! The vet said she is only going to live for another couple of months. I took her home and she isn't eating, she's just lying around the house.

COUNSELOR: And how does that feel?

CLIENT: Well, I feel guilty for keeping her alive. I'm thinking about having her put to sleep now so she doesn't have to suffer anymore.

COUNSELOR: Gee. So you feel responsible, right?

Even though the counselor's nonverbal attending skills are good, this client might actually feel unheard, because the counselor is asking questions when the implied client feelings seem obvious. Especially if this pattern of questions happens before there is solid rapport, a client might retort, "Well, how would *you* feel?" This questioning rut is clearly not conducive to establishing or maintaining a good therapeutic relationship. Another problem with the dialogue example above is that the counselor responded to only one of the feelings the client was expressing; there are also implications around feeling responsible and anticipating loss. Again, the result would likely be the client feeling not fully heard.

Confuse Thoughts and Feelings

This common mistake happens when we use the word *feel* when we really mean *think*. People often use the word *feel* when they are actually talking about a belief, thought, or decision. An example would be, "I feel it's best to vote for Bridget Smith for school council." This is a thought, which might very well have a corresponding feeling, but the statement itself reflects a thought. For the sake of semantic precision, as well as to become more adept at being aware of our own feeling states, it's important to differentiate in our own minds between thinking and feeling, and to gently correct those confusions when clients make them. Be sure that in your own reflections of feelings, you are actually identifying feelings and not thoughts.

CULTURAL CONSIDERATIONS IN FEELING REFLECTION

We have discussed culture extensively in this chapter. We'll turn now to Hofstede's model and the interface with feeling reflection. From that perspective, there are two ways cultural differences between you and your client may manifest. One of those has to do with the meaning that is made about situations or circumstances.

Our cultural characteristics of high or low power distance, for example, have implications for the feelings we have and the meaning that we make of a situation. Consider a hypothetical situation, such as a person's work supervisor making a disclosure during lunch about an extramarital affair she has been having for the past six months. If the subordinate is from a culture with high power distance, this situation could be a source of anxiety or other discomfort. To that extent, having an awareness of your client's cultural template with regard to the four axes will aid you greatly in understanding the meaning he or she attaches to particular events or situations.

The other way cultural differences will manifest will be the manner with which emotions are disclosed and discussed in the counseling session itself. Some cultures have clear rules about the nature of emotional expression. Those rules might be related to power distance or gender.

Power Distance

This is the axis that deals with the extent to which members of a culture accept and expect that there will be a power differential between those in authority and subordinates.

If you are working with a client from a culture with high power distance, it might be hard for him or her to openly emote with you if you are seen as being in a position of authority. Know that it might be a bad idea to push too hard for emotional expression under these circumstances; it won't help, and might hurt, your relationship with your client.

Gender Roles

Recall that this axis is concerned with two things: the way a culture distributes roles and jobs across both genders, and also the extent to which there is fluidity of values and behaviors in general across both genders. In other words, a culture with low masculinity would be accepting and supportive of androgynous values and nonverbal behaviors.

In a culture with high masculinity, gender roles are extremely clear with regard to who does which tasks, as well as which expressed emotions and behaviors are acceptable from each gender. In a culture with high masculinity, it is not acceptable for a man to cry or show weakness by admitting to feelings of hurt, inadequacy, or other feelings that might be associated with lack of virility and control. Therefore a male client with a cultural background of high masculinity may be disinclined to openly share feelings that are identified in his culture as unacceptable for males. The same would hold true for women from a high masculine culture; expression of feelings in those cultures is specifically prescribed for each gender.

Affiliation

This is the axis defined by the extent to which a person's culture defines allegiance to the collective as an important aspect of a person's behavior. High affiliation societies expect that an individual's actions be considered in a group context, as opposed to an individual context.

The degree of individual versus collective affiliation does not necessarily have direct implications for disclosure of about feelings in a counseling session, but it does have significant implications in terms of choices clients make, the steps of the decision-making process, and the meaning that is attached to particular situational contexts.

Uncertainty Avoidance

This axis has to do with a person's preference for structure and, to some extent, seems related to autonomy. People in cultures with low uncertainty avoidance are comfortable with ambiguity and unstructured situations. Cultures with high uncertainty avoidance have clear, explicit rules about right and wrong and rigid guidelines about acceptable behavior.

Again, this will most likely manifest in counseling in terms of the kinds of emotions that are causing distress for the client. People with high uncertainty have a lot of anxiety that they try to stave off by creating plenty of structure within which to operate.

FEELING REFLECTION IN THE CONTEXT OF THREE THEORETICAL STANCES

Humanistic

Feeling reflection is one of a couple of things that lie at the heart of existential, person-centered therapy. The whole point of humanistic counseling is to help a person be fully in touch with and aware of all the current aspects of his or her existence. To the humanists, that is really one of the points of being alive. From their perspective, as a person becomes fully aware and in touch with his feelings, the meaning he attaches to those feelings, and experiencing those feelings, growth and movement will inevitably happen.

Developmental

The developmentalists expect that across all people in a given culture, there will be a series of life situations accompanied by particular emotions, and emotional expressions in the contexts of those situations, all of which unfold in predictable ways for most individuals. Therefore, knowing what types of emotional conflicts are most likely to manifest at a given stage of development gives a counselor a means of anticipating and listening closely for recurrent emotional themes that are developmentally typical as clients discuss their experiences and concerns.

Cognitive-Behavioral

Feeling identification, especially identifying the meaning of feelings, is a central theme in a cognitive-behavioral counseling approach. However, whereas the humanists see the feeling identification in and of itself as the point of counseling, for cognitive behaviorists feeling identification is a means to an end. The client's feelings are the barometric indicator with which the counselor can target the cognitive distortions, irrational beliefs, and maladaptive behavioral patterns that are sustaining the problem.

Chapter Summary

We've covered a lot of ground in this chapter. We looked at the basic mechanics of a good feeling reflection. Those elements include:

- Making a statement that focuses on the client
- Accurately identifying the stated or implied feelings
- Permitting room for the client to correct you if your description of the client's emotional experience doesn't fit with the client's subjective experience of those emotions

From there, we looked at a few basic models of emotion processing, emphasizing that seven basic emotions occur for everyone: anger, fear, surprise, disgust, sadness, contempt, and happiness. However, the way these feelings are expressed and understood by observers, and the situational precipitants to which we give meaning and that are connected to the emotions, vary tremendously across cultures.

Some of your clients will be fairly willing and able to explore their feelings with you; others will not. When a client is coming for counseling willingly, and yet seems resistant to acknowledge or process feelings, there are multiple possible explanations. Regardless of the reason, it is extremely important that you use caution and refrain from pushing too hard. It could damage your therapeutic relationship with the client and, even worse, damage your client.

We also looked at some common errors novices make and gave some examples. With the conclusion of this chapter and your practicing the feeling reflection microskill, you now are well on your way to having acquired some of the foundational skills in becoming an effective counselor.

Questions for Class Discussion

1. How comfortable are you with your feeling word vocabulary? What are some strategies you can think of to expand it?
2. Talk with your classmates about what kinds of thoughts and feelings you experience when you are conversing with someone who is expressing intense feelings of anger, sadness, or other feelings that are uncomfortable for you.
3. Discuss a time when you shared some private feelings with another person and felt truly heard and honored. What did that person say and do that facilitated your sense of being completely validated?

Case Studies for Discussion

ADULT

Carole is a 37-year-old biracial woman of Caucasian and African American descent. She has been married for 8 years and has two children, ages 7 and 5. Her husband is a 43-year-old Caucasian man who is employed at a local automobile factory. Carole graduated from high school and has been employed periodically in unskilled labor jobs, but never for more than about a year at a time. She stopped working when she got married; her husband made it clear that her job was to tend to the house and have children. She is a homemaker and, while she loves her children dearly, she finds herself feeling very sad and lonely when the children are in school and her husband is at work. Her 7-year-old is in second grade while the 5-year-old attends an all-day kindergarten. Carole has been referred to counseling by her family physician due to her tearfulness, insomnia, and significant weight gain for which the doctor can find no physical cause.

COUNSELOR:	Last week when you were here, we talked a lot about your sense of feeling stuck in your situation of being at home and yet wanting to have some activities and involvements of your own, separate from your family responsibilities.
CAROLE:	Right.
COUNSELOR:	What thoughts and feelings have you had about this since we last talked?
CAROLE:	Well, obviously I decided to give counseling a try. You seemed like you might have some ideas and you know, even though we didn't solve anything last week, I felt a bit lighter when I walked out this door.
COUNSELOR:	I'm really glad you came back. And I think I hear you saying you felt like you had lightened your load a bit by talking about it, right?
CAROLE:	That's it!
COUNSELOR:	I think I also hear that you are feeling a glimmer of hope that there might be some solutions to your dilemma.
CAROLE:	I think so. But it's a little scary to hope because I can't imagine how things will ever change.
COUNSELOR:	On one hand, you want to feel this hopefulness, but at the same time it's risky because it hurts to be let down.
CAROLE:	I hadn't thought of it that way, but that's it. I don't think I can stand any more disappointment in my life.
COUNSELOR:	Sounds like there have been times in the past that you've been really let down. Tell me more about that, if you're willing.
CAROLE:	Well, I haven't told many people this, because it's private. When John and I got married I was already pregnant with Ariana. I think I mentioned that I'd had lots of minimum-wage jobs, then I worked at the deli and I met John. I was head over heels for him and we started dating and boom, I was pregnant. Before we decided to get married I had planned to go to community college to get my LPN certificate. For my whole life I've always wanted to go into nursing. I just never could get

it together to figure out how to pay for it. Then I found out about some tuition assistance I might be able to get. I actually went to the campus and got all the applications. But then I met John. After I got married and had the babies it was completely out of the question.

COUNSELOR: You had a career goal for a very long time, but when you met John and got married, even though you loved him so very much, you had to give up your goal. That sounds like a mixed blessing; joy on one hand but a pretty big loss, too.

CAROLE: Yep. (tears)

COUNSELOR: It's still very sad for you, isn't it?

CAROLE: Oh, yes! (sobbing)

Silence, then Carole's crying begins to subside

COUNSELOR: Tell me more about what the sadness and loss is like for you.

Questions for Discussion about Carole's Case Study

1. Discuss the complexity of Carole's ambivalence. What factors create the conflicted feelings? Talk about those factors with acknowledgment of the theoretical stance you are using to conceptualize her emotional experience.
2. What other thoughts and feelings did Carole imply that the counselor neglected?

CHILD

Derek is a 9-year-old boy of Latino descent being raised by his maternal grandmother. His father is in prison in Puerto Rico. His mother lives in a house across the street from Derek, and his grandmother is raising him while his mother is raising Derek's four younger siblings. His mother decided to send him to live with his grandmother because his behavior is so disruptive in the household and she felt she could not control him. Additionally, Derek has been exhibiting significant behavior problems at school and has been referred to you for help. Derek's disruptive behavior at home was primarily characterized by disobeying rules, staying out on the street at night past his curfew, hanging around the neighborhood with older boys who often are in legal trouble, and yelling when he doesn't get what he wants. At school, he has been aggressive in the lunchroom, taking other students' food, and has been suspended for fighting on the playground. His grades are C's, D's, and F's, and he frequently does not turn in or complete his homework.

COUNSELOR: Hi, Derek, glad to see you today! Are you going to beat me at Uno again?

DEREK: I hope so.

COUNSELOR: Before we get started with the game, I'm curious about what you remember from the last time we talked. Can you share what you remember about that?

DEREK: We played cards . . . and you asked me about yukky school . . . and then I told you about my skateboarding.

COUNSELOR: That's pretty much what I remember about it too. How about if you deal out the cards and while you're doing that you can tell me what you'd like to talk about today.

DEREK: (begins dealing cards) Well, I did my chores this week. Grandma didn't yell at me and I was allowed to stay up till midnight on Saturday.

COUNSELOR: Sounds like it felt better for you not being scolded.

DEREK: Way better!

COUNSELOR: What did you do when you stayed up till midnight?

DEREK: Played Mortal Kombat with George. I kicked his butt! He doesn't know how to do this one really cool move where you have to hit three buttons at the same time.

COUNSELOR: I can see how pleased you are with yourself. It was a specially good treat staying up because you got to beat your older cousin! I get the sense you don't usually beat him at things—am I hearing you right?

DEREK: Right on!

COUNSELOR: What else do you have to tell me about?

DEREK: Nothing. That's it.

Silence, playing cards without speaking

DEREK: What do you usually talk to kids about?

COUNSELOR: Lots of things. Most kids have things that they feel happy about, and also things that make them sad, mad, and scared. A lot of times when they come here, that's what they want to talk to me about.

DEREK: So I can talk to you about stuff that makes me mad?

COUNSELOR: Sure.

DEREK: Okay, here's what happened today with this girl Suzy at school. . . .

Questions for Discussion about Derek's Case Study

1. Do you agree with how the counselor conducted this session? Did it seem that the counselor adequately reflected Derek's emotional experience?
2. Which aspects of each theoretical frame seem to pertain the most in Derek's case?
3. What would you do differently with Derek at this point, and why?

CHAPTER 9

Reflection of Meaning

After studying this chapter, you should have a clear understanding of the following:

- The rationale for reflection of meaning
- The elements of a good reflection of meaning
- How to determine when a reflection of meaning would be a good choice of response to a client

The skill of reflection of meaning is defined as making a statement in response to material your client has shared, which reflects back to him or her the basic core beliefs or principles that have been communicated in his or her verbalizations. Reflecting meaning can serve several purposes:

1. Raising the client's awareness of his or her belief system
2. Raising awareness of the interpretations with which he or she makes sense of the world
3. Helping the client shift perspective from intense emotionality about one situation to a broader, generalized perspective that can help lessen emotional intensity
4. Providing a basis from which you can offer alternative interpretations of a situation

This last purpose is predicated on the assumption that there are many ways of interpreting and defining the same stimulus. This assumption is the basis of a postconstructive view of interpreting reality; from this philosophical viewpoint, reality is entirely a matter of individual perception.

Where the other microskills have hinged on concepts such as communication theory and/or affective awareness and processing, reflection of meaning is a microskill that is truly transtheoretical. *Acknowledging* the importance of meaning arises from existentialism; *articulating* meaning is a cognitive exercise; the *content* of the meaning one derives from an experience or situation is directly related to one's stage of development. Thus, the skill itself is defined primarily in the context of theory.

Reflection of meaning is a microskill that is most appropriately used after there has been enough of a counseling relationship established that you have a strong sense of knowing the client well. Following classroom practice of this particular skill, students frequently comment that discussion of meaning is very personal for them. Talking with another person about the meaning of their lives, their purpose, and their schemas is something they would only choose to do in the context of a firmly established, trusting relationship. There are two different video examples that are good illustrations of what a reflection of meaning looks like in a counseling session. The following links offer viewers a comparison of two applications of meaning reflection.

Video Lab > By Course >

⇒ **Theories of Counseling and Psychotherapy > Module 8: Existential-Humanistic Therapy > Goals, Expectations, and the Meaning of Life**

⇒ **Skills/Process/Techniques > Diagnostic Assessment > Reviewing Intake Information**

THE PERSONAL NATURE OF MEANING MAKING

The rationale for those participants' statement is that meaning making is an aspect of our being in the world that is foundational, underpinning a multitude of our beliefs, actions, and feelings. It takes considerable time with another person to learn enough about him or her to be able to accurately reflect the meaning he or she imbues in a particular issue (the issue could be a situation, interpreting someone else's behavior, certain feelings the person is having, or something completely different). Often a person's meaning making is implied, but like feelings, meaning making may not be explicitly stated in the course of a typical social conversation.

In general, the purpose of offering a client a reflection of meaning is to help him or her step back from the issue to understand what his or her core beliefs or assumptions are. This technique is important to the therapy process in cognitive theory, as well as humanistic and developmental theory. However, the rationale for *why* reflection of meaning is therapeutic varies among the three schools of therapy. One particular circumstance in which reflection of meaning will be instrumental is in the process of working through trauma, as a person is working to create an altered sense of purpose and meaning in the aftermath of a traumatic event.

ASPECTS OF INDIVIDUAL DIFFERENCE IN MEANING MAKING

Later in the chapter we will cover reflection of meaning from the vantage point of three schools of therapy. In the context of theories, there are multiple constructs that will illuminate meaning making. However, in addition to the axes of cultural variability and the three theory groupings, there are alternative aspects of individual difference that contribute to differences in the meaning people derive from situations. Additional sources of individual difference, which we will explore, are spirituality, level of cognitive ability, chronological age and level of psychosocial maturity, and resilience.

Spirituality

Sometimes meaning making is directly connected to a person's religious or spiritual beliefs. Religiosity and spirituality are facets of personhood that vary tremendously across individuals.

PERSONAL REFLECTION

To what extent do religion and spirituality play roles in your life now? What is the relationship between your spiritual beliefs and how you cope with stressors on a day-to-day basis?

The difference between religiosity and spirituality is that individuals who are highly religious place value and emphasis on the traditions and rituals of their chosen faith, for example, going to church. For example, a person who is an Orthodox Jew and highly religious is very observant of the rules about keeping a kosher diet and attending temple daily. People who are highly religious may attach meaning to aspects of their lives based on those religious beliefs.

Related to religiosity is the construct of spirituality. Spirituality is related to belief in a Higher Power. The two constructs of religiosity and spirituality are separate aspects of a person's worldview. Many people who are highly spiritual don't necessarily identify with a particular religion. Table 9.1 offers dialogue examples of reflection of meaning with a client who is highly religious, one who is highly spiritual, and one who is neither.

TABLE 9.1   Dialogue Comparison of Counselor Reflections of Meaning Across the Religious/Spirituality Dimension

Charlie: It's very clear to me that I'm supposed to be staying with Marlene. I've been around and around this in my head; it's not right for me to leave. I just need to figure out how to handle all this awful stress. I know things are going to work out if I hang in there and face my challenges.

High Level of Religiosity	**Counselor:** As you've mentioned before, Charlie, I know that you believe divorce is sinful and absolutely not a option. So if I'm hearing you correctly, you have a strong conviction that when you took your wedding vows, that meant you would hang in with Marlene no matter what because you made that promise to her and to God.
High Level of Spirituality	**Counselor:** I get the sense that you see this situation as a chance to rise to the occasion and meet your responsibilities. We've talked in the past about learning opportunities that arise in our lives and that you have a strong feeling that this situation right now is meant to be.
Low Religiosity and Low Spirituality	**Counselor:** You mentioned that you are "supposed" to be staying with Marlene. Let's take a look at those words "supposed to." When we talked before you shared that you don't believe in the Methodist teachings anymore, nor do you believe a higher power exists. So where do you suppose this idea of being supposed to came from? **Charlie:** I was raised to believe that only quitters get divorced and that you should stay with someone no matter what. **Counselor:** I can tell by your voice and facial expression that this clearly is a strong belief you have about the wrongness of divorce.

Level of Cognitive Functioning

A person's level of intellectual functioning will have bearing on the quality of, and extent to which, he or she makes meaning from events. Intelligence theory identifies one aspect of intelligence as the ability to create abstract categories that enable one to group disparate items or ideas (Aiken & Groth-Marnat, 2006). Abstraction, compared to concreteness, refers to the extent to which an individual can move beyond thinking about physical characteristics of an object or situation, into the realm of ideas and concepts *about* that object.

People who are cognitively impaired or developmentally delayed tend to think concretely; people with average to above-average cognitive ability are able to use abstract reasoning and logic. People at exceedingly high levels of cognitive ability are able to generate and manipulate abstract categories that are beyond the understanding of most others. The level of concreteness your client demonstrates will affect the degree to which he or she can reflect on the meaning of a situation. Table 9.2 offers dialogue examples of how a counselor might adjust his or her reflection of meaning to the level of concreteness of a client.

TABLE 9.2   Comparison of Counselor Reflection of Meaning Responses Based on Client's Cognitive Functioning Level

Bettina: I've had a horrible week. Let me tell you what happened. Last Thursday I walked into the Snyders' house to start cleaning. I didn't think anyone was home, and Delia gave me a key a long time ago so I could let myself in when she isn't there. I walked in and there was Dan standing in the kitchen in his underwear! And he yelled at me, "What are you doing here?" I ran out and got in the car and drove home. Delia called me that night and said she was really mad that she paid me and her house wasn't clean. Then she told me not to bother coming back and to mail her the house key she gave me.

High Cognitive Ability Level	**Counselor:** Seeing Dan in his underwear felt a little bit like you were being violated. Then Delia accusing you before you had an opportunity to explain yourself violated you even more. For her to fire you before you even had a chance to explain yourself sounds like the biggest violation of all. And I wonder if, also, you wondered what in the world he's doing home in the middle of the day walking around without clothes on.
	Bettina: Exactly.
	Counselor: What do you think you can take from this situation into other situations so this doesn't happen again?
Average Ability Level	**Counselor:** So on top of the embarrassment and discomfort of walking in on Dan in his underwear, Delia accused you of not doing your job and fired you, too. It sounds very unfair. From the way you're saying this I get the sense that you resent being accused when you made every effort to do your job.
	Bettina: Right! What do they expect me to do? Dan knows I clean on Thursday mornings. My name is right on the calendar. I was just trying to do my job!
Low Cognitive Ability Level	**Counselor:** Dan in his underwear and then Delia yelling at you on the phone caused you to have a very bad day.
	Bettina: Yep.
	Counselor: Have you talked to Delia since then?

PERSONAL REFLECTION _____

To what extent are you inclined to think mainly about a situation as a concrete incident, as compared to thinking abstractly about the meaning of events? Are you inclined to philosophize as a way of thinking about things? If so, what purpose does this style serve for you?

Level of Emotional and Psychosocial Maturity

In a manner related somewhat to concreteness, children and adolescents are generally more focused on the here and now than they are on long-term implications or consequences. Similarly, an adolescent, by virtue of life experience and overall maturity level, might be more inclined to make meanings that are concrete and short-term. Although some adults also tend to think in the short term and more about themselves than others, in general, as people mature their concerns and worldviews expand to consider long-term implications of actions or values. The dialogue comparison in Table 9.3 gives a statement and counselor response with an adolescent of 17 at various psychosocial stages of development ranging from below average to average to above average maturity. There is also an example of a dialogue with a 9-year-old child.

PERSONAL REFLECTION _____

Do you tend to think more about immediate needs or long-term implications of choices? If you have a balance of both, which of the two (short or long term) carry more weight when you are making big decisions?

Trauma

It is a simple fact of life that at some point we will experience life events that are traumatic. Death and other forms of loss, debilitating illness, natural disasters, and violence all exist as possible sources of trauma, some of which will inevitably touch us as we progress through our lives.

In the face of loss, many people move through a process of grieving and letting go. Kubler-Ross (1969) was one of the first to make accessible to the lay public the stages through which people progress when they have a terminal illness. Some of those same stages of grieving appear to be applicable to other types of grieving, such as death of a loved one, loss of a relationship through divorce or dissolution, or loss of a job. Kubler-Ross identified the stages as shock, denial, anger, bargaining, depression, testing, and finally acceptance. As a person progresses through these stages, the meaning he or she attaches to the unfolding events changes.

One group of people that has been the focus of research on recovery is parents who have had a child that died. Lister (2006) worked with a group of parents whose child had died after prolonged illness, in an attempt to understand the coping process and individual differences in grieving. While parents tried to make sense of the illness, none of them attempted to make sense of the child's death. The immediate emotional reaction following the child's death was, understandably, anguish, profound sadness, a sense of betrayal, and a sense of shattered assumptions. All of the participants underwent a profound questioning of their own beliefs immediately after the child's death. Over time, the parents who did use meaning making as a strategy for coping with the trauma came to a point of needing to decide how they were going to live their lives. Those parents who made the best adjustment

TABLE 9.3   Counselor Responses to Client Dialogue at Varying Ages and Levels of Psychosocial Maturity

17-year-old girl in 11th grade

Emily: First I found out that Joe has been calling and texting Mariah behind my back, and before when I asked him about it, he lied and said he barely even knew her and why would he be texting her. Then my friend Molly saw Joe and Mariah at the coffee shop sharing a caramel latte, with *two* straws in *one* glass! Lattes were my favorite drink I used to like to share with him. I can't believe he's out doing that behind my back with Mariah! What a *jerk*! I'm so glad I found out now.

Advanced Maturity Level	**Counselor:** I get the sense that you see this as a reflection of him being a jerk. Sounds like you are thankful that you got information that Joe is not trustworthy, before spending a lot more time and energy on your relationship with him. Trust is one of the most important things to you in a friendship, and if you don't trust the other person, it isn't worth having them as a friend.
	Emily: Even if I did accept his apology, I'd still always wonder if he was telling the truth.
	Counselor: In your experience, history repeats itself in relationships. So if it happened once, that's a good indication that it's probably going to happen again.
Average Maturity Level	**Counselor:** Joe went behind your back and is doing some of the things that you thought were special between you and him. Joe and Mariah both betrayed your trust.
	Emily: Right! How am I supposed to show my face at school? I'm never going into that coffee shop again.
	Counselor: Being lied to by two good friends was extremely embarrassing for you. You expect that other kids at school will look down on you because two of your friends lied to you.
Below Average Maturity Level	**Counselor:** You're really mad that they both went behind your back and Joe lied to you about it. Then they shared the drink you've always shared with him.
	Emily: Exactly. And now I want to figure out what to do to get back at them.
	Counselor: You think you'd feel better if you could get some revenge for your hurt feelings.
9-year-old girl in 4th grade	
Average Maturity Level	**Ariel:** I got in big trouble at school today because once again Zack Schlosser was slapping me on the shoulder, so I finally turned around and swatted his hand away. Then he started screaming "Ow! Ow! Ow! She hurt me!"
	Counselor: Looks like you're feeling pretty mad about this.
	Ariel: He bugged me first! I didn't hit him hard. All the kids around us said, "Oh Zack, quit being such a baby!" But he told and since he's the teacher's pet I'm the one who got the orange slip to take home. I can't stand how he gets away with stuff just because he's Mrs. D's favorite.
	Counselor: So from where you sit, Zack is a brat who gets away with things because Mrs. D doesn't hold him responsible the way she holds you accountable for problems.
	Ariel: Yep.
	Counselor: And that's not fair, but you and the other kids see that's how she runs her classroom.

after the child's passing validated their experiences through support groups with other parents and reworked their priorities, values, commitments, actions, and relationships. In other words, the trauma was a vastly transformative experience.

Illness and one's own death, or the death of a loved one, are not the only forms of trauma. Most readers are probably familiar with Post-Traumatic Stress Disorder, or PTSD. It is a disorder that causes a significant level of emotional distress to those people who suffer from it. The DSM-IV-TR (APA, 2000) has multiple and distinct sets of criteria, all of which must be met, in order for a person to be given a diagnosis of PTSD. The first set of diagnostic criteria includes being exposed to a traumatic event in which the person has experienced, witnessed, or been confronted with an extreme event that involved a threat of death or serious injury, and a response from the victim that included helplessness or terror. PTSD can result from exposure to a broad variety of antecedent events, including:

- Physical abuse
- Extreme emotional abuse
- Sexual abuse
- Physical or sexual assault
- Accidents with vehicles
- House fires
- Natural disasters such as floods, wildfires, or earthquakes
- Military experiences
- Witnessing any of the above even though the person witnessing was not the victim

Not everyone who is exposed to severe trauma develops PTSD; research efforts have focused, in part, upon the nature of the individual differences between those who develop PTSD and those who do not. For example, Park and Ai (2006) reviewed the research on meaning making in general and aspects of meaning making that mitigate the effects of trauma.

Park and Ai (2006) offer a cogent model for framing the crisis of meaning that follows a trauma. Essentially, what happens when a person is exposed to extreme trauma is that one's beliefs about life being mostly fair, God being a benevolent protector, and the expectation that bad things don't happen to good people, no longer appear to be true. Beliefs about fairness and invulnerability, as well as physical integrity or a continued relationship with someone, are disproven.

Extreme distress ensues when the reality of a situation is completely at odds with our expectations about how life works. Besides the physical and emotional damage that comes from being in fear of losing one's life, fear of losing our life as we know it, or sustaining profound physical insults to our bodies, when we are exposed to trauma we face another challenge too. That is the challenge of adjusting the meaning we make of the world that enables us to absorb and accommodate the new information. Being able to overcome this huge disparity between our beliefs and reality depends on our ability to become aware of and restructure our belief system to accommodate the new information that has been thrust upon us.

PERSONAL REFLECTION _____

How have traumatic events in your life affected the way you function in relationships? How have they affected the meaning you make of your life and your life goals or purpose?

Resilience

Recent years have seen quite a bit of attention in the professional literature to the construct of resilience. Lepore and Revenson (2006) offer a conceptualization of *resilience* that summarizes what authors are referring to when using the term. Their conceptualization enumerates three distinct themes.

RECOVERY: The first of the three is *recovery*: the individual's ability to return to a previous level of functioning after the trauma. Some people are much better than others at moving on and "getting back to the business of life."

RESISTANCE: The second of the three is *resistance*, meaning the ability to maintain a "normal" level of functioning in the midst of a trauma. This is the emotional and psychological equivalent of having a good immune system that resists infection. Another apt metaphor is having a car that has a good set of shock absorbers; resistance is akin to being able to tolerate the bumps in the road without being sent too far off course.

RECONFIGURATION: The last of the three is *reconfiguration*. This is the ability to broaden one's scope of beliefs, values, and worldview to take in and assimilate the new information that emanated from the event. This enables one to emerge from a trauma with increased strength and ability to use internal and external resources to cope.

It is the last of the three, reconfiguration, that has relevance to reflection of meaning in a counseling session. In the aftermath of a trauma, some individuals undergo significant transformations in the meaning they make of the situation and, more broadly, their lives. In fact, drawing on the theory of Frankl (1997), we have an inherent need to try to make sense of life events, and that need is perhaps most pressing in the face of recovery from trauma.

CULTURAL CONSIDERATIONS IN REFLECTING MEANING

Clearly, the meaning a person associates with a situation or issue is going to be strongly correlated with his or her position on each of four cultural axes. The very definitions of the axes explicate the meanings that hold importance for individuals. This will be most apparent to you by comparing dialogue samples representative of particular positions on the cultural axes.

Power Distance

The axis of power distance involves the extent to which subordinate people in a relationship with authority accept the unequal distribution of power. Table 9.4 is a dialogue example in which the same precipitating event is being discussed with a client who has high and low power distance, and an associated appropriate reflection of meaning is offered by the counselor.

Masculinity/Femininity

This is the axis on which a person's values will vary depending on the rigidity, or flexibility, of socially prescribed gender roles. The dialogue example in Table 9.5 offers a comparison of meaning attached to the same precipitant by two individuals who are high and low in masculinity.

TABLE 9.4   Power Distance and Reflection of Meaning

Cynthia: Our neighborhood has a homeowners' association. I received a certified letter in the mail that I am responsible for putting in a new drainage ditch because the one that was installed when my driveway got repaved caused my neighbor's basement to flood. I'm so upset about this! My roof is leaking and I have to put a new one on right away. I don't know how in the world I'm going to afford all this!

High Power Distance	**Counselor:** The finances are a huge concern for you. It's important for you to keep your home in order, and yet home ownership is a big expense and responsibility. **Cynthia:** I just don't know where I'm going to get the money to pay for this new drainage ditch on top of everything else. **Counselor:** Let's back up for a minute. You said that a letter informed you that it was your fault your neighbors have water in their basement, right? **Cynthia:** That's what it said. I should have brought the letter to show you, but I was so upset I left it lying on the table. I'll bring it next time. **Counselor:** I'm not sure how they can say for certain that it's your fault. Was there a surveyor or engineer who came to measure? **Cynthia:** Not that I know of. **Counselor:** If it's the neighbor's word against yours, you might have some recourse to fight this. **Cynthia:** Fight it? Oh no, I would never do that. **Counselor:** Because . . .? **Cynthia:** The association told me what to do. It's not my place to go against their directions. **Counselor:** I guess I'm confused. Isn't it a neighborhood association made up of all the people who live there? **Cynthia:** There is a board of directors. They make all the decisions. And they've given me directions that I must follow if I want to live there and get along with people. Which I do. I've only been there a short while and besides, they are the directors! I'm thankful that I saved enough to buy a house and be in that neighborhood at all. **Counselor:** I think I understand. You believe that it is not your place to question what you have been told to do because you were given an order by the directors. And that to maintain good relations with your neighbors, you must honor their request in a timely manner.
Low Power Distance	**Counselor:** The finances are a huge concern for you. It's important for you to keep your home in order, and yet home ownership is a big expense and responsibility. **Cynthia:** I just don't know where I'm going to get the money to pay for this new drainage ditch on top of everything else. **Counselor:** Let's back up for a minute. You said that a letter informed you that it was your fault your neighbors have water in their basement, right? **Cynthia:** That's what it said. I should have brought the letter to show you, but I was so upset I left it lying on the table. **Counselor:** Did that letter say how the neighbors know it's your fault? **Cynthia:** No, it did not, and to answer your question, I have no clue. **Counselor:** Seems like you might have some recourse if you want to fight this. **Cynthia:** I wondered about that. Here is yet another example of how, in my life, I have to fight for every little scrap I get. **Counselor:** You've had many struggles in your life. Most of the goals you've achieved have not come easily, and you see this as one more example of a challenge to your attaining the goal you set for yourself of buying and maintaining a home in that neighborhood. **Cynthia:** Bingo! If they want to accuse me of putting water in my neighbor's basement, bring it on! I'll take it to City Hall!

TABLE 9.5 Masculinity and Reflection of Meaning Dialogue Comparison

Bill: Here's what happened this week. Tuesday night I come home from work and once again, the house is a mess. It looks like a bomb went off in there! Toys all over the floor, dirty dishes all over the place, and dried-up oatmeal crusted on the table. Marie was nowhere around, and then I see this note that she'd gone over to Roberta's to babysit at the last minute. Something about Roberta having an emergency doctor appointment or something. It's great that she wants to help her friends out, but what about me? It's like Roberta is more important than keeping a nice home for us. And forget about dinner that night. We ended up ordering out that night, which I guess is okay once in a while. I know she's really busy.

High Masculinity	**Counselor:** To you it feels like when Marie lets the house go, it's a reflection of her not caring about you.
	Bill: Obviously. She knows that keeping a nice home is really important to me. And she isn't working because keeping the house is her job. That's why on our tax form we list her as a "homemaker." Making our home is her job.
	Counselor: I can see you feel quite strongly about her role in the family.
	Bill: We talked this out before we ever got engaged. She agreed with me. Martha Stewart is her hero. And that works for me completely. She wants to go to the craft store to get stuff for seasonal decorating in the house, go for it. I gave her her own credit card just for that stuff. So is it too much to ask to come home to a clean house and supper on the table?
	Counselor: Clearly it doesn't seem like too much to you.
	Bill: I don't think I'm being unreasonable here.
	Counselor: You guys agreed at the beginning of the relationship what each of your roles would be, and that those roles are very clear. So you should not be expected to help pick up around the house, because that's her job. And now she isn't holding up her end of the bargain.
	Bill: Precisely.
Low Masculinity	**Counselor:** To you it feels like when Marie lets the house go, it's a reflection of her not caring about you.
	Bill: Right. I know she's working part time and taking care of the kids too. And I know Roberta has been sick for a while. In fact, now they think it might be something really serious. But it still feels like she doesn't care about me when I come home to a house in shambles.
	Counselor: Tell me more about that.
	Bill: When I was growing up and my mom was drinking, she'd totally let the house go. We had bugs and mice, and it was more important to her to just stay obliterated than to take care of the house for me and the other kids.
	Counselor: She chose the bottle over you.
	Bill: Yes. And even though the thing with Marie is different, it still feels that way when I come home. I don't mind helping out picking up. In fact, that night I went ahead and made dinner so that when she came home supper was on the table.
	Counselor: You were able to separate out the situation this week from how it was growing up. But it was a similar feeling at first.
	Bill: I know Marie is not my mom and that she really does love me and makes an effort to take care of me. We take care of each other.
	Counselor: You don't have a problem with helping out around the house.
	Bill: Not at all. That's not the point.

Affiliation

The term *affiliation* refers to the extent to which a person identifies with a collective group of people as a primary consideration in life decisions. Concern for one's family or group versus concern for oneself as an individual, independent entity comprise the two ends of this continuum. The dialogue examples in Table 9.6 illustrate the difference in meaning reflection a counselor might offer as a result of a person's affiliation orientation.

TABLE 9.6   Reflection of Meaning by Degree of Individualism/Affiliation

Lina: I sat down with my parents this past weekend to talk about my school plans. I can see you're wondering how *that* went. . . . Well, it was okay, I guess. My dad is very strongly pushing me toward nursing or pre-med because of my science grades. I guess that's a good idea as far as my academic strengths go, but I love sketching. My friends all say I'm the artistic one in the group, and when I have alone time and want to do something to relax, I *draw*. I don't sit and do organic chemistry problems!

High Degree of Individualism/Low Affiliation	**Counselor:** So you're really good at the science stuff, but it doesn't bring you the joy that artwork does.
	Lina: Right. And here's Dad pushing the med thing, because he says then I'll be financially independent and won't ever need anything else from anyone.
	Counselor: It puts you in a bind that on one hand he's telling you to be independent, but yet he is telling you what to do.
	Lina: Yeah! If I'm so "independent" then shouldn't I be picking my own career path?
	Counselor: Sounds like you are leaning toward finding a career that brings you pleasure and satisfaction too, not just money.
	Lina: Life is too short to just spend it getting rich. For what? That's what Dad did, and I don't think he's too happy when it comes right down to it.
Low Individualism/High Affiliation	**Counselor:** The sciences come pretty easy to you, but it isn't as fun as the artwork for you.
	Lina: Yes. And yet, Dad's idea about making a good income is right. Not only do I need to take care of myself, but I need to get ready for helping my parents in their retirement, just as they are doing for their parents now.
	Counselor: So as you think about your career goals, you are considering not only your own needs, but also how you will be able to contribute to the family down the road.
	Lina: That's how we do it in our family. I see friends whose grandparents are in those horrible homes that smell bad and no one comes to see them because everyone is too busy. I would never, ever do that to my parents or grandparents. They are the bedrock of the family and deserve the highest honor.
	Counselor: Honoring your elders and respecting their advice is clearly an essential aspect of your life.

Uncertainty Avoidance

This axis encompasses the extent to which a person attempts to exert control over circumstances and life. Scheduling, planning, rules, laws, and other forms of structure have varying degrees of importance to different people. Religiosity with an emphasis on the rituals and traditions of a particular faith are related to a high degree of uncertainty avoidance. Table 9.7 gives dialogue examples for clients with high and low degrees of uncertainty avoidance.

TABLE 9.7   Uncertainty Avoidance and Reflection of Meaning

Diquan: This past week I stopped by Marco's Restaurant and put in an application to be a waiter or bartender. I think the bartender job will pay more in tips, because they have a big-screen TV and they get big parties in there for all the games and wrestling matches. The manager said he'd call me back Monday, but here it is Wednesday and I haven't heard from him yet. Ma keeps bugging me to call him, but I don't think I should do that.

Low Uncertainty Avoidance	**Counselor:** What makes you think you shouldn't?
	Diquan: Well, if you want to know the truth, I think he's going to say he doesn't want me because I'm black. I guess it just seems like, if that's how it is, then that's how it is. Life isn't always fair.
	Counselor: So where your Ma wants you to take initiative, your take on this is that the chips are going to fall where they will and there isn't much you can do about it. Life just is what it is and we need to roll with whatever happens.
High Uncertainty Avoidance	**Counselor:** What makes you think you shouldn't?
	Diquan: There might not be much point in doing that. He might not want to hire a brother. Doesn't matter, though, since I've put in five other applications and I already have a list of the guys I need to call back later on today. By the end of this week I'll have a job somewhere. That's just how I do things.
	Counselor: Sounds like you have a clear plan and a goal in sight.
	Diquan: Absolutely. Only person who's going to make things happen in my life is me.
	Counselor: So where some other people in your life, like your friend Darryl, hang out to see what's what, you take the bull by the horns and make things happen in your life.
	Diquan: You got it. I'm going places!

REFLECTING MEANING IN THE CONTEXT OF THREE THEORETICAL STANCES

We already mentioned that this microskill is quite different from the others with regard to the breadth of its focus. Although a reflection of meaning might look similar across a variety of therapists as they use it, a counselor's *intention* will vary greatly depending on whether the therapist's orientation is humanistic, developmental, or cognitive-behavioral.

There have been multiple dialogue examples of meaning reflection throughout this chapter. In fact, each of those are examples of how a reflection of meaning might be used by a therapist whose orientation is humanistic or existential. In both of those cases, the purpose of the meaning reflection is to make the client's meaning-making an object of his or her awareness. The intention of making meaning an object of a person's awareness is to facilitate the person being fully in touch with his or her experience in that moment.

Because the entirety of dialogue examples thus far have been illustrations of typical responses for a therapist who is either humanistic or developmental, we'll switch gears here. Rather than offering more examples of appropriate dialogue, we will examine some examples of inappropriate application of this technique. In the developmental and humanistic stances, undesirable counselor statements will be demonstrated, and possible client responses to those inappropriate statements.

Humanistic

Many of the existential theorists, for example, Frankl and Yalom, see meaning as a significant factor in our day-to-day functioning as humans. Frankl (1997) talked about the "existential vacuum" that he saw as reaching epidemic proportions in contemporary society. He stated, "the will to meaning is not only a true manifestation of man's humanness, but also . . . a reliable criterion of mental health" (p. 89). Frankl further cited numerous studies that identified meaninglessness as a significant factor in the increased rate of suicide over recent decades that has been observed among young adults, as well as self-reports among people with substance use disorders.

As a quick recap of the humanistic approach, the emphasis is on self-awareness. All the person-centered, existentialist, and Gestalt approaches place high value on a person being fully in touch with his or her experience in the moment. The very process of becoming aware constitutes a catalyst for change, even without an individual necessarily making overt behavioral change a goal.

The caveat, in this process of becoming self-aware, is that the client must be able to gain self-awareness in the context of an accepting, nonjudgmental relationship. Thus, a humanistic therapist would not be looking to change, modify, or restructure the meaning a client would make of a situation. First we'll look at an example of an appropriate sequence of meaning reflection.

MARK: I want to talk today about how pissed off I am at Brian and also at Mr. Sellers.

COUNSELOR: Okay, Mark, I'd like to hear about your anger. Tell me more.

MARK: I was walking down the hall and Brian came up behind me and pulled my backpack off my shoulder. It fell on the floor and a whole bunch of stuff fell out. My iPod broke. So I went after him. Mrs. G pulled us apart and sent us both down to the office. Mr. Sellers gave me detention. Brian got no punishment. I am so mad I can't stand it!

COUNSELOR: Let me make sure I have this. You were walking down the hall minding your own business. Brian came along, pulled on your backpack, and everything fell out. Your iPod broke in the process. Then, the two of you went to the office, but only you got detention. I can understand why you'd be so angry. Tell me more about what parts make you maddest.

MARK: I didn't start it. I was just trying to finish it. And who is going to replace my broken iPod?

COUNSELOR: Seems like you expect the discipline in this school to be fair.

MARK: Isn't that what they told us at the beginning of the year?

COUNSELOR: So your anger comes from being disciplined unfairly, and on top of it something that is very important to you got broken.

MARK: That's it. That's exactly it. This place stinks!

Here is another example of that same dialogue, but this time with the counselor making inappropriate judgment about Mark's meaning. We'll pick up most of the way through the dialogue from above. Keep in mind that from some theory viewpoints, the following dialogue would not necessarily be inappropriate. However, remembering the humanistic framework in which we are working, the final counselor statement would definitely be contraindicated.

COUNSELOR: So your anger comes from being disciplined unfairly, and on top of it something that is very important to you got broken.

MARK: That's it. That's exactly it. This place stinks!

COUNSELOR: Your mistake is that you expect life to be fair. The fact is, nothing about life is fair, and if you can come to grips with that, then you won't be disappointed when things don't go the way you think they should in a "fair" world.

PERSONAL REFLECTION

What do you think about this last statement from the counselor? Would you say that to a client in this situation? Why or why not?

Developmental

The stance of the developmentalists is that humans grow in myriad aspects in a process that is linear and hierarchical. Ego development is one such aspect of human growth that progresses through identifiable stages (Loevinger, 1976; Cook-Greuter & Soulen, 2007).

One well-known author who wrote extensively about the construct of ego development was Jane Loevinger. Her model of nine sequential stages is her theoretical representation of how we perceive ourselves in relation to the world. The stages begin with infancy in which there is complete nondifferentiation between the baby, her experienced needs, and the fulfillment of those needs by others in the environment. As the ego matures, there is an increasing ability to comprehend one's relationship to the environment as both integral and separate. From an interpersonal perspective, development begins with autistic self-absorption, then moves to receptive/dependent, manipulative, belonging and niceness, responsibility and mutual concern for communication, respect for others' autonomy, and finally, intense valuing of others' individuality as well as one's own.

When we consider our own stages of ego development, and the relationship between our own stage and our client's stage, the implications of this construct become more complicated. At any given stage of development, we can fully understand and comprehend meaning made by someone else who is at an earlier stage of development; although our own level of meaning making transcends the stage they are in, we can fully relate to their frame for understanding. However, when we try to comprehend the meaning made by someone whose level of development exceeds our own, we have no choice but to reduce the complexity to our own level in order to understand it.

The implications of this for counseling are that if we are trying to counsel an individual whose own stage of ego development exceeds our own, we will be unable to fully grasp and appreciate the complexity of his perceptions and thoughts. This could result in frustration for the client, perhaps a sense of "not being heard." It could also create some frustration or confusion for you as the counselor, and a view that the client is in denial, ambivalent, uncommitted, or otherwise resistant to your suggested interpretations. Here is a dialogue example of a mismatch between the ego development level of the client and counselor.

MARTIN: Bob came to me and told the truth; he is using some of his sick time to visit his daughter and her new baby in California. He already had to use all of his vacation time to take care of his wife after her surgery. My problem is that I have to sign off on his time sheet. I must approve his use of sick time, and if I follow the letter of the law at work, I must demand that he produce a doctor's note.

COUNSELOR: It looks as though this situation is causing a struggle for you. Tell me more about that.

MARTIN: Well, it basically comes down to me lying in order for Bob to do what I agree is right, or me being honest and then creating a situation where he won't be able to see his first granddaughter. He also could get a reprimand from the higher ups for trying to fraudulently use sick time. I hate to see that happen.

COUNSELOR: I guess I don't really understand why you have this dilemma. We've talked about how much you need your job. And it's clear that if you lie, you could lose your job and Bob could get in trouble too. Also, I know you've talked before about how important honesty is to you. This doesn't seem to me like a very difficult decision.

What are the subtleties and complications of this presenting problem from Martin's perspective? What competing values is he struggling to resolve? In what ways are this counselor's reflections of meaning failing to serve Martin's counseling needs?

There are a couple of possible solutions to the problem if a mismatch occurs in which your own stage of development is not as advanced as your client. One is to talk about that very issue, making it a focus of discussion in the counseling process. The other possibility is to refer the client to another counselor who seems to be a better match developmentally for your client.

Here is another example of an inappropriate reflection of meaning in which the counselor is not attuned to the ego development level of the client, but in the other direction. This counselor is attempting to work at a more advanced level of ego development than the client has attained.

ZOE: The coach acted like it was some really big deal that I scratched the trophy during the weekend I was allowed to have it at my house. I told him it wasn't my fault my stupid brother was doing yo-yo tricks in the living room. And besides, if coach was so worried about his precious little trophy he shouldn't be letting kids share it.

COUNSELOR: You are bewildered by your coach's anger about the damage to the trophy. But I think that perhaps to the coach, the trophy represents all the hard work and energy that your whole team put into winning the tournament. Allowing the trophy to be damaged while you had it is sort of like disrespecting him and the team.

ZOE: We all know how hard we worked. What does a scratch on the base of a trophy have to do with *that*? You can still read all the names that are on there. We still have the title too. So what?

The counselor in this case is reflecting an abstract level of understanding the presenting situation, while the client remains on a concrete level. Thus, the client continues to maintain a concrete interpretation, because developmentally, she can go no further at the present time. The appropriate remedy in this case is for the counselor to work with the client at the concrete level of understanding and problem solving, abandoning the broader and more abstract implications of the issue.

Cognitive-Behavioral

Counselors and therapists with a cognitive-behavioral orientation have a slightly different perception of meaning making. The cognitive literature refers to core underlying beliefs as *schemas.* Everyone has schemas; these are the frames with which we make sense of our world. There is a differentiation between automatic thoughts that occur soon after an event, and the underlying schemas that constitute one's cognitive framework. The automatic thoughts, or self-talk, are the most immediately apparent outcomes of a person's schemas. Our schemas, in contrast, are the basic structure of how we define ourselves. In a sense, our schemas are what give rise to our automatic thoughts.

Research has begun looking at schemas with regard to both ends of the continuum of emotional health. At the unhealthy end of the continuum, maladaptive schemas have been identified that create vulnerability to anxiety, depression, and other disturbances. At the healthy, adaptive end of the continuum lie optimism and hope, as well as other schemas we will discuss in more detail in future chapters, which create emotional robustness and re-silience to stressors and trauma.

With regard to the emergence of psychopathology, Young, Klosko, and Weishar (2003) proposed that early maladaptive schemas develop when core needs are not met during childhood. A child's core needs are: (1) secure attachment, (2) autonomy and a sense of identity, (3) freedom to express valid needs and emotions, (4) play and spon-taneity, and (5) appropriate limits, structure, and self control. Insufficient satisfaction of any of these core needs sets the stage for subsequent emotional disturbance in adoles-cence and adulthood.

The point of divergence between the cognitive theorists and the developmentalists is that in cognitive theory, these unmet emotional needs result in an individual arriving at faulty conclusions about how the world works. These conclusions and methods of coping are functional in the pathogenic or unhealthy environment in that they enable the child to survive. However, those schemas become ineffective later in life when the person has grown up and moved away somewhat from the pathogenic environment. Early maladaptive schemas become stable, enduring ways of interpreting reality that begin in childhood and can continue throughout one's life.

The schemas identified by Young, Klosko, and Weishar (2003) fall into five broad domains:

1. *Disconnection and rejection:* The schemas in this domain revolve around the ex-pectation that one's needs for stability and security will not consistently be met.

2. *Impaired autonomy and performance:* These schemas have to do with a fun-damental sense of inadequacy, resulting in either consistent failure or an expectation that one cannot independently handle the demands of life; that one will always need the help of others.

3. *Impaired limits:* These schemas manifest as an inability to set limits for oneself, disregarding one's responsibility to others, and lacking the ability to establish and attain long-term goals.

4. *Other-directedness:* The schemas in this domain are evident in a person's exclusive focus on the needs, feelings, and expectations of everyone else except herself. This is essentially an intense fear of fully expressing one's feelings or needs out of fear of rejection and emotional abandonment.

5. *Overvigilance and inhibition:* These schemas have in common the theme of rigidly suppressing one's feelings, urges, and spontaneity to meet rigid, external demands for behavior and observance of rules and ethical behavior.

One important point is that these domains are specifically targeting pathology and aspects of maladaptive behavior that result in personality disorders. That said, however, this author's life experiences and clinical observation suggest that even if a person doesn't meet the diagnostic criteria for a personality disorder, subclinical versions of these subtle themes may still influence the way our schemas develop and endure.

PERSONAL REFLECTION

Are you able to articulate one or two enduring themes in your life that have seemed to be stable over time?

Regardless of the setting in which you are working and the age group of the people you are helping, the constructs of self-talk, automatic thoughts, and schemas will be helpful in understanding the how and why of their emotional reactions to situations. In the context of cognitive-behavioral theory, identification and restructuring of a person's self-talk and schemas is one of two central foci of treatment.

To illustrate a cognitive approach to reflection of meaning, we will use one of the dialogue sequences from earlier in the chapter. In the current example you will see how a counselor would actually explain the cognitive model to a client in the context of cognitive restructuring.

MARK: I want to talk today about how pissed off I am at Brian and also at Mr. Sellers.

COUNSELOR: Okay, Mark, I'd like to hear about your anger. Tell me more.

MARK: I was walking down the hall and Brian came up behind me and pulled my backpack off my shoulder. It fell on the floor and a whole bunch of stuff fell out. My iPod broke. So I went after him. Mrs. G pulled us apart and sent us both down to the office. Mr. Sellers gave me detention. Brian got no punishment. I am so mad I can't stand it!

COUNSELOR: Let me make sure I have this. You were walking down the hall minding your own business. Brian came along, pulled on your backpack, and everything fell out. Your iPod broke in the process. Then, the two of you went to the office, but only you got detention. I can understand why you'd be so angry. Tell me more about what parts make you maddest.

MARK: I didn't start it. I was just trying to finish it. And who is going to replace my broken iPod?

COUNSELOR: Seems like you expect the discipline in this school to be fair.

MARK: Isn't that what they told us at the beginning of the year?

COUNSELOR:	So your anger comes from being disciplined unfairly, and on top of it something that is very important to you got broken.
MARK:	That's it. That's exactly it. This place stinks!

Additional cognitive dialogue starts here

COUNSELOR:	I totally see where you're coming from and I can see how it looks really unfair to you. What's especially frustrating is that the principal made such a big deal about this school being fair back at the beginning of the year.
MARK:	(*Silence*)
COUNSELOR:	Do you remember us talking back at the beginning about me helping you learn how to get a handle on how you talk to yourself as part of getting control of your anger?
MARK:	Yeah. So what am I saying to myself right now?
COUNSELOR:	Great question . . .
MARK:	Okay, I'm saying school stinks. It's not fair and I can't wait until I can drop out.
COUNSELOR:	What are some other things you could say to yourself that would be equally true?
MARK:	I don't know.
COUNSELOR:	Last week you said you were making Merit Roll. The first one in your family to do that. You also said Mrs. Smith had nominated you for the Most Improved Student award.
MARK:	So?
COUNSELOR:	So the fact that you have been studying and so committed, and that Mrs. Smith put you up for that award, *does* sound fair.
MARK:	I guess it does.
COUNSELOR:	What else could you do in this situation to get an outcome that would be more fair to you?
MARK:	What do you mean?
COUNSELOR:	I mean that you've identified property damage and another kid initiating aggression. You are not completely powerless here. What appropriate steps can you take to see that there is some justice done?
MARK:	I could talk to the principal about it. But he won't listen to me.
COUNSELOR:	What if we talked to him together?
MARK:	You'd do that for me?
COUNSELOR:	Absolutely. Let's practice what you might say to him.

(Toward the conclusion of the session)

COUNSELOR:	We've covered a lot of ground today. How is your anger level now compared to when you came in?
MARK:	At the beginning it was, like, really bad, and now I'm still ticked off, but at least I have a plan for what to do, so I feel better.

COUNSELOR: Let's focus for just another minute or two on the fairness thing. What are some examples of what you're saying to yourself now about that?

MARK: Okay, well, it's like some of the teachers here play favorites. But some of the people here are okay, like you. I can walk around and just take it or I can stand up for what's right. And I'm willing to give the school a chance to see if things are fair here like they promised it would be. But I don't know what's going to happen if the principal disses me.

COUNSELOR: Let's just take this one step at a time. Before we actually go to the principal I'd like to talk to you one more time to figure out a Plan B, just in case the meeting with him doesn't go the way you hope it will. Sound okay?

In this concluding sequence, several things are happening. The counselor is modeling a grounded, systematic problem-solving approach. He also is helping Mark become aware of how the self-talk is fueling his anger. Finally, the counselor is working on shifting the meaning and context with which Mark perceives the precipitating event. The process of cognitive restructuring happened in a way that was gently directive. That's one of the most obvious differences between the cognitive-behavioral approach and the other theories; the cognitive-behavioral work clearly directs the focus and the intervention toward a grounded, rational perception and interpretation of situations and events.

Chapter Summary

We began by looking at the various purposes that can be served by choosing to do a reflection of meaning. Sometimes it can be enlightening and empowering for a person to come to the realization of the meaning he or she is attaching to a precipitating event. As students in helping professions, many of you probably spend considerable time thinking about your own meanings, values, and schemas; the average layperson walking down the street probably does not. Therefore, the meaning your client imbues in an event might be completely outside the realm of his or her awareness.

Reflection of meaning can also be a way of helping a client move away from intense emotional experiencing to gain some distance and self-understanding. This, too, can be an empowering process, as it can help a client acquire a sense of self-control.

The essence of this microskill is to listen to your client's story and then to infer the core fundamental values or self-perceptions that are driving his or her interpretation of the event or situation. This is a skill that requires considerable knowledge of your client. If you try to use reflection of meaning before adequate trust and rapport have been established, you risk sounding presumptuous and overly familiar. Moreover, you could be wrong! These blunders have obvious implications for the therapeutic relationship.

There are multiple aspects of individual variability that bear upon the meaning a person makes; we touched upon a few of them. Individual differences we covered included the nature of the person's spirituality and religiosity, level of cognitive ability, level of psychosocial maturity, and resilience. Many people have an amazing capacity to recover from life's pain. For as many people who sustain significant emotional damage following trauma, there are just as many that somehow are able to accommodate and move on to a higher level of ego development and functioning.

Four axes of cultural variability were considered from the standpoint of how each might sound different, given a person's values on each of them. Note also that the discussion of meaning could itself be something that varies across cultures. That is, some families or groups may be comfortable frequently discussing "big picture" topics and issues, but for other groups this type of conversation might be considered intensely personal. This is another reason why reflection of meaning shouldn't be done until you know a client very well.

Finally, we compared and contrasted reflection of meaning from each of three theoretical positions. Reflection of meaning is seen as an important component of therapy in all three stances, but for different reasons. On this front, the humanistic and developmental models share the perspective of making a person's meaning simply an object of awareness. These models hold that awareness in and of itself eventually results in metamorphosis; that change and growth are naturally occurring processes. In contrast, the cognitive-behavioral model holds that faulty schemas and self-talk perpetuates itself as a by-product of our natural tendency to select those aspects of our environments that justify and prove the conclusions and beliefs we already hold.

A few points stand out as being most important for you to take from this chapter.

- As you counsel, you will need to reflect meaning at a level of development commensurate with your client's stage. This is a concrete example of the admonition some readers may have heard before: "Start where your client is."
- Once again, the issue of self-awareness is paramount. You need to be aware of what your own meaning making and schemas are, and also your own level of ego development.
- Recognize that your client may not share your interpretation of reality, and that the meaning he or she makes of a situation is every bit as valid to him or her as your own is to you.

Questions for Class Discussion

1. How do you feel about the idea of having big differences of interpretation of a situation between you and your client? Is your job to change his or her perception?
2. Among the four axes of cultural variability that were presented and discussed, what are some examples of values that will be difficult for you to accept in a client?
3. Think about the core emotional needs and early maladaptive schema domains. Talk with your classmates about people you have known that grew up in emotionally toxic environments and how those environments affected their views of themselves in the world.

Case Studies for Discussion

ADULT

In the last session, the counselor and Carole processed the strong and ambivalent feelings she had about raising her children and, in that process, giving up her career.

COUNSELOR: The last time we met, it was a very emotional session for you. I really appreciate you trusting me enough to share such personal information and to allow yourself to fully have the feelings you expressed. Over this past week, what other feelings and thoughts have you had about our last session?

CAROLE: This week has been really hard. I feel so guilty for wanting to have a career. Women in my family, or John's family for that matter, never work outside the home. It makes me a bad mom. I look around and I see that it's the children whose mothers aren't home after school that are out running the streets.

COUNSELOR: The fact that you don't find homemaking satisfying is a source of shame for you. Your dreams about a nursing career don't fit with what you believe you *should* be doing.

CAROLE: How can it? I don't think that mothers who work outside the home are good parents.

COUNSELOR: It's very understandable that you would be feeling so very hopeless and upset. You are in a situation where making either choice, a nursing career or a homemaker raising your children, eliminates the possibility of doing the other one. And they are both very important to you.

CAROLE: What can I do? There's no point in continuing this counseling, right?

COUNSELOR: Stopping counseling is always a choice. But to me it looks as though there may be other possibilities that would enable you to do both, perhaps possibilities you have not considered.

CAROLE: Really?

COUNSELOR: Yes. I can think of several alternatives. Would you like to talk about that today, or is there some other issue you'd like to focus on instead?

Questions for Discussion about Carole's Case Study

1. In what ways do your own values converge or diverge with Carole's values? How would that affect the way you feel about working with her?
2. The counselor alluded to alternatives for Carole to consider. What do you anticipate some of them might be?
3. Discuss application of each of the three theoretical stances and what the counseling goals would be for Carole from each of those perspectives.

CHILD

In the last session, Derek began sharing information about his interpersonal experiences, and there was some suggestion that perhaps he is aggressive in reaction to other students instigating events.

COUNSELOR: Last time you were telling me about Suzy making fun of your lunch because you don't bring Lunchables like the other kids. We came up with a plan for how you were going to handle it if it happened again. So did it?

DEREK: Oh yeah. I was sitting there eating my salami and Suzy said, "Too bad you're you. I got pizza Lunchables today." And then I said, "Whatever," and sat at the other end of the table with Jonathan.

COUNSELOR: So by doing that you avoided getting into another shouting match.

DEREK: Yep.

COUNSELOR: Wow, Derek, I think that's awesome! What do you think about it?

DEREK: I think I'm not going to get myself in trouble over some stupid girl.

COUNSELOR: The part that shows you are growing up is that you are able to recognize some steps you can take that will affect the outcome.

DEREK: Like things go more smoothly when I can stop and think about what I want.

COUNSELOR: Right. At home, when you do the jobs Grandma gives you to do, you get extra stuff like staying up. And at school, if you can stay out of fights in the lunchroom, then you can get to go out on the playground to play football.

DEREK: Football is about the only thing about school that I like other than playing Uno with you instead of going to reading class!

COUNSELOR: The thing you like best about meeting with me is getting out of reading?

DEREK: Well, yeah. But I guess you're okay, too.

COUNSELOR: I appreciate your honesty, Derek. Let's shift gears a little bit. Tell me about how it's been going at home with Grandma this past week.

DEREK: Okay, I guess.

COUNSELOR: If Grandma were here, what's your best guess about how she would say your week at home went?

DEREK: She'd say I had good days and bad days. The good days I did my chores and the bad days I didn't.

COUNSELOR: I want to understand more about how you decide when to do your chores and when not to. . . .

Questions for Discussion about Derek's Case Study

1. Do you agree that the focus on Derek's home life is appropriate, considering he is being seen in a school setting? Why or why not?
2. What are the advantages and disdvantages of getting Derek's grandmother involved in his counseling process? Considering those pros and cons, would you involve her?

CHAPTER 10

Confrontation

After studying this chapter, you should have a clear understanding of the following:

- When a therapeutic confrontation is appropriate
- The rationale for doing a confrontation
- How to effectively confront a client

This is the final chapter that focuses on microskills. The remaining chapters expand from microskills to the broader scope of counseling theory and process. Reviewing our exploration of the microskills, we began with attending. In the case of reflection of meaning, as well as confrontation and immediacy, the frequency with which you will use these latter microskills may be somewhat lower than the frequency with which you attend, question, observe, and reflect feelings.

Several aspects of confrontation may be helpful to deconstruct as you develop a mental image of challenging in the context of a counseling session. First, we will define specific aspects of a client's presentation that suggest that a confrontation may be an effective technique. Then we will take a look at how to ascertain whether the time is right to do a confrontation, and the intended outcome of a confrontation. Specific dialogue examples of appropriate and inappropriate confrontive counselor statements will be presented. Finally, we will consider confrontation in the context of the three theoretical stances, and implications of confrontation in the context of Hofstede's cultural axes.

PERSONAL REFLECTION _____

How often do you inform friends or family that you think they should do something different? How do you react when they argue or disagree with you?

SKILL DEFINITION: WHAT, WHY, AND HOW

Although some authors differentiate between *confrontation* and *supportive challenging*, we will use these two terms interchangeably in this chapter because from the perspective of counselor intention, they serve the same purpose. Confrontation consists of making an observation or otherwise bringing to a client's attention discrepancies that are apparent to the counselor in the client's behavior, feelings, or perceptions.

WHY COUNSELORS USE CONFRONTATION

Some authors who write about counseling techniques (e.g., McHenry & McHenry, 2007; Poorman, 2003; Young, 2005) have pointed out that contradictions in a person's thoughts, feelings, or behaviors create tension in the form of anxiety that the person is then energized to reduce. Those contradictions create *cognitive dissonance*, a term that derives from cognitive theory. The parallel Gestalt or person-centered terminology is that conflicting thoughts, behaviors, or ambivalent emotions create *incongruence* that the person is motivated to re-align or resolve. Therefore, when a counselor points out the client's discrepant thoughts, feelings, or behaviors, she or he is basically challenging the client to acknowledge the imbalance, thus resulting in increased anxiety.

The discrepancies a client exhibits may take one of several different forms, as noted by Hill and O'Brien (1999). Discrepancies may involve:

- Inconsistency between two spoken statements
- Inconsistency between words and actions
- Inconsistency between two behaviors
- Inconsistency between verbalized emotions and nonverbally expressed emotions
- Inconsistency between values and actions
- Inconsistency between reported perceptions and reported experiences
- Inconsistency between the "real self" and the "ideal self"
- Inconsistency in perceptions or thoughts between the counselor and client
- Inconsistency between client's behavior and societal external expectations

One example of a time that a counselor might use supportive challenging would be when there is a mismatch between the client's words and behavior. Sometimes the behavior is overt, such as not following through on something the person said is important. Here is an example. A counseling intern was working in a treatment program that offered substance abuse counseling to clients who were court-ordered to participate in treatment. One of his clients, "Adele," came to sessions twice a week talking enthusiastically about her success in abstaining from using cocaine, and how proud she was of her accomplishment. The student intern, too, was excited that his counseling efforts were so immediately helpful. However, when the intern received several weeks' worth of Adele's mandatory urine screen results, it was evident that Adele had been continuing to use cocaine throughout the entirety of her enrollment in the program. Thus, there was a substantial discrepancy between her words and her behavior outside of counseling.

Inconsistency in the way your client presents can also appear in a more subtle form: nonverbal and paraverbal behaviors that contradict the spoken words. This author once worked with a young man, "Mike," who was coming to counseling with career exploration needs and elevated anxiety. It quickly became apparent that Mike was experiencing significant pressure from his father, who was a high school soccer coach, to pursue a soccer scholarship for college. When the young man shared in a counseling session that he had received notification of being awarded the soccer scholarship, I asked, "So, how are you feeling about that?" He replied, "Well, I'm pretty excited," but while he spoke those words, his head was turning back and forth in a nonverbal expression of "no." He appeared to have no awareness that he was shaking his head as he was talking.

There may also be times when parts of a client's story or perceptions don't seem to match up. For example, "Kiara" was a 14-year-old girl who had been removed from her mother's custody due to neglect and placed with her biological father. Kiara had been complaining to the counselor that her father was also neglectful; she stated several times that he spent "*all* the time" on his computer. Later in the session, Kiara expressed frustration that her father insisted Kiara go out for dinner with him and then to a movie, when all she wanted to do was sit in her room and watch television. These two complaints about the father's behavior were discrepant and suggested that there were inaccuracies in Kiara's perceptions.

Yet another time that challenging can be effective is when a client is engaging in behavior that is likely to cause harm either to him or herself or others, including legal consequences. For example, confrontation has been found to be effective in group intervention with batterers (Silvergleid & Mankowski, 2006). Later in the chapter we'll come back to the client examples above and explore possible ways of confronting the clients in those situations.

The technique of confrontation is likely to intensify emotions (anxiety and possibly other emotions, too) during the counseling session. Depending on how skillfully you use this strategy, this emotional intensification can result in significant movement toward growth on the client's part, or it can result in significant resistance and pulling back from the counseling relationship.

PERSONAL REFLECTION

Has there ever been a time when you were trying to act a certain way that wasn't reflective of your true feelings, and someone called your bluff? What did that feel like? From your perspective in the present, did something positive come from that experience?

The term *significant movement toward growth* could be defined variously as broadened awareness of conflicted feelings, acknowledgement of self-defeating behavior, or a more accurate and integrated perception of self, others, or external situations. A person's reaction to confrontation can range from flat denial and refusal to acknowledge any discrepancy, to a superficial or partial acknowledgement, to surprise, bewilderment, or acceptance/admission. Regardless of the outward reaction, internally the client may experience an intense rush of emotion.

HOW TO EFFECTIVELY CONFRONT A CLIENT

Video Lab > By Course > Skills/Process/Techniques >
⇒ **Module 6: Cognitive and Behavioral Intervention >**
Challenging Clients' Incongruent Messages
⇒ **Module 7: Psychodynamic Intervention >**
⇒ **Confronting Client's Resistance and Responses**
⇒ **Continuing to Confront Client's Behaviors**

The links listed above provide two contrasting examples of a client confrontation, from two different theoretical approaches. Viewing both will give you a concrete sense of what a confrontation looks like when effectively used by a competent counselor. Skillful use of confrontation requires ability in several realms: a good sense of timing (your ability to gauge whether the time is right for a confrontation), delivery (the verbal and nonverbal manner in which you present the confrontation), and the manner in which *you* respond to your client's response to your confrontation. We will take each of these factors and discuss them in more detail.

Timing

Multiple aspects of timing are important. These include the stage of the counseling process (early, middle, or end), the client's emotional stability, the quality and extent of the client's external resources, the riskiness of the behavior that you are confronting, and the client's stage of readiness for change.

STAGE OF COUNSELING PROCESS   It is not generally advisable to challenge a client early in the counseling relationship. It takes time for trust and rapport to develop in *any* relationship; a therapeutic relationship is no different. As you develop rapport with a client, a level of trust begins to emerge on the client's part; a knowledge that you are concerned about his or her well-being. This trust usually emerges gradually over an extended period of time. Although *you* know, as the counselor, that you have the client's best interests at the heart of your intention and effort, a new client does not necessarily know this to be true. Over the course of time, as you demonstrate your active listening skills and, most importantly, your unconditional positive regard, many of your clients will come to see that you are trustworthy.

PERSONAL REFLECTION _____

Have you ever been questioned by a health care professional who expected you to share private or highly personal information before you felt ready to disclose it? How did that affect your feelings about working with that person?

Attempting to develop a counseling relationship is like tending to a seed that you hope will germinate and grow. Growing the plant requires favorable conditions: adequate light, water, and warmth. If a gardener tries to prune and reshape the plant before the root system is adequately established, the plant will die. Confronting a person with the intention of precipitating change parallels pruning a plant; the relationship needs to be firmly established to sustain the potential threat a client may experience when being challenged by a counselor.

Some populations of clients may be more likely than others to use denial of personal responsibility to justify their behavior. These populations include people who perpetrate domestic violence, people who are pedophiles or other types of sex offenders, people who abuse substances, or people who are criminals. One commonality among these groups is that they are likely to be court-ordered for counseling, as opposed to being self-referred. Even among groups of clients whose behavior is quite harmful to others and themselves, research has suggested that confrontation is far more effective when the clients perceive the counselor as supportive and trustworthy, after therapeutic rapport has been established (Bratter, 2003; Dutton, 2003; Kear-Colwell & Boer, 2000; Nakayama, 2003; Silvergleid & Mankowski, 2006).

THE CLIENT'S EMOTIONAL STABILITY   This term, *emotional stability*, requires some explanation. It originates from one factor of a commonly known model of personality organization, the 16 PF, by Cattell (Cattell, 1943, 1990). This model organizes personality into 16 factors hypothesized by Cattell to comprehensively describe human traits, tendencies, and behaviors. Each factor is represented on a continuum, and one of those 16 factors is emotional stability. One end point of the emotional stability continuum is "high ego strength," in which a person is emotionally stable, mature, and able to cope with life's stresses. The other anchor of the continuum is "low ego strength," in which a person is highly reactive emotionally and becomes easily upset. People with low ego strength seem to struggle with taking life's ups and downs in stride, becoming emotionally disrupted by events that others would find relatively minor.

Clearly, if a client has low ego strength, a counselor challenging him or her will need to be very gentle in the confrontation. An alternative to confrontation with a client who has low ego strength would be to first work on developing more skills for coping.

On the other hand, a client with high ego strength and emotional robustness may be more capable of being confronted without reacting angrily or defensively. People with high ego strength are less susceptible to self-doubt in response to situational stressors. Therefore, an individual with high ego strength may be more likely to respond to a direct challenge with either flat denial (if he is completely unaware of his discrepancies) or willingness to explore the contradiction in a nondefensive way.

THE CLIENT'S EXTERNAL RESOURCES   When you confront or challenge a client in a way that suggests you think she should change her behavior, you are placing subtle conditionality on the counseling relationship. Even if you are careful to say, with your words, that it doesn't matter to you what choice your client makes, she may nevertheless have the perception that she is letting you down by not doing what you seem to be challenging her to do. If your client's external resources are severely limited, there may in fact be few options for behavior change until other, healthier alternatives are first established.

An applied example will help illustrate this point. "Heidi" is a 27-year-old woman who relocated 10 months ago from another city far away, in order to move in with her boyfriend, whom she met online. The boyfriend works in a bar, drinks heavily, goes on weekend binges with cocaine, brings people from the bar to their home to drink and use drugs all through the night and into the next day, behaves very suggestively with other women when he is inebriated, and lies on the couch watching television when he is home. Heidi drinks occasionally but does not use drugs, and she typically spends minimal time in the bar. The boyfriend has stated clearly to Heidi that he sees no problem whatsoever with his behavior, and he has no intention of changing anything. Heidi is depressed, not performing well in her job at a theater box office, and is worried about her boyfriend developing an addiction problem.

Here is a situation where it seems fairly obvious that the relationship is not a healthy choice for Heidi. Heidi recognizes this, as she comes into counseling sessions and tells stories to the counselor about the boyfriend's latest antics. She asks for the counselor's validation that his behavior is inappropriate and that her anger is justified. On the other hand, though, she says, "But the rest of the time he's a really good guy!" It might seem that Heidi needs to end the relationship immediately. However, her only friends are people she met through her boyfriend when she relocated to this city. Those are all people he knows from the bar. She has recently lost one of her two part-time, minimum-wage jobs.

Heidi is a person with very few external resources. She has no healthy support system of people in her immediate geographic area, is estranged from her family of origin, has a minimal source of income to support herself, and because of her depression, she has little energy to work on developing new friendships. Even though she needs to leave this relationship with her boyfriend, if the counselor confronts her about making a decision to get out of the apartment immediately, it could be extremely detrimental to Heidi. The counselor is one of the few healthy, stable individuals in Heidi's life. If the counselor puts Heidi in a position of feeling that she must leave the boyfriend in order to maintain the counselor's approval, Heidi may feel that she needs to discontinue the counseling relationship. Discontinuing counseling or leaving her boyfriend before she has generated another plan for herself as far as income, shelter, and development of a healthier support system could create additional vulnerability for Heidi.

THE RISKINESS OF THE BEHAVIOR   Level of risk is a mitigating factor that must be considered in the counselor's decision about appropriate timing for a confrontation. Some contradictory client behaviors might be minimal or low risk. For example, Mike's ambivalence about the soccer scholarship might be causing a minor to moderate amount of emotional distress for him. If his conflict is not appropriately resolved, it may result in his unhappiness with his choice of colleges. However, he is not suicidal, and his conflicted feelings do not generate an elevated risk of legal or physical harm in the short or long term. Thus, in Mike's case, the need for confrontation and/or rapid behavior change on his part is low.

On the other hand, in the case of Heidi, her boyfriend's behavior and her own ambivalence about leaving the relationship *do* carry significant potential risks. For example, his use of illegal drugs in their home could implicate Heidi as well, if he were arrested for drug possession. She could also be charged with possession because she lives at the same address. As well, he is sexually promiscuous and has unprotected sex, again potentially placing Heidi in harm's way as far as contracting a sexually transmitted disease from him; even though she is monogamous, he is not. In Heidi's case, then, although she has minimal external resources, other aspects of her circumstances suggest the importance of some rapid changes on her part in order to reduce the likelihood of harm to her.

THE CLIENT'S STAGE OF READINESS FOR CHANGE   Prochaska and others (Prochaska, 1999; Prochaska, Velicer, DiClemente & Fava, 1988) developed a model for conceptualizing how ready a client is to make behavioral changes in counseling. Although their model initially focused on addictive behavior and smoking cessation, it has since been expanded and investigated for use with a variety of presenting problems. We will spend more time on this model in Chapter 12, "The Counseling Process." Here, we provide just a brief explanation of the stages.

Prochaska and colleagues discovered that even clients who come to counseling of their own volition have varying degrees of commitment to make behavioral changes that will eliminate or reduce their presenting problem. They proposed that a counselor's choice of which intervention strategies are most appropriate for a client should not necessarily be based on the counselor's theoretical orientation, but instead on the client's stage of readiness for change.

The stages of readiness are precontemplation, contemplation, preparation, action, and maintenance. In the precontemplation stage, the client does not believe the targeted problem is really a problem; for him or her, the advantages of maintaining the problem behavior greatly outweigh the disadvantages. In the contemplation stage, the client begins to consider the ways in which the problem behavior is costing him or her and to consider those costs in relation to the benefits. In the preparation stage, he or she has begun to recognize and accept that a behavior change would be desirable and is thinking about specific plans for making the change. In the action stage, steps are actually taken. Finally, in maintenance, the client takes steps to create internal and external conditions that will enable him or her to sustain the behavior changes that were made during the action stage.

For some clients who are heavily entrenched in the precontemplation stage, a direct, critical confrontation may simply be completely ineffective. For other clients it takes a counselor speaking bluntly, in plain English, to get their attention and break through the barrier of denial. This is particularly the case when you have a client who has repeatedly had substantial negative consequences, yet persists in problematic behavior.

Some readers may be familiar with the term "hitting rock bottom," often used among people who are addicted to substances. This refers to a person having had such magnitude and severity of negative consequences that he or she finally becomes aware of the ways the substance abuse is creating loss or other problems. For some who are addicted, receiving a reprimand from a boss or a teacher is sufficiently upsetting that it is their "rock bottom" point; they decide they want to stop using. More often, though, a person must experience extensive losses before he or she is willing to consider substance use as "problematic."

This same model can be used to conceptualize other types of behavior problems, for example, anger management problems for a youngster in public school. Assuming frustration tolerance and impulse are the only problems (i.e., in the absence of other psychological diagnoses), temper outbursts and low tolerance for frustration may result in behavior that is problematic and costly for other people in the child's environment. However, until the student himself experiences cost, such as loss of privileges that occurs when he demonstrates impulsive anger outbursts, he will have little reason to change the behavior. In fact, the student may be getting secondary gain for exhibiting a tantrum. An example of secondary gain would be getting sent home from school, so the rest of the day can be spent playing video games or watching television. This child is unlikely to have any emotional investment in making changes until the consequences of the behavior also change.

A client who is further along in the readiness process, and in the contemplation stage, may be more amenable to confrontation and challenging because the person is less likely to respond with denial of a problem. An individual in the contemplation stage may be more open minded and willing to consider multiple aspects of a problem, and more open to the idea of making behavior changes.

In the preparation, action, or maintenance stages, gentle confrontations may be more likely to have an impact on the client's thinking, because he or she is more emotionally invested in making changes. Therefore, your evaluation of where your client lies on the continuum of readiness for change may have some bearing on whether, or how, you confront.

Carrying Out the Confrontation

Two aspects of actualizing this particular counseling strategy need to be in your conscious awareness as you supportively challenge your clients. One aspect involves the words you use when you confront, and the other is the paraverbal and nonverbal behavior you exhibit as you are challenging.

WORDS   Choose your words carefully *before* you speak. Don't be afraid to let a few moments of silence elapse as you gather your thoughts and decide how to express your challenge. Some people are, by nature, more blunt than others; if the recipient is a person with high ego strength, he or she may be able to respond to your bluntness without being defensive or overly apologetic. If the recipient has low ego strength, however, a blunt challenge from a counselor could be devastating.

There are myriad ways to confront. Regardless of the particular method you use, it is probably most helpful to use concrete, behavioral observation, preferably as succinctly as possible. Sometimes a description of the contradictory behavior, thoughts, or feelings is enough. One option is to simply state your observation and then wait in silence for your client's response. You also can follow your observation with a statement or question that will structure your client's response.

Examples include the following:

- I know you're telling me _____, and yet over the past couple of weeks, I've seen you _____. (*Here is where you could stop, or then proceed with the following phrase*) I want to make sense of this and I'm wondering if you can help me understand it.
- At one time you've said _____, and at another, I've heard you say_(*Stop here or go on with the following*) How do these two things go together for you?
- Although you're saying you feel _____, your facial expression and body posture suggest that you feel _____. Tell me more about that.

Several clients were described earlier in this chapter. For each of those individuals, we will briefly review his or her situation, examine an example of inappropriate confrontation, explain why that confrontation is inappropriate, and offer an example of a more appropriate confrontation.

ADELE   a woman who has been court-ordered for substance abuse counseling and had multiple positive drug screens

INAPPROPRIATE CONFRONTATION:

COUNSELOR: Adele, what were you *thinking*? Didn't you remember the paper you signed saying I'd be writing a report for the court?

This counselor statement is inappropriate because it is somewhat demeaning to Adele. Additionally, this particular question about the counselor's report going back to the court is a closed question. The client is likely to respond with a single "yes" or "no" and then be either sullen or argumentative.

APPROPRIATE CHALLENGE:

COUNSELOR: Adele, I was very confused when I got the urinalysis report back today. I saw several positive results, and this didn't match at all with what you've been saying in counseling.

This is a counselor statement that, although direct and blunt, is not accusatory, nor does it imply stupidity on the part of the client.

MIKE   the teen who is trying to decide about college and is being pressured into a soccer scholarship by his father

INAPPROPRIATE CHALLENGE:

COUNSELOR: Mike, when you talk about this scholarship thing, your facial expression gives me the impression that it's more about what your dad wants than it is what you want. I really think you should just stand up to him and tell him it's your life. What's stopping you?

This is inappropriate for a couple of reasons. First, the counselor is assuming that his interpretation of Mike's facial expression is correct, and he has not given Mike the opportunity to verify the accuracy of his perception. Second, he is giving the client a directive as to what he should
do, which is not respectful of the client's autonomy. Ironically, the *counselor* is telling the client
what to do: that the client should speak up and not let his *father* tell him what to do. This is truly
a conundrum! It certainly is not conducive to Mike learning how to come to his own conclusions
and plan of action, which, in this case, seems to be centrally related to the presenting problem.

Following is a more gentle, respectful, and appropriate way to confront Mike's
discrepancy.

COUNSELOR: Mike, as you tell me about this scholarship, I note that your voice tone
is sort of flat and there is a furrow on your brow. It doesn't look to me
as if you are feeling excited or enthusiastic about it.

This is an example of a place where silence could have more impact than continued
talking. By simply offering his observation of the discrepancy, he gives the client room and
time to more fully get in touch with his ambivalent feelings, of which Mike may not be completely aware.

KIARA   the teen who perceives her father as both neglectful and too invasive in
wanting to spend time with her

INAPPROPRIATE CONFRONTATION:

COUNSELOR: Kiara, you've complained at length about your dad spending too much
time on the computer and neglecting you. I would think you'd be thrilled
to have him ask to take you to the movies and dinner. So which is it?
Does he neglect you, or does he bug you and not give you time alone?

These questions might be precisely what is going through the counselor's mind, and with
good reason. However, the phrasing of the question puts Kiara in a bind: Her perception
must be one or the other. Asking, "Which is it?" makes this a black-and-white issue without
room for nuances of emotion. As we discussed in the feeling reflection chapter, emotions
are often complex and involve more than one quality. In this case, it is possible that because
Kiara was neglected by her mother, she is particularly sensitive to and attuned to someone
not giving her full, undivided attention. At the same time, though, she may also desire autonomy. At Kiara's chronological age, it is developmentally typical to have ambivalent feelings about spending time with a parent.

APPROPRIATE CHALLENGE:

COUNSELOR: I can hear the sadness you express when you talk about your dad spending so much time on his computer and not giving you attention. And I
also can hear, and see, the frustration you felt when you just wanted to
spend time alone in your room, and he insisted you go out for dinner and
a movie with him. But I'm a bit confused and I'm hoping you can help
me understand: How can he be neglectful and invasive at the same time?

HEIDI   the woman in an unhealthy relationship with the substance-abusing,
promiscuous boyfriend

INAPPROPRIATE CHALLENGE:

COUNSELOR: Heidi, it's clear from what you've said that the relationship with Greg is so bad for you. I see *so many* potential risks for you, staying with him. Do you realize that *you* could be arrested for drug possession even though you don't use? You could contract a sexually transmitted disease from him, and perhaps worst of all, his behavior toward you completely discounts your value. How much worse does it have to get before you bail out?

This counselor may feel justified in her bluntness because of the elevated risk for Heidi if she remains in the relationship. However, obviously in Heidi's perception it's not yet "bad enough," because Heidi is still there. She has yet to hit "rock bottom," which can be scary because rock bottom might be a dangerous crisis of some sort. Nevertheless, the last sentence implies that the counselor has attachment to Heidi making the decision to leave. Change in Heidi's relationship with her boyfriend will not occur until Heidi herself is emotionally and mentally prepared to carry out different behaviors. Therefore, it would be more effective for the counselor instead to help Heidi explore her conflicted feelings and the emotional and other barriers to leaving.

APPROPRIATE CHALLENGE:

COUNSELOR: Heidi, as I was thinking back over our last couple of sessions, I realized that we spend a lot of our time talking about Greg's behavior and how upsetting it is for you. Yet you've also stated that other than his cocaine use, messing around with other women, and accusing you of being "paranoid," your relationship is good. When you say that otherwise your relationship is good, what do you mean? Like, what's good about it?

NONVERBAL AND PARAVERBAL BEHAVIORS DURING CONFRONTATION   It will come as no surprise that once again, you are strongly advised to be mindful of your paralinguistics during a challenge. Conflicted thoughts, feelings, and behaviors elicit anxiety for our clients, which leads to their inconsistencies. Know that even though a particular solution to their problems might seem obvious to you, the solution is not so obvious or easy to them. Consider how you like to be spoken to when you are struggling with a dilemma. A soft voice tone and an open posture, perhaps leaning in, all can help create the least threatening atmosphere possible. These nonverbal behaviors are an invitation for your client to slow down and reflect upon, or explore, the discrepancies you are trying to bring to his or her awareness.

As noted above, even with clients whose behavior is egregiously harmful to others, the most effective methods of challenging are supportive, not aggressive. Remember that in the context of behaviors harmful to others, such as sexual or physical abuse, a confrontation can be firm and simultaneously supportive, as opposed to accusatory or shaming. In these cases, the confrontation is likely to take the form of insisting that the client take personal responsibility for choosing the harmful behaviors rather than blaming some external source (e.g., the victim, or the circumstances).

Some therapists find it impossible not to be angry or offended by a client's behavior. You may find yourself unable to separate your personal feelings about the client's behavior from your interaction with the client. If this is the case, it will be extremely important for you to process your feelings with your supervisor, and to decide whether it would be in your best interest, and therefore the client's best interest, for your client to work with a different counselor.

How You Respond to Your Client's Response

At first glance, this may seem like an odd thing to identify. Nevertheless, it is an aspect of confrontation that may have significant bearing upon the impact your confrontation has on your client. Counselors, especially when they are new to the field, may experience a dilemma when they see a client acting in a way that seems self-defeating or that seems to undermine his or her efforts to live more effectively.

Observing a client's contradictory behaviors or thoughts may be a source of frustration for a counselor. The frustration could be the result of any of several factors:

- The counselor is very invested in effectively helping the client.
- The counselor believes that the source of the conflict and the "right" solution are obvious.
- The counselor is worried about the possible risks to which the client is exposing him- or herself.
- The counselor is tired of the client continuing to come to counseling expressing desire for change, but persisting in the problematic behaviors between sessions.

AUTHOR'S REFLECTION _____

When I first began seeing clients who were paying for the therapy I was providing, I felt a huge responsibility to make sure clients were getting their money's worth. Thus, when clients would struggle for many sessions or over an extended period of time, but not take action, I often became frustrated and perceived their lack of progress as a reflection of my inability to be a "good" therapist. I had a strong investment in my clients choosing, or behaving, in a particular way. Subsequently, if my confrontation was met with denial or with partial acknowledgment but no behavior change, I struggled to suppress my frustration.

Counselor frustration might be most likely to emerge when a client is in a state of pre-contemplation or partial awareness of the problem. However, responding with frustration is unlikely to result in a client's willingness to look more honestly at his or her own conflicts. Because you may find yourself in a state of frustration about your clients' denial of contradictory behavior or ambivalent feelings, it makes sense for us to discuss possible responses.

In this section we are going to take another look at Adele, because her behavior is not only most contradictory, but also most risky. This time we'll begin with an appropriate confrontation of Adele. This example will begin with the appropriate counselor challenge, as it appeared above. It will follow with responses from Adele that are representative of each of three degrees of acknowledgment, and then appropriate and inappropriate counselor responses to each of those. This dialogue is diagrammed in Table 10.1.

IMMEDIACY

We will look now at one of the most advanced of the microskills, immediacy. It is advanced in that when used properly, it can serve as a tremendous catalyst in the counseling process. However, use of immediacy can also be risky because if the counselor has not accurately

TABLE 10.1   Counselor Responses to Different Levels of Client Acknowledgment

Counselor:
Adele, I was very confused when I got the urinalysis report back today. I saw several positive results and this didn't match at all with what you've been saying in counseling. What are your thoughts and feelings about that?

Adele (in denial):
Well, my thought is that that lab doesn't know what they're talking about. Do you know how many hundreds of people go there for testing every day? I'm sure they mixed up my results with someone else's.

Counselor inappropriate:
You are lying. I honestly don't think there is any more point in our continuing the work together. I'll send the letter to the judge saying you've failed the program. We can end this meeting now.

Counselor appropriate:
I do know how many people go there, and I also know for a fact that their system is set up in such a way that there is a 99% chance for accuracy in a single report. In your case, there are actually three positive results, so for all three to be wrong, the chances are pretty much nonexistent. So, Adele, imagine you were in my shoes right now. Knowing the judge is expecting a report about a client who gave us this urine profile, what would you say?

Adele (partial acknowledgment):
On that one that happened on the Monday after I'd been out that weekend, I hoped maybe I'd get lucky. But I only used one time and the other times, I don't know what to tell you. I think the lab made a mistake.

Counselor inappropriate:
To say "lucky" is ridiculous. There is no luck involved in recovery. It's about working hard to get straight and stay straight. Looks to me like you just don't have the willpower to do that.

Counselor appropriate:
There are a couple of issues here. I have to be candid and tell you that I don't know, now, when you are and aren't telling me the truth. We can come back to that at some point. First, let's talk about hoping you'd get lucky. What do you mean by that?

Adele (acknowledgment):
I can't believe you got that report. I heard that it would be out of my system before I had to submit my urine sample. I really don't think I'm going to be able to kick.

Counselor inappropriate:
Well, believe it. We run a tight ship around here and to think you'll get away with anything is just completely clueless. You'll be able to kick when you decide you're ready to kick. Haven't you been listening to the group leader? It's up to you.

Counselor appropriate:
Adele, I really appreciate that you're finally being honest with me. I hear that you are scared about trying to quit. Tell me about that—what's scary?

assessed the client's ability to tolerate immediacy, using immediacy could be detrimental to the therapeutic alliance.

Immediacy, a form of confrontation that also integrates counselor self-disclosure, refers to bringing the client's awareness and the focus of discussion to the present moment in the counseling session. Use of immediacy may have the effect of intensifying whatever emotions are being processed or focused upon as the client's awareness of present experiencing is accentuated. One way to use immediacy, according to Patterson and Welfel (2005), is for the counselor to share his or her reaction to changes in the client's engagement or participation in the counseling. When this type of immediacy is used, appropriate implementation would take the form of the counselor using an "I" message, rather than a "you" message. Here is a dialogue example:

> COUNSELOR: Sue, one of the things I've noticed about our discussion today is that you are much more forthcoming as you shared information with me. It seems like it was hard for you; in the past I've noticed that we talk a lot about other people in your life. Sometimes it seems to me that when you and I sit down to talk, a crowd of people comes along, and that I can't see you behind all those other people. What do you suppose is different about today?

This counselor is bringing attention to the perception he has of the client in that moment. This is a strategy that can be either fruitful or quite off-putting for a client. Some prior studies (e.g., Hill, Thompson, Cogar, & Denman, 2001) have found that clients often leave things unsaid, either related to things happening between the counselor and client in the counseling session, or related to their feelings and thoughts. For example, sometimes a client may perceive a counselor as trying to change a client's feelings about a particular issue.

Skilled counselors tend to be more aware of client reactions in session (Thompson & Hill, 1991), and in one study, this awareness was related to the clients subsequently giving higher ratings of therapist helpfulness. When a counselor senses that a client is feeling some discomfort with the counseling relationship, or that there are things between the counselor and client that have not been said, it is best to initiate with an "I" statement rather than a "you" statement. This will reduce the chance of the client reacting defensively. Here are two examples of how to do that:

Example 1

> COUNSELOR: If it's okay, I'd like you to tell me more about what your experience was with your mom this past week.
>
> ABIGAIL: I can't tell you that. It's too hard.
>
> COUNSELOR: I can see how much pain you have as you share this. *(The counselor chooses to use immediacy instead of doing a feeling reflection because the client just said it's too hard)* I guess my dilemma is that in the past when I've pushed you a little bit to share, you've been relieved afterward that you were able to get it out. So I'm wondering now whether I should just accept your answer that you can't tell me, or encourage you to tell me more.
>
> ABIGAIL: *(Silence, shoulder shrug)*
>
> COUNSELOR: Perhaps instead you could tell me what's hard about telling me.

Example 2

> CLIENT: Just now, when you said it's my choice, it makes me feel like you think it's my fault I'm staying in this bad marriage.
>
> COUNSELOR: What did I say that made you think I blame you?
>
> CLIENT: You don't understand what it's like to be in my family and have your parents expect you to just stick it out.

COUNSELOR: I was raised to see women as able to choose their own paths. I hear you saying you feel as though I've used my own learning to judge your behavior. Am I hearing that correctly?

This type of interchange might be beneficial in those counseling situations where there are differences between the counselor and client on some essential values. Making those differences overt and a topic of discussion may increase the chance that the client feels heard. This will particularly be the case if the counselor is willing to acknowledge that her or his values do not represent an absolute right way of seeing the world.

CULTURAL CONSIDERATIONS IN CHALLENGING

We have talked in prior chapters about the impact of a mismatch in the axes of cultural variability. In the context of confrontation, it seems prudent to focus on how a cultural mismatch might affect the *process* of confrontation in a session rather than the *content* of a confrontation. Two of the four cultural variables are most likely to influence how the process of a confrontation might unfold. Following are brief summaries of each of the four axes, and then examples of how process could be affected for two of them: power distance and gender roles.

Power Distance

This axis deals with the extent to which members of a culture accept and expect that there will be a power differential between those in authority and subordinates.

A client who holds a value of high power distance might feel apprehensive or fearful if he or she thinks the counselor is negatively judging his or her conflicted thoughts, feelings, or behaviors. Therefore, if you are aware that your client has a high power distance, it will be important to be very gentle and as neutral as possible when you do the confrontation.

Table 10.2 gives examples of dialogues with high and low power distance.

Gender Roles

Recall that this axis is concerned with two things: the way a culture distributes roles and jobs across both genders, and also the extent to which there is fluidity of values and behaviors in general across both genders. In other words, a culture with low masculinity would be

---

TABLE 10.2   Dialogue Responses to a High Power Distance Client

Client (with a value of high power distance): So on one hand, my boss tells me I must make my job a priority, but at the same time he announces that other people will have to cover for him because he is taking his family on a cruise for the next two weeks.

Inappropriate counselor response from a counselor coming from a low power distance value:

Counselor (projecting a low power distance): I can see how distraught you are about this, since you'll have to miss your son's first birthday party to work. I guess I'm confused about why you would just take that lying down when your boss's behavior is so hypocritical. Why not just tell him how you feel about this?

Appropriately culturally sensitive response to the same client statement:

Counselor: I'd be very upset, too, if I were in that spot. I get the sense that you see this as very hypocritical on your boss's part, yet at the same time you feel unable to do anything about it. In what ways does that stuckness take a toll on you?

accepting and supportive of androgynous values and nonverbal behaviors. In a culture with high masculinity, the gender roles are extremely clear with regard to who does which tasks, as well as which expressed emotions and behaviors are acceptable from each gender.

Perhaps the main way gender roles would play a role in the process of a confrontation would be if the counselor were female and the client were a male with a high masculinity orientation. A male client with high masculinity might believe that it is untoward for a female to challenge a male for any reason. A confrontation in this situation might result in the client being offended or alienated.

Affiliation

This is the axis defined by the extent to which a person's culture defines allegiance to the collective as an important aspect of a person's behavior. High affiliation societies expect an individual's actions to be considered in a group context, as opposed to an individual context.

The variable of affiliation does not seem to carry much in the way of implication for process regarding confrontation. We do need, to reiterate, though, that particularly if the counselor has a Western, individualistic orientation, a client whose affiliation is highly collective will have a divergent view about where his or her responsibilities lie. This is a topic that could be a source of inappropriate challenging on the part of the counselor.

Uncertainty Avoidance

This axis has to do with a person's preference for structure, and to some extent, it seems related to autonomy. People in cultures with low uncertainty avoidance are comfortable with ambiguity and unstructured situations. People from cultures with high uncertainty avoidance live in societies with clear, explicit rules about right and wrong and rigid guidelines about acceptable behavior.

Here again, uncertainty avoidance in and of itself does not seem to have implications for process in confrontation. On the other hand, differences between counselor and client in this variable, as in affiliation, could definitely be a basis for significant disagreement and a perception on the part of the counselor that a confrontation is in order.

CONFRONTATION IN THE CONTEXT OF THREE THEORETICAL STANCES

Earlier in the chapter we talked about a person's state of internal tension and considered the various terminology used to describe that tension. The internal tension, or disequilibrium, that gives rise to contradictory behavior or ambivalent feelings and thoughts may be the very thing that motivates a person to seek counseling. A challenge or confrontation would not necessarily look or sound any different regardless of which theory base a counselor was using. Instead, the theoretical objective of the confrontation is the part that would vary. Therefore, comparison tables of confrontation from the three stances have not been included.

Humanistic

In this group of theories, humans are perceived as having a drive toward congruence and alignment. However, when the presenting situation (contradictory feelings, thoughts, or experiences) is too anxiety provoking, we generally try to achieve alignment by disowning or suppressing the parts of ourselves that aren't aligned. Thus, in the humanistic realm of approaching counseling, the overarching goal is helping the person to move toward congruence and alignment within him or herself.

The main technique for helping a client achieve this alignment is to bring the suppressed parts into his or her awareness. Where a person-centered counselor might want to help the client achieve congruence, a Gestalt counselor's goal would be achieved if the client were simply fully aware of and owning all the disjointed parts. From a Gestalt perspective, the very process of acknowledgment and ownership is enough to catalyze integration.

Developmental

Developmental crises are often fraught with conflicts (e.g., Erikson's stages) and those conflicts take the form of ambivalent feelings and contradictory behaviors and thoughts. Thus, the goal is to help the client achieve resolution of the conflict by fully exploring all the aspects and angles of the conflict, and possibly to gently guide the client toward a healthy, effective resolution.

Cognitive-Behavioral

When a person's talk and behavior are inconsistent, the behavior may be a more accurate reflection of his or her true thoughts and feelings. In the cognitive-behavioral approach the therapist is not necessarily looking for contradictions. Instead, the focus is more upon elucidating the cognitions and behaviors that are contributing to and maintaining the client's difficulties. There might be efforts made to identify contradictory or incompatible self-statements, or self-statements that contradict the reality of a given situation. In this approach, the counselor would work to help the client create realistic, rational self-talk and interpretations of external situations and of self-appraisal. In the cognitive-behavioral context, confrontation often centers around issues of compliance with homework assignments and commitment to the goals of treatment.

Chapter Summary

Confrontation and challenging are counseling techniques that can be extremely effective when used judiciously. Whereas some of the earlier microskills, such as paraphrasing, could be comparatively benign if done inappropriately, a confrontation can be quite detrimental if used inappropriately. It should be used with caution.

When a client comes to counseling in a state of incongruence or conflict, he or she may have varying levels of awareness about (1) the nature of the conflict, and (2) what he or she is doing to reduce the conflict. Your role as a counselor will be to help your client become fully aware of the conflict, be able to articulate the nature of the contradiction, and then possibly reestablish some balance with a reduction of the psychic tension associated with the conflict.

A number of variables will play a role in determining the effectiveness of your confrontation. These variables include timing, carrying out the challenge, and how you respond to your client's response. Despite a significant degree of distress because of ambivalence, if the timing is not right, the client will be unable to appropriately resolve the ambivalence. In the process of delivery, paraverbals are extremely important in ensuring that the client will be able to hear and respond appropriately to your attempts to confront. Particularly if the client is emotionally fragile, you need to be extremely mindful of how you are giving the challenge. Finally, if you respond indignantly or resentfully to a client who is maintaining denial, you risk damaging what rapport you have worked to establish.

Your own frustration with your clients' ambivalence is something with which you must cope. Coping with your feelings that are engendered in counseling and also related to other aspects of your life will be one of our discussion topics in Chapter 16, when we talk about self-care. For now, the important thing is that you need to be adequately self-aware that you are not permitting your expectations of someone else's behavior to inappropriately influence the way you are reacting to him or her. On the other hand, if you are able to master this skill, a well-timed, appropriately phrased confrontation might be one of the most influential strategies you will implement with a client.

Questions for Class Discussion

1. How was conflict handled in your family of origin? Did people face it head on or avoid it? How did that affect the family interactions?
2. What do you see as your primary responsibility as a counselor? That is, is it your job to actively point out the places where your client is contradicting himself or acting in self-defeating ways?
3. Think back over your own life and the times when you made some kind of big change. Did your internal process of becoming aware and then making the change parallel Prochaska's readiness model? In what ways was your process consistent with the model, and in what ways did it differ?
4. On a scale of 1 to 10, with 10 being completely comfortable and 1 being extremely anxious or uncomfortable, what number best describes your comfort level with confronting people? What do you see as your personal assets and liabilities regarding confrontation?

Case Studies for Discussion

CLIENT CASE EXAMPLE: CAROLE

In the last meeting with Carol, she was struggling with whether to continue in counseling. The counselor suggested that there might be some possibilities for Carole to meet her needs for having some role and activities outside of the home, and also be able to be a "good mother and wife."

COUNSELOR:	Last time, Carole, I offered you the possibility of looking at alternatives to your having to choose one or the other. What thoughts and feelings have you had about that over this past week?
CAROLE:	Part of me is excited and part of me is afraid to be excited, because I don't see how it could possibly be true. But I guess I would like to hear what you have to say.
COUNSELOR:	Okay. Let's start with what, for you, defines being a "good mom" and a "good wife"?
CAROLE:	A good mother is someone who is home when the kids come home from school. She has cookies and milk waiting on the table and is ready

to sit down with them to talk about their day. She's the person the children come to first when they are sad, scared, or upset. She puts healthy home-cooked meals on the table every night.

COUNSELOR: In your view, are you a good mom now?

CAROLE: Yes.

COUNSELOR: And what parts of that role do you imagine you would have to give up if you got trained in nursing?

CAROLE: I'd be working different shifts all the time. They would come home to an empty house. I wouldn't know what was going on in their lives. They would start to run the streets and there would be no one here to stop them.

COUNSELOR: Here's what I wondered about. Have you ever considered finding someplace to start out by doing some volunteer work, maybe just one or two mornings a week?

CAROLE: How can I do that?

COUNSELOR: What do you mean?

CAROLE: Like where would I go to volunteer? How would I get there? I have nothing to put on an application! Why would they want me—I mean, what do I have to offer anyone?

COUNSELOR: I hear the fear and discouragement in your voice. On one hand you would like to have a career and believe that your family is what holds you back. But just now, the fears and questions you raised sounded to me like it has a lot more to do with whether someone else will think you are good enough.

CAROLE: (*Silence and tears*)

COUNSELOR: Did you know that this part of your feelings was in there?

CAROLE: No! I used to be a poor student, but I thought I'd gotten over that. Now here I am feeling like a failure and I haven't even started yet.

COUNSELOR: Let's suppose I could put you in touch with a clinic that would be interested in having you do some volunteer work. Would you be willing to give it a try?

CAROLE: What if I failed?

COUNSELOR: Great question! Let's talk about that. In what way might you fail?

Questions for Discussion about Carole's Case Study

1. How would this line of questioning be beneficial to Carole?
2. What would you do differently with her than the counselor did in this session, and why?
3. To what extent should the counselor get involved with helping Carole make the arrangements for volunteer work?

CLIENT CASE EXAMPLE: DEREK

In the last session, Derek was able to implement some improved coping strategies in order to avoid overt conflict at school. He also admitted that his main motivation for seeing the school counselor was getting out of class. However, his behavior at home has not been consistently positive or appropriate.

COUNSELOR:	We came up with a plan last week about what you were going to say and do when Grandma gives you your chores for the day. How did that plan go?
DEREK:	Okay sometimes. Not okay other times.
COUNSELOR:	Tell me about the times it did work.
DEREK:	I was in a pretty good mood, and I figured I might as well just get it done so I can go out to play.
COUNSELOR:	You chose to just go along with the program.
DEREK:	Yep.
COUNSELOR:	And what about the "not okay " times?
DEREK:	Sometimes I get really ticked off when she's all up in my face, so I just ignore her.
COUNSELOR:	What is it about those times that makes you ticked off?
DEREK:	I don't know. Just depends on the day.
COUNSELOR:	So I hear you saying that on one hand, whether the day goes okay is pretty much in your control, and at the same time, when it's not going okay, you don't know why.
DEREK:	Yep.
COUNSELOR:	Hmmm. That's confusing to me.

(Prolonged silence. Derek gazes out the window.)

COUNSELOR:	Take today, for instance. Is this an okay day or a not okay day?
DEREK:	I'd say more not okay.
COUNSELOR:	Let's go back to this morning when your alarm went off. Did you know then that it was going to be a bad day?
DEREK:	I don't know.

(Silence)

DEREK:	I guess I woke up mad.
COUNSELOR:	How come?
DEREK:	*(Eyes filling with tears)* I miss my mom! I miss my old school! I don't want to be here.

Questions for Discussion about Derek's Case Study

1. What is your first reaction to Derek's disclosure?
2. How does his disclosure affect your theory framework for conceptualizing his issues?
3. Do you think the counselor pushed Derek too hard with the challenging questions? Why or why not?
4. What would be the very next thing you would say to Derek?

CHAPTER 11

Counseling Theories

After studying this chapter, you should have a clear understanding of the following:

- Major conceptual differences among three major groups of theories
- How treatment techniques are embedded within a theoretical framework
- How differences in theories relate to differences in the way microskills are used
- The relationship between your chosen theory and sensitivity to variables of diversity in your clients

INTRODUCTION

A theory is a working set of principles that are constructed to offer an explanation for a phenomenon. It is a series of assumptions that are recognized to be assumptions, but are, at least temporarily, accepted to be true in order to have a conceptual framework with which to perceive, understand, and explain phenomena. Theory development and empirical investigation to prove or disprove theories, occur in many academic disciplines; counseling and psychology are no exception. There have been a multitude of theories developed and tested to account for various aspects of human development and behavior. The terms *theory* and *model* are often used interchangeably.

This chapter provides an overview of some foundational theories in the field of counseling. After the overview of theories, we will touch briefly upon some of the other, more recent developments related to theory. Please bear in mind that this chapter is intended as a very brief glimpse of these theories so that, if you have not yet taken a course in counseling theories, you will understand some of the basic counseling theories and how a counselor's theoretical leaning will influence the choice of how, and especially *why*, to employ a particular microskill at a given time.

Numerous authors (Bergin & Garfield, 1994; Hubble, Duncan, & Miller, 1999) have noted that there are over 200 models of therapy in existence, and over 400 different techniques associated with those models! Beyond the fact that there are such a huge number of them, one of the aspects of theories with which many beginning counseling students struggle is that different theories offer learners a variety of ways to consider and understand a given behavior. Rest assured that you are not alone if you feel confused about how to select a theory. Weinrach (2006) noted, "Unfortunately, the state of the art of theory construction is such that even well-informed scholars rarely agree among themselves. The theories are complex, and the empirical evidence is often sketchy" (p. 157).

As an applied example, we might observe a woman attending a loud, lively party and note that she is acting quiet and withdrawn, sitting in a corner with her head down. The model developed by the person-centered theorists to explain her behavior is substantially different from the model developed by the theorists who are focused on human development. As well, the strategies about how best to help that woman overcome her social withdrawal will look very different.

Consideration of different theories is of great relevance to you as early learners of basic counseling skills, because whatever theory we use will influence not only our understanding of the woman's party behavior, but also will determine how we define counseling goals. Moreover, counseling techniques and strategies arise out of the tenets of a theory; to use a counseling technique without understanding the overarching theory is not an acceptable standard of practice.

PERSONAL REFLECTION

Based on your life experiences, including classes and observing yourself and others, articulate your thoughts about what makes people "tick." What do you believe motivates and shapes us? How much of our tendencies and temperaments are we born with ("nature") and how much are we taught ("nurture")?

The Relationship Between Theory and Microskills

The basic counseling microskills being covered in this text have potential application across a variety of counseling models. However, the *manner* in which the skills are used, the *intention* behind choice of particular skills, and the decision about *when* to use them are driven by the choice of theory or combination of theories the counselor is using. Thus, it is essential that we cover some basic, common counseling theories so that, when we discuss pros and cons of using particular microskills for a given client, we can place those pros and cons in the context of a theoretical conceptualization. Training programs typically require a course in helping theories; in that course, these models are examined in much greater detail.

We cannot escape theories, just as we cannot escape our cultural templates. Many years ago, Ginter (1988) noted, "Therapy cannot exist without theory" (p. 3). It is difficult, if not impossible, to understand another person's experience and behavior without having some form of a mental model of how and why people do what they do. Even when we are not consciously aware that we are using a particular model for understanding human behavior, we nevertheless are using some internal theoretical conceptualization about people, their choices, and their behaviors.

Understanding our own mental models, as therapists, and bringing these internal representations acutely into our awareness is imperative in becoming a great counselor.

Despite the fact that there are so many different theories (Miller, Hubble, and Duncan, 1996, documented a 600% increase in theories since the 1960s), they can generally be grouped on the basis of key features of the models. A full discussion of the different ways to classify counseling theories is beyond the scope of this chapter. However, there are some broad categories of theories that represent three schools of thought that emerged in psychology and counseling. These categories represent what have historically been standard approaches (e.g., Zook & Walton, 1989) to training counselors.

The fields of counseling and psychology are continually growing and evolving; numerous approaches have emerged recently that appear to offer benefits for particular types of clients and presenting concerns. Toward the end of the chapter, we'll look at some of the current trends in the realm of theory.

Three Schools of Counseling and Therapy

The general schools of counseling theories we will cover are developmental, humanistic, and cognitive-behavioral. This sequence roughly parallels the temporal emergence of key theories over the mid and later 20th century. Freud's psychoanalysis was the dominant mode of helping people with emotional problems and was very influential as a basis for the emergence of many other theories that are developmental in nature. The humanistic-existential movement and the behavioral and cognitive movements (a subset of which merged to become cognitive-behavioral) primarily arose as the result of psychologists' frustration and discomfort with the Freudian psychoanalytic model of treatment (Archer & McCarthy, 2007; Corsini & Wedding, 2005).

The developmental models will include Adlerian theory, Erikson's model of psychosocial development, and attachment theory. The realm of humanistic theories will include person-centered, existential, and Gestalt. The cognitive-behavioral section will cover behaviorism, cognitive theory, and the cognitive-behavioral model. Table 11.1 provides a quick overview comparison of how each of the three schools conceptualizes the emphasis of counseling, and the corresponding microskills that would be highly instrumental in that process.

This chapter is divided into three sections that discuss each of the three broad schools of thought. The sections will have identical features for ease of comparison:

1. A description of the essential elements of that theory cluster
2. A presentation of three representative theories within the theory cluster
3. A description of two or three theories within that cluster; for each theory there will be sections titled:
   - Essence of the theory
   - Definition of psychopathology from that theory viewpoint
   - Goals of treatment and treatment strategies
   - Microskills in the context of that theory

DEVELOPMENTAL MODELS

We will begin by first talking about what the developmental models have in common, and then consider specific descriptions for a few of the commonly recognized theories. Commonalities of the developmental theories include the following assumptions:

- Human development occurs in stages over time.
- Relationships early in life become the template from which we establish relationships as adults.

TABLE 11.1   Comparison of Theory Groups

Theory Group	Nature of Relationship	Emphasis of Treatment (Prominent Themes)	Microskills Most Likely to Be Used Frequently
Developmental (Adler, Erikson, Bowlby)	Moderately directive Alliance is important; provides client a chance to resolve emotional needs not met during earlier development	• Healthy development • Focus on past experiences in family of origin and relationship to present difficulties • Resolution of conflict • Understanding and self-awareness	• Active listening • Client observation • Paraphrasing • Feeling reflection • Supportive challenging • Reflection of meaning
Humanistic (Person-Centered, Existential, Gestalt)	• Varies from nondirective (person-centered, existential) to highly directive (Gestalt) • Alliance is extremely important; is the basis of the treatment (person-centered, existential)	• Experiencing present moment • Accepting personal responsibility • Emphasis on freedom of choice • Authenticity, fully in touch with oneself	• Active listening • Client observation • Feeling reflection • Reflection of meaning • Supportive challenging (Gestalt)
Cognitive-Behavioral (Behavioral, Cognitive, Social Learning)	• Highly directive • Alliance only important to extent client feels engaged to participate in assignments	• Identification of behavioral excesses and inadequacies • Identification of reinforcers • Manipulation of the reinforcers to change the behavior and thought process	• Active listening • Questioning • Reflection of meaning • Supportive challenging

- All humans develop and progress in a predictable sequence with regard to emotional functioning.
- Disrupted development (including trauma or neglect) at a particular stage results in predictable behaviors, symptoms, and/or problems.
- Counseling and psychotherapy aim to recapitulate or correct earlier, disrupted development in order to affect change in the client.

The theories covered in this section are Adler's Individual Psychology model, Erikson's psychosocial model, and attachment theory (originated by Bowlby and Ainsworth). Table 11.2 provides a comparison of particular differences between theories on key points such as definition of psychopathology and treatment goals and techniques.

Both Adler and Erikson were initially trained in Freudian psychoanalysis and then moved away from pure psychoanalytic theory to articulate their own theories. Attachment theory is included in this section because in the past few decades there has been a vast amount of professional literature about attachment and attachment disorders (e.g., Buchheim, George,

TABLE 11.2 Developmental Theory Comparison

Theory	Definition of Pathology	Goals	Techniques	Evidence/ Support	Criticisms
Adlerian	Striving for superiority but with faulty goals Focus on self Lack of social interest	Increasing social interest Decreasing inferiority Overcoming discouragement	Focus on client's subjective experience Acting "as if" Task-setting Imagery for metaphors Push-button	Common therapeutic factors Research about family constellation with contradictory findings	Weak in empirical support (Archer & McCarthy, 2007)
Erikson's psychosocial model of development	Inadequate resolution of developmental tasks stalls progression	Recapitulation of early learning, resolution of developmental dilemma	None specified	Rejected the RCT model of data collection	Inadequate definition of some concepts
Attachment	Insecure or ambivalent attachment in childhood	Emotional regulation and ability to self-soothe	Treatment focus on the caregiver's response to the child	Research lies in area of associating attachment disorder with many forms of adult psychopathology (Myer & Pilkonis, 2006)	Lack of consensus about how to assess treatment or outcome (Stafford & Zeanah, 2006)

Kachele, Erk, & Walter, 2006; Schore, 2001; Stafford & Zeanah, 2006). Any counselor working with children is likely to work with youngsters who are exhibiting behavioral problems, such as oppositionalism or difficulty with peers; some of those clients will also have experienced a significant degree of neglect or trauma.

All developmental theorists have shared the concept that the nature and quality of our relationships in infancy and childhood set the stage for our ability in adulthood to establish and maintain relationships. Theorists vary in their definition of the most salient aspects of psychological development; for some, it has to do with ego development (e.g., Erikson, Loevinger, Maslow); for others, development of the ability to establish and maintain emotionally healthy relationships (e.g., Adler, Ainsworth, Bowlby).

Adlerian Theory

ESSENCE OF THE THEORY Early in Alfred Adler's career, he worked closely with Freud. However, Adler began to develop opinions about human nature that deviated significant from Freudian theory (Archer & McCarthy, 2007). In contrast to Freud's deterministic and somewhat pessimistic view of human development, Adler saw people as having control over their lives, rather than as victims of circumstance. Whereas Freud saw people as driven primarily by biological instincts from which there is no escape, Adler observed humans to be driven by social relationships and a deep need for interpersonal connectedness. For Adler, social interest was a core feature of being human.

Adler's theory, which he called "Individual Psychology," holds that our behavior always serves a purpose, and that we all possess innate striving for competence and adequacy. Adler saw human development and our striving as always embedded within a social context. Our ability to achieve goals we set for ourselves arises out of a basic sense of inadequacy.

It is important to note that what is most influential is our *perception* of our family's expectations. Our self-perception of inadequacy originates in our family of origin, and that self-perception gives rise to the creation of fictional goals. These goals represent to us the ultimate demonstration that the inadequacies have been overcome. With regard to the development of self-perception, Adler heavily emphasized birth order and family constellation as influential forces. Adler was the author who identified particular personality characteristics associated with ordinal position/birth order in the family of origin.

PERSONAL REFLECTION

What effect, if any, did your birth order in your family of origin have on your development? Can you identify particular ways that your birth order influenced your parents' (or caregivers') expectations for you? How has your perception of their expectations affected the adult you have become?

The inherent human striving for competence results in people being in a constant state of becoming (developing), moving toward fictional goals they set for themselves (Mosak & Maniacci, 2005); thus, we construct our lives to make meaning of our efforts to achieve competence. The way we construct (create) our lives is referred to as our *lifestyle*. In Adlerian theory, "lifestyle" is the very framework by which we live, including our most basic, core beliefs about the meaning of our existence, our corresponding values, and our perceptions of others and ourselves. The goals toward which we strive were referred to as fictional because they exist only in our own minds. Degree of social interest is a primary barometer of mental health (Mosak & Maniacci, 2005).

PSYCHOPATHOLOGY FROM AN ADLERIAN PERSPECTIVE   The choices we make and the behaviors we exhibit arise from our own private logic about how we can best improve our condition from inadequacy to adequacy. Thus, one of the ways that the Adlerian model can be helpful to counselors is to remind us to ask, "What purpose does this behavior (or symptom, or problem) serve this person?" Further, Nystul (2006) noted that this frame could be quite helpful in understanding a child's misbehavior.

GOALS OF TREATMENT AND TREATMENT STRATEGIES   An Adlerian counselor sees the process of counseling as educational (Nystul, 2006). From this theoretical standpoint the counselor will work with a client to discover the nature of her or his feelings of inadequacy as well as to uncover mistaken assumptions that are creating problems in the person's lifestyle. The counselor does this primarily by attempting to take the perspective of the client, seeing the world through his or her eyes, to fully understand what the client is attempting to achieve through the maladaptive or inappropriate behavior. Then the counselor will work to help the client become aware of what needs are being met through inappropriate behavior, and to then identify better ways to meet the needs. Eventually, as the individual moves toward appropriate need reduction, development of social interest is important.

MICROSKILLS IN AN ADLERIAN CONTEXT   An Adlerian would likely use attending skills, client observation, and questions. Restatements in the form of paraphrasing and summarizing could also be helpful in illuminating a client's fictional goals that drive the choices. Because the working alliance is an important component of the counseling process, minimal encouragers and immediacy might also be microskills an Adlerian therapist would be likely to implement. The following links on the MyHelpingLab website will provide you with two examples of how an Adlerian counselor would use this theory in a session.

myhelpinglab

Video Lab > By Course > Theories of Counseling and Psychotherapy > Module 3: Adlerian Therapy >
⇒ **Discussing Family Constellations**
⇒ **Establishing Lifestyle Themes**

Erikson's Psychosocial Development Theory

ESSENCE OF THE THEORY Erikson departed from pure Freudian theory to incorporate culture and society, beyond biology, as additional forces in the determination of human behavior. Erikson worked with people of many different chronological stages who were functioning at varying levels (Schuster & Ashburn, 1980).

Erikson (1980) said, "[The epigenetic principle] . . . states that anything that grows has a ground plan, and that out of this ground plan the parts arise, each part having its time of special ascendancy, until all parts have arisen to form a functioning whole" (p. 53). The essence of Erikson's theory of psychosocial development is that people develop in a sociocultural context, highly dependent on interaction with other people. Our cumulative life experiences create our *ego identity*, which is defined as the view we hold of ourselves.

Our life experiences and ego identities evolve throughout our life. Beginning in infancy, there are particular psychosocial challenges that parallel cognitive and neurological development. These challenges manifest within us as emotional needs and ambivalent feelings about our needs. Erikson's developmental progression is presented in Table 11.3.

One key aspect of this theory is the nature of stage progression. It is possible for an individual to struggle with two stages simultaneously. It is possible for development to

TABLE 11.3 Erikson's Model (Erikson, 1980)

Stage	Developmental Task	Successful Resolution	Outcome of Delay in This Stage
Infancy	Trust	Drive and hope	Basic mistrust
Early childhood	Autonomy	Self-control and willpower	Shame and doubt
Play age	Initiative	Direction and purpose	Guilt
School age	Industry	Method and competence	Inferiority
Adolescence	Identity	Devotion and fidelity	Identity confusion
Young adulthood	Intimacy	Affiliation and love	Isolation
Adulthood	Generativity	Production and care	Stagnation
Mature age	Ego integrity	Renunciation and wisdom	Despair

advance at an uneven rate, or for a person's level of development to regress to an earlier stage in reaction to trauma. Factors beyond a person's control, such as genetics and the environment, can influence the rate of progression. Lack of appropriate resolution of a conflict results in the appearance of the negative counterpart and mental illness (Schuster & Ashburn, 1980).

PSYCHOPATHOLOGY FROM AN ERIKSONIAN PERSPECTIVE   Table 11.3 features a column entitled, "Outcome of Delay in This Stage." In the Erikson model, pathology is equated with unsuccessful resolution of a crisis at a given stage of development. The way in which pathology is evident will depend on the nature of the unresolved crisis. Whereas a person with unresolved trust issues may have trouble sustaining long-term relationships, a person with unresolved identity issues may be able to maintain relationships but struggle with finding a satisfying career.

GOALS OF TREATMENT AND TREATMENT STRATEGIES   The essence of treatment is successful resolution of the developmental crisis, enabling a person to move on to the next stage. For example, if a young man were struggling with whether to make a significant emotional commitment to his girlfriend, the developmental dilemma would be intimacy or isolation. Upon making his decision to commit to her and propose marriage, the question of commitment, for him, would fade into the background. The Eriksonian model does not specifically prescribe a particular approach to treatment or specific strategies. The applicability of this model in our present context has most to do with conceptualizing the developmental context in which clients will experience distress or demonstrate competent, developmentally appropriate behavior.

Attachment Theory

ESSENCE OF THE THEORY   John Bowlby and Mary Ainsworth originated attachment theory; this model holds that crucial bonding needs to occur between a child and the primary caregiver during infancy and early childhood. The infant's relationship experiences create the emotional template with which he or she develops all subsequent relationships throughout life.

This theory is essentially an exclusive focus on Erikson's basic trust versus mistrust crisis. A "secure attachment" occurs when a child is dependent on a caregiver and the caregiver reliably meets the child's needs. In this process, the caregiver provides for some of the child's impulses to be met while other impulses are restricted. Gradually, throughout maturation, the child acquires the ability neurologically and emotionally to be independently responsible for regulating and meeting those needs (Bretherton, 1992).

PERSONAL REFLECTION _____

What is your reaction to the attachment theory view of human functioning? Is the caregiver/child bond so central that it influences the nature of relationships for the rest of a person's life? How did your own relationship with your primary caregivers set the stage for your later relationships?

The construct of attachment may be one of the few frameworks that actually have a diagnostic category in the DSM-IV stipulating a set of symptoms directly related to the definition of the theory itself. Whereas many other types of disorders stand independently, with a set of symptoms that can be understood from a variety of theoretical lenses (e.g., anxiety disorders or mood disorders), the very DSM-IV-TR diagnosis of reactive attachment disorder (APA, 2000) is predicated on acceptance of attachment theory as a viable interpretation of observable reality.

Due in part to substantial advances in medical technology, recent research has illuminated a great deal of new data about the interdependent nature of the self and the relationship environment in the realm of neuropsychological development (Schore, 2001). *Attachment* has been identified as "a biologically based behavioral system that influences motivational, cognitive, emotional, and memory process with respect to intimate relationships" (Buchheim, George, Kachele, Erk, & Walter, 2006, p. 136).

PSYCHOPATHOLOGY FROM AN ATTACHMENT PERSPECTIVE   In attachment theory, when the bonding does not occur in a manner that consistently meets the child's needs, impairment occurs in the child's ability to trust others in relationships. It is likely that over the course of your time working with students or clients, you will work with individuals who have had disrupted attachments that correspond with significant relationship and adjustment problems.

Some studies have suggested a significant relationship between insufficient attachment during childhood and adult psychopathology. Examples of disorders correlated with attachment disruption include addiction (Flores, 2004; Schindler et al., 2005), anorexia nervosa (Zachrisson & Kulbotten, 2006), general vulnerability toward psychopathology (Ward, Lee, & Polan, 2006), and borderline personality disorder (Aaronson, Bender, Skodol, & Gunderson, 2006; Meyer, Ajchenbrenner, & Bowles, 2005). The evidence suggests that when a child's ability to emotionally attach is impaired, the vulnerabilities may contribute to compromised emotional functioning later in life.

GOALS OF TREATMENT AND TREATMENT STRATEGIES   It follows, then, that the purpose of the therapeutic relationship is to essentially recreate the parent–child relationship, enabling the client to relearn that it is safe to trust others, and to learn how to be separate, and yet connected, in an emotionally close relationship. In treating children with attachment disorder, interventions are often aimed at caregivers, teaching them how to respond to the child's distressed and inappropriate behavior. For example, a 7-year-old girl diagnosed with the inhibited type of reactive attachment disorder (DSM-IV-TR, APA, 2000) might display symptoms of extreme stranger anxiety, hiding behind the caregiver or completely avoiding eye contact when introduced to a stranger. Stranger anxiety is developmentally expected when a child is 2 years old, but not developmentally typical at age 7. The counseling intervention for this child would include working with the caregiver on how he or she feels and reacts internally when the child demonstrates this stranger anxiety, and might also focus on what to say and do with the child when she exhibits this avoidant behavior. However, the process of relearning how to attach is long and arduous. Despite the inclusion of reactive attachment disorder as a diagnostic category in the DSM-IV-TR (APA, 2000), consensus has not yet emerged in the professional literature about the precise definition of attachment disorder or how to assess it, nor is there a coherent body of evidence as to the most effective treatment approaches (Hughes, 2003).

MICROSKILLS IN ATTACHMENT THEORY   The overriding emphasis of therapy from an attachment perspective needs to be provision of a secure attachment figure. That would mean attending skills, reflection of feeling, paraphrasing and summarizing, and possibly questioning. There would probably be minimal supportive challenging and perhaps a reduced emphasis on client observation and feedback about those observations.

HUMANISTIC MODELS

The humanists are theorists whose models emanate from a shared philosophical approach. For the humanists, as with as the developmentalists, Freudian psychoanalytic theory is one influential historical context from which humanistic theory emerged. Where "successful" Freudian therapy required a therapist to be emotionally removed and neutral toward a client, humanists saw warm, caring, therapeutic relationships as essential to the recovery or growth process for people in distress.

Carl Rogers was one of the first to express the idea that the therapeutic relationship and the transparency and genuineness of a therapist were critical to client growth. Besides Rogers's client-centered theory, other humanistic models we will touch upon include existentialism (Viktor Frankl and Irving Yalom) and Gestalt. Some of the commonalities among the humanistic models include the following:

- A philosophical stance that sees humankind as basically good, and as people having the inherent capability for self-direction and growth if given the right set of circumstances
- Use of the present, here and now, as a therapeutic tool
- Congruence and alignment among thoughts, feelings, and behavior as a definition of mental health
- Treatment goals centering around establishing congruence and acceptance of personal responsibility
- The process of having an authentic human relationship between the client and counselor being itself therapeutic

In general, the humanists see a person as functioning in a healthy manner when he or she is fully aware of internal experiencing and is able to consciously choose when and how to express that to others. People possess an inherent drive toward growth and increasing levels of psychological and emotional sophistication that, according to Rogers, unfolds in a predictable way. In this respect, the progressive and systematic unfolding is similar to the developmental view of human functioning.

PERSONAL REFLECTION _____

Can you think of a time when your own increased self-awareness resulted in your making significant changes in your behavior, relationships with others, or feelings about yourself?

Table 11.4 provides information for comparison between some theories categorized as humanistic. The following sections will offer more detailed views of selected humanistic/existential theories.

Client-Centered Counseling

ESSENCE OF THE THEORY   Carl Rogers was the primary person who developed client-centered counseling; he has been tremendously influential in the field of counseling and psychotherapy. His clinical work, writing, and research shifted the focus in therapy to clarification and refinement of the feelings and thoughts the client was expressing in the present moment. He made a huge contribution to the field in his recognition that his own personhood had influence on the counseling process. Rogers was adamant in his belief

TABLE 11.4   Humanistic Theory Comparison

Theory	Definition of Pathology	Goals	Techniques	Evidence/ Support	Criticisms
Client-centered (Rogers)	Inauthenticity	Genuineness, authenticity, risk-taking	Active listening Unconditional positive regard Feeling reflection Immediacy Self-disclosure Relationship it-self is conducive to growth	Lies in realm of "common factors and core conditions" Momentum for research on efficacy has waned (Hazler, 2007)	Requires insight Requires counselor self-awareness (Hazler, 2007) Lengthy Some clients need more directiveness (Corey, 2005) Unconditional positive regard difficult for most people
Existentialism (Frankl, May, Yalom)	Philosophical worldview that honors pain at many levels Suffering is an achievement	Centered aware-ness of being Self-responsibility Vulnerability is chance to become more authentic Unpredictability is incentive for responsible choices and behavior	Feeling reflection Active listening Reflection of meaning Relationship it-self is conducive to growth	Lies in realm of "nonspecific fac-tors" Practitioners believe integrity of therapeutic relationship su-percedes political and scientific argument	Vague; no sys-tematic state-ment of princi-ples and techniques of treatment Insight does not necessarily equate with ex-ternally observ-able behavior change Limited applica-bility for non-verbal clients
Gestalt (Perls, Wertheimer)	Faulty bound-aries between individual and environment; excessive or insufficient dif-ferentiation and contact be-tween self and others	Awareness and integration of disjointed parts of self Ability to main-tain contact and differentiation Acceptance of personal responsibility	Location of feeling Empty chair Confrontation and enactment Unfinished business Rehearsal Minimization	Evaluation is idiographic; self-report only Common factors	Intense emo-tional expres-sion may require cogni-tive work too

that as long as certain core therapeutic conditions are met, people are entirely capable of healing and growth without any intervention techniques other than a transparent, gen-uine listener who is able to value and prize the client. This valuing was termed *unconditional positive regard* and was, in Rogers's view, one of the primary cornerstones of human growth.

Rogers (1961) said, "The more I am open to the realities in me and in the other person, the less do I find myself wishing to rush in to 'fix things'" (p. 21). He went on to describe the directions that he commonly observed his clients to take. Those directions included:

- Movement away from a fabricated presentation of who one is, and toward more genuine expression of thoughts and feelings
- Movement away from notions of what behaviors and feelings are expected by others, and toward the ability to set one's own course
- Movement toward awareness of the complexity of emotions that one is experiencing at any given moment
- Movement toward a willingness to have new experiences and take risks

PSYCHOPATHOLOGY FROM A CLIENT-CENTERED PERSPECTIVE   In this model, psychological disturbance is the result of a person being out of touch with all aspects of his or her feelings. Dangerous emotions are threatening because they do not fit our existing view of ourselves, and so we suppress them. When we suppress those aspects of our experience that are too threatening or uncomfortable, we become *incongruent*. Incongruence leads to a life of inauthenticity and disconnection. Rogers believed that people could not change until they become aware of, and accepting of, what they are. In his belief system, self-awareness and self-acceptance are absolutely necessary for growth to occur.

Mental illness or disease (dis-ease) occurs when a person is not authentically experiencing the emotions and thoughts that are occurring, or when an individual experiences incongruence among what is felt, what is known, and what is expressed.

GOALS OF TREATMENT AND TREATMENT STRATEGIES   Rogers (1961) saw therapy as intensive and extensive, the therapist entering an intensely personal and subjective relationship with the client, person to person. Ownership of feelings, increasing tendency to live fully in each moment, and increasing willingness to trust in oneself are the means of arriving at the most satisfying behavior.

The therapist must bring unconditional positive regard and genuineness, fully open to empathizing with the client with no internal barriers on the therapist's part.

In response, the client is then able to explore increasingly strange and dangerous feelings in him or herself. As those feelings are more fully experienced in the context of therapy, the client discovers that he or she *is* those feelings, and can thus more fully experience who she is as a total person, with openness to awareness and acceptance of all of herself.

Treatment strategies are intended to help a client to do two things: (1) articulate his or her true feelings and thoughts, and (2) live life in a manner that reflects those feelings and thoughts. From Rogers's perspective, there are often reasons that people feel unable to live that way, and the goals of treatment are to discover the courage and willingness to take the risk of being transparent to others in the world. The goal is honesty and authenticity with oneself and others.

MICROSKILLS IN A CLIENT-CENTERED CONTEXT   The client-centered approach to counseling has become one of the basic stances from which a variety of other approaches can be added. You will learn and practice numerous microskills that emanate from a client-centered perspective. It is important to note that the microskills approach itself is not from Rogers; while Rogers emphasized active listening, subsequent authors (Allen Ivey and others) that came later were able to take the active listening approach and break it down into small component parts for ease of learning and mastery. The microskills most frequently used by a client-centered therapist include attending behavior, paraphrasing, summarizing and clarifying, and feeling reflection.

Existentialism

ESSENCE OF THE THEORY   A host of figures in the field contributed to the literature on existentialism. Two influential authors have been chosen for illustration in this text, one a historical figure (Frankl) and the other a contemporary therapist and author (Yalom). Existentialism is more of a philosophical approach to conceptualizing the human condition than it is a model for treatment per se.

Viktor Frankl survived being a concentration camp prisoner during World War II. Rather than becoming embittered by that experience, he was able to use his life experience to articulate a philosophy of human functioning that is a hopeful observation of the human process. He referred to his approach as *logotherapy*. Frankl wrote extensively about the search for meaning, which is the heart of existentialism (e.g., Frankl, 1997, 2004). The existentialist philosophy emphasizes the universal human struggles. There is a corresponding deemphasis on explicating therapeutic techniques for helping people to grow.

In Frankl's model, the driving force among humans is to discover the purpose of our lives, and to then live accordingly. For some people, this need is met through spiritual and religious beliefs, which permits them to make meaning of the events that transpire around them. For others, there is some other means of attaching meaning and purpose to their lives. We might define our purpose as making a contribution to a better world, alleviation of human suffering, acquisition of political power, acquisition of material possessions, creation of a healthy family unit, or some other purpose that has become apparent to us through the course of our lives.

PERSONAL REFLECTION

Most large organizations have a mission statement that defines their purpose and vision. What is your mission statement? To what extent do you think lack or loss of one's mission statement relates to subsequent emotional disturbance?

YALOM'S EXISTENTIALISM   For Yalom, lack of meaning is one of several major crises we all must face. Yalom (1980) talked about the necessity of coming to accept the "existential givens," and the tremendous emotional angst that we experience in the face of each of them. He identified four inescapable existential givens:

- Death
- Freedom
- Isolation
- Meaninglessness

Our struggle with these issues plays out internally, and our outward behavior is the externalized expression of that struggle.

GOALS OF TREATMENT AND TREATMENT STRATEGIES   Given the assumptions made by the humanists about emotional disturbance, it follows that the process of counseling and therapy will entail helping people to become more congruent, authentic, and aligned. It may also entail them becoming aware of and articulating their beliefs about the purpose of their lives.

This is an insight-oriented treatment approach in which clients focus on internal feeling experiences, emotional suffering, and the meaning they attach to those phenomena.

MICROSKILLS AND EXISTENTIAL THERAPY APPROACHES   From an existentialist perspective, the primary microskill that takes one to the goal of treatment is reflection of meaning. When any client's angst is followed to its logical and emotional source, the angst will emanate from one of the four core struggles articulated above. By using attending, paraphrasing, feeling reflection, and immediacy, a therapist can bring a client to a place of verbalizing his or her struggles or fears about the core issue and ultimately come to some resolution. The following links on the MyHelpingLab website offer examples of how an existential counselor would use silence and bringing incongruence into a client's awareness.

Video Lab > By Course > Theories of Counseling and Psychotherapy > Module 8: Existential-Humanistic

Therapy >

⇒ **Using Silence in Session**

⇒ **Relating Nonverbals to Congruency**

Gestalt

ESSENCE OF THE THEORY   Perls and Wertheimer were both heavily influential in development of Gestalt theory. Gestalt theory is focused mainly on process. That means that what happens between parts of your client, and between your client and other people, including yourself, are the main grist for the therapy mill. The Gestalt model sees the human experience as a continuously flowing process of self-awareness, contact with others, new experiences through that contact, and withdrawal to integrate and incorporate the new feelings and experiences that occurred during that contact. This cycle of interpersonal contact is similar to the movement of the tide in an ocean.

PSYCHOPATHOLOGY FROM A GESTALT PERSPECTIVE   Returning to the Gestalt emphasis on self-awareness, when aspects of the self are too disturbing or threatening, they are pushed out of our awareness. This suppression of awareness results in limiting our ability to be in full contact with all the aspects of an interaction with another person. Suppression is an expression of pathology to the extent that any degree of reduced awareness equates to a less than optimal level of interacting with our environment.

Another related concept in Gestalt theory is *unfinished business*, in which we have feelings and thoughts about a situation or person, but we have been unable to express and resolve them. When we are functioning well emotionally, as we move away from contact to withdrawal, part of the process involves resolution and closure, meaning that we have awareness of our feelings and thoughts, we ascertain where in our internal landscape they can fit, we make what sense of them we need to, and then we put them away. This is referred to as *termination and closure,* and is a very important part of an interaction.

PERSONAL REFLECTION

Have you ever had a friendship with someone that ended badly, or with one or the other person drifting away without saying goodbye? Has that experience left you with a sense of needing more closure? If so, how did that lack of closure affect you?

One example of a situation that creates unfinished business would be having someone end a relationship with you and then your subsequently having things to say but no opportunity to do so. A similar thing happens when someone close to us dies before we have a last chance to say goodbye or express our love for him or her. This can result in a sense of extreme frustration, guilt, or resentment, as well as a need to say some parting things to the other person. This creates unfinished business; we are held captive by our unexpressed feelings, and subsequently we are prevented from fully moving forward in our lives. Alternatively, we may *try* to move forward to find that in later relationships we carry the residual unresolved feelings from the prior relationship that was not adequately concluded.

GOALS OF TREATMENT AND TREATMENT STRATEGIES The goal in Gestalt is integration. Integration occurs when a person is fully self-aware, fully able to maintain contact with others while maintaining a sense of self, and capable of making that contact with authenticity and honesty, and with closure of past feelings from earlier relationships. Emphasis is fully on the here-and-now relationship and interaction between the therapist and client.

In contrast with person-centered therapy, a Gestalt therapist might be quite directive in suggestions about where to focus the therapeutic interaction. The Gestalt therapist seeks to help a client become aware of those aspects of him or herself that have been pushed away from awareness. Gestalt therapists believe that the behaviors a client is exhibiting in the counseling session are avenues that can be followed to find the suppressed emotions. The purpose of the therapist's actions with the client is to help the client to move from *dis-integration*, that is, nonownership of feelings and experiences, to *integration*, thereby allowing more full contact and more aliveness.

The therapeutic techniques are referred to as *experiments*. One Gestalt technique is to bring a client's nonverbal behaviors to his or her attention by having the person further exaggerate the movement, and then do an internal scan to identify the feelings that emerge. Another Gestalt technique is to do an empty chair dialogue. There are a couple of ways the empty chair can be used; one would be to have the client identify the different parts of herself that are in conflict (i.e., the "good" Kathie and the "bad" Kathie), and then have her sit in each of those chairs and talk as though she is fully that person. In another empty chair version, the client sits in different chairs that represent different parts of himself, or sits in a chair with an empty chair facing him.

MICROSKILLS IN A GESTALT CONTEXT The microskills necessary for effective Gestalt intervention heavily emphasize careful client observation, immediacy, and feeling reflection. These may be the crux of the Gestalt approach, because Gestaltists believe that what is happening in the here and now between the client and therapist is the gateway to exploration and discovery of the client's aspects of disintegration and fragmentation. Examples of techniques related to Gestalt interventions can be seen on the following MyHelpingLab links.

Video Lab > By Course > Theories of Counseling and Psychotherapy > Module 7: Mind-Body Therapy >

⇒ **Exploring Dreams with Clients**

⇒ **Staying in the Moment; Focus on Sensations**

⇒ **Exploring the Meaning of "Control"**

COGNITIVE-BEHAVIORAL MODELS

Behavioral therapy and cognitive therapy with a behavioral component started out as separate approaches. There remain a number of counselors and psychologists who are theoretical purists, meaning that their emphasis is exclusively on behavioral or cognitive interventions. In practice, though, many therapists subscribe to the cognitive-behavioral approach, which incorporates conceptualization and strategies from both behavioral and cognitive models.

This section of the chapter will talk about both models, and then present an explanation of how they are integrated in the cognitive-behavioral approach. The cognitive, behavioral, and cognitive-behavioral models of therapy have in common the following assumptions:

- Human beings are living organisms that are subject to the same learning principles that were established in animal research.
- The basic principles of conditioning (both classical and operant) continue to account for an individual's behavior and cognitions throughout his or her life.
- Psychopathology occurs as the result of distorted self-talk that results in maladaptive behavior; both the self-talk and undesirable behaviors continue to be reinforced and thus persist.
- The therapist's task lies in conducting a sound analysis of how reinforcers are maintaining problematic self-talk and behavior(s).
- Treatment consists of modifying the schedules of reinforcement and restructuring the self-talk to be more rationally based.
- The therapist is the expert, although the therapist and client have a working alliance in which the client must be actively engaged.

Readers can review a comparison of the behavior and cognitive theories in Table 11.5.

TABLE 11.5 Cognitive-Behavioral Theory Comparison

Theory	Definition of Pathology	Goals	Techniques	Evidence/Support	Criticisms
Behavioral (Watson, Pavlov, Skinner, Wolpe)	Behavioral excesses or deficits are result of problematic conditioning	Eliminate maladaptive behavior; condition adaptive behavior	Systematic desensitization Progressive relaxation Exposure and response prevention Shaping	Extensive body of empirical support for these techniques (Wilson, 2005)	Disallows construct of unconsciousness Insufficient focus on feelings (Kalodner, 2007) Insufficienc attention to client's past (Corey, 2005)
Cognitive (Beck, Ellis)	Inaccurate or distorted internal dialogue results in emotional distress	Client's awareness of cognitive distortions; rewording of self-talk to reduce affective intensity	Socratic dialogue Cognitive restructuring	Extensive empirical evidence for effectiveness	Requires abstraction ability on client's part Imposes some value-laden assumptions on counselor's part

We will first review the principles of classical and operant conditioning, both of which are subtypes of behavior theory, and then focus on cognitive theory.

Behavior Theory

ESSENCE OF THE THEORY   *Classical conditioning* is a neurological process first discovered by Ivan Pavlov in the early 1900s. His initial research was conducted on dogs, but it was found that his model was also applicable to other creatures such as pigeons, rats, and humans. The essence of classical conditioning is that if an organism is presented with a neutral stimulus, such as a bell ringing, in the presence of some other salient stimulus, such as food or electric shock, after a short period of time the neutral stimulus elicits the same response as the salient stimulus. This classical conditioning model has been applied to the understanding of how people develop phobias for particular stimuli such as spiders or heights.

B.F. Skinner went on to develop a related model, *operant conditioning*, which also has been demonstrated to be applicable to a variety of animals. The essence of the operant conditioning model is that all behavior is subject to the principles of *reinforcement*. Behavior is determined by the environmental conditions that either reinforce, or fail to reinforce, a given behavior.

A *positive reinforcer* is any event that occurs after a behavior is exhibited, which increases the probability that the behavior will reoccur. One obvious example is receiving pay after a period of work. The pay greatly increases the likelihood that the work behavior will continue; in the absence of pay, the behavior will likely stop if too much time elapses. Removal of the reinforcer (in this example, the pay) results in extinction (removal) of the behavior.

One other key term is *negative reinforcer*, in which the removal of an aversive stimulus occurs when the desired behavior is exhibited. One example of a negative reinforcer would be a parent scolding a teen, who is sitting on the sofa watching television, to get up and take out the garbage. When the teen stands up from the sofa to take the garbage outside, the parent stops scolding, and the teen's behavior has thus been negatively reinforced. The scolding was aversive, and when the teen exhibited the desired behavior, the aversive stimulus was removed.

Negative reinforcers are used in society; one instance is the use of home monitoring in the legal system, in which a person on probation is permitted to wear a radio transmitter ankle bracelet and remain at home; if her or his behavior is lawful for a specified period of time, the ankle bracelet is removed. The removal of the ankle bracelet following appropriate, lawful completion of probation is a negative reinforcer.

PSYCHOPATHOLOGY FROM A BEHAVIORAL PERSPECTIVE   Behavior is pathological if it is maladaptive. *Maladaptive* means it causes discomfort or unfavorable consequences either for the client, or for others in the client's environment. Maladaptive behavior develops according to the learning principles of either classical or operant conditioning.

GOALS OF TREATMENT AND TREATMENT STRATEGIES   The goal of behavioral treatment is to reduce the frequency and intensity of undesirable behavior and to increase the frequency of adaptive, socially appropriate behavior. This requires a careful behavioral analysis, in which a therapist identifies a target behavior and then gathers baseline data about the antecedents and consequences of the behavior. This behavioral analysis yields information about what consequences are serving as reinforcers in maintaining the undesirable behavior.

The behavioral treatment strategies are also based on established principles of learning and conditioning. Each of the techniques was developed with the intention of disrupting the relationship between the undesirable behavior and the subsequent reinforcer, while simultaneously introducing a new desirable behavior and pairing it with positive reinforcers. Representative behavioral techniques include shaping, progressive muscle relaxation, guided imagery, behavioral rehearsal, and exposure and response prevention.

MICROSKILLS IN A BEHAVIORAL CONTEXT A counseling session focused on behavioral intervention is highly directive. The therapist asks many questions with the intention of gathering specific information about the parameters of the targeted behaviors and the loop of antecedent, behavior, and consequence. The most likely microskills that would be used in this context would be paraphrasing, summarizing, and questioning.

Feeling reflection might also pertain here, but only in the context of specifically quantifying the level of subjective distress experienced by the client (referred to in Chapter 8 as a "scaling" question). Behavioral therapists typically use the Subjective Unit of Distress measurement (SUD) as one baseline number against which to compare the effect of treatment; a therapist would then perform a behavioral intervention and then get another SUD report from the client to determine the success of the intervention.

Herein lies a subtle difference between counseling approaches. In a humanistic approach, the exploration of the feeling and meaning of the feeling would be the focus of the counseling interaction. A behaviorist, in contrast, uses the feeling exploration as one means of quantifying the extent to which the behavioral interventions are effective. For humanists, exploration of the feeling is the endpoint; for behaviorists, it is a means to an end.

Cognitive Theory

ESSENCE OF THE THEORY The basic premise of cognitive theory is that although internally, we have the experience of external situations as causing us to feel certain emotions, there actually is an intermediary process of how we *perceive* and *interpret* the external situation, which results in our subsequent feelings. This process of perception and interpretation is referred to as *internal dialogue, self-talk,* or *automatic thoughts,* and in the cognitive model it is one of the primary determinants of the emotions we experience.

The same principles of reinforcement that were described in behavior theory apply in the cognitive model as well. When we hold given beliefs and expectations, we select and focus on those aspects of our environment that confirm our belief system.

PSYCHOPATHOLOGY FROM A COGNITIVE PERSPECTIVE Beck (Beck & Weishar, 2005) referred to a number of cognitive distortions that serve to maintain a faulty belief system. One example of a cognitive distortion is *generalization.* In this instance, we take one incident that is distressing and generalize from it to make broad conclusions. For example, perhaps we call a friend to have lunch the following day, and we must leave a message on the friend's voice mail. If the friend doesn't call us back, and we are interpreting this outcome rationally, we might say to ourselves, "Gee, I'm disappointed Joe didn't call back. I guess he didn't get the message in time or maybe he's really buried in work. That's too bad, I'd have liked to see him." If, on the other hand, we use the cognitive distortion of generalization, we might say to ourselves, "I *knew* it! He can't stand me. No one else can either, that's why I *never* get invited to do anything with anyone." After reaching either conclusion, we will be on the lookout for other instances in our daily lives that support whichever self-talk we used.

Finding such confirmation serves as a positive reinforcer, which results in our strengthening our convictions and beliefs. In cognitive theory this cycle is referred to as a *self-fulfilling prophecy.* Studies clearly support the observation that people who are depressed consistently tend to have negative self-talk around the *cognitive triad,* another concept articulated by Beck. The cognitive triad refers to our beliefs about three key components; oneself, the world, and the future. The cycle of cognitive distortions, self-talk, and emotions can have relevance to many degrees of emotional disturbance, ranging from mild annoyance or sadness all the way through clinical levels of disturbance in any number of different kinds of disorders.

GOALS OF TREATMENT AND TREATMENT STRATEGIES   The focus of cognitive therapy is on identifying the cognitive antecedents of the intense and distressing emotions, because the distortions result in intensification of negative feelings. Cognitions basically function like a volume knob on a radio. Although it is neither realistic nor healthy to expect that a person will never experience negative feelings, the intention of cognitive therapy is that (1) a person's feelings will be realistically and rationally based, and (2) the intensity of feelings will be appropriately proportional to the situation. Thus, although we might be sad or lonely when we can't find anyone to go to the movies with us, most people do not become so overwhelmed by sadness that they can only sit and wring their hands, becoming immobilized by the sadness.

The main treatment strategy in cognitive therapy is Socratic dialogue, or as Ellis called it, disputing irrational beliefs. This requires that a client share with the counselor the language and words he or she uses in self-talk. Then the counselor looks for the distortions and specifically discusses those distortions with the client. Clients are then taught how to reword their self-talk in a manner that is more rational.

Cognitive-Behavioral Theory

ESSENCE OF THE THEORY   The cognitive and behavioral theories fit together well, and a number of theorists integrated the two approaches. One of the first to do so was Albert Ellis, who was the founder of Rational-Emotive Behavior Therapy (Ellis, 2005). Examples of more recent cognitive-behavioral theorists are Donald Meichenbaum and Steven Hayes.

Ellis's theory was heavily focused on identifying the erroneous components of a client's belief system, referred to as *irrational beliefs,* and then modifying those beliefs and prescribing behavioral "homework" in which the client would intentionally alter his or her behavior based on the new, restructured belief system. One instance of an irrational belief many people hold is, "Everyone must like me all the time, and if they don't, I can't stand it and that's awful."

PSYCHOPATHOLOGY FROM A COGNITIVE-BEHAVIORAL PERSPECTIVE   The cognitive-behavioral view of emotional distress and behavioral disorders is that they arise out of an interaction between faulty interpretations of events (distortions or irrational beliefs) *and* schedules of reinforcement and conditioning. The incorporation of faulty belief systems as well as conditioning and reinforcement occurs due to environmental influences, not only in our family of origin, but in other aspects of our environments as well.

One of the extrafamilial sources of irrational beliefs is the media, evident in a variety of areas. For example, Dyer (1995) listed several song lyrics with irrational messages that perpetuate cognitive distortions, such as, "I can't live if living is without you." Media influence on body image and subsequent distortion of self-perception has been well documented in research.

PERSONAL REFLECTION _____

Think about some of the advertising jingles you see or hear on television or the radio that imply you will feel better about yourself if you purchase some product. Consider the underlying message being communicated to you about yourself. What are the ways that the media messages have influenced your self-perception?

GOALS OF TREATMENT AND TREATMENT STRATEGIES   The goals of cognitive-behavioral treatment are development of a healthy, stable, rational belief system that supports and drives healthy, stable emotional regulation and general functioning. Sometimes a client is able to identify and clearly articulate a problem (e.g., "I know I shouldn't be so anxious and avoid dating, but I just don't know how to get over it"). Other times a client may be aware that parts of her or his life are not working, yet be unable to articulate exactly what the discomfort is, in which case a cognitive-behavioral therapist will be active and directive in the process of problem identification and definition.

Treatment strategies are an integration of cognitive restructuring through literally rewording what clients say to themselves and behavioral techniques such as progressive relaxation, exposure, and shaping. The basis of the cognitive-behavioral treatment approach is the assumption that data and *empirical evidence* about the client's response to treatment are as important as the *client's self-report* that he or she is feeling less distress. There are multiple examples of applying cognitive-behavioral techniques, which you can view via the following MyHelpingLab links.

_____ myhelpinglab

Video Lab > By Course > Theories of Counseling and Psychotherapy > Module 5: Cognitive Behavioral Therapy

⇒ **Exploring Feelings, Thoughts, and Behaviors**

⇒ **Shedding Light on Automatic Thoughts**

⇒ **Connecting Thoughts to Behaviors/Feelings**

⇒ **Helping Clients Become More Assertive**

Because this approach is empirical, it is important at the outset of counseling to gather *baseline data* about key aspects of the problem. Baseline data typically include information such as the antecedents and consequences of the problematic feelings or behaviors; the frequency, intensity, and duration of the feelings and behaviors; and the client's internal dialogue throughout this process.

As one might imagine while reading this description of gathering baseline data, the process depends on the client following through on "assignments" between counseling sessions. The counseling relationship is seen in this approach as a collaborative venture, and one that will only work if the client is motivated and willing to follow through. The client is seen as the expert reporting the data about his or her own behavior and cognitions. However, the therapist is the holder of extensive clinical expertise.

The counseling process is educational and the therapist is the individual who directs the focus of each treatment session. So while, like the other approaches, the counseling relationship is important, it is seen as important for a very different reason than in a developmental or humanistic approach. The counselor often takes a teaching or coaching role; the counselor educates the client about the cycle of self-talk and subsequent behavior that perpetuates the cycle of distress and maladaptive responses to the distress. The counselor also takes an active role in explaining and educating the client about how the course of treatment will progress, including how and why particular things are going to be recommended and prescribed for the client from one counseling session to the next.

One excellent example of how this can be effective is in the strategies that are suggested at a well-known weight-loss program. The program leaders, who offer a weekly meeting for participants, teach the participants how to identify and modify their faulty beliefs around food and body weight. At the same time, the leaders offer many specific suggestions about making changes in one's home environment to positively reinforce healthy food choices and eating patterns. For example, one suggestion for managing portion size while eating a bowl of ice cream might be to use small but pretty custard cups that hold a smaller amount than a typical cereal bowl.

One other quick example is smoking. When someone is quitting smoking, one means of eliminating an antecedent ("trigger") for wanting to smoke is to completely discard all the ashtrays in the home. This removes all the environmental cues that are serving as conditioned stimuli for the person and resulting in a conditioned response, which in the case of smoking might be anticipation of the physical sensations associated with lighting a cigarette.

The techniques described above are examples of stimulus control, in which a person consciously controls the antecedents in his or her environment as a means of controlling the problem behavior. As you might imagine, depending on a client's presenting concern, there are a multitude of ways that a person can learn to manage his or her environment in a manner that results in more satisfying behavior patterns and a subsequent sense of success and/or mastery. This is an opportunity for the client and counselor to collaboratively think about the cycle of reinforcement and to creatively restructure the environment to support healthy behavior and choices.

In cognitive-behavioral approaches, partially because there is such emphasis on empiricism, the recommended process for helping a client has been heavily researched. Cognitive-behavioral approaches have been identified as very effective for certain types of disorders, including anxiety disorders such as panic disorder and simple phobias, and mood disorders.

MICROSKILLS IN A COGNITIVE-BEHAVIORAL CONTEXT   There are some microskills more likely than others to be apparent in a cognitive behavioral treatment session. This model emphasizes making good use of time. Typically there are specific pieces of information the therapist needs to obtain from the client, while simultaneously established a solid working alliance. Therefore, attending, actively paraphrasing and summarizing, and questioning are key microskills. On the other hand, immediacy may be of minimal value unless the problem behavior involves social skills. Reflection of meaning is of value to the extent that it enables exploration of core beliefs that could illuminate cognitive distortions.

INTERPLAY OF MULTICULTURAL ISSUES AND THEORIES

Early proponents of a culturally sensitive approach to counseling individuals who are members of cultural, ethnic, or racial minority groups justified their position by criticizing traditional counseling theories that were developed on white, middle-class, European or

European American values and belief systems. All of the theories we covered in this chapter could justifiably be classified as falling in that category.

The implied problem with the ethnocentricity of the traditional models is that each model makes critical assumptions about the definitions of mental health, mental illness, and what people need to get better or grow, without the recognition that those assumptions are based on *values*, not facts. So, for example, the cognitive approach might be of minimal benefit to a client whose belief system, couched in his culture, appears to a culturally different counselor to be "irrational."

CURRENT TRENDS IN THEORY DEVELOPMENT

One notable trend in the last several decades has been for researchers to conduct meta-analyses of the hundreds of treatment outcome studies to look at overall trends in the findings. The need in our field for identification of specific treatments that are effective for specific types of clients and problems has become a major concern. Increased need for accountability, as well as awareness of variables of diversity that mitigate counseling effectiveness, have resulted in the movement toward empirically validated treatment (EVT).

Power Distance	
High	**Low**
More comfortable with a directive approach	More comfortable with a collaborative approach
Either behavioral or Gestalt	Client-centered, psychoanalytic, or cognitive-behavioral if presented as a collaborative undertaking
Uncertainty Avoidance	
High	**Low**
Client may be cognitively rigid and respond well to behavioral interventions but struggle with cognitive restructuring	Client may tolerate any approach
Individualism	
High	**Low**
Traditional Western approaches are individualistically oriented	Cognitive approaches may be contraindicated due to the emphasis on community beliefs and values
Gender Roles	
Masculinity	**Femininity**
Rigid belief systems probably contraindicate cognitive intervention	Fluidity of gender roles suggests some cognitive flexibility and ability to accommodate a variety of counseling approaches

FIGURE 11.1 Hofstede's Axes of Cultural Values and Implications for Use of Particular Theories

As a consequence or possibly co-occurrence with meta-analysis and the push for EVT, some therapeutic approaches have emerged that integrate a variety of theories and treatment techniques. A transtheoretical approach is one that integrates multiple theoretical frameworks. Examples of current transtheoretical treatment approaches are dialectic behavior therapy (Linehan), Lazarus's multimodal therapy, and the readiness model (Prochaska).

Integration of Traditional Theories with Hofstede's Model

Each of the three schools we have discussed has potential to be used, at least in part, with clients whose cultural backgrounds differ significantly from our own. This potential can best be actualized if we are sensitive to times and ways that each of these approaches might be either particularly *helpful* or particularly *distasteful* or unhelpful to a given client.

Our knowledge based on the research about cultural characteristics of specific groups of people enables us to have some generalized expectations about the needs of the group, as well as about the efficacy of a particular theory/approach. In addition to the extant information available about group characteristics, Hofstede's axes of cultural variability may offer further insight about the possible interactions that might occur between theoretical counseling approaches and techniques, on four of the axes. Figure 11.1 provides the continua of four axes and examples of places where particular approaches might be effective or specifically ineffective or offensive.

Chapter Summary

As was stated at the beginning of this chapter, one challenging aspect of learning how to work with clients is to experience the ambiguity of realizing that counseling and therapy are as much art as they are science. A counselor or counseling strategy that might work wonderfully for one client might be completely ineffective or aversive for another. The phenomenon of individual differences, both between counselors and between clients, makes each counseling relationship and interaction a unique experience.

This chapter has described the basic schools of developmental, humanistic, and cognitive-behavioral theory. The major points of difference across those schools have been identified, with one major goal being to illustrate that while many different counselors might use the same technique of asking questions, the intended purpose of asking questions varies significantly depending on the therapist's theory base.

You have likely been able to find some aspects of each theory that resonated with you personally. Each model offers a different avenue for perceiving and defining the same phenomenon. Although some therapists are trained specifically in one particular theory and approach through specialized training programs such as a Psychoanalytic Institute or the Gestalt Institute, many therapists are eclectic, using a combination of several theories.

There are two summative points intended for you to take from this reading. First, there are many ways to perceive the same client, and the theories you choose will greatly affect the way you conceptualize what is wrong and how you can and should help. Consequently, the way you choose to apply the microskills we have covered in the book will be driven in part by the theories to which you subscribe.

Second, recognize that the theories presented in this chapter are not inherently sensitive to cultural differences. This issue is usually covered at great length in a course on social and cultural foundations in counseling.

At the time many of the theories presented in this text were emerging, little attention was paid to the role played in the counseling process by the interaction of cultural templates between the counselor and the client. Presently, there are many books and articles in the professional literature focusing specifically on recommended treatment approaches for particular populations of clients. There exist some indigenous counseling approaches that are far more culturally sensitive than any of the theories presented in this chapter.

The movement for sensitivity to variables of diversity has arisen in large part because these foundational theories, based on traditional white, western European values and ways of seeing the world, were identified as nonapplicable for many people. The people for whom the models did not fit were clients whose descent or values placed them in a minority group.

The criticisms about the ethnocentrism of the traditional theories make it even more important that you be aware of the assumptions made by each model, and aware that the individual sitting before you might not fit neatly into a particular theoretical conceptualization about aspects of existence such as the importance of early development and relationships, the significance of self-talk, and the importance of discussing and processing here-and-now issues in the present moment.

Having this awareness and entering each counseling relationship as a new experience with an individual about whom you know little until he or she teaches you will do much to mitigate the possible pitfalls of making quick assumptions or judgments about a client. Know that you may have some general knowledge about cultural and social influences on your client, and yet the specifics of how they manifest may not fit into your general expectations. In other words, be able to generalize, but also maintain a stance of cognitive flexibility.

Case Studies for Discussion

For each of these cases, take one general school of counseling and then apply the principles of that school to identify the specific components of the case description that fit the model. Then discuss how those features of the client's case would relate to the counseling goals and the strategies you would use to attain the goals. Also discuss specific techniques you would *not* use and why, in your estimation, they would be contraindicated.

CASE DESCRIPTION—ADULT CLIENT

Carole is a 37-year-old biracial woman of Caucasian and African American descent. She has been married for 8 years and has two children, ages 7 and 5. Her husband is a 43-year-old Caucasian man who is employed at a local automobile factory. Carole graduated from high school and has been employed periodically in unskilled labor jobs, but never for more than about a year at a time. She stopped working when she got married; her husband made it clear that her job was to tend to the house and have children. She is a homemaker and, while she loves her children dearly, she finds herself feeling very sad and lonely when the children are in school and her husband is at work. Her 7-year-old is in second grade while the 5-year-old attends an all-day kindergarten. Carole has been referred to counseling by her family physician due to her tearfulness, insomnia, and significant weight gain for which the doctor can find no physical cause.

CASE DESCRIPTION—CHILD CLIENT

Derek is a 9-year-old boy of Latino descent being raised by his maternal grandmother. His father is in prison in Puerto Rico. His mother lives in a house across the street from Derek, and his grandmother is raising him while his mother is raising the four younger children. His mother decided to send him to live with his grandmother because his behavior is so disruptive in the household and she felt she could not control him. Additionally, Derek has been exhibiting significant behavior problems at school and has been referred to you for help. Derek's disruptive behavior at home was primarily characterized by disobeying rules, staying out on the street at night past his curfew, hanging around the neighborhood with older boys who often are in legal trouble, and yelling when he doesn't get what he wants. At school, he has been aggressive in the lunchroom, taking other students' food, and has been suspended for fighting on the playground. His grades are C's, D's, and F's, and he frequently does not turn in or complete his homework.

Questions for Class Discussion

1. Which of the theories or general models of treatment is most closely aligned with your own view of the world? Which is the least appealing to you, and why?
2. What are your thoughts about the best way to determine which theory and techniques to use with a given client?
3. What are the limits of unconditional positive regard? At what point should a counselor "draw the line"?
4. The developmental and humanistic schools of theory place heavy emphasis on the counseling relationship, while the cognitive-behavioral models do not view it as the primary curative factor. What are your views about the relative importance of the therapeutic relationship?

CHAPTER 12

The Counseling Process

After studying this chapter, you should have a clear understanding of the following:

■ The difference between counseling process and outcome

■ The change process

■ The variety of ways in which counseling sessions can vary

■ The constructs and relationship between homeostasis and client readiness for change

INTRODUCTION

This chapter examines the broad picture of the counseling process. We shall begin by discussing the difference between counseling process and outcome, and then look at aspects of each. Client resistance and homeostasis are concepts that are best discussed in this context. Examples will be offered of the myriad ways that clients, settings, and circumstances of a referral can vary the counseling process. Through the lens of homeostasis, we will examine the work of Prochaska and DiClemente, who have made a significant contribution to the knowledge base with their model of client readiness for change.

COUNSELING PROCESS AND COUNSELING OUTCOME

The relationship between process and outcome is comparable to travel; the outcome is the final destination, and the process is the means of transportation by which we get to the destination. Outcome, according to Patterson and Welfel (2005), is the "intended results of counseling" (p. 31). Process goals, on the other hand, have to do with aspects of your relationship and pattern of interaction with your client as you work toward the outcome goals. Both process and outcome are integral components of counseling.

In Chapter 11, we reviewed a few of the theoretical frameworks for understanding the nature of the counseling relationship and the process of helping. Comparison of those theoretical positions reinforces the observation that most aspects of counseling, including the semantics that are used in describing counseling, and articulation of treatment goals are inextricably intertwined with theory.

As we have established throughout this text, the view held by a person-centered counselor regarding what goals a client should be working toward can vary substantially from the view that a cognitive-behavioral counselor holds. Hackney (1992) posits that in reality, few clinicians are theoretically "pure," meaning that many practitioners integrate multiple theoretical perspectives in their conceptualization of process and counseling goals. Indeed, an eclectic, transtheoretical approach seems in some ways to offer the most utility.

We are going to explore counseling process from multiple angles. First, we'll look at the typical course and progression of counseling, including progression of interaction within a given session, and also across the span of the entire counseling process. We will then explore possible differences in situational circumstances and compare how they may affect the counseling process; these include adults versus minors, voluntary versus involuntary clients, agency versus school settings, and scheduled counseling versus emergency crisis counseling.

Typical Stages of the Counseling Process

There are a number of ways that the stages of counseling can be conceptualized. The term *process* can refer either to the interaction and how the relationship unfolds within one particular session, or to the overall progression of counseling throughout the counselor/client involvement. The process in a single session parallels the process that occurs over the long-term working relationship. In both cases, the most simplistic conceptualization would be a three-stage process. The three broad stages are warm-up, working, and termination/closing down. We will look first at a single session.

STAGES WITHIN A SINGLE SESSION

Warm-Up The warm-up is a stage in which both individuals make small talk or otherwise ease into the process of communication. This small talk happens on the walk to the counselor's office, either from the waiting room of the counseling center, or possibly from the classroom to the counselor's office, if it's a school setting in which the counselor has taken a student out of class. Examples of small talk might include a comment about the weather, asking your client if he or she had any trouble finding your office, or some other benign and impersonal comment or inquiry. The purpose of initiating a brief amount of small talk is to help the client feel at ease.

It is advisable, in a first meeting, to explain to your client about your limits of confidentiality. Knowledge of the reporting requirements in your state is very important; there is some variability as to the conditions under which you will be required by law to break confidentiality.

In general, the two conditions for breaking confidentiality in working with an adult are when the client is a danger to himself or a danger to others. When working with children, or elderly or dependent adults, states often have additional mandatory reporting requirements if the counselor has knowledge or suspicion of abuse or neglect. The variability between states has to do with how detailed and concrete the information must be before a therapist is compelled to report, and to whom the report should be made. We will cover mandatory reporting in Chapter 13 on intake. For now, recognize that you need to be aware of your state's laws about breaking confidentiality. Pabian, Welfel, and Beebe (2007) conducted a survey and found that 75% of the 300 responding psychologists across multiple states were misinformed as to the particular reporting requirements for their state.

If the counselor's orientation is humanistic/existential, the client will be solely responsible for determining the process and direction of each session. A completely nondirective counselor might not say anything whatsoever and wait for the client to initiate a conversation about whatever is on his or her mind. A slightly more directive yet still person-centered opening question might be, "So what's been going on for you (or, how have you been feeling) since I saw you last?"

A counselor whose orientation is cognitive-behavioral may take a more active, directive role in establishing the goals for a given meeting. For example, the therapist might state, "I'm curious about what happened as you began recording some of your self-talk about your anxiety." This immediately sets the session focus in a particular direction.

Regardless of their orientation, some counselors may work with their client to come to some agreement about what will be accomplished in the meeting that day. The counselor's theoretical orientation of directiveness, collaboration, or nondirectiveness influences the emphasis for the session. This practice is referred to as "contracting for a piece of work," meaning that there is explicit discussion about what the client's goals and hopes are for the session. An example of why it is important to contract follows.

Case Example

A confederate "client" in a counseling skills class was role playing a practice counseling session with another student. The "client" said he was seeing the counselor to discuss a problem with his future mother-in-law. He further explained that his fiancée's mother was overly involving herself in the couple's wedding planning. The counseling student spent the entire 20-minute practice session trying to help the client solve his problem by telling his fiancee's mother how he felt about her behavior. The "client" finally exclaimed, exasperatedly, that all he really wanted from counseling was to get his feelings off his chest, not to do anything about the problem.

Contracting for a piece of work can take the form of one of several questions you may ask your client. Examples include the following:

- What do you want to work on today?
- What do you think would be the best use of our time?
- What shall we start with?
- What is the most pressing part of this problem for you right now? and then, Would you like to work on that?

In agency settings, a standard session time may be 50 to 60 minutes. Given a 50-minute block of time, about 5 minutes at the beginning might be spent on small talk, then about 35 to 40 minutes working on the goals that have been set, and then the last 5 to 10 minutes reviewing what was accomplished in the meeting and discussing any directives ("homework") or outside activities the client might do before the next counseling session.

In a school setting, counseling often happens somewhat differently. If the school counselor is typically accessible to the students, the procedure might simply be that if students have a concern they are welcome to just stop by. When a student does stop in to talk to a counselor, he or she may have a specific problem or issue to discuss. In this case it would be the client who would be setting the goals.

Through mindful use of your client observation skills discussed in Chapter 5, during the initial warm-up interchange, you can be assessing the client's demeanor and the range of affect. Observe the nonverbal and paraverbal behavior, and mentally compare that to how the client appeared on previous occasions as part of your data collection.

Working Stage   A variety of things could happen in the working stage. If the contact is the first one or two meetings with the client, the counselor may be mostly actively listening, gathering information, or trying to help the client articulate and define what the overall counseling goals are going to be.

It is throughout the working part of the session that your own orientation and values will influence what you define as "helpful" intervention. A complete discussion of specific counseling techniques is beyond the scope of our present discussion. For the sake of example, though, the "work" might be focused on thought logs and cognitive distortions (cognitive therapy), or it might be on gaining insight and understanding the antecedents of the client's feelings (person-centered or existential), or on what the client would need to express or do with another person in order to gain closure on some unfinished business (Gestalt).

Video Lab > By Course > Skills/Process/Techniques >

⇒ **Module 11: Practical Issues: Ethical Dilemmas > Two Different Methods for Ending a Session**

Termination   There are a variety of ways that counselors choose to end a session. Two such examples are provided on the MyHelpingLab website by following the links provided above. As the allotted time with your client is drawing near the end, make sure to allow time for you and the client to review what occurred in the session. This provides a means of closure and consolidation, and also gives you the opportunity to ensure that the client is sufficiently composed emotionally to go on with his or her day. One gentle way to initiate the closing process is to make the statement, "Well, (*client's name*), we have about 10 minutes left together, so we need to begin winding down." Here are some reasons it is important to signal the gradual closing down of the session. This will

- Model boundary setting
- Provide relief for the client:
  - The client may have other another appointment or somewhere else to be, yet feel uncomfortable saying he or she wants to end the session.
  - The client may be struggling with the emotional intensity of the session and need to put it away.
- Maintain your established schedule as an aspect of your own self-care

PERSONAL REFLECTION

What are your feelings about closing a session when a client is in obvious emotional pain? On a scale of 1 to 10, with 10 being impossible, what rating would you assign to your comfort level with keeping a session to the set time? How does this relate to your definition of what your role is with your clients?

Keep in mind that if your client is in acute distress or for some other reason is clearly not able to begin closing down, you must carefully work with him or her toward gaining some composure and emotional control. Some clients will have an event or circumstances that legitimately constitutes an acute state of distress. Other clients, though, may be chronically in crisis and consistently push the time boundary. Differentiating between "state" and "trait" is a skill that you will hone through work experience and good supervision.

Assuming that your client is not in an acute crisis, consider the following comments. Although it may feel as though you are cutting your client off, it is important for you to observe the time boundary. Additionally, the client may be relieved that you are watching the time, so he or she doesn't have to worry about keeping track of the clock. Sometimes people are emotionally capable of focusing on difficult, painful issues only for small blocks of time; some clients will welcome your move toward closure of the session. It also provides a model for your client of how to set appropriate boundaries with another person.

Another, completely pragmatic reason to carefully observe the time is to manage your own work day and stress level. You may be on a tight schedule; if one session extends beyond the time you have allotted by 10 minutes, and you continue to exceed the scheduled time for each session by 10 minutes in every meeting, by the end of the day you could be working at least one extra hour. This will inevitably happen occasionally, but it is not advisable on a regular basis; self-care on your part is necessary and adhering to your scheduled times is one way to provide yourself with self-care.

Following your initial statement that time is growing short, it can be quite informative to then ask, "As you think back over our meeting today, what stands out the most?" You may discover that *your* perception of what you said or what had the most impact and your *client's* perception of those things could be worlds apart. This can be enlightening to you as you discover more about how your client perceives you and the nature of your interaction with him or her. The information gained can provide an opportunity for you to clarify or correct any misperceptions your client may have.

If it becomes apparent that your client chronically runs over the allotted time, it will become especially important that you begin the session by listing the concerns he or she wants to work on that day. There are a couple of different strategies you might use after a list of concerns has been constructed. One would be to prioritize which of those items is the most important, and then to decide together what amount of time will be spent on it. This author has sometimes said to clients, "I need to be very mindful of our time today and make sure we finish at the scheduled time." How the client reacts to that statement can become part of the process that unfolds over the duration of the working relationship.

Process Across the Course of Counseling

If we look at the *overall* process of counseling over the entirety of treatment, we see a parallel progression of the process that occurs in an individual meeting. The initial stage is the intake and assessment phase (during which time a working alliance also needs to be developed), the middle stage is the working phase, and termination occurs when the counselor and client agree that the goals have been achieved and the client is satisfied with the outcome.

INTAKE, ASSESSMENT, AND RELATIONSHIP DEVELOPMENT   Chapter 13 is devoted entirely to a discussion of intake and assessment. We will touch upon initial contact here only from the standpoint of process. Concomitantly with gathering objective intake information and getting information that will help inform an accurate diagnostic impression, establishment of a solid working alliance needs to occur in this stage.

The following is a case example of what *not* to do. A colleague who is very active in the local Greek community shared the following true anecdote.

Case Example

"Adara" and "Cal" were a married couple, both in their mid-30s who went to a counselor to get assistance with parenting their difficult preteen. Both spouses were second-generation Greek Americans, who strongly identified with their cultural heritage, values, and beliefs. When Adara and Cal went for their first counseling session, the counselor informed Adara that she was excessively focused on taking care of everyone else in the house. The counselor adamantly advised that Adara needed to quit doing that and start worrying more about herself.

The counselor's comments caused extreme discomfort for both Adara and Cal; so much discomfort, in fact, that on the ride home in the car, Cal apologized to Adara for the counselor's behavior, which both Adara and Cal had experienced as an attack. Adara went on to disclose to her friends that she felt violated and completely unheard by the counselor. The couple never returned for help to this or any other counselor, stating that they would handle their problems within the Greek community at their church.

PERSONAL REFLECTION _____

Often, counseling sessions demonstrated in the popular media (e.g., "Dr. Ruth" Westheimer, "Dr. Phil" McGraw) depict a therapist providing specific directive advice after seeming to gather minimal background information about the client. What do you see as the advantage and disadvantage of doing this?

Unfortunately, Adara and Cal's counselor never got the feedback that her counseling behavior was inappropriate, because Adara and Cal never returned for a second appointment. People don't return for a variety of reasons; sometimes they aren't ready, can't afford it, have transportation problems, or as in the case of Adara and Cal, they aren't comfortable with their counselor.

The example of Adara and Cal illustrates how lack of cultural competence can undermine the counseling process. Although we discussed how multicultural incompetence can harm your clients, it is important to discuss it again here in the context of counseling process. The source of counselor incompetence in this case was differences on the individualism/collectivism axis of Hofstede's culture-bound values.

One of the overriding process goals in a first session is to adequately engage your client so he or she will want to return to meet with you again. A recent study (Vogel, Wester, & Larsen, 2007) explored psychological factors that inhibit people seeking help. Your awareness of these factors, coupled with your awareness of the Client Readiness Model (later in this chapter) could be helpful to you in addressing with your client the potential resistance and reluctance he or she might be feeling. The factors identified by Vogel, Wester, and Larsen that inhibit people seeking counseling are:

- Social stigma and fear of negative evaluation by others in their social network
- Fears about what treatment involves
- Fear of having to discuss painful emotions that are more easily avoided or suppressed

- Low expectations as to how helpful it will be (a low cost-benefit ratio)
- Discomfort with self-disclosure and a preference for privacy
- Social norms—how socially acceptable it is to have a therapist
- Self-esteem—not being willing to admit one needs help

Be aware that even if your client voluntarily scheduled an appointment with you, some of the above listed factors may contribute to ambivalent feelings about coming to counseling. It may ease the client's ambivalence somewhat if you are attuned to these possible reasons for reluctance, and if you validate rather than minimize your client's concerns about being a client.

HOMEOSTASIS   One additional source of resistance or reluctance that is sometimes observed among clients, but was not mentioned in the Vogel study, is *systemic* resistance to counseling. As we learned in Bronfenbrenner's ecological model, clients are always embedded in social systems; many of them will be embedded at varying degrees of emotional connection to family systems. The concept of *homeostasis,* borrowed from physiology, refers to the process by which an organism regulates its internal environment to maintain a stable, constant condition. When one member of a family system makes changes, other members of the system must flex to accommodate the new behavior patterns. If a member within a system makes changes that are too big or dramatically different from prior patterns of behavior, other system members may attempt to exert energy to reestablish the earlier balance of the system.

PERSONAL REFLECTION

Think about the extent to which you have changed since your childhood. If you have changed substantially, do you still have family members or friends who think of you and see you the way you were when you were much younger? If so, how does this affect your interactions with them?

Consider the case example with Adara and Cal presented above. Besides the mistake the counselor made in ignoring cultural value differences about affiliation, the counselor completely ignored the possible ripple effects in the system had they followed her advice. What might have happened in that family system if Adara had, in fact, gone "on strike" and simply stopped grocery shopping, doing the laundry, cleaning, and handling family members' appointments and arrangements? Perhaps the first results would have been family members trying to push Adara back into the role she had formerly been filling. Had that not worked, a family crisis might have ensued until a new, different level of homeostasis became established.

When you have an individual client, he or she may be faced with some degree of systemic resistance to whatever changes he or she is trying to make. It might not be to others' advantage, for example, for your client to become more assertive and vocal about his or her needs. The client may consequently experience some amount of negative reaction, or systemic backlash, in response to efforts to change.

So how can we make sure our new clients want to come back for the next session? First and foremost, knowing that you could potentially make a faux pas or clinical mistake that would impair your relationship with the client may help you to remember the importance of proceeding respectfully and carefully. Don't mistakenly assume that because you are familiar with the diagnosis of the client or the life circumstances that you already know how he or she feels, or what he or she needs to do to fix the problem. Look and listen for places where you can sincerely validate their experiences and give them the sense of being heard by attending, paraphrasing, and reflecting their feelings. The book by Nichols (1995), *The Lost Art of Listening*, offers additional insight about this.

It seems to make intuitive sense that clients who are similar to us on some key variables, might feel more comfortable or connected with us. There have been studies that support this supposition (e.g., Towberman, 1992). However, more recent data suggest that there is not necessarily a clear pattern of clients' preference regarding similarity to their counselor (Anderson, 2005). Perhaps what is more important than similarity on demographic variables is being a nonjudgmental listener, including giving the person room to talk about aspects of coming to counseling that are hard for them.

TERMINATION   When, and under what circumstances, does a counseling relationship end? Interestingly, despite all the research about counseling process and outcome, there has been very little work done in the area of termination after successful goal attainment, and how clients and counselors come to agreement in that regard. Ideally counseling ends when the agreed-upon goals have been attained. Jakobsons, Brown, Gordon, and Joiner (2007) identified a small number of studies that have investigated reasons for termination.

One notable finding (Todd, Deane, & Bragdon, 2003) arose from a study that used matched pairs of clients and counselors. The authors reported that although 28% of the counselors stated that termination was due to the clients' goal attainment, only 14% of the clients cited goal attainment as the reason for ending counseling. However, the number of clients reporting that they terminated counseling due to dissatisfaction with counseling was quite small (8%), whereas the most frequently endorsed reason had to do with external factors. The external factors included the client moving away (the setting was a college counseling center), financial cost, and schedule conflicts. This is a finding consistent with some of the counseling outcome literature about the degree of influence of extratherapeutic factors in treatment outcome.

A set of structured, identifiable criteria may be of assistance in deciding when the time has come to end counseling. Jakobsons et al. (2007) offered the following signals as indication that termination is appropriate:

- Decrease of the symptoms with which the person initially presented
- Stable symptom decrease for at least 8 weeks
- Decrease in functional impairment
- Evidence that the client is using new skills, which is resulting in less frequent or intense symptoms
- Ability to use new skills at times when the person formerly would have been vulnerable to symptom exacerbation
- A sense of pride about new skills (self-perception of increased self-efficacy)
- Ability to use new skills in areas other than those specifically targeted in therapy

AUTHOR'S REFLECTION

I chose this profession because I aspired to teach people methods of healthy coping, help people have effective and satisfying lives, and walk with them through their suffering. Many of you may have similar intentions for your own careers in the helping professions. Because I strongly desired to be helpful, there were benefits to my self-esteem and ego to have a client say to me, in our final meeting, "I couldn't have done it without you." It was extremely validating because those words appeared to be tangible evidence of my contribution to the world. However, I eventually came to realize the importance, in this particular context, of not succumbing to my need to feel indispensable to my clients.

PERSONAL REFLECTION _____

What are your thoughts about sharing the credit with your client when treatment is successful? What are some advantages of your taking credit for the work? What are your own internal needs in that regard?

Terminating with clients who have grown, or successfully processed and integrated their pain or other difficulties, can be hugely rewarding.

However, we must be humble when a client attributes his or her growth to us. Providing good counseling has some similarity to being a good parent. Some theories of counseling actually do conceptualize counseling as a process of re-parenting, giving clients an opportunity to receive the unconditional regard and guidance they were not fortunate enough to receive in their family of origin. Regardless of whether you think of the counseling process in that way, one of the overriding goals is to teach your clients how to function and cope independently, the same way parents teach their children how not to need them. The counselor's intent must be for clients to develop and hone their skills to successfully navigate life's challenges in a healthy, adaptive way.

The learning process requires both a teacher (or guide) and a student. As the counselor, you may offer or guide the learning experiences to facilitate the growth process. Nevertheless, the decision about how to respond to what you have offered rests with your client. Individual autonomy always guarantees everyone the latitude to make that choice, regardless of whether we have been forced into treatment or come voluntarily.

Thus, success in counseling is most accurately seen as largely the result of the *client* working, not the counselor. When a client says, "You saved me" or "I couldn't have done it without you," it is more honest to respond with a statement that acknowledges the client's contribution to the process. One example of a constructive response could be, "The way I see it, I asked you some tough questions and you trusted that your painful search for those answers would help you. *You* chose to rise to the occasion and do the hard part."

Recent observations (Weinberger & Rasco, 2007) support the belief that gains made in therapy are most likely to be maintained over the long term if the client completes counseling with a sense of mastery and self-efficacy. Otherwise, when the person encounters the next set of inevitable life challenges, she may believe herself to be incapable of coping with those challenges without you (or some other professional helper).

Situational Factors That Influence Process

The way a counseling session unfolds, and the relevant forces and factors that influence the counseling process, vary tremendously as a function of many circumstantial factors. At the risk of explaining the obvious, we need to touch upon some of the situational variables that are mitigating factors. Such external variables include client characteristics (minors or adults; general level of functioning), the setting in which the client is being seen, and the nature of the counseling referral (voluntary or involuntary; emergency or scheduled).

MINORS OR ADULTS Working with adults as clients, either individually or as couples and families, might be considered to be "easier" to the extent that adults are consenting, and to some degree are independently capable of making decisions and taking action. On the other hand, working with children offers multiple unique rewards. The caveat of counseling young people is that children and adolescents below the chronological age of 18 are under the legal authority of their parents or legal guardians; they have somewhat less autonomy.

From a legal perspective, a therapist must have signed parental consent to counsel a minor. A child cannot refer her or himself for counseling and then come for sessions without parental or guardian consent. The specifics depend on the jurisdiction and the laws; in some states a child may be seen for a limited number of sessions without parental consent but likely not for more than a few sessions before parental consent must be granted. From a more practical perspective, a minor may be dependent on a parent to get to the session, may not be able to help it if a parent is not committed and doesn't keep an appointment, frequently has no control over his or her living situation, and may be unable to discontinue counseling if he or she doesn't want to come. For all of these reasons, a youngster's autonomy may, in some cases, be significantly impeded. These impediments represent potential barriers to the process of successful treatment with a minor.

Another potential impediment to the counseling process among minors is that the parent or guardian is the "holder of the privilege." This term refers to a client's legal guarantee for confidentiality and privacy of information shared with a therapist. Among adult clients who are consenting and voluntary, the information contained in medical and counseling records belongs first to the client. Treatment data cannot be released to anyone else without a release of information, in which the client gives written permission for treatment information to be disclosed (the only exception being if the adult presents with indication of danger to self or others). In contrast, a child's counseling records belong not to the child, but to the parent or guardian. Technically, if a parent demanded that a counselor disclose the content of his or her child's counseling session, the counselor would be compelled to make that disclosure.

Imagine a surly, angry adolescent who has not requested counseling and has been dragged by his parents to your office; after several stilted meetings with him, he finally is beginning to share some information and engage with you. If his parent insisted that you disclose what the teen told you, in most jurisdictions you would be legally obligated to divulge what the young man had said to you in session.

The implications and necessity of this dilemma about confidentiality and holder of the privilege are obvious from the standpoint of relationship development with this young man. Issues of trust and confidentiality are especially a consideration in working with children because technically you cannot promise confidentiality to a child.

How do counselors navigate this dilemma? One way to work around it is to spend time at the outset of the counseling relationship forging a working alliance not only with the child, but also with the parents. Part of that rapport development should focus on establishing the counselor's credibility and trustworthiness, and for the counselor to explain to parents how *very important* confidentiality and trust are in counseling. It can be helpful for a counselor to state that he or she will probably be able to do more with and for the child if the child could be assured that the parent would not be demanding an itemized accounting of what had been disclosed in a counseling session. Parents are generally willing to agree to respect their child's privacy, as long as they can be assured that if there is information the counselor believes they need to know, they will be advised of it. You need to be completely honest with your minor clients about limits of confidentiality.

In a school setting, the counselor's relationship with the parents may or may not be as relevant as it is in an agency setting. For school counselors, the degree to which parental involvement is a factor in the counseling process depends a lot on the presenting problem. For example, career exploration and investigating colleges for a high school junior might not require much, if any, contact between the school counselor and the parents. In contrast, if a child is being bullied or experiencing other social problems in school, contact between the school counselor and parental involvement could be more pertinent.

Many school counseling interns have at least one or two students on their caseloads who are growing up in seemingly hopeless circumstances with parents that are neglectful or abusive. This seems to happen more frequently in a school setting than in an agency because children are required to be in school; therefore, a child or family who might otherwise not be seen by a therapist may be well known to the school counselor. The unfortunate reality of working with children is that many grow up in the context of relationships or homes that are pathogenic, although the condition of the home situation is not of sufficient severity that the child can be removed from the home by Children's Protective Services. These are among the most difficult circumstances under which to work. Sometimes a counselor has few options for helping a child, beyond offering support and teaching coping skills that might help to offset the negative impact of the home experiences.

If you find yourself working with a client in this type of situation, it may feel discouraging to you; however, *don't underestimate* the value of your relationship with the young person. We will soon be looking at the relative contribution of the counseling relationship in positive counseling outcomes. Furthermore, for some of your clients, you may be one of a very few people who provide to him or her unconditional positive regard, offer the time to listen, and offer an emotionally safe place to be validated. That, in and of itself, can be a great service.

VOLUNTARY AND INVOLUNTARY   The term *voluntary* means either that the client is the one who made the decision to pursue counseling, or that he or she is in agreement with whoever did make the decision that counseling could be helpful. In contrast, *involuntary* generally refers to a person being forced or required to participate in counseling.

A person can be required to enter counseling under any one of a number of circumstances. One context in which involuntary counseling occurs is through the court system. There are a variety of legal charges for which a judge might decide the best consequence is counseling. For example, many jurisdictions have diversion programs for people who are convicted of their first DUI (driving under the influence of alcohol). In a diversion program, the offender is required to participate in a counseling intervention for a specified length of time (often a group counseling program), and if he or she does not participate appropriately, he or she is sent to jail. Another type of legal conviction, the punishment for which may include counseling, is domestic violence.

Dutton (2003) discussed the dynamics of providing court-ordered counseling to men who inflict violence on an intimate partner. He found that of particular note was the clients' anger and defensiveness in the first meeting, which typically gave way to shame as group members shared their stories with one another.

Yet another example of mandatory counseling is when a child has been removed from a parent due to abuse or neglect, and the parent is attempting to regain custody of the child. In these cases, Children's Services or a Juvenile Court judge often will require the parents to participate in group or individual counseling. Parents are also required to demonstrate specified behaviors and skills before the child is returned to the home.

Many prisons have staff psychologists or counselors whose role is to provide counseling to those inmates who want it, and some of those inmates are court-ordered to participate in counseling during their incarceration. Court-ordered counseling during incarceration may be most likely when the client's presenting problem is directly related to the reason for the criminal conviction, for example, sex offenders or people with addiction problems who are serving time for drug-related offenses.

Mandatory counseling as part of a disciplinary response to unacceptable behavior also happens in school settings, including higher education. Kiracofe and Wells (2007) pointed out that it is essential for a school to differentiate between a disciplinary sanction for a violation of the student conduct code, and counseling intended to produce behavior change.

PERSONAL REFLECTION

Have you ever had a friend or family member forced into involuntary treatment? Did that person benefit from the treatment? What factors, in your perception, resulted in the success or lack of success of the treatment?

Any time a person is forced into treatment, it creates a potential tension in the power balance between the counselor and the client. A counselor appointed by some external source, such as a judge, may have been granted some authority over the client. Even if the counselor does not have authority, he or she will still be expected to submit some type of documentation as to the client's participation and degree of benefit at the conclusion of the forced treatment. It can be challenging to maintain one's authority and professionalism and at the same time make the honest, unavoidable acknowledgement that ultimately the decision to engage and participate rests with the client. This is a situational variable in which knowledge of Prochaska's readiness for change model can be of use. That model will be presented shortly.

EMERGENCY APPOINTMENT OR SCHEDULED APPOINTMENT   Circumstances related to being seen on an emergency basis shift the interpersonal dynamics substantially from a scheduled appointment. An emergency, unscheduled appointment implies some type of crisis that is reaching a crescendo.

Understanding these differences in dynamics requires that we look at crisis theory. Numerous circumstances can precipitate crises: a traumatic event like a natural disaster or violence, and other possible sources as well. Crises can be thought of as emanating from two broad categories of precipitants: developmental or situational.

Developmentally Precipitated Crises   When a crisis is developmental, a person is experiencing life events that are *developmentally typical*, for example, graduating from high school and moving away to college, having a baby, an elderly parent dying. Note that typical developmental challenges are culture-specific. Regardless of the details of the typical developmental challenge, the person's response to the developmental event is not adequate to cope with the situational demands, and an emotional crisis ensues.

Situationally Precipitated Crises   The other type of crisis is situational, and these are the types of scenarios most people envision when they think of a crisis. There are many examples of different kinds of situational crises. Some crises occur when an event happens that is outside the realm of typical human experience. Such events could include violence against a person (assault, rape, murder of a close person), accidents (e.g., automobile or farm equipment accident, a house fire), or natural disasters (Hurricane Katrina, earthquakes, mudslides). Think about a counseling session with a person who the day before lost all his earthly belongings in a house fire, and how that session might unfold differently than it would with a person who scheduled an appointment to discuss his worsening depression.

Crises can arise not only from some dramatic precipitating event, but also at any point when we perceive ourselves as unable to cope, or further accommodate *any* set of stressors or precipitants. Sometimes the precipitant may not be one single event or issue, but rather an accumulation of several smaller things that individually might be tolerable, but taken together create an intolerable level of demands for coping. This is like "the straw that breaks the camel's back." When our usual strategies no longer satisfy the environmental demands and our lack of coping becomes increasingly problematic, a crisis may ensue.

When someone is in crisis, a counselor needs to assess the severity of the person's stress symptoms and to be more directive than usual. MacCluskie and Ingersoll (2001) listed the following characteristics of people in crisis:

- Lowered attention span—the person becomes almost exclusively focused on the crisis
- Introversion—the person turns inward and becomes less aware of others in her environment
- Emotional reaching out—the person might come across as significantly more emotionally "needy" than he normally is
- Impulsive and unproductive behaviors—the person might be trying to engage in behaviors to deal with the problem but be going about it in a disorganized and unproductive way
- Subjective sense of extreme vulnerability—the person may be feeling tremendous sense of helplessness and anxiety in the face of the life event over which she has no control (p. 160)

PERSONAL REFLECTION _____

Think of a time in the past when you had a crisis. Which of the listed characteristics did you experience, if any? How did you navigate through the crisis to resolution? Was there someone in your support system who became very directive with you in the decision-making process?

Appropriate steps for treating people in crisis will be enumerated in Chapter 13. Usually when a client has scheduled an appointment, there is a precipitating event, but the level of distress and extent to which it is an acute crisis is somewhat lower.

Length and Frequency of Meeting Time   Length of meeting time, frequency of meetings, and duration of counseling vary substantially across settings and clients. In general, more severe symptoms or impairment necessitate more frequent, intense contact (Beutler & Johannsen, 2006). Thus, a person who is severely depressed and somewhat suicidal might benefit from counseling contacts more frequent than weekly; perhaps meeting every other day might be necessary until the symptoms begin to improve. Agency clients who chronically require frequent meetings may be referred to a Partial Hospitalization Program where a group of clients are able to be given significantly more contact and support than would be possible to offer them individually by a single therapist.

The length of the session is determined by the nature of the client/situation, or it may be determined by the organization. For example, in an emergency situation, a meeting might extend beyond the standard 50-minute hour. Conversely, a school counselor working with a kindergarten student in a nonemergency meeting may only meet with the child for 15 or 20 minutes, considering the child's developmental level and ability to sustain attention and focus.

SELF-DISCLOSURE

Two aspects of your interaction with clients bear mention in this chapter on counseling process. They are not microskills, and yet they will have an impact on your counseling relationships and the nature of your client interactions. These two counselor behaviors are self-disclosure and immediacy. We covered immediacy in Chapter 10. Here, we'll look at counselor self-disclosure.

Video Lab > By Course > Skills/Process/Techniques > Cognitive and Behavioral Interventions > Example of Counselor Self-Disclosure

"Counselor self-disclosure" means exactly what the words imply: sharing with a client aspects of your personal experience. Self-disclosure can take many forms (Wells, 1994). The categories enumerated by Wells include the following:

- Information about the therapist's training or practice, e.g., level and location of education, types of clients served
- Information about personal life circumstances, e.g., relationship status, religious beliefs, sexual orientation
- Personal reactions to the client, e.g., liking or disliking the client, perceptions and feelings about the client's behavior
- Admitting to mistakes made in counseling, e.g., expressing regret for having said something

The training and credentials category of information should, in my opinion, be readily available to any client. Practitioners in many disciplines ranging from medicine, to law, to mental health frame their diplomas and hang them on the wall of their office. Welfel (1998) stated that description of one's credentials is advisable because many clients want this information to decide whether they want to work with you; also, many state licensing boards require counselors to disclose their credentials as part of informed consent for treatment.

Our subsequent discussion of self-disclosure is focused on the other categories of personal information that are more personal or intimate than a summary of your professional training. You might wonder how much to disclose, or whether you should ever disclose anything about your personal values, history, or internal experience. Know first, that there are significant differences among counselors in this regard, and that you will need to find your own comfort level. Although I can offer guidelines for those individuals who do intend to use self-disclosure, you have no obligation to give *any* self-disclosure to your clients. Indeed, if you are not comfortable sharing any information about yourself, you should not do it; your discomfort could result in stiltedness or other nonverbal and paraverbal signals that your client may misinterpret, thereby doing more damage than benefit to your alliance.

A great deal has been written about the impact that counselor self-disclosure has on the client's perception of the counseling process. Many authors emphasize consideration of the ethics related to self-disclosure, and there is also considerable research examining the extent to which clients perceive counselor self-disclosure to be beneficial to the treatment process. Regarding the extent to which self-disclosure is ethical, Peterson (2002) noted that the ethicality of a disclosure is a direct function of the content disclosed. The counselor's intention when making the disclosure is an important consideration. Any intent on the counselor's part to obtain reassurance from the client, or to meet the counselor's need rather than the client's, puts the self-disclosure in the realm of unethical behavior. Unfortunately, though, it can be challenging for a therapist to discern whether the desire to self-disclose to the client is based on the therapist's own needs, or whether it will be in the client's best interest.

Many studies have found self-disclosure to be an effective technique for enhancement of the counseling process. However, it has also been demonstrated to have negative effects if it is used too infrequently, too much, or with poorly chosen content. Several authors (Knox & Hill, 2003; Myers & Hayes, 2006) have summarized research results of many empirical studies about therapist self-disclosure and have generated guidelines to assist therapists in their decision as to when, and how much, self-disclosure is advisable.

- Self-disclosure *is* beneficial to the therapeutic relationship, but only when used mindfully and infrequently.
- The content and level of intimacy of the self-disclosure must be carefully evaluated.

The following case example occurred for one of my counseling interns:

Case Example

Nicole was an agency counseling intern working with "Kim," a young woman who had had a "troubled relationship" with her father. Beyond making that vague disclosure, Kim was reluctant to disclose her childhood experiences with him. Although Kim wondered out loud whether she had been abused, she would change the subject if Nicole asked any questions about Kim's wondering. One day, Nicole accidentally spilled a glass of water during the session, and made a comment about her own clumsiness and how often she spilled things. Both she and Kim started laughing about it, and they continued to laugh and giggle for the last 10 minutes of the session. As Kim was preparing to leave the session, she spontaneously leaned in toward Nicole and said, "I think I'm ready to talk in our next session about what my father did to me." Looking back on it, Nicole was certain that their relationship had become closer because she had spilled water and then made a joke about herself. It seemed to her that it gave Kim a chance to see Nicole as more "human."

Nicole's admission that she often spills drinks because she is distractible is an example of a moderate level of intimacy of information. Following are two additional examples of low, moderate, and high levels of intimacy in a counselor self-disclosure to a client:

Example 1

Low level: I have worked with many clients who have struggled, like you are struggling, with friends bugging them to use drugs.

Moderate level: When I was in high school a lot of my friends started drinking heavily and it was very hard for me, so I think I really do understand what you are going through right now.

High level: Once when I was in high school, a friend and I were driving around. He had a bad drinking problem and we got pulled over and both got charged with under-age drinking. My temporary driver's license was suspended.

Example 2

Low level: I need to reschedule for next week because I have another commitment.

CLIENT: Oh, okay.

Moderate level: I have to reschedule with you for next week because I have a doctor's appointment.

CLIENT: Is everything all right?

COUNSELOR: Well, we're not sure, but I can't say much more about it right now.

High level: I have to reschedule with you because next week I'm going to the doctor for a colonoscopy and biopsy.

CLIENT: Is everything all right?

COUNSELOR: Well, no, I've been having a lot of symptoms and the first biopsy came back questionable, so now I'm being sent to a specialist who is going to do some additional diagnostic work down at the Metro Clinic. I've been there several times before for other cancer scares.

The counselor disclosures at the high level of intimacy are too much information, and both of them offer degrees of detail that are unnecessary for a client to know. In both cases, the information at the high level of intimacy likely is not pertinent to the client's needs. On the other hand, a sketchy description of a past experience or a current issue as a means of expressing empathy or showing that one is a human with frailties and challenges might, for some clients, be helpful.

- Fit the disclosure to the particular client's needs and preferences.
- Make sure the purpose is to help the client and not because it will meet your needs.
- Return the focus to the client after counselor self-disclosure.
- Consider using self-disclosure as part of the termination process.

AUTHOR'S REFLECTION _____

As I was terminating with one client, Kevin, we were discussing the changes that had occurred in his life over the months we had worked together, and the ways he had grown. In that context, I observed that I perceived Kevin to have demonstrated healthy growth in his ability to set boundaries and to be aware of and express his own needs. Kevin expressed surprise at my observation of his behavior, of which he had been peripherally aware. For him the process of change had been so gradual that it wasn't until it was brought to his attention that he was able to contrast his behavior prior to therapy with his behavior at the conclusion of therapy.

Sharing with your clients your own perception of their growth can be instrumental in consolidation of their self-perception.

Multicultural Considerations in Self-Disclosure

Several authors have identified the need for counselors to be aware of differences in preference for degree and type of self-disclosure across particular groups such as ethnic minorities (Cashwell, Shcherbakova, & Cashwell, 2003; Constantine & Kwan, 2003). The relationship between client ethnicity and client preference for therapist self-disclosure is complicated; multiple variables affect the correlation. It appears that the most need for self-disclosure occurs in cross-cultural dyads, meaning that when the counselor and client are of visibly different ethnicities, the client may have increased need for counselor disclosure. Particular cultural groups, though, may have specific preferences that differ from that general statement. For example, some Asian American clients have reported preference for low-level intimacy disclosures, and Hispanic clients may similarly prefer a formal relationship with the counselor including low-level disclosure, especially in the early stages of the counseling process (Constantine & Kwan, 2003).

Other authors have examined the relative benefit of a gay or lesbian therapist self-disclosing about aspects of sexual orientation, such as his or her process of coming out, in the context of working with clients who are gay or lesbian (Bashan, 2005; Kronner, 2005; Satterly, 2004). Counselors who have an area of specialty, such as working with survivors of rape, may believe it to be highly important to disclose their own history with the particular treatment focus. In these cases, the counselor's self-disclosure might serve to establish that he or she fully understands the depth of the client's pain, and also that there is hope for recovery.

One of the consistent themes in working with clients who are in minority groups is counselor awareness about various forms of discrimination, oppression, and microaggression (Sue et al., 2007) to which minorities are exposed with frequency. This includes ethnic minorities, sexual minorities, people with particular disabilities, and particular religious affiliations. One coping response to being socially minimized or marginalized is mistrust of others who do not share one's minority characteristic (Sue & Sue, 2003). It would seem that, especially among clients who have been oppressed or have experienced overt or subtle discrimination, there may be less likelihood to trust a counselor. In working with such people, the research seems to support a correspondingly higher client need for the counselor to be transparent and human.

Chapter Summary

This chapter covered topics that constitute a broad perspective of the counseling process from a variety of angles. We began with a definition and comparison of counseling outcome and process, and looked at the stages of counseling within a session as well as across the duration of a counseling relationship. The remainder of the chapter considered a number of factors that influence the process.

Process refers to the relational and interactive aspects of counseling. Multiple situational variables have tremendous influence on the counseling process; while the aspects we covered are not intended to be an exhaustive list, they should be pertinent to you in your thinking about how to proceed with a given client. Some of the obvious differences between clients or settings include whether your client is a minor or an adult, whether the client is in counseling voluntarily or has been forced by a third party, and whether the counseling is being done on an emergency basis or was previously scheduled.

All of these variables contribute to the overall dynamics that will influence and shape the nature of your counseling interactions with your clients. Having reviewed the wide breadth of variables that affect how and the extent to which a therapeutic relationship unfolds, it is easy to see how each counseling relationship will be a unique experience, not only for your clients, but also for you.

Questions for Class Discussion

1. Under what circumstances, if any, should a person be court-ordered for therapy? To what extent do you agree with the "tough love," confrontational approach to working with clients that are forced into counseling, and why?

2. To what extent is establishing a relationship with a minor client's parents an essential aspect of a good counseling outcome? If you believe that it is important, what are some ideas about how to maintain a minor's trust if he or she perceives you as being aligned on the parents' side?

3. What is your own feeling about counselor self-disclosure? What level of private information are you personally comfortable sharing with your clients? What circumstances would cause you to deviate from your comfort level, either toward more or less personal self-disclosure?

CHAPTER 13

Intake Interviews and Initial Assessment

After studying this chapter, you should have a clear understanding of the following:

- The purpose of an intake
- The importance of explaining limits of confidentiality before any other conversation transpires
- The relationship among assessment, diagnosis, and treatment planning
- Essential elements of an intake
- Specific techniques for getting accurate intake information
- Risk assessment for violence and suicide prevention
- The controversy around diagnosis
- The difference between diagnosis and case formulation
- The connection between case formulation and multicultural competence

This chapter covers aspects of first sessions with a client. Chapter 12 talked about what happens in a first session from a counseling process perspective. In contrast, the emphasis in this chapter is upon acquiring objective information.

Table 13.1 summarizes the broad questions you should be seeking to answer in a first session with a client as well as the techniques or actions one can take to answer the corresponding question. This chapter discusses those techniques.

A good intake interview will enable you to answer these broad questions and generate a comprehensive, culturally sensitive conceptualization of your client. Gathering background information about the client and about the presenting concern forms one basis for a good first session. This data then will enable an accurate case conceptualization, a preliminary goal that is appropriate for every individual with whom you work, regardless of the setting. Note also that the question about technical skill is an aspect of service delivery we haven't talked about yet; the ethical imperative is to be aware of our own limits of

TABLE 13.1   Broad Intake Questions and Ways to Acquire the Information

Broad Question	How to Acquire the Information
How much distress is this person in right now, and how imminently does something need to be done about it?	Assess subjective distress and objective impairment
Is anyone in potential danger as a result of this person's disturbance, and if so, how imminently do I need to do something about it?	Assess potential for risk of harm to self or others
To what extent is this problem "state" or "trait" for this person?	Risk assessment and diagnostic conceptualization
Based on my other counseling experiences and base rates in the general population, how unusual is this person's presentation?	Knowledge of human development and developmental typicality
Do I know enough about his or her cultural context to assess the developmental typicality of this person's problem?	Application of multicultural ethical principles as well as the Bronfenbrenner and Hofstede models
Do I have the technical skills to help with this problem, or should this client be referred to someone with expertise that I lack?	Treatment planning, honest and accurate assessment of one's skills

competence and know when it is proper and appropriate to send a client to another counselor or specialist.

It may be helpful to begin with a brief definition of three terms explored in the remainder of the chapter. *Assessment* means collecting data and evaluating that data on the basis of some normative comparison. *Diagnosis,* a term that emanates from a medical model, refers to the process of identifying and labeling a disorder. *Treatment planning* is the process by which the outcome goals for treatment are identified. We move now to each of those in turn.

ASSESSMENT

This stage of interaction is the information-gathering stage. Actually, a counselor's information gathering does not stop over the entire course of time he or she is working with a client. However, the process of gathering background information and developing a sense of the client's context is especially important at the outset of the counseling relationship.

There are many different types of data you can obtain. The types of data you may have the option to use include client verbal and nonverbal behavior, self-report, and in some cases collateral report, test results, prior treatment records, or school records. One way data is differentiated is self-report (subjective) and other-report (objective). The relevance of differentiating subjective from objective data is to enable you to compare the client's perception of the problem with others' perception (including your own perception of his or her issues). A great deal of disparity between the subjective and objective suggests several possibilities. It could be that the client lacks insight, may be out of touch with what is happening, or that you have not gotten sufficient contextual information.

Precipitating Events

Perhaps one of the first questions that a counselor may ask a client, once the pleasantries have been proffered, is, "What has brought you in today?" or "What's been going on that prompted you to schedule this appointment?" The purpose of asking this type of question is to identify the precipitating event. A *precipitating event* is whatever occurrence resulted in the client seeking counseling. Precipitants can be anything. Sometimes your client will not be able to articulate one specific occurrence, instead reporting a gradual increase in stress, or a gradual accumulation of stressors that are no longer manageable.

Multicultural Considerations

There are several aspects of precipitating events that are subject to misunderstanding due to cultural differences between a counselor and client. First, there is the obvious impediment imposed by language and communication problems if both individuals are not fluent in the same language. Second, there are the more subtle impediments that can be introduced by the counselor using his or her own cultural frame of reference for evaluating the "health" or "disturbance" inherent in another person's behavior. This issue will be covered in greater detail later in this chapter.

In the present context, we are looking only at techniques for eliciting a client's description of the presenting issues. Assessment questions can be posed in a manner conducive to multicultural sensitivity. These queries are phrased to lend a clear understanding of the person's worldview. Lonner and Ibrahim (2002, p. 356) suggested the following culturally sensitive questions:

> What do you call the problem?
>
> What do you think has caused the problem?
>
> Why do you think it started when it did?
>
> What do you think the sickness does? How does it work?
>
> How severe is the sickness? Will it have a short or long course?
>
> What kind of treatment do you think the patient should receive?
>
> What are the chief problems the sickness has caused?
>
> What do you fear most about the sickness?

When the client *is* able to name the precipitant, you have a piece of data. This data offers a preliminary clue as to the nature of the client's disturbance.

Organic or Medical Conditions

One thing that needs to be ruled out as early as possible is whether evidence suggests there could be an organic or medical cause for the client's emotional or psychological symptoms. Pollack, Levy, and Breitholtz (1999) stated that as many as 10% of the clients who present at a mental health center for psychological symptoms are in fact suffering from a physical problem that is generating the psychological symptoms. In some cases, the physical problem may be a very serious condition, such as a metabolic disorder, a seizure, or a brain tumor. Even if the medical problem is not imminently dangerous, an undiagnosed medical condition that is causing the client's symptoms will result in the client appearing to have persistent problems that are not responsive to the treatment strategies you are using. A careful assessment of your client's presenting problem, including the pattern of onset and history of similar episodes, will give you some insight as to whether there should be further investigation as to possible physical origins for the symptoms. Following are some characteristics of presenting issues that have a significant correlation with medical conditions, according to Pollack, Levy, and Breitholtz (1999):

- *A first episode of severe symptoms such as catatonia, psychosis, or extreme mood disturbance*

When there is no pattern of prior psychiatric involvement, a first episode of dramatic symptoms should always have a rule out of physical cause for the symptoms.

- *An abrupt change in symptoms, especially when the change involves a noticeable shift in mood or behavior*

Case Example

Jonathan was a 43-year-old male who had always been stable and highly functioning. However, over the course of several days, Jonathan became increasingly moody and overly reactive to minor events. Then one evening he began hearing voices. His wife took him to the emergency room where a blood test revealed that he had a severe bladder infection and prostatitis, even though he did not complain of physical pain.

- *First onset of symptoms after age 40*

It is typical, if a person has a major psychiatric condition, for symptoms to emerge earlier in life than middle age. For example, schizophrenia usually first appears among males in their late teens to early 20s, and for females in their 20s and 30s (National Institute of Mental Health, 2008)

- *Symptoms of mental illness that emerge close in time to a major medical illness, particularly when the illness involves a fever*
- *No identifiable situational stressors to account for the symptoms*
- *Symptoms that are disproportionately severe for the intensity of the stressor*
- *Vegetative and cognitive complaints that are unusually severe for the magnitude of the stressor*

Case Example

Isabelle was a 77-year-old Caucasian woman who had recently experienced the death of her beloved toy poodle. She complained of sadness and guilt related to the dog's illness, but her main complaint was that she noticed a great deal more forgetfulness and difficulty concentrating on her needlework projects. Lab work conducted by her physician determined that she had a folic acid deficiency, and with vitamin supplements, her memory and concentration improved significantly.

- *A rapidly evolving shift in level of consciousness, such as fluctuating levels of alertness, spells of disorientation, confusion, or short-term memory loss*

- *Hallucinations that are not auditory (visual, tactile, gustatory, or olfactory hallucinations are not typical symptoms of psychosis)*
- *Changes in motor functioning, such as development of a tic, dysarthria (trouble with clear pronunciation of words), tremor, or coordination impairment*
- *Experiential anomalies such as déjà vu (a sense of familiarity in a new situation), the opposite of déjà vu, which is jamais vu (an experience of unfamiliarity in familiar surroundings), or depersonalization (losing the sense of who one is)*
- *Signs of neurological dysfunction, such as inability to name familiar objects (agnosia), language disturbance (aphasia), or apraxia (inability to perform familiar motor sequences such as signing one's name, despite intact muscle functioning)*
- *A history of multiple medical disorders that can be associated with mental status change*
- *Symptoms of organ failure that can be associated with brain function, such as jaundice related to kidney function, or dyspnea (difficulty breathing) associated with cardiac or pulmonary disease. In these cases, the body's inability to cleanse itself of toxins, or properly oxygenate the blood, can affect neurological functioning in a way that produces psychiatric symptoms.*
- *Headaches in the absence of a headache history with an acute, recurrent, or chronic progressive pattern (this is more likely to be related to an underlying medical condition if the headaches are accompanied by other severe symptoms such as vomiting, cognitive impairment, or visual changes)*

Some of the most commonly occurring medical disorders that are misdiagnosed as psychological disorders, according to the authors, include hyper- or hypothyroidism, temporal lobe seizure disorder, HIV/AIDs dementia, multiple sclerosis, and sleep apnea. There are also some neurodevelopmental disorders that may initially look like mental disorders; these include attention deficit disorder, Asperger's disorder, and nonverbal learning disability syndrome.

Assessment of the above characteristics may seem straightforward and clear. Nevertheless, it can be very difficult to differentiate symptoms that are unique to a given episode from symptoms that are common for your client. Additionally, some characteristics that may seem strange or unfamiliar to you may be commonplace in your client's culture of origin. This is where some knowledge about different levels of groups/systems to which your client belongs will help give you some normative data.

For instance, perhaps in your junior high school counseling job, you are accustomed to seeing students who are being excluded by other students and subtly teased throughout the day. A seventh-grade student might arrive at your office in tears over comments classmates made about her clothing. While this student's response is very strong, or perhaps even unusual in that adolescents do not often cry in front of other people at school, the precipitant itself is *developmentally typical*. Many individuals at her developmental stage are faced with similar challenges. On the other hand, if a seventh-grader is referred to your office because he is having a loud conversation with an invisible friend, this precipitant is developmentally *atypical*.

The thought of a "counseling session" may conjure an image of a client and counselor sitting down together in some private space, discussing topics of concern to the client. In the context of an intake interview, though, a number of circumstances may necessitate getting ancillary information from individuals in addition to the identified client. For example, if a child has been referred to the school counselor due to disruptive behavior in the classroom, and the child flatly denies any difficulty as well as denying awareness of a problem, it will be helpful to have some information from the teacher regarding the specifics of the acting out behavior. Likewise, if a family member has brought a client who is extremely depressed to a counseling center, and the client is only minimally responsive to the counselor, it could be extremely important to get information from the collateral family member about the client's symptoms and current behavior.

Inconsistent Reports Between People

If the circumstances of counseling are such that you can gather information from a collateral individual, note the degree of consistency between the reports of the client and the collateral. When there is inconsistency, is one or the other of these individuals selectively perceiving or disregarding things? Or is there purposeful misrepresentation of information, and if so, for what reason?

Sometimes there is inconsistent reporting between collaterals. For example, some agency counselors who work with children obtain behavioral ratings on a standardized form from a parent and also from the child's classroom teacher. The behavioral ratings given by a parent are sometimes quite inconsistent with those given by the teacher. When this happens, it is important for the counselor to further speak with all the reporting individuals to get as much information as possible as to why there are discrepancies. The child's behavior may be radically different at school than at home. Perhaps one or both of the raters has unrealistic expectations for behavior among children who are the client's age.

AUTHOR'S REFLECTION _____

When I was in training, I wondered how I could know whether what my client was telling me was really true. One client in particular came to sessions complaining about "manipulative" things her husband was doing around the house, and I wondered about the extent to which her stories were true. I wondered if I should somehow try to verify the accuracy of the client's statements. My supervisor's response to me was, "Work within your client's world." In other words, adopt the client's view of reality as reality and work from there.

From a person-centered, phenomenological perspective, it makes sense to honor and respect the client's view of reality. However, if the client's sense of reality is grossly discrepant with the views of most other people, there comes a point where the discrepant perception represents a thought disorder. It requires clinical judgment to accurately ascertain where that line is.

Personality Style and Typicality

Part of the assessment process is to get a general sense of this person sitting before you and his or her typical way of being in the world. It can be challenging at first to discern your client's style of perceiving his or her environment. There are general personality styles of optimism and pessimism, degrees of awareness of emotional aspects of situations, and so on, which represent "trait" patterns as opposed to "state." In the context of the Big Five personality model, there are five aspects of each individual's personality structure, all of which occur on a continuum. Use of an instrument such as the NEO-PI-R is sometimes useful in distinguishing between state and trait aspects of your client's situation.

Besides the person's style of personality, a skilled clinician also needs to have some knowledge about healthy development and the developmental stages through which many people progress over the lifespan. Some readers will be required to complete a course in lifespan development as part of their graduate program for that very reason.

Stages of lifespan development can have cultural variability. As an illustration, for Latinas, turning 15 years of age represents moving into womanhood, and a party called the *quinceanera* celebrates the transition. In a Latino family, there may be some shifts in family roles and the expectations for the young woman; this role shift would not necessarily be present in a family of European descent. Be careful not to assume that your client's patterns are atypical responses or behaviors if you are not thoroughly familiar with the cultural background and culturally based role expectations for your client.

Precipitants That Constitute Crises

We talked in several earlier chapters about crises, both developmental and situational. A developmental crisis is essentially an exacerbation of dynamics or symptoms that are sequelae of typical developmental issues. In contrast, a situational precipitant is a circumstance that is not necessarily a typical event for most people. The range of possible situations is as infinitely variable as individuals are. A given precipitant that might be easily taken in stride by one person can be a life-shattering event for another person. Being able to have a client describe the precipitant and how it has affected him or her is another piece of data that is pertinent to assessment.

As defined previously, ego strength and resilience are essentially the psychological equivalents of shock absorbers on a car. As you listen to a person talk about the precipitant, try to have some awareness of what his or her presentation suggests about his or her level of resilience and ego strength; you will need to consider and integrate these in the eventual treatment planning.

There have been several attempts to develop a rating scale that would help clinicians assign numerical values to various life events that are common precipitants of stress. For example, Holmes and Rahe (1967), the first to try to quantify the impact of life stressors, developed the Life Events scale. Topping their list for stressors was death of a spouse, followed by incarceration, divorce, and death of a close family member. It's hard, though, to come up with a definitive list of stressors that is universal, because the meaning one attaches to a given precipitant affects the level of stress it generates. Note that in addition to the negative connotation of "stress," there also is "eustress." *Eustress* is the term for the energy required in adjusting to a shift in life circumstance, even if it is a "happy" or desired shift. Relocation to a new city, getting married, a job promotion, or the arrival of a new baby can all take a toll on a person's coping resources and contribute to less emotional energy available for accommodating other stressors that may arise.

CURRENT IMPAIRMENT

One useful combination of measures for determining the acute severity of a person's disturbance is (1) the subjective level of distress, and (2) the degree of impairment in the person's daily functioning.

Subjective Distress

The *subjective level of distress* reflects how much emotional discomfort the person is reporting, while the degree of impairment in daily functioning can be somewhat estimated by integrating the client's report and your observation of aspects of the person's behavior in your presence. An example of a means by which you can get a sense of the intensity of a person's emotional discomfort is to have him or her rate it on a scale of 1 to 10 or 1 to 100. If you use a rating scale, define what the two anchors of the scale indicate. The number that a client offers as a description of his or her discomfort is specifically referred to as a *subjective unit of distress*. Here is an example:

COUNSELOR:	John, I know you said you've been quite depressed and discouraged for the past several months. If you were going to assign the intensity of your depression on a scale of 1 to 10, with 1 being almost none and 10 being so bad you can't do anything but sit, what number would you give it?
JOHN:	It's about a 7.5.
COUNSELOR:	Has there been a time in your life that it was a 0?
JOHN:	Of course!
COUNSELOR:	When was that?

This dialogue example also includes a question intended to gauge the client's *premorbid level of distress*. It can be useful to get some sense of the extent to which the current emotional experience is a departure from how the client usually feels. Use of the subjective unit of distress is a behavioral technique, and it can serve dual purposes. In addition to informing you of the client's self-reported present measurement, the level of distress at which he rates himself can also serve as a baseline point of comparison, so that after several more sessions, you may again ask the client for a self-report of the intensity of the emotion.

Impairment in Daily Functioning

The other aspect of impairment is ability to meet daily demands. There are a number of ways you can ask about this. Following is an example of how to assess a person's level of daily functioning:

COUNSELOR:	John, since you've been depressed, have you still been making it to class every day?
JOHN:	Well, I've been able to drag myself in most days, but every once in a while I just lie in bed and think, "Oh, what's the point?" so then I don't go to work. If I failed the course, who would care?
COUNSELOR:	Sounds like some days you are so discouraged and down you can't even get out of bed.
JOHN:	Yep. And that's really awful. I hate feeling like this.
COUNSELOR:	Besides not going to class, have you been able to keep up with things around your apartment?
JOHN:	What do you mean?
COUNSELOR:	Well, I'm wondering about your day-to-day tasks like fixing food to eat and doing laundry so you have clean clothes to wear. Sometimes when people get very depressed they stop taking care of themselves. Do you eat your meals at regular times?

JOHN:	Mostly.
COUNSELOR:	What do you usually eat for lunch and dinner? How about dinner?
JOHN:	Doritos and French onion dip is the only thing that tastes good to me.
COUNSELOR:	How different is your eating now, compared to how you ate before you were depressed?

The counselor is looking here for a description of whether the client's behavior has changed in the context of the presenting problem. "Impairment" in daily functioning and meeting daily demands depends on what typical demands are for a person of that developmental stage. In the case of John, above, because he is a full-time college student and not working, his pattern of staying in bed and not attending class represents a moderate degree of impairment as a result of the depression.

We've talked at length about client observation; it may be helpful to briefly refer back to Chapter 5, "Client Observation," to refresh your recollection of the aspects of your client's behavior that can offer information. Essentially, *all* of your client's verbal and nonverbal behaviors are potentially sources of information about him or her.

INTAKE INTERVIEWS

These categories of information, adapted in part from MacCluskie and Ingersoll (2001, p. 150), are recommended as important for inclusion in an intake:

- Client description of the precipitant
- Relevant history of the precipitant
- Family history
- Legal history
- Employment or academic history
- Mental status
- Suicidal/homicidal ideation/plans
- Medical history
- Current medications
- Allergies
- Drug/alcohol/tobacco/caffeine history and current use
- Previous mental health contacts

A variety of standardized instruments are available for a counselor to gather this comprehensive breadth of information. Many agencies have a standard intake form that must be completed on a client. Even when there is standardized information you need to acquire, however, there are some questions and ways of asking questions that will give a more accurate set of data.

In Chapter 7 on asking questions, I talked about asking questions in a way that gives implicit permission for the client to admit to socially unacceptable behaviors and symptoms. When I'm asking a client about the family system in the client's household of origin, rather than asking a closed question like, "Was your upbringing a happy one?" I say, "Would you give me three words that best describe what it was like growing up in your family?" Then I record the three adjectives and follow up with open-ended inquiries for the client to elaborate on those words. This often yields a wealth of information.

Among the list of information categories are numerous items related to physical and medical aspects of your client's current picture. This relates back to our earlier discussion about conscientiously accounting for medical and physical components that may be significantly affecting the clinical picture.

There is not room here to cover specific questions to ask regarding those categories. However, getting comprehensive information across so many aspects of a person's past and present is important for two reasons. First, it gives you a maximum amount of data about past events that could have set the stage for the present picture. Second, even if past events did not necessarily contribute to the current problem, you will nevertheless have the best chance of fully understanding the various contexts and levels of context in which your client exists.

One category of intake information in particular does merit further expansion here because of the implications of the information; this is the item on suicidal or homicidal ideation and plans. In the following section, we will talk about how to assess risk. The next chapter, which covers choosing treatment strategies, will offer you suggestions about strategies for working with clients who present some degree of risk for harm to themselves or to other people.

ASSESSMENT OF SUICIDE RISK

One of the questions in Table 13.1 is identification of possible risk. The purpose of considering the degree of risk is to ascertain how imminently you need to take steps, and how drastic your steps need to be, to prevent self-inflicted harm. If a client tells you, or you become informed, that he or she has the intention to harm him or herself, in most states you are required by law to take action to prevent that harm from occurring. The specific details of *when* and *how* you must report vary between jurisdictions; you will need to be aware of the laws in your particular state. One exception would be if you were to assess a client who disclosed that she or he engages in self-mutilation behavior such as cutting. While self-mutilation carries risk, it can be differentiated from a suicide attempt in that a person who self-mutilates typically does not intend to kill herself; the cutting is a coping strategy.

The whole purpose of suicide risk assessment is to generate an estimation of the likelihood that the person will actually follow through with plans for behavior intended to result in serious or fatal harm. Know that it is never possible to predict with 100% accuracy what another person will choose, but with empirical information about risk factors that correlate with suicide, we can learn to make good, educated guesses. So the following information about how to assess probability is the first of two steps; after assessing probability, the next phase is to take steps to avert the suicide attempt from occurring.

Even though you may feel uncomfortable broaching the topic of suicide with your clients, it will be necessary for you to do so, especially in an intake. Sometimes novice counselors express fear that by inquiring about suicide, they will give the client ideas that hadn't previously occurred to him or her. However, some people at least fleetingly have thoughts about their own death, and suicidal thoughts for someone who is significantly distressed are not unusual. Clients who have suicidal ideation often have one of two intentions: either to end their own emotional suffering, or to extract revenge on someone who has hurt them. A counselor's accurate understanding of the client's motivation for suicide offers clues about where the focus of treatment, at least initially, needs to be.

Because suicide is a subject with which some people feel uncomfortable, it may be valuable to initiate your questions about suicidal and homicidal ideation in a way that implicitly gives your client permission to admit that he or she thinks about it. If you ask a person, "Do you ever think about killing yourself?" you are asking for an admission of a behavior that, for some people, is not socially acceptable. Thus, it may be more embarrassing and therefore less likely that your client will say yes. On the other hand, if you ask, "*How often* do you think about killing yourself?" you've communicated that you already assume it happens, so the person will be less likely to be afraid of shocking you if he or she admits it. If you are wrong in your assumption and the person actually does not engage in suicidal thoughts, he or she will just say something like, "I *never* do" or "I don't" or, "Oh I couldn't do that—it's a mortal sin!"

Through careful research and analysis of completed suicides, it has been possible for researchers to identify risk factors that are associated with a suicide attempt. The presence of multiple risk factors may correspond to an increased likelihood that the client will make an attempt. Note that these factors correlate with suicidality, which means that they often co-occur. There is no causal relationship implied here, simply recognition that presence of any of these risk factors may correspond to presence of suicidal ideation or attempts. According to Rogers (2001, p. 260), the risk factors for suicide include

- Cultural and religious beliefs
- History of psychiatric problems
- History of substance abuse
- Suicidal ideation, including a plan and a suicide note
- Prior suicide attempts
- Access to a means of attempting suicide that could be lethal
- Social isolation (absence of an appropriate, healthy support system)
- Feelings of worthlessness
- Hopelessness
- Depression
- Impulsivity
- Hostility
- Intent to die
- Marital stress and family factors
- Environmental stress (either real or anticipated)
- Physical illness
- Family history of suicide
- Lack of access to mental health services

Table 13.2 offers a synopsis of information (Schwartz & Rogers, 2004) regarding how to estimate the overall suicidal lethality of a client.

PERSONAL REFLECTION

Have you ever known or personally known of someone who either attempted or completed a suicide? How many of the above listed risk factors were part of that person's clinical picture?

Please note that when a client initially presents as severely depressed and suicidal, there may be a great deal of lethargy and inertia. Because antidepressant medication can carry a side effect of agitation, coupled with the increase in energy that occurs after someone has been medicated for a short time, the likelihood of carrying out a suicide plan can actually increase even when it looks on the outside as if the person is getting "better." Thus, when a client has disclosed suicidal ideation, it is important for you to continue to assess his or her thoughts and feelings about it over an extended period of time throughout the individual's treatment.

TABLE 13.2 Assessing Suicidal Lethality (from Schwarz & Rogers, 2004)

Low lethality	• Thinking about it but no intention to carry it out • No specific plan • No prior attempts
Moderate lethality	• Presence of more than one risk factor • Thinking about it and intention but no specific plan • Motivated to feel better
High lethality	• Client has several risk factors in clinical picture • Thinking about it, talking about it, intent to do it • Clear, concrete plan • Access to the means to carry out the plan
Very high lethality	• Thinking about it • Clear plan including immediate access to the means • Black-and-white thinking with no hope for improvement in the future • Lack of recognition of any social support • History of prior suicide attempts

ASSESSMENT OF VIOLENCE RISK

We will shift the focus here from suicide risk to risk of violent, aggressive behavior directed at others. Haggard-Grann (2007) made an important point, observing that the purpose of risk assessment is to *prevent* violence, as opposed to predicting it. There are frequent stories in the media about random shootings and other acts of violence across the United States, such as the campus shootings at Virginia Tech in the spring of 2007. Given the prominence of these stories, the stakes now seem higher than ever when it comes to mental health professionals being able to identify risk factors in anticipating possible violent behavior among their clients. Truscott, Evans, and Marshall (1995) noted more than a decade ago that a legal precedent was becoming established holding mental health professionals responsible for their clients' behavior outside of a counseling session.

Counselors are faced with a real dilemma between being aware of ethical responsibility to their clients, and yet also respecting the need to protect intended victims. Some authors report a substantial improvement in the empirically based tools for risk assessment (Douglas & Kropp, 2002). For example, a variety of normed, standardized assessment instruments are available for risk assessment. Examples of such instruments include the Violence Risk Appraisal Guide (Harris, Rice, & Quinsey, 1993), the HCR (Historical, Clinical, and Risk Management Scheme) (Webster, Douglas, Eaves, & Hart, 1997), the Static-99 (Hanson & Thornton, 1999) for sexual offending, and the Sexual Violence Risk-20 (Boer, Hart, Kropp, & Webster, 1997). All of these instruments were developed from empirical investigation of variables that carry statistically significant predictive value in the realm of violent behavior.

A number of studies have examined other aspects of individuals with proneness to violence. One study tabulated the informal criteria and strategies most frequently used by experienced clinicians (Odeh, Zeiss, & Huss, 2006). Interviews with 80 psychologists, psychiatrists, social workers, and nurses (20 in each respective group) revealed a set of

13 risk cues commonly used to estimate risk of violence. They are listed here in descending order of frequency:

- Past assaults
- Compliance with prescribed psychotropic medication
- History of substance abuse
- Presence of psychosis
- Ideation about assault
- Prior psychiatric admissions
- Paranoid delusions
- Mental illness
- Uncooperativeness
- Poor impulse control
- History of using a weapon
- Family problems

From a contrasting angle, Welches and Pica (2005) interviewed 9 men who had been hospitalized for potential dangerousness to others, thereby establishing constructive narratives of their prehospitalization experiences. The aspects of their subjective experiences shared by almost all the interviewees included having a sense of being alone, having long-standing feelings of inadequacy, being fearful of losing control, and having a sense of being depressed, unloved, and misunderstood. In all cases, the precipitating situation just prior to their hospitalizations involved circumstances that threatened their self-esteem and an increased level of anxiety about "becoming nothing."

Once again, as with assessment of risk potential in suicidality, the higher the number of risk factors that are present, the more likely that some violent behavior will occur. Truscott and Evans (2001, pp. 272–273) identified a "fictional modal person," meaning a description of the individual with the most commonly occurring characteristics, and other risk factors for violent behavior.

Individual Characteristics

- Male, late teens to early 20s, history of opiate or alcohol abuse
- Low IQ and level of education
- Unstable residential and employment history
- History of violent behavior—the more recent, severe, and frequent the prior violent incidents, the lower the threshold for current risk (red flags are juvenile or adult court involvement for violence, psychiatric hospitalizations for violent behavior, and self-reported violence)*
- Combat or martial arts training, or very strong

*Those variables related to history are the single most powerful predictor of proneness to future violent behavior.

Situational Characteristics

- Intended victim known to the client
- History of aggressing toward a particular type of person or in a particular setting
- Intended victim accessible to the client
- Client actively inebriated with alcohol
- Stress related to family/relationship, peer group, money, or job

When you are assessing a person for potential to commit violence toward another, Truscott and Evans (2001) suggest two components to consider: violence threshold and therapeutic alliance.

Threshold for Violence

As mentioned in the section about precipitants, everyone has a breaking point. The same can be said for potential for violence; virtually every person has a threshold that when crossed, will result in violent behavior. Given this awareness, the question in risk assessment becomes not whether a person will be violent or not, but rather, at what level is this person's threshold?

Research on this topic has led us to the recognition that violent behavior is the result of two interacting dynamics: stable traits possessed by an individual, coupled with particular situational characteristics of the environment. Truscott, Evans, and Marshall (1995) noted that with regard to exhibiting violent behavior, "individual characteristics are neither necessary or sufficient whereas in most cases situational characteristics can be" (p. 485). Thus, stable characteristics lower a person's threshold; someone who demonstrates many of the traits typical of violence-prone people will be at high risk for violent behavior in response to relatively fewer situational precipitants.

Therapeutic Alliance

The other aspect of risk assessment is the treatment alliance; this is a variable that can potentially help raise the person's threshold. In an intake session, before you have had much opportunity to establish rapport, you will likely have less of a therapeutic alliance than you will have with a client you have worked with longer.

Nevertheless, even in a new counseling relationship such as an intake session, awareness that a solid counseling relationship can mitigate risk of violent behavior points to the importance of expressing empathy and concern for the client. In the study by Welches and Pica (2005), all 9 individuals who were hospitalized due to danger to others reported similar emotional themes. These might be similarly prominent themes for a client you are assessing for violence. Those clients reported feelings of aloneness, long histories of feeling inadequate, fear of loss of control, and a perception that precipitating situations represented threats to their self-esteem. Thus, their fantasies about aggression essentially represented their efforts to become empowered and adequate.

The next chapter on treatment strategies devotes space to empirically based suggestions for intervention. In either case of suicidal or homicidal/violent intent, many factors must enter the decision-making process about exactly how to proceed. Although we may envision ourselves as immediately phoning 911 when a client discloses thoughts about perpetrating violence, there are many shades of gray and intermediate steps between doing nothing and calling the police. The presence and extent of your therapeutic alliance with your client is one of those variables, and as stated previously, there are differences between state jurisdictions as to what the laws stipulate for reporting suspected violent or suicidal intent.

DIAGNOSIS

Diagnosis is the process of identifying a disorder. As you read the material that we just covered in the assessment portion of this chapter, perhaps you were struck by the breadth and volume of information that may be acquired in an intake. After all that information has been gathered, a counselor must then sift through the accumulated data and prioritize which aspects of the story are most relevant to the diagnostic and counseling process.

When a client presents a multitude of behaviors, symptoms, concerns, and aspects of personal history that are potential foci for counseling, prioritization requires judgment on the counselor's part. There is also judgment required when the counselor must make a decision, in the face of suspicion about danger to self or others, as to how to proceed with a client. The judgment involved is an inherent component of the diagnostic process. Many third-party payers, in an effort to be as cost-effective as possible, expect a clinician to generate a diagnostic impression very shortly after beginning with a client. Sometimes a diagnosis is expected at the end of a first meeting! Many Western physicians use the same process every time a patient comes to their office complaining of various physical symptoms.

Counselors are faced with finding a balance between trying to be as efficient as possible, yet also delaying generation of a diagnostic conceptualization until it is clear that all relevant information has been evaluated and accounted for in the final diagnosis. In the mental health field diagnosis is often accomplished using the medical model of comparing a person's symptoms to the criteria that are put forth by the DSM-IV-TR (*Diagnostic and Statistical Manual,* 4th edition, Text Revision; American Psychiatric Association, 2000). If the person's symptoms meet the diagnostic criteria, then a diagnostic label is assigned to the person's disorder.

DSM-IV-TR Multiaxial Diagnosis

Some psychiatric diagnoses frequently appear in the media. Numerous television advertisements and movie characters give wide exposure to psychological disorders such as clinical depression, substance dependence, and anxiety disorders (such as obsessive compulsive disorder). Less commonly known is that there are five axes on which mental health professionals assess and diagnose human functioning. The diagnoses mentioned above (clinical depression, substance dependence, obsessive compulsive disorder) represent only a diagnosis on the first of the five axes. A proper DSM-IV-TR diagnosis involves diagnoses or provision of data on all five axes. Please note that not everyone will have a diagnosis on every category; there is a provision for a counselor to note "No diagnosis" on axes I through III if the person has no relevant conditions. The five axes are:

Axis I: Clinical Disorders and Other Disorders That May Be a Focus of Clinical Attention

Axis II: Personality Disorders and Mental Retardation

Axis III: General Medical Conditions

Axis IV: Psychosocial and Environmental Problems

Axis V: Global Assessment of Functioning

The axes provide the following information:

AXIS I: CLINICAL DISORDERS AND OTHER DISORDERS THAT MAY BE A FOCUS OF CLINICAL ATTENTION   This is the axis on which the vast majority of mental and emotional disorders would be assigned. The explicit diagnostic criteria ("rules") that must be met in order to make the diagnosis are provided for each diagnosis in the manual.

AXIS II: PERSONALITY DISORDERS AND MENTAL RETARDATION   This axis reflects those disorders that have been present developmentally and represent a longstanding, impaired level of functioning in comparison to the person's chronological peers. Again, explicit symptoms and characteristics are listed and must be met for the diagnosis to be made.

AXIS III: GENERAL MEDICAL CONDITIONS   On this axis clinicians are able to identify physical conditions regardless of whether those conditions are visibly impinging on the person's psychological functioning. Sometimes the medical condition will be the direct cause of mental disorders, whereas other times it may have bearing on the mental disorder without being directly connected.

AXIS IV: PSYCHOSOCIAL AND ENVIRONMENTAL PROBLEMS   This axis provides a vehicle with which to account for circumstances external to the individual that nevertheless are implicated in the diagnosis, treatment, or prognosis for that person. There are a variety of categories offered that include, for example, problems with primary support group (e.g., death of a significant family member), educational problems (e.g., interpersonal problems with a teacher), occupational problems (e.g., job loss), and problems with access to health care services (e.g., lack of transportation to medical appointments, lack of health insurance).

AXIS V: GLOBAL ASSESSMENT OF FUNCTIONING   On this axis the clinician is called upon to make an educated judgment as to the extent to which the individual can effectively meet daily demands. It enables one to review all the pertinent aspects of the individual's problems and then estimate how functional the person is. The Global Assessment of Functioning (referred to as the "GAF") score can range from 100 ("superior functioning in a wide range of activities") to 1 ("persistent danger of severely hurting self or others OR persistent inability to maintain personal hygiene OR serious suicidal act with clear expectation of death").

The entire DSM-IV-TR is devoted to providing clinicians with descriptive criteria for diagnosing clients on each of these five axes. Regardless of whether you are a clinician who is diagnosing clients, or one who is not legally permitted to diagnose and treat mental and emotional disorders, it will be important for you to have an understanding of how to interpret a five-axis diagnosis. It is extremely likely that you will be working with people who have been given a full five-axis diagnosis at some point.

There are advantages and disadvantages to using a DSM-IV diagnosis. During our discussion in Chapter 5, "Client Observation," one point frequently emphasized was the importance of trying to refrain from judgment in your observations. When you enter the stage of the counseling process in which you must formulate a diagnostic impression, you actually *do* need to exert some judgment upon the total accumulation of data about your client.

You will likely take a course on diagnosis or case conceptualization as part of your curriculum. Rather than going into great detail here about the process of diagnosis, we will discuss issues *related* to diagnosis.

Not everyone in the counseling professions agrees that diagnosis is either helpful or necessary. We will look at two of the major issues surrounding the disagreement about diagnostic process, and then you will be presented with some questions to ask yourself in order to mitigate the impact of those issues in your own practice. Two noted areas of problems related to diagnosis are (1) the arbitrary sociopolitical factors endemic to diagnosis, and (2) the high rate of frequency with which clinicians make errors in clinical judgment.

The Sociopolitical Nature of Diagnosis

The practice of using an established manual such as the DSM-IV-TR to diagnose clients with emotional concerns is highly controversial in the discipline of counseling (Ivey & Ivey, 1999). Many authors believe that rather than being helpful, it actually is detrimental and demeaning to reduce a person's problem to a label; some psychiatric labels carry a negative social connotation. It sparks debate in other mental health disciplines as well, but because the origin of counseling was developmentally oriented, with emphasis on healthy development as opposed to pathology, many authors believe that counselors' use of the DSM-IV-TR is anathema to the very foundations of our specialty.

The philosophical approach of constructivism, or in anthropological terms the emic approach to understanding another's behavior, questions the accuracy and advisability of categorizing anyone as "normal" or "abnormal." The case can be made that all diagnoses in the DSM-IV-TR are sociopolitical in nature, as evidenced by the way diagnostic categories change over successive revisions of the DSM. For example, in earlier versions of the DSM, homosexuality was a diagnosis, thereby relegating homosexuality to the realm of psychopathology. It has since been removed.

Critics of the DSM (Raskin & Lewandowski, 2000) note that labeling a person with a psychiatric diagnosis "contributes to certain clinical realities" (p. 18). The label ascribes to that person a definition as a psychiatric patient, which carries a host of implications. For the client, it increases the likelihood of a self-perception as "mentally ill." It also increases the likelihood of others' expectations that the person will behave in a somewhat abnormal way.

In 1973, Rosenhan conducted a study in which a group of 8 "sane" people (confederates in the research), including a college student, a pediatrician, and several psychologists, presented themselves at psychiatric hospitals on the East and West coasts of the United States, vaguely complaining of hearing voices. When the confederates were admitted as inpatients in the hospitals, they immediately stopped complaining of their auditory hallucinations and acted as they normally would. Despite the fact that the confederates resumed acting "normal," their status as inpatients resulted in their behaviors being perceived by hospital personnel as pathological.

The point of the Rosenhan study is that the professional staff in the hospitals expected these clients to be "crazy" because they were inpatients, even though when the confederates were in the hospital they did not act "crazy" at all. Rosenhan used these results to justify his hypothesis that a significant part of our identification of a person as "disturbed" comes not from the individual's present behavior but instead from our expectation that the behavior will be crazy.

However, the reality of clinical work for an agency counselor, or a school counselor working with students who have special needs, is that diagnosis using clinical, diagnostic nomenclature is a integral part of the job (Hinkle, 1999). Regardless of whether one agrees or disagrees with the advisability of making clinical diagnoses, in order to interact with other mental health professionals or educators, some ability to use diagnostic labels is required.

CASE CONCEPTUALIZATION   There are other ways, too, to make a "diagnosis"; use of any theoretical model allows a clinician working within that theory framework to consider that person's symptoms and the corresponding indicated course of treatment. The medical model posits that there is an illness that is afflicting an individual. Moving beyond the constraints of "diagnosis" in the classic sense of that word, the use of any theoretical model, such as a developmental or existential theory, enables a counselor to define, within that theory, which key issues and aspects of the individual's situation require closer attention.

ERRORS IN CLINICAL JUDGMENT

Multiple sources of bias and error exist that could detract from your ability to accurately diagnose a client. You know from our prior coverage in this text how your own values, beliefs, and cultural framework can color your view of the world and of other people. You know also that a key to reducing the extent to which your own values detract from your effectiveness is to be aware of what your values are. We will take a look at some other common sources of bias or diagnostic error, again to reduce the likelihood that they will happen for you.

There has been a great deal written about the diagnostic judgment errors committed by counselors and psychologists. Dumont and Lecomte (1987) noted that when a client initially presents with a multitude of information, the process of trying to discern what is truly clinically relevant from what instead is simply a distracter or a secondary issue is a process ripe for error. This process is referred to as *inferential judgment error.* The authors offer several explanations as to why inferential judgment leads to diagnostic errors; we will look briefly at two of them.

One source of inferential judgment error is the *availability heuristic.* Random events occur regularly in everyone's life, including the life of a counselor. We may be having lunch with a coworker who makes a comment about a certain disorder, or we might have recently attended a seminar about a particular clinical topic. These events can affect our thinking during the diagnostic judgment process; we may be most inclined to seize upon the aspects of a person's presentation that we perceive as evidence of that particular clinical symptom or diagnosis. For example, if we just came from a workshop on attachment disorders, we may become highly attuned and primed to be listening for evidence of an attachment disorder in our clients.

Another source of judgment error is *causal attribution of symptoms.* Research has solidly established that the cause we attribute to problems varies, depending on whether we are the observer or the person who is experiencing the problem. An individual who is an observer or helper is much more inclined to attribute the cause of a person's problems to individual characteristics of that person. An individual who is experiencing a problem, on the other hand, is much more likely to perceive the problem to be the result of external, situational variables.

More recently, Hill and Ridley (2001) listed a variety of errors that have been empirically identified to occur frequently. Common diagnostic errors include failure to use base rates for occurrence of a disorder within the general population, diagnostic overshadowing, age and health biases, and confirmatory hypothesis testing. Confirmatory hypothesis testing means that a therapist generates a diagnostic impression and then selectively seeks those aspects of the clinical presentation that support the diagnosis, while simultaneously disregarding any contradictory evidence.

It could be argued that awareness of various symptoms and disorders is an important aspect of being a skilled clinician. What Dumont and Lecomte (1987) are saying, though, is that we can prioritize a particular disorder so much that we disregard other aspects of the clinical presentation that should be given at least as much weight in the diagnostic process. Hill and Ridley (2001) suggest that delayed diagnostic decision making is another good way to reduce errors in judgment. If you can find a way to spend some counseling time with your client while refraining from making a final diagnosis, it's more likely that you will be open to seeing and considering additional details and symptoms that could be helpful in ruling in, or ruling out, a given diagnosis.

Perhaps the most compelling reason that accurate diagnosis is such an issue is that your choice of the most appropriate techniques and strategies is predicated on the assumption that the diagnosis is accurate. If you misdiagnose your client, he or she may not benefit from your work together. Additionally, continued symptoms could worsen, creating secondary or exacerbated problems. After you have generated a accurate diagnostic conceptualization, the next step is to identify the treatment plan.

TREATMENT PLANNING

Treatment planning is the logical conclusion of assessment and diagnosis; it simply means articulation of goals that will indicate counseling has succeeded. Again, how the goals are defined can depend on what the client hopes to gain, on the theory frame of the counselor, possibly on the objectives identified by some third party (e.g., parents, the court system, an employer), or some combination of all the above.

In a school counseling situation, there can be varying degrees of formality with which treatment plans are established. Some students, whose symptoms or conditions have a substantial impact on their educational process, have an IEP (Individualized Educational Plan) that identifies counseling as one component of the intervention. Other students, however, might see a school counselor for a few meetings and then have a resolution of the problem. While the school counselor in that case might have assessed the problem thoroughly, there would probably not be a formal treatment plan developed with the student.

The next chapter is devoted to a presentation of some ways that therapists decide what strategies to use with particular clients or presenting problems. Many contemporary authors are talking about counselors using results obtained from treatment outcome studies. A large number of authors state unequivocally that it would be unethical to treat a client with an uninvestigated technique if there were clearly proven techniques to treat a particular disorder.

Chapter Summary

We have looked at a number of strategies and recommendations for conducting an intake interview. Intake interviews ideally can serve a dual purpose of being the beginning of a good counseling relationship, and also a means by which you begin gathering important information about the client and his or her concerns. Despite the need to obtain objective information, it can be helpful to take the time to respond to some of the client's statements using active listening, including paraphrasing and feeling reflection.

The various aspects of the client's story, as well as the nonverbal and paraverbal behaviors exhibited during the interview, all are pieces of data that are highly pertinent to the intake process. As well, consideration of not only the client individually, but also the systems of which the client is a part, are components of data. The whole process of information gathering is similar to assembling pieces of a jigsaw puzzle. Taking one isolated piece of information without the context of all the other information is like making an inference about what the image will be when the completed puzzle is assembled.

This process of considering a broad compilation of information before making a final decision about a client's diagnosis is important in order to avoid making errors of judgment. In fact, counselors often make judgment errors, and we covered a number of ways that such errors can be minimized. A couple of ways that we looked at included not rushing to make a decision about a diagnosis too soon, and also being aware of possible biases you might have.

We also looked at three things in particular that you need to be on the lookout for, especially with new clients that you do not know well yet. Those things are possible medical conditions that could be the source of psychiatric symptoms; suicide risk assessment; and finally, violence risk assessment. The point was made that in most of these cases, the intent is not simply to assess the risk, but to *prevent* harm to the client or an intended victim. Knowledge of risk factors is quite important and it might be beneficial for you to be thoroughly familiar with them. It is also extremely important that you know the laws in your state regarding your duty to warn intended victims, and also the procedures that you should follow if you determine that a client is suicidal.

Question for Class Discussion

1. In the case of the Virginia Tech shootings, a young man had been seen for counseling, and a number of adults who had worked with him expressed concerns about his emotional stability. However, he had never been in court-ordered treatment for any length of time. What do you see as the advantages and disadvantages of incorrectly identifying a client as "dangerous"?
2. What is your reaction to the statement that everyone has a threshold for violence? Where does your own threshold lie?
3. What are your thoughts about diagnosis? To what extent will you need to diagnose your clients in your intended professional position, and to what extent are your thoughts at odds with what your job may require?

CHAPTER 14

Empirically Supported Techniques and Common Psychotherapeutic Factors

After studying this chapter, you should have a clear understanding of the following:

- The difference between common factors and empirically supported techniques
- The research designs used to empirically determine effective counseling techniques
- The historical bases for both the empirically supported technique and common factor movements
- The strengths and limitations of each approach
- Current models that integrate both approaches

Currently, there is a highly visible debate in our profession around the advisability of using only those counseling and therapy techniques that have been scientifically proven to be effective in treating clients with a particular disorder or presenting problem. Such techniques are referred to in the professional literature by several different names, including Empirically Supported Treatments (ESTs), Evidence Based Mental Health, and empirically validated therapies. The push, among many authors, is to use research as the justification for treatment selection, which will be referred to in this chapter as the EST movement.

The EST movement has provoked a great deal of dialogue in the professional literature due to differing views among researchers, practitioners, and scholars on some fundamental interpretations of the accumulated data. Proponents of the EST movement believe that when research exists that supports use of a particular treatment strategy for a particular disorder, practitioners are obligated to use that treatment technique first, regardless of their own personal views or biases about that technique.

Another group of authors believe that there are common factors in the therapy process that are *always* present, regardless of the treatment strategy used. These authors cite numerous arguments favoring an emphasis on common therapeutic factors rather than specific techniques for specific symptoms.

Yet another group has more recently postulated that advocating for *either* a common factor or EST approach to the exclusion of the other creates a false dichotomy that does not adequately incorporate all the research findings. These authors propose that instead, an integrated treatment approach that factors in therapeutic relationship, therapeutic technique, and participant (both client and counselor) is a model that more efficiently and satisfactorily incorporates both the EST and common factor research results.

This chapter is divided into three sections; the first section covers the aspect of the debate encompassing evidence-based mental health interventions, including the basis of that perspective and corresponding strengths and weaknesses. The second section focuses on the other side of the debate, namely the common factors, or therapeutic factors that have been determined to be common denominators across all therapeutic approaches. Again we will explore some historic antecedents, strengths, and weaknesses. The final section covers integrative models and recommendations for counselors who wish to stay current with the advances in techniques and knowledge to inform their work with clients.

EMPIRICALLY SUPPORTED TECHNIQUES

The core value upon which the EST movement is based is that the scientific method represents a "gold standard"; it is the main avenue by which all of our modern technological advances have been possible. Therefore, scientific techniques need to be implemented to ascertain the most effective techniques for helping people alleviate or reduce their suffering.

The models of behaviorism and cognitive behaviorism arose out of an effort to systematically, scientifically understand principles of human behavior. John Watson, B. F. Skinner, and Joseph Wolpe were all prominent researchers in the field of behaviorism whose explications of behavioral principles moved the field of psychotherapy forward significantly. The principles that they established have formed the basis for many highly successful behavioral therapy techniques. Behaviorists, more than professionals in any other theoretical orientation, place a premium value on empirical investigation of treatment techniques with each client, beginning the therapy process with precise baseline data, and ultimate concern for maximizing therapeutic efficiency and effectiveness.

Historical Antecedents of the EST Movement

Three factors gave rise to the EST movement among mental health professionals (Foley, 2004). The first force was pressure from insurance companies, particularly managed care organizations, to increase value and decrease cost. This increase in value and decrease in cost are aspects of therapist accountability. While at first glance improving quality and decreasing cost seem to be appropriate goals, many therapists unfortunately equate "accountability" with managed care (Sexton & Liddle, 2001). For example, because Axis II Personality Disorders (a particular category for diagnosis in the DSM-IV-TR) are very difficult and costly to treat, since therapy often involves years of treatment, some insurance companies specifically exclude paying for therapy for their subscribers if the subscriber has been diagnosed with a personality disorder. Thus, managed care is often perceived by mental health practitioners as intrusive and not in clients' best interest.

The second force was the growth and prominence of biological psychiatry, which views psychotherapy as comparable to pharmacological treatment and places psychotherapy on par with any other medical intervention to be investigated scientifically. The Western medical model views the body as a complex mechanism and illness, affliction, and symptoms as conditions upon which an external, learned expert exerts treatment or other intervention for the purpose of reducing or eliminating the affliction.

The third force was the researchers and psychologists with scientific interests, who have increasingly developed the means to identify particularly effective treatments for particular populations of clients. Clinicians and researchers seem to hold a mutual disregard for one another, though, and there seems to be a disconnection between the information published about efficacious treatments and clinicians' willingness to actually use that information (Sexton & Liddle, 2001, Beutler, 2000).

In 2007, the *Journal of Counseling and Development*, which is the main journal for the American Counseling Association, ran an article that introduced a new journal feature: "Best Practices." The inclusion of this new section was initiated with an article written by Marotta and Watts, but which was comprised mainly of contributions by four well-known authors. One of those contributors, Thomas Sexton, made the critical point that it is just as possible to do harm as it is to do good in counseling. Furthermore, Sexton reiterated what numerous prior authors have admonished: that we as professional helpers have an ethical, legal, and moral obligation to bring the best available information about treatment to our clients.

PERSONAL REFLECTION

If you were suffering from a disorder, physical or emotional or both, from which you were experiencing great pain, would you want your helper (doctor or therapist) to have knowledge about the most recent research results on what helps your condition?

The seminal EST project that became the impetus for a flurry of articles and books on ESTs was a project done by a task force from the American Psychological Association that undertook a major meta-analysis of the treatment outcome literature. What resulted was a list, published in 1995 (Division 12 Task Force, 1995), that identified treatment techniques as falling into one of three categories. The categories were "well-established treatments," "probably efficacious treatments," and "experimental treatments." The individuals who supported use of ESTs advocated for clinicians using only the techniques that had been identified as well-established or probably efficacious.

We will first define terms commonly used in the EST literature. When a study is defined as *efficacious*, it means that it has been proven, in a controlled laboratory study, to be more effective than some other treatment technique, or more effective than placebo or no treatment (Nathan, 2007). A technique identified as *effective* has been found to be effective in applied, naturalistic settings. There is a big difference between treatment conditions in a lab setting and treatment conditions in a naturalistic setting, for a number of reasons. The importance of doing laboratory investigations is that clinical intuition has been demonstrated to be frequently inaccurate (Hollon, 2006).

In a controlled laboratory experiment, true to scientific form, in order for an independent variable to be proven as *causing* a dependent variable, all other variables must be controlled. If any variables in the project vary in an uncontrolled way, they are *confounding variables* and they render the results meaningless.

Here is an applied example of a confounding variable. Suppose a school counselor needs to compare students' responses to two different peer-mediated conflict resolution programs used in schools in two different areas of a city. If the counselor/researcher does not account for the location (suburban vs. urban) or the number of years of education of the people training the students in each program, it will not be possible to conclude that the *program* is the reason for difference in effectiveness. A number of possible confounds exist; the students could be tougher in one area than in the other, there could be differences in level of expertise between the two program instructors, there could be differences in tolerance among school administrators, or there could be differences between the actual conflict resolution training programs.

In the case of a treatment outcome study, then, the variables that need to be controlled would encompass everything except the treatment technique being studied. These variables would include a client having only one diagnosis of the disorder in question, a specified number of counseling sessions, the therapist only saying or doing specific things. This type of tightly controlled research design is referred to in the literature as a *randomized clinical trial* (RCT).

Here is an applied example of an RCT. Let's say a researcher wants to compare two different treatment techniques for depression. One of those techniques is "tough love" where the therapist basically admonishes the client to "snap out of it" and begin acting as if he or she is not depressed. The other technique is a skill-building approach where the client learns how to use encouraging and supportive self-talk and also begins increasing physical activity level. In order to see which of these techniques are most effective, each technique needs to be implemented on similar people. For our results to have even more significance statistically, we might want a baseline comparison group of people who are depressed but are not in treatment at all. Because both treatments can't be used on the same client, we need different clients. Thus, to make sure we have a fair comparison among the approaches, we must create groups of clients that are very similar in all three groups, the control group and the two treatment types. We also need very similar therapists for both treatment conditions; to be as tightly controlled as possible, we might have the same therapist implement both techniques with both groups of clients. If we used the same therapist in both groups, though, there could be two possible confounds. One is that the therapist might personally be more comfortable with one of the two approaches. The other is that the therapist might have strong expectations that one or the other is what is expected by the researcher. In either case, the conditions might be predisposed to go in a certain direction.

Most of the controlled outcome studies that are published in the literature are some variation on the above theme for research design. There are other types of studies that are more descriptive in nature, such as research that identifies a high degree of relationship between two variables. An example would be the relationship between history of sexual abuse and psychological difficulties in adulthood, or between a diagnosis of bipolar disorder and a history of substance abuse. However, correlational studies cannot establish a causal link. While two characteristics co-occur at a frequency higher than we would expect in random occurrences, we cannot say definitively that sexual abuse causes psychological disorders, or that bipolar disorder causes substance abuse, because the data are only correlational, not causal.

Other published outcome studies use a case analysis approach with a small number of clients, or a larger *n* but with a less tightly controlled participant group. These "naturalistic" studies are less rigorous scientifically, but are another important step in the process of investigating whether a technique is effective, because naturalistic studies are much closer approximations to what happens in real life than are the controlled laboratory experiments.

Strengths of the EST Approach to Treating Clients

Authors who advocate the EST approach have identified a number of strengths and rationales with which to justify limiting treatment of clients to those techniques that have been proven to be effective. The benefits of using ESTs include the observation that a large number of studies appear to support the superiority of ESTs over non-ESTs, the ability to identify a treatment technique as causally effective when everything else is tightly controlled, and the fact that scientific investigation is the most fruitful means of acquiring knowledge. We will look at each of these in more detail.

A LARGE NUMBER OF STUDIES SUPPORT ESTS   Several authors have had the opportunity to look at counseling outcomes with large numbers of clients, some of whom received EST interventions and some of whom did not. In one study (Cukrowicz et al., 2005), a community mental health center that had been operating for years made a policy change that required all therapists to begin using only ESTs with their clients. The shift in policy enabled the researchers to review client records to analyze the extent to which clients stayed in counseling and improved, stayed the same, or got worse, both pre- and post–policy change. The individuals who analyzed the clients' records were not informed until after the chart review about the hypotheses of the study. Chart reviews were conducted in a way that would minimize bias in rating to control for researchers finding what they expected to find in the charts. Nevertheless, the clients who were treated following the policy change showed more improvement by the end of counseling than those clients treated prior to the policy change.

IDENTIFYING TECHNIQUES AS CAUSALLY EFFECTIVE   One of the basic differences in research designs is the extent to which it enables a researcher to identify one variable (the independent variable) as causing another variable (the dependent variable). I have given you examples above about correlational studies that identify two variables that seem to have a relationship to each other. Correlational studies are descriptive, meaning that by the nature of the way they are designed, it is not possible to say with confidence that one variable causes the other variable, even though it might look obvious that one does.

Although there is a great deal of information about comorbidity and relationships between adverse life events and psychological problems, precious little of the data proves a direct causal relationship. The difficulty of descriptive, correlational studies is that there may be an active, causative variable that causes the presence of one characteristic to generate the presence of another characteristic. Without a research design that permits direct observation of one variable causing the other variable, though, questions remain as to exactly what the mechanism is and how it operates. Therefore, advocates of ESTs maintain that the only research design that enables that level of surety is the randomized clinical trial.

Criticisms of the EST Approach

Considering the fact that scientific rigor is significantly responsible for advancing our knowledge to where it is today, it is hard to imagine that anyone would be opposed to using scientific method to illuminate variables that result in therapeutic change. Indeed, the authors who are opposed to exclusive use of ESTs are not necessarily against outcome research on therapy. What they take issue with are aspects of the research process, and the assumptions that underlie those aspects. Critics of ESTs have identified the following limitations and problems with the exclusive EST approach.

Limitations of the EST approach exist because of certain critical assumptions that are made in the process of conducting a randomized clinical trial. Westen, Novoty, and Thompson-Brenner (2004) identified a set of assumptions on which RCTs are based that are problematic from the standpoint of adopting ESTs as a standard for practice. We will take a look at those assumptions that comprise the limitations of EST usage.

PSYCHOPATHOLOGY IS EASILY MOLDED AND CHANGED   Most of the RCTs use a treatment protocol that completes the treatment process quickly, typically between 6 and 16 sessions. The reason for keeping the intervention period brief is that it reduces the chance that extraneous, chance factors would occur that could influence the degree of therapeutic change. However, Westen and colleagues point out that psychiatric relapse is high, meaning that people's responses to treatment is often neither rapid nor permanent. Further, a dose-response relationship in therapy has been demonstrated, meaning that in general, longer duration of treatment results in better client response to treatment. Therefore, the research studies that use 6 to 16 treatment sessions are actually not a particularly good comparison to how treatment occurs in the "real world."

MOST PATIENTS HAVE ONE PRIMARY PROBLEM OR CAN BE TREATED AS IF THEY DO   Elsewhere I have noted that while the DSM-IV is used as the primary basis for nomenclature of disorders in our field, use of the DSM-IV is not necessarily endorsed by everyone. One of the criticisms of the DSM-IV is that the diagnostic categories are based only on evidence of symptom clusters. The disorders have not been empirically analyzed for interrelationships, nor are the disorders necessarily empirically supported. Therefore, according to Westen and colleagues, somewhere between 33% and 50% of the people who seek treatment do not fit neatly into a DSM diagnostic category. However, the RCT studies use tightly controlled groups of participants, all of whom each have only the disorder being studied. This narrow window of diagnosis serves the purpose of strictly isolating particular variables.

While this practice is a strength from the perspective of adequately controlling variables, it is a weakness in that many clients do have more than one diagnosis. Therefore, the RCT participant groups are not directly representative of the client populations that exist in reality. Between 50% and 90% of the people who have Axis I disorders also present with another Axis I disorder as well. Again, considering the very tight control by using only research subjects with a single diagnosis, there is a problem with trying to apply those research results to clients whose problems and symptom constellations are considerably more complex.

PSYCHOLOGICAL SYMPTOMS CAN BE UNDERSTOOD AND TREATED AS BEING SEPARATE FROM TEMPERAMENT OR PERSONALITY   The first two of the five DSM-IV-TR axes on which clinicians diagnose clients are Clinical Syndromes, and Developmental Disorders and Personality Disorders, respectively. Even when a person has only an Axis I disorder and no apparent personality pathology, research has established that Axis I disorders are still related to personality; personality characteristics influence response to treatment. For example, a person who is generally extroverted and optimistic will likely have a different response to treatment than a person who is characteristically nervous and pessimistic. Most treatment manuals that have been developed for implementation of ESTs do not give practitioners the option of accounting for these personality idiosyncrasies despite the fact that personality characteristics have significant impact on the course of treatment.

CONTROLLED LABORATORY EXPERIMENTS SHOULD BE THE "GOLD STANDARD" THAT DEFINES A TECHNIQUE AS HAVING "EFFICACY"   Westen and colleagues' problem with this assumption is that the RCT studies are not a representative sample of how psychopathology really manifests, in terms of co-existing disorders or in terms of length of treatment. Another opponent of ESTs (Wampold, 2006) noted that a treatment that does not appear on a list of

ESTs does not necessarily mean the treatment does not work; it may simply be that the treatment in question has not yet been subjected to the EST test.

ESTS ARE NOT ESTABLISHED AS EFFECTIVE FOR MINORITIES   Multiple other authors have expressed the opinion that ESTs are not useful for working with clients who are not identical to the white, female, heterosexual, middle-class, educated, physically able people that are usually research subjects (Bernal & Scharron-del-Rio, 2001; Sue & Zane, 2006). Bernal and Scharron-del-Rio (2001) made the point that therapy itself is a cultural phenomenon and called attention to the extensive literature that supports the role of culture and ethnicity in treatment.

Ironically, ethnic minorities often lack the financial resources to afford to choose their treatment or therapist; if they did have the resources they would be better able to choose a counselor versed in the client's cultural preferences. They also are more exposed to the stressors associated with poverty and low social status, placing them at disproportionately higher risk than the mainstream population for psychiatric and emotional disorders. Despite these facts, ethnic minorities are generally not the targeted participant groups in efficacy studies. Bernal and Scharron-del-Rio stated, "Thus, a list of treatments based on a literature that has an ethnocentric bias is at best of limited use to ethnic minorities" (p. 332).

Another group of people, namely, members of sexual minorities—lesbian, gay, bisexual, transgendered—are similarly exposed to substantial social stressors as the result of their characteristics. Because of their sexual minority status and the associated discrimination and lack of social support, these groups use psychotherapy at least twice as much as the heterosexual population (Brown, 2006). Yet, sexual minority groups are not represented in the treatment outcome literature on ESTs, and ESTs should not be assumed to be generalizable to this group of people.

As mentioned at the beginning of this chapter, the above listed issues have been the focus of an ongoing debate among many contemporary researchers and scholars. Note that for each of the advantages and limitations listed above, there have been counterpoints written by authors taking opposing views.

We turn now to the other side of this debate, namely, the case in favor of a common factors approach to counseling and psychotherapy. The same general format will be followed: First we will explain the common psychotherapeutic factors position, then examine the strengths and limitations inherent in this approach.

COMMON PSYCHOTHERAPEUTIC FACTORS

The body of research regarding common psychotherapeutic factors is sometimes referred to in the professional literature as *specific vs. nonspecific therapeutic factors*. Even though this debate is current, common psychotherapeutic factors are not a new concept. We will begin this exploration of common factors by recognizing some of the pioneering authors to introduce this construct. Historically there have been several forerunners; two of the early, influential individuals were Saul Rozenzweig and Hans Strupp.

Saul Rozenzweig

One professional journal exclusively devoted to commonalities in treatment is the *Journal of Psychotherapy Integration*. That journal published an interview of Saul Rozenzweig conducted by Barry Duncan (Duncan, 2002). Rozenzweig's landmark 1936 article, "Some Implicit Common Factors in Diverse Methods of Psychotherapy" (cited in Duncan, 2002) was, according to Rozenzweig, the first to present the common factor concept. In recounting his early thought process, Rozenzweig talked about his extensive knowledge of history, classic literature, and anthropology, all of which informed his thinking in the development of his common factors concept. In the Duncan interview, Rozenzweig said:

> . . . the common factors came out of my awareness that there was such a variety of methods trying to reach the mind and doing mental tricks of various kinds—like the evil eye, the royal touch, the revolving chair, and so on and so forth. All seemed to have more in common, implicitly, than not. All those precursors to psychotherapy from the panorama bear a resemblance to each other and later forms of healing like psychotherapy. (Duncan, 2002, p. 19)

Rozenzweig's contributions are compelling; his vision and scope, integrating cumulative knowledge bases across numerous academic disciplines and bodies of knowledge, seem to make intuitive sense. The contributions from anthropology, philosophy, religion, classic literature, and history all point to the universality of core features among helping relationships, transcending mere psychology and looking more broadly at the myriad ways people in different cultures help one another.

Hans Strupp

Another prominent author in the common factor movement was Hans Strupp. Strupp's research, which began in the 1950s and continued for many decades, emphasized the impact of aspects of the patient-therapist relationship and the potential for therapeutic change to occur (Society for Psychotherapy Research, 2008). Strupp (1973) stated, "There is little doubt that the totality of the therapist's personality—his age, sex, experience, maturity, attitudes, and a host of other factors—is subtly intertwined with his therapeutic techniques and the theoretical framework he brings to bear upon his therapeutic operations" (p. 287).

Ironically, managed care, with its emphasis on accountability and efficiency in service delivery, was also one of the catalysts in the reemergence of common factors as a focus in the professional literature. The statistical technique of meta-analysis enables researchers to compare treatment effects across many different types of coefficients and numerical results. Meta-analysis has been highly instrumental in quantitatively confirming that common treatment factors clearly are a component of positive therapeutic outcome.

Some of the contemporary authors who have been at the forefront in current meta-analytic research are Beutler, Duncan, Lambert, Norcross, and Wampold. These individuals have identified the relative contribution of multiple variables to the outcome of treatment. One publication in particular, *The Heart and Soul of Change*, by Hubble, Duncan, and Miller (1999), lends itself well to other concepts that will be presented; however, please note that this book is just one of many that cover this topic.

At the very core of the common factors movement is the postulate that common factors such as therapeutic alliance can *never* be separated from therapeutic technique, thereby establishing that common factors remain a prominent component of any treatment strategy. Probably the biggest criticism the common factors proponents have of the EST movement is that in publications such as the Division 12 Task Force Report, there is not sufficient emphasis on the contribution of the common factors upon treatment outcome, instead unilaterally emphasizing technique.

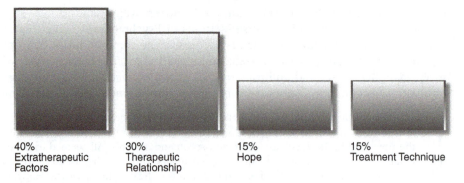

40%	30%	15%	15%
Extratherapeutic	Therapeutic	Hope	Treatment Technique
Factors	Relationship		

FIGURE 14.1 Proportion of Contribution to Treatment Outcome

Source: Hubble, Duncan, & Miller, 1999. © American Psychological Association (APA).

According to Hubble, Duncan, and Miller (1999), the following four categories of variables (Figure 14.1) account for the treatment effects reported in treatment outcome studies:

Client/extratherapeutic factors: 40% (these include client strengths, environmental support, i.e., support system, and some chance events

Relationship between therapist and client: 30% (these include caring, empathy, warmth, encouragement of risk-taking)

Hope: 15%

Model or technique used by counselor: 15%

We will examine each of these factors in further detail.

CLIENT EXTRATHERAPEUTIC FACTORS—40% OF THE OUTCOME VARIANCE Note that the largest influence upon treatment outcome is exerted by client factors and external factors, all of which lie completely outside the realm of counselor control. These external factors range from events as mundane as being unable to get a ride to the counseling appointments, to the adequacy of the person's support system, to complex internal psychological factors that influence the person's readiness for change.

This high degree of contribution by extratherapeutic factors to outcome variance is the very reason that researchers doing RCTs strive to use brief treatment interventions. Once a client begins treatment, the more time that goes by, the more likely it is that external variables that may have nothing to do with treatment will nevertheless affect treatment outcome.

RELATIONSHIP—30% OF TREATMENT OUTCOME The main relationship components identified in the Hubble, Duncan, and Miller (1999) analysis are caring, empathy, warmth, and encouragement of risk-taking. Other authors (Weinberger & Rasco, 2007) articulated several additional components of a successful therapeutic alliance. One is agreement between therapist and client as to the treatment goals. The bulk of the microskills we have studied in this text are used with the intention of establishing and enhancing a strong therapeutic alliance. Other therapist strategies include being highly attuned to the client's experience of the therapeutic intervention, and a therapist's willingness to take responsibility for her or his own contribution to the therapeutic interactions. Note that a therapist taking responsibility for her or his part of the therapy interaction can be seen as one form of self-disclosure, a topic we covered in Chapter 12.

An additional caveat in the present discussion is the frequently occurring theme of benevolence toward your client, and your belief that there is hope for your client, which you will communicate to him or her through many channels. Sometimes clients come to counseling already hopeful, but many may be feeling defeated and hopeless. Frank and Frank (1991) observed that people's failed attempts to adequately cope with a problem results in their feeling demoralized; they have tried to solve their own problems and have "failed." Some clients may present for counseling feeling ashamed that they have to see a mental health professional for help. Your ability to provide essential ingredients for a successful therapeutic alliance will therefore influence the eventual outcome of counseling.

Authors differ in the semantics they use to define a "successful" therapeutic relationship. Carl Rogers wrote at length about the necessary conditions for change; more recently, others have enumerated additional conditions that must be present for a client to benefit. For example, Frank and Frank (1991) identified the following four conditions for successful treatment:

1. An emotionally charged relationship, meaning an interaction with a helper who is both caring and hopeful
2. A therapeutic setting, meaning an environment that conveys that the helper has successfully helped others
3. A therapeutic myth, meaning that the helper must use some coherent model that he or she can both explain and subscribes to, explaining the presence of symptoms
4. A therapeutic ritual; a rationale and method defining the techniques to eliminate the symptoms

One compelling aspect of these four features is that they are applicable across a number of helping situations, including some of the healing rituals that are used in indigenous cultures.

HOPE AND PLACEBO EFFECT—15% OF TREATMENT OUTCOME The definition of *placebo* is an inert substance given to a patient used to reinforce the patient's expectation that he or she will get well. It is becoming more acceptable in Western medicine to acknowledge the role that our expectations and thoughts play in our physical health and bodily functioning. Across many different lines of research inquiry, ranging from psychology to physiology and medicine, it has been solidly established that some degree of the positive effects of medication or other palliative treatment often is the result of an individual's expectation about the medication. Items 3 and 4 from Frank and Frank (1991; above) point to the therapist establishing a structure in which a technique is presented in such a manner that it essentially functions partially as a placebo.

Hope is a construct that is worth looking at in detail, because if you understand the cognitive mechanisms behind hope, you may be better able to help your clients develop or enhance their sense of hopefulness. Snyder, Michael, and Cheavens (1999) conducted a meta-analysis of the treatment outcome literature and found that in many studies, anywhere from 56% to 71% of the total treatment outcome occurred in the early stages of the counseling process. The authors concluded that since those changes happened early in counseling, they could not be attributable to specific treatment strategies, and so instead were a reflection of the clients' expectations and hope.

Snyder and colleagues (e.g., Shorey, Little, Snyder, Kluck, & Robitschek, 2007) have researched hope extensively, with an emphasis on the cognitive components. Two aspects of the thought process must be present for a person to experience hope. The first is *agency*; we must see ourselves as being capable of achieving the goals we have set for ourselves.

The second is *pathways*; we must see ourselves as capable of generating alternative, attainable ways to achieve the goal.

Reflecting back to the essential elements of treatment identified by Frank and Frank (1991), it is perhaps most important at the outset that the helper be hopeful and believe that he or she can help the client. Clients may, in the very early stages of counseling, be looking to the counselor for that hope, because the client him or herself may see no way out of the suffering.

AUTHOR'S REFLECTION

In my work as a therapist, my first session with clients usually focused on gathering a multitude of background data as well as processing the presenting problem. Toward the end of a first session I routinely gave clients a chance to ask questions of me. Frequently, the question the client would ask is, "Well, am I hopeless?" or "So, doc, do you think you can help me?" What they really were expressing was a need to believe that their situation could be helped, and to know that I was a person who could help them (agency component) and give them the skills to navigate their way out of the problem (pathways component). Even then, before I knew of Snyder's research, intuitively it seemed important to the counseling process that I could honestly say to my clients, with conviction, that I *believed* I could help them reduce their symptoms and improve their quality of life.

INTERNAL REFLECTION

Think of a time when you saw a physician for a condition about which you were quite concerned. When the doctor said, "Yes, I can treat this" or "I'm sorry, there is nothing we really can do for you," how did that response affect your perception of the condition? If it was something untreatable, did hopelessness become part of your emotional experience about the condition?

TREATMENT TECHNIQUE—15% OF THE TREATMENT OUTCOME VARIANCE   Clearly there is a need for a counselor to accurately identify and diagnose a client's problem or condition, and then implement treatment techniques that have been empirically found to be effective for treating the condition. Here is where the EST outcome data pertains to interventions for specific disorders. You will likely be taking additional coursework that focuses specifically on diagnosis and selection of treatment strategies.

A unique contribution of counseling has historically been an emphasis on the person's strengths, assets, and developmental aspects of the issues, not just negatives of the symptoms, problems, deficits, and areas of compromised functioning. This fits nicely with hope theory. Additionally, the emerging specialty of positive psychology has much to offer, and in the future it may prove to be as significant a moderator variable of treatment outcome as the strategies that focus on symptom reduction.

Strengths of the Common Factors Approach

At least on the surface, the common factors model seems to be more easily adjustable to meet individual needs and characteristics of each client, regardless of ethnicity and other variables of diversity. Owing to the general nature of the principles of this model, it can be readily tailored to unique situations.

The common factors approach represents a more diverse means of integrating diverse knowledge bases, as pioneered by Rozenzweig. Empiricism in and of itself places external observation of readily measurable phenomena as the pinnacle of scientific enterprise. On the other hand, non-Western cultures have for centuries embraced other means of acquiring knowledge and information, and have well-established traditions for multiple aspects of cultural characteristics.

Criticisms of the Common Factors Approach

The same authors who advocate for ESTs are the people who most strongly express two primary concerns about a common factors approach. The common factors approach has not adequately accounted for the extensive data that identify particular treatment strategies as superior in outcome for particular disorders. Empiricists believe that if a variable such as treatment technique is, in fact, causative, then manipulation of that variable should consistently yield the same results. However, the common factors studies tend not to be as tightly controlled with regard to various aspects of the research design, and so the data yielded are not viewed as being as scientifically compelling.

The other criticism of the common factors approach is that while the EST proponents perceive themselves as, in fact, recognizing common factors as contributors to treatment outcome, the common factors in and of themselves are not sufficient to consistently produce favorable therapeutic change. Many RCT studies use, as their comparison, a group of clients receiving "treatment as usual," and if the common factors alone were the causative agents, then there would be no difference in treatment outcomes between the experimental and control groups. However, this is not the case. Some specific treatment techniques have consistently been demonstrated to yield significantly better treatment outcomes for clients than for the client in the comparison, "treatment as usual" group.

Summary of ESTs and Common Factors

This debate began to acquire heightened visibility in 1995 with the APA Task Force report. While the empiricists and behaviorists have advocated for a quantitatively based approach to intervention since Watson and Skinner, the issue of empiricism has gained visibility and the debate has gathered tremendous energy on both sides of the argument over the past couple of decades. There have been books written that consist entirely of point/counterpoint arguments around various points on this issue, for example, Norcross, Beutler, and Levant (2006), *Evidence-Based Practices in Mental Health: Debate and Dialogue on the Fundamental Questions.*

For each point of argument that either side articulates, there are highly intelligent, informed authors on the other side who present cogent, evidence-supported arguments to discredit the other side's claims. Recently, efforts have been made by some authors to find a middle road that enables a rapprochement and integration of the strengths of each respective position.

Some readers may be familiar with the parable about several men who are blind and an elephant; numerous religious traditions have a version of this story. A brief recounting of an American version by J. G. Saxe (1816–1887) is given here. Six men who were blind all examined an elephant and offered their interpretations of the creature. The first man placed his hands on the elephant's side and exclaimed, "An elephant is like a wall"; the second man felt the tusk and declared, "This animal is as a spear." The third took the squirming trunk in his hands and said, "The elephant is like a snake," while the fourth felt the elephant's knee and said, "It's like a tree"; the fifth felt the elephant's ear and said "It's like a fan"; and the sixth felt the tail and declared the elephant was like a rope. Each of the men based his interpretation on his own experiences, and each was partly but not completely right.

Some authors (e.g., Clinton, Gierlach, Zack, Beutler, & Castonguay, 2007; Foley, 2004; Marotta & Watts, 2007; Sexton & Liddle, 2001; Westen & Bradley, 2005) have begun to advocate that counselors and psychologists strive to develop and use models that successfully integrate the strengths of ESTs *and* common factors, hypothesizing that perhaps the seemingly contradictory evidence is contradictory because neither position alone adequately accounts for all of the observed phenomena.

THE PROCESS OF CHANGE

Two authors and their various associates have been extremely prominent in the research endeavors to understand exactly how the process of change unfolds in counseling and therapy. Those two authors are James Prochaska and Larry Beutler. Whereas Prochaska has looked only at variables within a client and in the context of work with particular presenting problems such as weight control or smoking cessation, Beutler and his colleagues have looked at three sources of variability that all interact in a complex way. We will explore both of these models briefly. It is suggested that you consider ways to use the information afforded from *both* of their models.

Beutler and colleagues (Beutler & Johannsen, 2006; Castonguay, 2007; Clinton et al., 2007) have advocated for a research-based treatment approach that simultaneously accounts for participant variables (therapist *and* client), the therapeutic alliance, and the treatment techniques. This approach enables use of empirically derived knowledge, seen by many as critical, while simultaneously accommodating the unique characteristics of each client and client situation, as promoted by a client-driven, constructivist approach. The model is called Systematic Treatment Selection (Beutler & Clarkin, 1990; Beutler, Clarkin, & Bongar, 2000).

Systematic Treatment Selection

This model was created by initially conducting a series of comprehensive reviews of the literature. These literature reviews enabled the authors to generate a list of principles regarding aspects of clients, treatment, and the therapeutic alliance. There were many subsequent steps of progression in refinement of this model; it began with assembling a panel of experts to sift through published results of treatment outcome studies, with emphasis on conducting meta-analyses of the cumulative findings. After compiling a set of hypotheses that accurately represented all the research findings, the next step of this study involved doing a chart review of completed client cases. The purpose of the chart review was to ascertain whether the identified hypotheses were upheld by the data in clients' treatment records. The end result of this broad-scale project was the creation of a set of principles for Systematic Treatment Selection. The basic principles give guidelines across many categories, including prognosis, level and intensity of care, strategies for reducing risk, characteristics of effective therapeutic relationships, basic principles for exposure and extinction, principles for determining sequence of interventions, and principles for determining which types of treatments to use and when to use them. The principles in each of these categories are applicable and pertinent independent of a theoretical orientation. For example, in the category of "Risk Reduction," the principle stipulates that, "Risk is reduced and patient compliance is increased when the treatment includes family intervention" (Clinton et al., 2007, p. 145).

We segue now to the client readiness model for two reasons. Not only is readiness for change a noteworthy client factor; additionally, development of the therapeutic relationship (the second strongest influence on treatment outcome) will hinge to some extent on how proficient you are at accurately gauging your clients' readiness to change. By accurately assessing this and then choosing intervention strategies accordingly, you are implicitly communicating that you have awareness of the client's experience in the counseling session. This implicit communication can augment your other efforts to explore and acknowledge your clients' perceptions and feelings about the counseling process.

The Readiness for Change Model

Prochaska (1999) has done extensive research with various colleagues (e.g., DiClemente and Vellicer) to examine and elucidate exactly how people make the decision to make change, what the process of change looks like as it is happening, and which treatment techniques work best at each stage of the change process. Table 14.1 offers a comparison of the client's perceptions, typical statements, and suggested interventions at various stages of client readiness.

TABLE 14.1 Stages of Change, Characteristics, and Representative Statements (Prochaska, 1999)

Stage Name	Characteristics	Representative Statements
Precontemplation	• The individual does not perceive the behavior to be problematic • Complete denial and lack of problem recognition	• "My drinking is no problem whatsoever; my husband's just mad because I stayed out too late." • "So I go out for a few beers to watch the game. So what? I have to do *something* to unwind."
Contemplation	• The individual is willing to consider possible ways the behavior is causing problems • The individual begins to wonder about possible solutions	• "I never really thought about how my drinking was affecting my husband and our marriage." • "I suppose I could find other ways of relaxing. I just don't think it's going to be as fun as going to the bar to watch the game."
Preparation	• The individual has a definite intention to change the behavior and is getting ready to make behavior changes • The person is willing to look at elements of her environment or lifestyle that contribute to the problem behavior, and to identify alternative behaviors	• "Next Monday I'm going to attend my first AA meeting." • "Instead of going to the bar to watch Monday night football, I've invited some friends over to watch a movie."
Action	• The person actually carries through the plans made	• "Last night I dumped all the beer down the drain." • "I went to my first AA meeting and I already have a sponsor."
Maintenance	• The person works to maintain the gains made in the action stage • Willing to look at the triggers or situations that make a return to earlier behaviors likely, and to develop a plan for what to do if that happens	• "My brother-in-law invited us over to watch baseball but I knew they'd all be drinking. So, I accepted the invitation for dinner, and then made other plans for later so we'd have to leave before the drinking started."

Included in the table is an applied example of statements that might be made by a person with problematic drinking to enable concrete comparison of the stages. These same types of general perceptions and statements could be applied to many different kinds of presenting problems.

The authors (Prochaska, 1999) go on to recommend specific treatment techniques especially suited for people demonstrating thoughts and behaviors indicative of a particular stage of readiness. We will explore one or two techniques from each readiness stage and give examples of how they pertain to that stage.

PRECONTEMPLATION   People in this stage see no need for change; from their perspective, things in their life are working just fine. Consciousness-raising means helping a client acquire increased awareness about the causes, consequences, and cures for the problem or the implications of the problem. This might entail client observation, confrontation, interpretation, and education. Because confrontation is often best used in later stages of relationship development, it is not recommended for use with clients who are just beginning the counseling process and do not see themselves as having a problem. At this stage of readiness, a skilled counselor will gently probe, reflect, and with sensitivity make some observations about the client's circumstances, with the intention of helping him or her become aware of some ways that the problem is resulting in unwanted consequences.

CONTEMPLATION   Emotional arousal is about getting to the very heart of what emotional factors are inhibiting a person becoming energized to change. In other words, emotional arousal can help an individual become fully aware of the emotions that contribute to maintaining the problem or symptoms. Emotional and social purposes are being served by maintaining the problem behavior. We talked before about secondary gain and therapeutic resistance; both of these factors are very important to fully explore with clients who are in the contemplation phase of change. For example, a person who is trying to lose weight might need to explore and process the emotional needs that are being met by staying obese.

Underlying feelings around any problem behavior might include feelings of guilt, resentment, inadequacy, fear of failure, or shame. Immediacy, client observation, experiential techniques such as a split chair, cinematherapy, or bibliotherapy can all serve to heighten a client's awareness of feelings, especially when there is ambivalence about an issue.

Environmental reevaluation involves looking honestly at the aspects of one's environment that maintain the problem behavior, and how one's environment would be affected if one made the anticipated changes. We talked before about homeostasis—dynamic balance is often a factor here even though a problem exists.

A common theme among people who use substances, for example, is the need for developing a new group of friends who do not use substances. Concomitantly, it might come as a surprise to some clients that all the significant people in their life drink heavily, and that if the client stops drinking it will change the relationships significantly. Additionally, a person who stops drinking may find him or herself without any social support, if all the friends are also heavy drinkers and encourage one another to drink. Thus, the prospect of giving up old, unhealthy friendships and finding a new circle of associates can be overwhelming for some people.

PREPARATION   In the preparation stage, a therapist can use principles of cognitive-behavior theory to begin working with the client on developing concrete plans for making changes. Inherent in the counseling process at this point is the client fully investing in the belief that change is possible, and coming to a place of hopefulness that he or she will accomplish the goal no matter what. Hope theory plays a role here; hope and expectancy were identified as one of the main contributors of treatment outcome, even though at a lesser rate than the other factors. The agency (capability) and pathway (concrete steps) both become clearer and more tangible to the client during this stage.

ACTION   We arrive, finally, at the action stage. Here is the stage where visible behavior change will begin to emerge. The counseling techniques at this stage correspondingly should become much more behaviorally focused, and principles of positive and negative reinforcement can be of great utility. These are the reward and counterconditioning techniques, wherein the client sets up structured plans for him or herself and then gives himself rewards for successfully complying with the plan.

An example of creating a reward would be that after 4 weeks of successful compliance with a diet, taking oneself on a weekend getaway with one's partner or a few friends. The key here is helping the client identify specific rewards that will be salient (meaningful and motivating) as ultimate goals.

Also in the action phase, clients need to be highly aware of the environments and situations that make a return to old problem behaviors more likely. A plan for how to avoid those situations, and specific steps to take once a person actually finds herself in a high-risk situation, is imperative. This is referred to as creating a *relapse prevention plan.*

MAINTENANCE   In some ways, maintenance might be the hardest stage of all. The excitement and frequency with which one receives praise/positive reactions from others begins to taper off. The reality of losing the payoffs of the problem behavior might become more apparent, and there may be times when clients pine and mourn for the "good times," "back in the day." Successfully remaining at the maintenance stage requires continued commitment and refusal to return to the problem behavior, not giving in to the self-talk of "Oh, it will be okay just this once."

MISMATCHING OF STAGE AND COUNSELING TECHNIQUE

AUTHOR'S REFLECTION _____

My early training in counseling was cognitive-behavioral, which is a directive treatment approach. I routinely gave my clients homework assignments to collect baseline data related to their targeted problem. I found that many of my clients would return to their second or third appointment with their homework not completed.   Some therapists might attribute the client's lack of follow-through to a lack of commitment to counseling. An alternative perspective, though, is that some of the clients who did not follow through were not at a stage of readiness to begin taking action, even if only in the form of recording information about the problem.

You may have clients who verbally state that they are ready to make changes, and yet be demonstrating behaviors more typical of someone in the precontemplation or contemplation stage of readiness. You could potentially address this incongruence in the form of a supportive challenge, although you need to make sure you are as mindful as possible about preserving the therapeutic alliance. For example, it might be helpful to validate, or even give the client permission, to be having the ambivalent or resistant feelings about making changes. Sometimes people stay stuck in the unaware or minimally aware stage for long periods of time; some never get past it.

A mismatch between the client's stage of readiness and the techniques the counselor is implementing results in the client not achieving maximum benefit from counseling.

Someone who does not believe his or her shoplifting habit poses any problems will not engage in behavior change if shoplifting is serving some purpose (which it very likely is). Similarly, someone who is ready to find a treatment group for shoplifters may feel frustrated by a counselor who wants to continue to focus on how the shoplifting has cost the client financially and emotionally; this client already knows that and needs to make concrete plans and take behavioral steps. This client would probably value a directive therapist.

Interested readers who would like to learn more about how to implement the readiness model are encouraged to explore the numerous books by Prochaska and his colleagues. Some, such as *Changing for Good* (1994), are specifically written for clients and consumers, and use language that is easily understandable to a layperson.

RECOMMENDATIONS FOR NEW COUNSELORS

On one hand, being a new counselor and seeing the multitude of outcome studies can be overwhelming, especially for agency and school counselors who are working with a wide variety of clients who present with diverse issues and concerns. On the other hand, contemporary counselors have a huge advantage over mental health practitioners in the past, from the standpoint of having ready access to the latest research findings about the best ways to help people.

It may not be realistic to expect that counselors will have the ability to themselves conduct meta-analyses of all the literature. Fortunately, though, there are authors and sources that do offer compilations of results.

Readers may consider perusing several books that are available to help determine the best treatments for disorders. This is by no means an exhaustive list, just a brief set of suggestions to help readers with ideas of where to start.

- *Evidence-Based Interventions for Students with Learning and Behavioral Challenges*, by Richard and Nancy Mather (2008)
- *Selecting Effective Treatments (rev. ed.)*, by Linda Seligman (1998)
- *Prescriptive Psychotherapy: A Guide to Systematic Treatment Selection*, by Larry Beutler and T. Mark Harwood (2000)
- *Handbook of Psychotherapy and Behavior Change* (5th ed.), by Michael Lambert (2004)

Besides consulting in compendiums of treatment principles and strategies, other authors have offered some suggestions, too, for how to stay current with recent research findings. Sexton and Liddle (2001), who strongly advocate for evidence-based mental health, suggested three concrete steps mental health practitioners should take to stay current with the latest evidence.

- First, be aware of the articles published in the professional literature that are meta-analyses offering observations of general trends in research findings.
- Second, be aware of and use evidence-based treatment strategies for particular clients who have particular disorders that have been researched. Examples of disorders that have had a lot of research conducted on treatments include anxiety disorders, mood disorders, and substance abuse.
- Third, maintain a commitment to keeping your own outcome data in order to continually inform and refine your own intervention attempts.

We talked earlier in this chapter about the Marotta and Watts article (2007) introducing the new section of the *Journal of Counseling and Development*. In their introduction, Marotta and

Watts noted that in contrast to a strictly scientific mind-set in examining research, there is also significant benefit from exploring case-based research, which lends itself to a multimethod, multidimensional perspective. This is consistent with the recommendations made by numerous others (e.g., Westen & Bradley, 2005) who have been so concerned about only using results from controlled experiments. Therefore, in the Best Practices section of the *Journal of Counseling and Development*, a variety of techniques, research methods, and treatment outcome findings will be readily accessible to counselors. Hopefully we will begin to see more studies using participants who are minorities or represent other groups of clients who have significant stressors and need of help.

Chapter Summary

The chapter has provided an overview, both historic and current, of the debate in our field about empirically supported treatment, common factors, and integrative approaches. The EST movement has resulted in benefits for clients in the form of therapists having available information about the best methods for helping people with a particular problem. However, use of an EST approach also comes at a cost; ESTs have not been researched for effectiveness with clients who are minorities, and there are some philosophical assumptions that undergird the empirical approach in general that some authors see as anathema to the intent of counseling.

An alternative way to explain and understand some of the outcome research is to consider the common factors that all therapeutic approaches share, even though they may be defined using different terms. Advocates of common factors state that those common factors cannot be isolated from other, more circumscribed treatment techniques. For that reason, common factors proponents perceive the common factors to be more representative of the curative aspects of a counseling or therapeutic intervention.

We concluded the chapter by looking at two integrative models: Prochaska's Readiness for Change model, and Beutler and colleagues' Systematic Treatment Selection, as viable and accessible sources for practitioners. The idea of "evidence-based practice" as advocated by Westen and Bradley was differentiated from "empirically supported" in that evidence-based practice more broadly encompasses treatment outcome results that are derived from other research besides just random controlled trials.

Questions for Class Discussion

1. Any approach has advantages and disadvantages. What, if any, do you imagine could be disadvantages of using an evidence-based, integrated approach to working with clients?
2. What ideas do you have about how you will go about getting the latest information on evidence-based treatment approaches?
3. Do you agree that it is unethical to use a treatment strategy that has not yet been researched for effectiveness? Why or why not?
4. In your own perception, to what extent do you think emphasis in treatment should be on relationship versus technique? What is the relationship between your own temperament, ethnicity, and other personal characteristics, and your client's temperament, ethnicity, and personal characteristics, in the establishment of a therapeutic alliance?

CHAPTER 15

Integrated Case Conceptualization

After studying this chapter, you should have a clear understanding of the following:

- How to use the assessment categories to elucidate case material that is pertinent to treatment
- How to use the cultural values paradigm to inform your rationale for counseling approaches
- The role of Bronfenbrenner's ecological model in conceptualizing treatment in applied cases
- How to use the client readiness and integrated treatment paradigms to inform your choice of counseling techniques in applied cases

The purpose of this chapter is to illustrate the application of multiple frameworks for conceptualizing a client's concerns. We are going to work in a more focused manner on analyzing and discussing Carole and Derek, the two client cases that have appeared at the conclusion of each microskill chapter. Because the text has not been working specifically on case conceptualization and treatment techniques, we are at a bit of a disadvantage. Nevertheless, you have read the case descriptions of Carole and Derek over multiple counseling skill chapters, and we now have the opportunity to explore how we would actually use a variety of client information and apply it to the several models that have been presented in this text. There are multiple benefits that can be served by this case analysis.

1. We will extract data from the previous counselor/client interactions to demonstrate how data can be used in an applied way to the categories suggested for intakes in Chapter 13.
2. We will use the client-generated data to discuss the aspects of the counseling process that have transpired thus far in each case. We will apply multiple models that were used elsewhere in this text to demonstrate how the models can be implemented.
3. We will identify a treatment plan and, just as occurs in reality, discuss some of the possible impediments that may occur in counseling, and outside of counseling, that could affect treatment outcome.

The six chapters covering microskills gave dialogue examples of a counselor working with two clients, Carole and Derek. With the progression of each microskill chapter, the interactions between the counselor and the clients represented subsequent sessions. Thus, over six chapters, the excerpts represented six meetings between Carole and Derek and their respective counselors. Across the initial client descriptions and the six following sessions, a picture of the clients and their histories began to emerge.

This chapter is divided into two parts, one focusing on Carole, our adult client, and one focusing on Derek, our child client. Each respective client discussion will provide information extracted from their dialogue excerpts. In addition to the bits of data gleaned from those dialogues, other data will be offered, and an illustration of how to apply those data to several models we have covered. These include the suggested assessment categories, relevance of each of Hofstede's axes, Bronfenbrenner's ecological model, and the Prochaska information about stages and levels of change. We will then see what possible treatment plans might look like, as well as potential barriers or impediments to the counseling process in each case.

THE CASE OF CAROLE

Where it is relevant, direct client quotes have been extracted. Following those quotes will be an explanation of how those quotes relate to objective application. The logical place to start is with intake assessment data.

Individual Assessment/Intake Information

SUBJECTIVE DISTRESS   Carole came to counseling at the suggestion of her family physician. During a routine physical, Carole complained to her doctor of impaired concentration, terminal insomnia (early morning awakening at 3 A.M.), feeling "squirrely," sadness, and a significant weight gain over the past year. In response to the counselor asking Carole to rate the intensity of her sadness on a scale of 1 to 10, Carole described herself as being a 7.

IMPAIRMENT IN DAILY FUNCTIONING   Following are several direct quotes and then a brief discussion of how to assign a level of severity.

"I'm trying to make their breakfasts and get their lunches packed and it all seems overwhelming. I stand there in the kitchen looking around and can't get myself organized to get their things ready. Lately I started giving them lunch money because I can't get their lunches made."

"After I get the kids to school and John leaves for work, I come home and sit. There's all this work piled up around me. Laundry, dishes, yard work, and I do all of it. I'm tired of being the pack mule and the workhorse in the house. I love them, but I'm just so darned tired. And there's no help for me, I just have to do it."

A *mild* level of impairment would be slightly reduced efficiency, a *moderate* level of impairment would be noticeable decrease in efficiency and level of functioning but still maintaining capability to meet some daily demands, whereas a *severe* degree of impairment would be either vegetative (lying in bed or sitting in a chair) or agitated (pacing purposely and not accomplishing anything) behavior. These self-descriptions Carole has provided would suggest her current level of impairment is moderate.

CLIENT DESCRIPTION OF THE PRECIPITANT   Carole describes the onset of her difficulties as occurring over the past year; she identifies her husband's possible promotion to middle management and youngest child starting school (all-day kindergarten) as being two significant changes in the household. She sees herself as shirking her responsibility and not being a good mother, because she doesn't find enjoyment in being home all day taking care of the house.

RELEVANT HISTORY OF THE PRECIPITANT   Carole's husband John has always held a traditional view of "appropriate" gender roles. She thought she agreed. However, in the past year Carole has begun feeling increasingly anxious and guilty and has wondered about what her conflicted feelings say about her ability to adequately fill her assigned role as wife and mother in this family.

FAMILY HISTORY   Carole is the third of five children in her family of origin. Her mother is Caucasian; her father, now deceased, was African American. Her parents had a rocky relationship in which they were intermittently together and estranged. During Carole's childhood, her mother was loving but often seemed sad and lethargic, did not work outside the home, but didn't do much inside the house either. The children were expected to do the chores, meal preparation, and so on. Her father was employed as a mechanic in a neighborhood garage. She experienced her father as a stern disciplinarian who otherwise was somewhat disinterested and uninvolved with the children. The parents did not drink, although both of her older brothers drank and "ran the streets."

Carole has a close relationship with her younger sisters, while her two older brothers both left home at 18 and currently don't have much contact with Carole or either of her sisters. Carole's father died of a heart attack when she was 25. Her mother lives near Carole and John. Carole and her two sisters maintain contact with their mother and share the responsibility for making sure their mother is okay. One of Carole's concerns has been what arrangements will be made when her mother is no longer able to manage her own needs, which Carole anticipates is coming in the next several years.

Carole's family of origin attended church regularly and had a good support system of extended family and the community of the congregation of their church.

There is a positive family history of depression in several maternal aunts and reported history of depression in her mother, as well, although her mother was never "officially" diagnosed as being clinically depressed. There is no history in the family of suicide or homicide.

Carole currently resides with her husband John, her daughter Ariana, and her son John Junior ("JJ").

LEGAL HISTORY   Carole has no significant legal history other than a couple of speeding tickets.

ACADEMIC AND EMPLOYMENT HISTORY   Carole graduated from high school but reports that she was "not a good student," meaning that she earned mainly C's and D's. Following high school she began working as a waitress. She continued to live in her parents' home until she was about 22, at which time she was making enough money to get an apartment with some friends. Carole went from job to job, always seeking to make more money. At the age of 26, she began to think about what she wanted to do with her life and started dreaming of becoming either a pediatric nurse or a pre-school teacher. Carole was in the process of meeting with a counselor at the local community college, discussing financial aid options and possible majors, when she met her husband John. When they got married, she stopped working outside the home and did not pursue community college any further.

MENTAL STATUS   Carole was oriented to person, time, and place. Her range of affect was blunted, and she was frequently tearful for the first several sessions. She never smiled, typically kept her eyes downcast, sat slumped in her chair, and was very still.

SUICIDAL/HOMICIDAL IDEATION/PLANS   Carole denied suicidal or homicidal ideation or plan. She did, however, report that there have been days she wished she would just not wake up.

MEDICAL HISTORY   No significant medical conditions.

CURRENT MEDICATIONS   No medication currently.

ALLERGIES   Pollen and hay fever.

DRUG/ALCOHOL/TOBACCO/CAFFEINE HISTORY AND CURRENT USE   Carole has a history of heavy alcohol consumption in her early adulthood, but she stopped drinking with her first pregnancy and denies any current use of alcohol. She reduced her caffeine consumption when she began having consistent terminal insomnia, but her abstinence from caffeine has not helped the insomnia problem. She began drinking coffee in the morning again to get going because she wakes up in the morning so tired. She smokes one to one and a half packs of cigarettes per day and has since she was 19. Carole denies current or past use of street drugs or any other psychoactive substances.

PREVIOUS MENTAL HEALTH CONTACTS   No prior mental health contact.

Carole's Value Preferences (Hofstede's Cultural Axes)

POWER DISTANCE   There is indication that Carole's values support a belief in democracy and that people get places in life as the result of two things: hard work and the grace of God. She was raised to believe, and continues to believe, that hard work will be rewarded and that people in authority are there because they worked hard and deserve to be there. This achievement is something that is possible, from her perspective, for anyone who is committed to working toward that goal. These perceptions would be consistent with someone who has *low power distance.*

MASCULINITY   In Carole's family of origin, there were clearly differentiated gender roles between men and women. Although she worked to support herself in early adulthood, she always imagined that she would only support herself if she had no other choice; that is, if she had not gotten married and would not be supported by a husband.

Here are dialogue examples that indicate a masculine gender role value:

> "John comes home exhausted and expects a square meal on the table in a clean house. That's not really too much to expect, considering how hard he works all day."

> "My husband tells me I have no business looking outside the house for a job. He is more than capable of supporting our family and for me to get a job is a disgrace to him as a provider. In fact, he forbade me from getting work outside our house."

When Carole and John got married, they both believed that the man's role was to financially support the family and it was the woman's role to support the family in every other way, by making a comfortable home, preparing good, healthy meals, and so on. However, prior to meeting John, Carole had begun to dream about having a career in either pediatric nursing or early childhood education. Carole had envisioned working either as a preschool teacher or as a nurse and then working her way into management in a health care facility. However, she never considered having professional employment of that nature and also being a wife and mother; she had thought of homemaking and career as mutually exclusive.

Interestingly, both of her possible career goals are consistent with a role of caretaking and nurturing, which is congruent with a traditional view of women's roles.

Carole's values on this axis are a source of internal and external conflict for her and are contributing to her current distress. She has surprised herself by realizing that she would like to have a career outside of her family life, but this is not at all congruent with the way she expected her life would be, nor does it fit with what she believes is "right."

AFFILIATION   Carole has a fairly high level of collectivism, which is another source of distress for her, in that she sees her responsibilities to her family of origin to outweigh her needs as an individual. Therefore, the gender role responsibilities identified above, in concert with her high degree of affiliation, create a life circumstance that she sees no way to escape.

At the same time, though, part of her yearns to individuate somewhat and to have her own life. "I think I've been walking around the house feeling sorry for myself because everyone has a life except me. They all leave every day to go do their things and the only thing I can do is clean up and do laundry. I need to find something to do with myself."

However, the idea that she would have any inclination for a career outside her family caregiving is a source of guilt and embarrassment for her, as she sees it reflecting poorly on her commitment as a wife and a mother.

UNCERTAINTY AVOIDANCE   Carole and her family are Baptist and their church is Fundamentalist. She firmly believes in "right" and "wrong," and while she is careful not to judge or condemn anyone else for their choices, she holds very high standards for herself and her family. Carole also firmly believes that God gives opportunities to all those who are deserving, and that illegal or un-Christian behavior will be punished.

Carole's Spheres of Influence in the Ecological Model

MICROSYSTEM   The primary dyad that impacts on Carole's issues is her marriage. There are other dyadic interactions as well at this level, including her relationships with Ariana and J.J., both of which Carole finds positive, as well as her relationships with her two sisters. Carole talks to both sisters every day. Both of them have had concerns about Carole's symptoms and have offered to help with child care.

Although her relationships are generally positive, Carole experiences some dissonance as emanating from these dyadic interactions, too. For example, from John she feels pressure to fulfill her wifely duties. On the other hand, her two sisters are both very supportive and encourage Carole to "branch out" and get some activities/employment outside the home. Her sisters see John as "using" her.

MESOSYSTEM   In Carole and John's life, there are two main mesosystems in which they are heavily involved and which exert influence. One is the elementary school their children attend, and the other is their church. Carole occasionally volunteers at the elementary school as a room mother, chaperoning on field trips, and so on.

Carole and John both are involved with their church and participate in several committees for increasing the size of the congregation and also doing community service.

EXOSYSTEM   The exosystem that currently exerts the most bearing on Carole's life is John's employer, which is an automobile factory. John has been working at the same plant since he was 18. He has been a shift supervisor for the last several years, and he has been given indication from his manager that he is being considered for further promotion into middle management. Because of that, he is very conscientious about being available to cover over-time, volunteer for additional tasks, and so on. While Carole is completely in favor of John's career advancement, the extra work and time away from the family puts even more responsibility on her for managing everything else in the household.

MACROSYSTEM   The shared beliefs and values that Carole and John hold are reflections of the macrosystem. The values and beliefs of their church, namely, that God provides for those who help themselves, are central in their lives. They also highly value social contribution and helping other people, and both were raised in homes with traditional, clearly defined gender roles. These prescribed gender roles encompass not only tasks and jobs in the family, but also acceptable and unacceptable experience of and expression of emotion.

DIAGNOSTIC IMPRESSION AND READINESS FOR CHANGE

Carole's life was going well until fairly recently when her youngest child began school. This transition to school age is a typical developmental stage through which all parents progress, and so the precipitant can be seen as developmentally typical. It was shortly following both of her children beginning school that Carole began having numerous symptoms of depression, including weight gain, impaired concentration, feelings of sadness, and early morning insomnia. Her presentation and constellation of symptoms are consistent with a vegetative depression.

The source of Carole's depression appears to be conflict and incongruence that are occurring for Carole both intrapersonally and interpersonally. Internally, the main source of Carole's problem is that she is dissatisfied with her current life role as a wife and mother, yet this dissatisfaction is a source of guilt and tremendous conflict. Carole believes that she should be satisfied with remaining in her current role as a full-time homemaker, but in reality she feels unfulfilled and frustrated that her only role is to support everyone else's activities and efforts.

There are external sources of conflict too. Carole's husband, while loving her very much, expects her to uphold the implicit "contract" they have had in their marriage regarding their roles in the family. John expects her to continue being responsible for all the household chores, food preparation, and so forth, and he has expressed concern and frustration that she has not been getting as much done around the house. Additionally, Carole's sisters place some pressure on her to "stand up" to John and tell him what she wants.

These internal and external conflicts have begun to manifest in the form of depression. Carole's growing awareness of the problem suggests that she is in the contemplation phase of change, in which she is realizing that her life is not going completely smoothly. Yet, the prospect of giving up old ways in favor of growth and change is scary and overwhelming to her, and when she thinks about change she thinks mainly of all the ways it will be difficult and that it will cost her, both emotionally and financially.

TREATMENT PLAN

If you want to practice generating a treatment plan yourself, you can use the treatment plan template included at the end of this chapter. Read on to see one example of how to formulate a treatment plan for Carole.

Carole's Treatment Plan

To supplement Carole's treatment plan in Table 15.1, we can add additional detail about each of the problems/strengths/strategies.

TABLE 15.1   Carole's Treatment Plan

Problem	Strengths	Goal	Strategies
Depression	• Generally happy • No prior history of depression • Previously high level of functioning	• Reduce depression rating from a 7 to a 0 • Eliminate insomnia, increase concentration • Increase sense of well-being	• Modify self-talk; work toward less rigid thinking • Process conflicted feelings • Generate satisfying hobbies or volunteer work • Consider referral for possible antidepressant medication if symptoms persist
Marital conflict/mixed messages from husband	• Previously strong marriage	• Find a compromise that will enable husband's comfort and also Carole's • Process John's concerns about Carole	• Involve husband in sessions • Explore feelings and thoughts related to family roles • Identify areas where compromise might be possible • Increase number of activities and sources of pleasure for them as a couple
Career indecision	• Has some idea already of her preferences • Motivation is emotional, not financial	• Identify goals for vocational or avocational activities	• Explore places to volunteer

PROBLEM: DEPRESSION   Carole's low power distance supports presenting the overall counseling process to her as a collaborative effort with the counselor basically in the role of educated coach. Empirically supported treatment indicates a cognitive-behavioral approach to her depression, and her belief that people can and should help themselves will be conducive to a structured cognitive-behavioral approach. Her black-and-white thinking has contributed to her feeling "stuck" and not being able to see any compromises for her current predicament, resulting in depression. Therefore, helping Carole become aware of her rigid thinking and how she has basically created her own prison mentally needs to be a first step in moving toward a more balanced style of internal dialogue.

Paired with the modification of her self-talk, helping Carole to identify and then pursue some behavioral techniques for increasing pleasure in her daily life could help her depression. One possibility would be to teach Carole how to create a list for herself of household tasks, and then choose one or two easy tasks to do before providing herself with a rewarding activity. Mild exercise may serve multiple purposes simultaneously. Doing a physical activity could mitigate depression and help her to expend more physical energy so she will sleep better.

If Carole's depressive symptoms were to persist despite her following through with the above strategies for coping, it might be advisable to refer her to a psychiatrist for possible antidepressant medication. The rationale for this suggestion is that if her insomnia persists, it could exacerbate her concentration impairment and also her melancholia.

PROBLEM: MARITAL CONFLICT AND MIXED MESSAGES FROM JOHN   Historically, Carole and John have had a strong relationship and John has recognized and respected what a great wife she has been. Carole fell head over heels in love with John and continues to describe loving him deeply. This would be an important foundational strength to identify and emphasize at the outset of Carole's counseling. I would discuss John's ambivalence with Carole from the standpoint of deciding what she believes would be the best way to communicate with him about her struggle. There are three apparent options: helping Carole practice how to talk with John about what she is feeling and thinking, inviting John to accompany Carole to some counseling sessions, or having John come for a session without Carole. While the counselor might have strong preferences for one of these options, I believe it would be most culturally sensitive and person-centered to discuss each of the options with Carole and fully explore advantages and disadvantages of each choice, before deciding how exactly to address this particular presenting problem.

There would be several purposes for involving John. First, because he is the most proximal individual in her life, he exerts much influence on her thinking and feelings. He has shared in her perceptions and thoughts about roles in the home, and a change in her behavior will certainly affect him. One point that will be important for John to understand is that Carole having a career outside the home is not a reflection of John's inability to support the family.

PROBLEM: CAREER INDECISION   One alternative for helping the couple gradually make the adjustment to Carole having some responsibility outside the home would be for her to consider volunteer work. Volunteer work could be advantageous from the standpoint that she could ease into it and not necessarily feel the pressure or obligation that she might if she were employed or had paid tuition to be in school. Volunteering would also give her the option of exploring possibilities to see which of her two choices, nursing or early childhood education, actually seems to be a better fit for her preferences.

This is the main problem area in which Carole has highly ambivalent feelings about making changes. So, from a readiness for change perspective, the appropriate treatment strategies here need primarily to be dramatic relief and full exploration and experiencing of the myriad, contradictory feelings she is having about the prospect of doing something outside the home. For Carole, the idea of doing that is such a major departure from how she expected to live her life that working through these feelings is essential before taking any action steps to become involved in volunteer work or schooling.

Potential Impediments to Successful Counseling

One other thing to identify and consider preemptively are the potential barriers to Carole's success in counseling. Once again it can be helpful to think about impediments that might arise for Carole within herself as well as potential external barriers. There are several possible barriers that readily come to mind in her case.

NEEDING TO TAKE RESPONSIBILITY FOR HER MOTHER   Carole has repeatedly expressed concern about caretaking for her mother. Her mother is already somewhat dependent on

Carole and her sisters for meeting some needs. If her mother's health takes a turn for the worse, Carole might need to spend more time and energy doing additional care for her, and if she has other responsibilities too, such as being in school or working, this could become a overwhelming prospect.

RESISTANCE/NONSUPPORT FROM HER HUSBAND   John might be completely nonsupportive of Carole's pursuing outside interests. Because he has tended toward rigidity historically, he may perceive her desire to differentiate as a betrayal of his wishes, or a violation of their implicit contract in the marriage. Resolution of this dilemma could become one of the focuses of the treatment plan.

HISTORY OF LOW ACADEMIC ACHIEVEMENT   Carole's history of being a poor student raises a question. Her low grades in high school may reflect a low average level of cognitive ability, a low degree of interest in academically related activities, or they could simply indicate a lack of effort. If she has low average cognitive ability, a return to school could be extremely stressful and difficult as well as costly. Therefore, when the time comes to make a decision about going back to school, it would be advisable for Carole to work with someone in Assessment Services at the community college to ascertain her level of academic functioning.

FEAR OF FAILURE   Carole has expressed some thoughts that reflect a fear of failure. If these fears are not adequately addressed and processed, this fear could very well become a self-fulfilling prophecy.

THE CASE OF DEREK

Individual Assessment/Intake Information

Derek is being seen by a school counselor, and so the degree of contact and involvement with his grandmother will be at a much lower level of intensity than if they were being seen in an agency setting. Nevertheless, we will apply the same categories of client data that we have for Carole, because the information has bearing on the rationale about how to proceed with him.

Subjective Distress

COUNSELOR: Take today, for instance. Is this an okay day or a not okay day?

DEREK: I'd say more not okay.

COUNSELOR: Let's go back to this morning when your alarm went off. Did you know then that it was going to be a bad day?

DEREK: I don't know.

COUNSELOR: *(Silence)*

DEREK: I guess I woke up mad.

COUNSELOR: How come?

DEREK: *(Eyes filling with tears)* I miss my mom! I miss my old school! I don't want to be here.

Derek reportedly has good days and bad days. He is not able to identify specific precipitants, but is aware of waking up feeling "bad" on some days, and those are usually the days he gets into trouble. He reports that on days he feels bad, his distress rating is about a 9 and on good days his distress rating is a 0.

IMPAIRMENT IN DAILY FUNCTIONING   There is a moderate degree of impairment in his day-to-day functioning. The collateral information from his teacher, Ms. Neill, is consistent with Derek's self-report of good and bad days.

CLIENT DESCRIPTION OF THE PRECIPITANT   Derek reports that he has never really liked school. He was previously enrolled in another elementary school, and although he states he did much better there, his academic records reflect a history of grades and behavior very similar to what he has demonstrated at his current school.

RELEVANT HISTORY OF THE PRECIPITANT   Derek is a 9-year-old boy of Latino descent who has been exhibiting significant behavior problems in school. Since the beginning of the school year, he has been aggressive in the lunchroom, taking other students' food, and has been suspended for fighting on the playground. His grades are C's, D's, and F's, and he frequently does not complete or turn in his homework.

FAMILY HISTORY   Derek's family came to the mainland United States when Derek was an infant, with the intention of joining other family here and in the hope of finding stable, better-paying employment. However, about two years ago Derek's father received a court summons to return to Puerto Rico and upon his arrival was arrested and convicted of receiving stolen property. He is serving a 7-year sentence. His mother promptly divorced his father.

Derek's mother is trying to single-handedly raise the five children. There are some cousins who live in the area and sometimes help his mother with her financial needs and child care. However, despite the tradition in Puerto Rican culture of the oldest male child helping with child care, Derek has flatly refused to participate in contributing to the family's functioning. Derek's disruptive behavior at home was primarily characterized by disobeying rules, staying out on the street at night past his curfew, hanging around the neighborhood with older boys who often are in legal trouble, and yelling when he doesn't get what he wants.

Derek has been disruptive and defiant for most of his life; it was his oppositionalism that prompted his mother to send him to live with his grandmother. His mother could not control his behavior, and she felt unable to manage him and the other children.

Derek's grandmother believes that Derek is angry and upset that his father had to return to Puerto Rico and was then incarcerated there. Although Derek has not identified his father's absence as a precipitant, his grandmother believes Derek needs a strong male in the household to teach him how to "act like a man." Derek does not have a stable consistent relationship with any significant adult males.

LEGAL HISTORY   Derek himself has no history of involvement in Juvenile Court, but numerous friends from his neighborhood are well known to the local police.

ACADEMIC HISTORY   Derek's grades and school behavior have been marginally acceptable throughout his academic history. He has never been referred for any type of educational intervention, nor have teachers expressed any perception of possible learning problems.

MENTAL STATUS   Consistent with his self-description of "good days" and "bad days," Derek's presentation does seem to fluctuate from meeting to meeting. On some days he is quite animated and energetic, while on other days he seems sullen and downcast. At those times, his range of affect is constricted, his responses are minimal, he makes little eye contact, and he offers little information.

SUICIDAL/HOMICIDAL IDEATION/PLANS   Derek denies any current or past suicidal or homicidal thoughts and also denies a history of having been abused physically or sexually.

MEDICAL HISTORY   Derek has asthma for which he uses an inhaler. There are no other known medical conditions.

CURRENT MEDICATIONS   Derek has an asthma inhaler, which he uses as needed for wheezing and breathing difficulty.

ALLERGIES   Dust and cats.

DRUG/ALCOHOL/TOBACCO/CAFFEINE HISTORY AND CURRENT USE   Denies any use of any of these.

PREVIOUS MENTAL HEALTH CONTACTS   None.

Derek's Family's Value Preferences (Hofstede's Cultural Axes)

Note: In working with young children, the cultural axes are probably most pertinent from the standpoint of what the parents' values are. In Derek's case, because his grandmother is functioning as essentially the single parent who is raising him, it might be helpful to get some sense of where her values are on each of these axes.

Especially since we may have limited time to meet with his grandmother, it could be an efficient use of time to become educated about general characteristics of Puerto Rican culture prior to talking with her. Upon perusing the Hofstede website that lists data for countries, found at http://www.geert-hofstede.com/, we note that Puerto Rico does not have a set of numerical values because it is a U.S. territory. Therefore we may need to do other research to get insight as to likely value preferences that we then could further explore in our meeting with Derek's grandmother.

POWER DISTANCE   In general, we know that there is high power distance in some Latino cultures. High power distance equates to deference to authority and an expectation that children will also be deferential and respectful. This is a possibility that would definitely need to be explored with Derek's grandmother; what, in general, the family expectations are regarding children's obedience. Derek's disregard for punishment and rules in the home may be especially significant given this cultural component. In other words, Derek's overt oppositionalism may be a behavioral expression/indication of his anger and pain about what he experiences as abandonment by his mother and father.

MASCULINITY   Puerto Rican culture is strongly patriarchal. *Machismo* is highly valued. Older male children are often expected to be responsible for younger siblings. Again, this is a point that would be important to explore with the grandmother; to what extent did Derek's mother expect that Derek would be helping to care for his younger siblings?

AFFILIATION   Puerto Rican culture generally holds a collective orientation toward extended family. The grandmother's offer to raise Derek and assume legal custody of him is one indication of the family's involvement in helping and supporting one another. Similarly, to the extent that it is possible, it will be important to include family members (especially Derek's grandmother) in the intervention techniques.

UNCERTAINTY AVOIDANCE   Many people who are Puerto Rican are Catholic, which would suggest a high level of uncertainty avoidance.

Derek's Spheres of Influence in the Ecological Model

MICROSYSTEM   Derek's key microsystems are his interactions with his grandmother and his teacher. He has minimal contact with his mother or younger siblings. Derek's relationship with his grandmother is fairly close; he seems to be motivated, at times, to meet her expectations. His relationship with his teacher is not particularly positive; she sees him as a "troublemaker" and he sees her as a "grouchy old lady who just wants to scold kids." Her frequent corrections of him in class have had a negative impact on his perception of being in school. He also has begun developing friendships with other boys in his neighborhood, some of whom are "rough." His grandmother is extremely concerned about his association with these peers.

MESOSYSTEM   The mesosystem is a web of many microsystem interactions, which consists of interconnections between the dyads and triads of the microsystem. A meeting among Derek, his grandmother, the school counselor, and his classroom teacher would be an example of a mesosystem that could exert influence in his life.

EXOSYSTEM   The exosystem is the set of environments that have indirect influence on a person's internal experience, such as parents' place of employment, policies in a school, and local politics. In Derek's case, despite his teacher's frustration with his classroom behavior, the school principal has been very supportive and positively inclined toward Derek. The principal is aware of Derek's family situation and is very much in favor of the school trying to serve not only as the source of Derek's formal education, but also as an ancillary support to his grandma's parenting efforts.

Derek's grandmother is not employed, she is a full-time homemaker who is currently receiving a pension and Social Security from the death of her husband many years ago.

MACROSYSTEM   The family does attend church, and for the most part they have continued to adhere to traditional Puerto Rican customs as far as holidays, food preparation, and collective, extended family.

DIAGNOSTIC IMPRESSION AND READINESS FOR CHANGE

There are a number of issues going on for Derek. He is demonstrating externalizing, disruptive behavior at school; he is disruptive and disobedient at home; and he has neighborhood friends that are negative influences. The dynamics and forces that are contributing to his symptoms appear to have originated environmentally and situationally. His father's leaving the home and subsequent incarceration are likely to have been an extremely traumatic stressor. It is notable that in all Derek's interactions with the school counselor, while he verbalizes some feelings including missing his mother, there has been absolutely no mention of his father. A father's incarceration is not a typical developmental event, and it represents a traumatic incident.

Derek's disruption and lack of achievement in school are also a concern. In conceptualizing the reason for Derek's low achievement, it is very difficult to differentiate the roles played by his feelings about his father's absence, his mother's giving custody to his grandma, and possible learning difficulties he may be experiencing for other reasons. While it appears that his poor school behavior is an expression of his overwhelming feelings about each parent, his lack of achievement and classroom misbehavior could also be related to boredom and lack of comprehension.

Additionally, Derek has now begun to have an identity at school as a "tough" kid who fights on the playground and hangs around other tough kids in his neighborhood. It seems as though he may find it easier or more comfortable to present this persona to people in his world rather than trying to "succeed" in a more traditional sense.

There is some suggestion that Derek may be experiencing a mild to moderate adjustment reaction to his father's absence and his mother's struggles. As is typical for children, Derek does not necessarily perceive himself as needing to change; from his perspective, all his problems are occurring outside of himself. Therefore, Derek's stage of readiness for change is precontemplation.

TREATMENT PLAN

You may wish to try your hand at generating a treatment plan for Derek by using the blank treatment plan template at the end of the chapter. Alternatively, a suggested treatment plan has been provided (see Table 15.2) that represents what a school counselor, working with Derek and the adults in his life, might generate.

TABLE 15.2   Derek's Treatment Plan

Problem	Strengths	Goal	Strategies
Not doing homework	Likes the tutor	Increase homework completion and submission to 100%	Schedule Derek to come early to school 4 days a week to work with the tutor for 20 minutes
			Give him a breakfast treat while they are tutoring
Fighting with peers	Has demonstrated some self-control	Reduce physical altercations completely	Reinforce successfully coping such as walking away
		Develop some positive friendships with peers	Get him involved in Boy Scouts
Disobedient with Grandma	Loves her and has a close relationship with her	Become compliant with chores and rules	Behavioral plan of earning privileges such as later bed on weekends and video game time; loss of privileges for noncompliance
Missing Mom	Prior to Dad's leaving, had a close relationship with mother	Give him opportunity to have contact with Mom	Schedule time to do something fun together on a regular basis, e.g., park on Saturday afternoons to rollerblade
Grieving Dad	Had a close relationship with father	Give opportunity to verbalize his feelings of abandonment and rejection	Artwork Bibliotherapy Writing letters together in a counseling session
		Give opportunity to have Dad be part of his life through letter writing or possibly a phone call	

Derek's Treatment Plan

Each of the presenting problems is addressed with additional supplemental detail beyond what appears on Derek's treatment plan. One general comment, first, is that if Derek were an adult and were in the precontemplation stage of readiness for change, emphasis on consciousness-raising and insight would be indicated. However, again as is typical for children, emotionally based insight-oriented counseling may not be beneficial to him because many 9-year-olds are not particularly insightful about the implications of their behavior. Therefore, Derek's treatment plan incorporates techniques that will give him a chance to process his feelings, but also take responsibility for structuring a behavioral plan out of his hands and into the purview of key adults in his life: his teacher and his grandmother.

Following is a further elaboration of Derek's treatment plan.

PROBLEM: NOT DOING HOMEWORK There are a couple of reasons why this is the first problem listed on the treatment plan. First, because this counseling is happening in the context of a school setting, it seems appropriate to have his school behaviors be a focus. Second, because the school does have tutors available, if Derek and his grandmother are agreeable to getting him involved with the tutor, the likelihood of success here is quite high. This is favorable from the standpoint of creating positively reinforcing school experiences fairly quickly. Also, because the goal is not a particular letter grade, but instead emphasizes effort, it places a greater amount of control in Derek's hands, which again is especially valuable in this early stage of counseling.

The school counselor might also consider periodically discussing Derek's classroom behaviors with Ms. Neill, his classroom teacher. One purpose would be to give her an opportunity to vent about her own frustration with having him in class. If she has that opportunity to express her feelings about him, it might be more possible for her to work with the school counselor on developing a behavior plan for his behavior in the classroom similar to the behavior plan that will be suggested for home. Ms. Neill has been teaching for many years and some school personnel believe she is burned out. However, she does take interest in some of her students, and historically she seems to respond best to those students whose families express interest in collaborating with her to maximize their child's educational benefit.

PROBLEM: FIGHTING WITH PEERS This is obviously a pressing concern. If Derek's fighting continues, he will be suspended or expelled from school. Also, harm could come to him or someone else. Acquisition and appropriate use of conflict resolution skills and behaviors are clearly necessary. It is possible that his inclination to fight may be exacerbated by some of the boys with whom he is spending time in his neighborhood. In addition, his inclination to fight might be an externalization of his feelings of anger about the issues in his family of origin.

If Derek has excessive physical energy secondary to anger, alternative physical outlets would probably be helpful. Boy Scouts, which are offered at school one evening a week, could be a means for Derek to establish new friendships with other peers under adult supervision. Boy Scouts is free to attend; they perform a number of service activities in the community; and they also have other activities such as camping and outdoor survival skills. In addition, the Boy Scouts are run by several fathers who are interested in serving as appropriate male role models for boys who do not have anyone in their lives to fill that role. While it is obviously not the same as having a father in the home, the presence of appropriate adult male role models could be beneficial to Derek.

PROBLEM: NONCOMPLIANT WITH GRANDMA   Until recently, Derek's relationship with Grandma was positive and loving. His frustration and anger have recently begun to dominate multiple aspects of his life, and the anger and disobedience he expresses toward Grandma may actually be a displacement of the feelings he has for his dad.

Grandma needs support and help with understanding how to establish and follow through with behavioral contracts for compliance. A behavior contract at home would be a fairly easy thing for the school counselor to offer to Grandma, and it could be helpful to involve Derek in the contract process.

Establishing clear expectations about the chores he must perform and the house rules may provide him some comfort; often when things feel out of control, having external structure established can give a child a sense of security. It will be important for Derek to identify what he wants to work toward; the behavioral rewards he earns must be highly desirable to him. Grandma could be shown how to place the behavior chart on the bulletin board in her kitchen, and to have Derek check off his chores as he completes them.

When he is noncompliant, he loses privileges; the costs associated with misbehavior should similarly be identified by Derek and Grandma together.

PROBLEM: MISSING MOM   Even though he was angry and belligerent with his mother before moving to his grandma's house, at 9 years of age Derek still has emotional need for contact with his mother. Given Grandma's role as the main disciplinarian, it should be easier for Derek and his mother to reestablish their emotional connection. I would recommend that Mom and Derek have scheduled time together each week, and that Derek be given time with his mother regardless of whether his behavior through the week has been appropriate and acceptable. Perhaps his behavior through the week could determine what activities with Mom he can choose, but access to her should not be denied whether he is behaving or not. In this way, the message being communicated is that his mother will be available unconditionally, but the allowable activities will be within Derek's control, determined by whether he chooses to follow the behavioral contract.

PROBLEM: GRIEVING FOR DAD   Derek's grief over Dad's loss has been completely ignored/avoided. The dynamic that is causing Derek's feelings to remain unspoken is not clear—perhaps Derek feels guilty (not uncommon in children), or believes he should not be angry, or perhaps Derek has told himself he hates his father and will never forgive him. In any case, this is an area where perhaps the school counselor can gently probe periodically to explore whether Derek is willing and able to verbalize his feelings about that. It is likely that this topic, because it is so highly sensitive to Derek, should not be pushed by the counselor until a long, stable helping relationship between Derek and the counselor has become firmly established. Given Derek's family history and ability to attach to significant adults, the prognosis for developing a strong working alliance with Derek is good.

Potential Impediments to Successful Counseling

GRANDMA MIGHT NOT FOLLOW THROUGH ON THE TUTORING, BOY SCOUTS, AND BEHAVIOR PLAN   One potential problem with this overall treatment plan is that Grandma plays a key role; a great deal of the responsibility for follow-through rests on Grandma's shoulders. As is so often the case working with children, given Derek's age, he is unlikely to initiate any of the remedial activities that were identified as treatment strategies. Therefore, if Grandma is too tired or otherwise unable to become fully invested in and energized about the treatment plan, the likelihood of success is greatly compromised. Thus, I cannot overemphasize the importance of the school counselor establishing a solid relationship not only with Derek, but also with Grandma.

MOM MIGHT BE DEPRESSED AND UNABLE TO EMOTIONALLY ENGAGE WITH DEREK   We are assuming that Mom will be interested and able to give Derek some individual attention, based on Grandma's report that Mom wants to do that. This could be wishful thinking on Grandma's part; until we talk directly to the mother to form our own impression, we will not know. Rather than having Derek make the request of his mother, it would be better for the request to come from either Grandma or the school counselor, so that in the event his mother declines, Derek is not overtly exposed to yet another "rejection."

DAD MIGHT NOT WRITE BACK   In encouraging Derek to express his feelings about his dad and possibly begin a correspondence with him, again we must be careful not to assume his father will respond in a particular way. If Derek were to write and not get a response, it could mean that his dad doesn't want contact, or it could mean Dad never got the letter. Here is another example of where the school counselor could "run interference" and perhaps get some additional information about rules for letter writing at Dad's prison, which could mitigate further emotional trauma for Derek.

DEREK MIGHT STILL DEMONSTRATE ACADEMIC PROBLEMS   There may be additional learning difficulties beyond those that are the result of Derek's emotional turmoil. After the emotional and situational issues have been worked on and resolved somewhat, it will be important to continue looking at the academic achievement to ascertain whether further assessment and possible remediation are indicated.

Chapter Summary

There are significant differences between these two cases; obviously because of the clients' respective ages, the approach a counselor takes will be vastly different. In addition, I have tried to demonstrate how cultural factors and consideration of various levels of systems may affect the counselor's conceptualization of the client and also the selection of counseling technique.

   Another significant point of difference between Carole and Derek is the setting for the counseling. School counselors often try to communicate with key family members, but time constraints and other role responsibilities place school counselors in a position of having limited time to do intensive, focused counseling interventions with students and families. Thus, in Derek's case, I have attempted to illustrate how the process of counseling and the focuses of an intervention would look if this work were occurring in a school setting.

   One aspect of case conceptualization to which I have alluded throughout the book has been how one's thinking about a client is shaped by one's own values and theoretical orientation. Perhaps even more importantly, a recurrent theme in the book has been sensitivity to the client's characteristics and preferences. I hope that through these applied cases, the complexity of undertaking these responsibilities became apparent to you.

   The questions for class discussion at the conclusion of this chapter were developed for you to consider and to engage in dialogue with your classmates about the counseling process with Carole and Derek. You may have very different opinions or perspectives as to what the counseling priorities should be for each of these clients. I strongly encourage you to discuss it; there certainly are multiple ways and means by which a counselor could help each of these individuals.

Questions for Class Discussion

1. What aspects of Carole's or Derek's case presentations do you think are not adequately addressed by the diagnostic impressions and suggested treatment plans?
2. What would you do differently in your treatment approach with each of them and why?
3. What approaches do you think are specifically contraindicated (absolutely should not be done) based on their case information?
4. If the possible barriers were to arise in either of their cases, what would you do about it?
5. On a scale of 1–10, with 10 being extremely favorable, what do you believe each of their prognoses are for benefitting from counseling, and why?

TREATMENT PLAN TEMPLATE

Problem	Strengths	Goal	Strategies for Goal Attainment

CHAPTER **16**

Self-Awareness and Self-Care

After studying this chapter, you should have a clear understanding of the following:

- The sources of stress for counselors and therapists
- Compassion fatigue and professional burnout
- Why self-care in our profession is such a critical issue
- What your self-care plan might look like

This text began with a lengthy discussion in the first chapter about the importance of the book's themes and learning them simultaneously. By now you should have a clear understanding of how each of the specific skills you have learned is influenced by mitigating variables such as one's theory frame and one's cultural frame of reference. Chapter 16 is devoted to a culmination of the self-awareness strand, with an emphasis on self-care. The self-care discussion will include raising your awareness about specific sources of stress common to practicing counselors (work environment, client-induced, and self-induced); strategies for self-care that have been found helpful; and an opportunity to begin considering what you anticipate are going to be your particular points of vulnerability to stress or compassion fatigue.

THE SELF-AWARENESS STRAND

The personal reflections that were posed to you throughout most chapters and the concluding questions from each chapter were intended to amplify your self-awareness. The questions were posed in a way that necessitated a consideration of your personal meaning, which is your context when perceiving objective information. I hope that through the process of participating in those personal reflections and maybe discussing them with your classmates, you now have an enhanced sense of how your own characteristics and attributes interface with the techniques you will be using with your clients.

Cultural influence is an extremely broad concept that has far-reaching implications; beyond the conventional construct of "culture" in the anthropological sense, there are also a multitude of other variables of diversity that have similar impact on levels of social influence vis-à-vis Bronfenbrenner's ecological model. Our discussion and your personal reflections in this regard should have enhanced your understanding of how these forces can shape the form and direction of your counseling interactions with your clients.

Your career goals may include some form of working with clients as a professional helper; taking a course in counseling skills is a step along the path toward that goal. When you have finished your graduate education, you will have completed another stage in your process of becoming. Even after you finish your graduate education, though, the developmental progression of learning about yourself and learning new, advanced, or enhanced skills and techniques will be ongoing. I hope you will be open to continued feedback about your techniques and ability, and also open to new learning related to your work. If you eventually obtain a license to practice as a mental health professional, you will be required to maintain ongoing training in order to periodically renew your license.

PROFESSIONALISM

A *professional* individual is someone who has completed specialized training to perform a particular type of job that requires specific preparation. When we consult with any professional, such as an attorney or an accountant, we expect that person to behave in a manner that is consistent with how most other people with those same credentials and qualifications would conduct themselves. For example, if we were consulting with a lawyer to whom we had paid a retainer, we would not expect her to be eating a sandwich and talking on the phone to a friend during our meeting with her.

Professionalism refers to conducting oneself in a manner that would be expected for someone with a graduate degree and a license to work with the public. This encompasses many aspects of your conduct, ranging from your dress to the way you talk to and interact nonverbally with your clients, coworkers, and supervisors. It also refers to the language you use in your written documentation such as case notes, letters, announcements, and reports.

PERSONAL REFLECTION _____

Have you ever met with a trained professional whose behavior was unprofessional? What specific things did that person say or do that you would call "unprofessional"? Generate a list of behaviors that, to you, constitute "professional behavior."

One of the things that differentiates professional relationships with clients from your personal relationships with friends, family, or work colleagues is the nature and purpose of your relationship. Whereas in a personal relationship with someone you are dating or to whom you are married there is some expectation of intimacy and mutual needs being met, in a professional relationship the concern should only be about the needs of the client. When we go to a doctor because of physical symptoms and compromised health, we do not expect or want the doctor to disclose to us *his* symptoms and compromised health; we want the focus to be on our own problems. Similarly, when a client comes to us with symptoms or needs, we must be able to set aside our own symptoms and problems to make the client's concerns the priority.

This ties in, to some extent, with the material covered in Chapter 12 about self-disclosure. As stated then, you will need to make a decision about your own level of comfort in sharing personal information with your clients. Regardless of how much or how little you disclose to your client, the intention that must always remain clear is that the only person whose needs should be considered is the client. It is your responsibility to manage your own needs completely outside of and separate from your relationships with your clients.

The conundrum is that if we are completely honest, we *do* have needs that are met in our counseling relationships. We all have needs that are met through our employment, some of which are financial and some of which are psychological. Some theories about career choice include an element of need reduction as one component of why people choose the careers that they choose. We talked at length in Chapter 1 about your motivation for becoming a professional helper. The key is to be highly self-aware of our needs for contribution, being needed, and so on, at all times. By having clear and honest self-awareness, we can greatly reduce the chance that we will have emotional needs inadvertently or inappropriately being met by our clients.

ETHICS, BOUNDARIES, AND IMPAIRMENT

The topics of relationship boundaries and counselor impairment are of such vital importance that they are among the section headings of our ethical guidelines for behavior. In the following section, we will discuss the definitions and issues related to these topics as well as exploring their relationship to ethical issues.

ACA Code of Ethics, Section A.5, explicitly addresses what the parameters of a counselor/ client relationship are expected to be. These parameters can alternatively be referred to as boundaries, which will be discussed below. This includes not only sexual or romantic involvement, but also friendships or business relationships, such as going out for a social lunch with a client or having a client who happens to be a contractor work on your house.

ACA Code of Ethics, Section C, which is about professional responsibility, includes counselor impairment. Impairment is an aspect of self-care that warrants a closer look as well, in the context of self-awareness.

Boundaries

A *boundary* in a relationship refers to the degree and nature of limits and differentiation between two people. This involves communicating with the other person about your own feelings and the acceptability or unacceptability of his or her behavior. In an emotionally and physically close relationship, the boundaries are typically quite different than they are in a relationship with an acquaintance.

With a relationship partner, we might make disclosures about our feelings and perceptions that we consider to be private and that we would only share with someone to whom we feel very close. Although in some sense you will have emotional intimacy with your clients, it is a pseudointimacy, meaning that it is a contrived relationship based on professional services (Welfel, 1998).

Another thing unique about boundaries in a counseling relationship is that there is a significant imbalance between the two participants with regard to the degree of disclosure and the power distribution. Regardless of whether *we* see ourselves as being in a position of authority with our clients, the facts that (1) we are professionals with extensive education in our specialty area, and (2) the client is working with us because of our training, place us in a position of authority. Conversely, there is an expectation that the client will be making disclosures to us about information that to him or her may be intensely personal and private.

Observation of appropriate boundaries in our roles as professional helpers is perhaps more important than in other professions because of the nature of our work. Counseling can be emotionally demanding for a counselor. Many of your clients will be in significant emotional pain and will have suffered many abuses physically and emotionally. They will have significant emotional needs. Whereas during the counseling session, you are to make yourself wholly available to the client, it is neither healthy nor advisable to make yourself wholly available to all your clients all the time. If you were to make yourself continually available without discretion, you would become emotionally depleted at some point.

Rothschild (2006) devoted most of a book entitled *Help for the Helper* to understanding the process of empathy and its effect on the listener/helper. We will cover more about that later in the chapter. Related, Figley (2002) talked about *disengagement*, which is similar to the concept we discussed earlier: setting boundaries. In this case it refers to the therapist's ability to disconnect from the empathic experience of suffering between therapy sessions, thereby obtaining a reprieve from the emotional pain. He points out that this is, to a large extent, a cognitive technique in which the counselor consciously and intentionally makes a distinction, through his or her self-talk, between the client's life and the counselor's life.

In a more concrete sense, one boundary that many professional counselors set is not disclosing to clients one's home phone number or home address. Unless you live and work in a very small or rural community, you might not want to share your home address with clients. What is the rationale for this suggestion?

Clients who generally have a hard time discerning what is and is not appropriate in relationships might not be able to make good decisions about when and under what circumstances they can spontaneously stop by your house. And why might it be problematic for a client to just stop by your house? Here are several possible reasons:

- You may feel that your home is a sanctuary, a place that is to be kept separate from work.
- You may not want your children or family members to have contact with your clients.
- You may want to wear some clothing or be engaged in some behaviors that you do not want your client to see.
- You could be doing something during which you do not want to be interrupted, such as practicing yoga or eating dinner, yet feel obligated to let the client in and also feel obligated to meet the client's needs rather than your own.
- A client could arrive at your door in crisis or inebriated, and you would be responsible for handling it. If you have been dealing with crises all day at work, you need a time and a place in which you are *not* dealing with crises.
- You may have a client with a history of substance abuse and violence who has not been honest about that history and could be violent toward you or your family members.

One of the main ways to ensure that you will be able to stay in the profession and maintain physical and emotional health will be for you to establish and maintain very clear boundaries with your clients. This will be beneficial for them as well as for you.

Impairment and Self-Care

Counselor impairment and self-care are essentially two sides of the same coin. Self-care is an aspect of optimal professional functioning that is as important as self-awareness. It is hypocritical to advocate self-care for our clients if we have ourselves been unable to find balance in that regard. This was one of the rationales for advocating that you participate in your own counseling as part of your own professional training. We will explore sources of stress, some of which are endemic to the helping professions. As you may recall from Chapter 13 on intake assessments, each of us has a finite amount of coping ability available at any given time. If the stressors we are about to explore go unchecked, or if they intensify to a breaking point, subsequent emotional problems could develop. The importance of healthily coping with stressors cannot be overemphasized if you hope to have longevity in the helping professions. With that cautionary statement in mind, we move now to an exploration of four categories elucidated by Kottler (1992) that are sources of stress for helpers. Those sources are the work environment, event-related stressors in your personal life, client-related stressors, and self-induced stressors.

The term *impairment* as it is used in the ACA Code of Ethics refers to physical, emotional, or mental problems that impede one's ability to do one's job. While one common source of worker impairment that comes to mind is problematic substance abuse, there are many other reasons and causes for a therapist to become impaired. Among the four stress sources to be discussed, problems of sufficient magnitude as to result in impairment could occur.

WORK ENVIRONMENT STRESS   Multiple authors have identified work environment characteristics as contributing to work stress (Kottler & Schofield, 2001; Sherman, 1999; Stadler, 2001; Welfel, 1998). One of the biggest environmental stressors occurs when a discrepancy exists between what your job demands and what you are realistically capable of effectively doing. There may be work-related obligations and yet not enough time in the work day to meet all of those obligations. This results in either chronically not meeting work demands, or working longer hours than one is being paid for in order to get the job done.

AUTHOR'S REFLECTION

I worked at an agency that was having financial problems due to cuts in state funds. The clinic administrators began to steadily increase the number of billable contact hours that therapists were required to have with clients. The production requirements got so high that it was not possible to attain the contact hour requirements unless we worked through our lunch hour and frequently scheduled two clients for the same time slot, expecting one of them not to appear for the appointment. An inevitable by-product of the increased number of client contact hours was an exponential increase in paperwork, which necessitated often working several hours past "quitting time" or going to the office on a weekend to stay current with progress notes, treatment plans, quarterly reviews, and correspondence.

School counselors in some settings face similar demands, needing to divide their time between helping students who are severely struggling and performing many administrative tasks, unrelated to school counseling, for the building. Other school counselors are required to divide their work week across several buildings, leaving the counselor no option but to deal only with the most pressing and severe of student problems.

It is easy to imagine how these kinds of working conditions, coupled with a caseload of students or clients in great distress, could create an intolerable work situation for a counselor. Excessive environmental demands are not always the case; however, it could be advantageous for you to be aware of the precise work demands when you are interviewing for a particular position. A school or agency with a high frequency of staff turnover may have that turnover because the working conditions are not conducive to longevity in the position, and by accepting that job you could be placing yourself in a high-risk environment.

Job Burnout   Job burnout is closely associated with one's work environment. Burnout happens when a person has not only experienced chronic job stress, but also sees absolutely no hope for improvement. Any kind of worker can experience burnout, although service professionals, who spend their work lives attending to the needs of others, are definitely at higher risk for burnout than other types of professionals. This is particularly the case if work puts them in frequent contact with the dark or tragic side of human experience: working in a prison, investigating child abuse, or working with rape victims are examples. A person is also at high risk for developing burnout if he or she is underpaid, unappreciated, or criticized for matters beyond his or her control. One source of burnout can be setting unrealistic goals for yourself or having them imposed upon you; you may feel that you are expected to do too many things for too many people. There could be occasions on which you believe you are working under rules that seem unreasonably coercive or punitive, or you are doing work that causes you to violate your personal values. Perhaps the least desirable circumstance would be if any of the above were a characteristic of a position, and you were stuck in that job for financial reasons.

It is probable that in the course of your mental health career you will have colleagues or supervisors who are burned out in their jobs. It is also possible that you could find *yourself* in a position of being burned out. Characteristics of burnout include the following:

- Frustration and powerlessness
- Hopelessness
- Being drained of emotional energy
- Detachment, withdrawal, isolation, feeling "too tired" to socialize
- Being trapped
- Believing you've failed at what you're doing
- Irritability—snapping at people or making snide remarks about them
  - Sadness
  - Cynicism (believing that people act out of selfishness and nothing can be done about it)

EVENT-RELATED STRESSORS   Sometimes we will experience stressors in our personal lives that impinge on our ability to work effectively with other people having problems. There are myriad stressors, ranging from separation and divorce, to personal or family illness, or death of a loved one. Recall that we each have a finite amount of emotional and psychic energy to cope with daily demands. Some of us have more energy (resilience) in reserve than others, but no one has an endless supply. When we have stressors outside of work, we may still be able to perform competently at work. However, our available margin for accommodating stressors is reduced, so that if excessive work stressors present themselves when we are already in a compromised emotional state, our level of functioning may deteriorate.

CLIENT-INDUCED STRESS   There are particular types of client problems and client populations that are recognized as among the most challenging and difficult. Stadler (2001) summarized research findings across multiple studies that have identified particular clients as being among the most stressful to work with, according to therapists. These include clients with chronic substance abuse, clients who have HIV, clients who are sex offenders, clients who are abusive males. She further enumerated client suicide as an extremely stressful event for many therapists.

Beyond particular client populations that are challenging to work with, a variety of idiosyncratic events may happen in the context of your work with students and clients that can be highly stressful.

AUTHOR'S REFLECTION

I once saw a 77-year-old gentleman for an emergency assessment in a mental health center in a small town. He was sent directly to the mental health center by a hospital emergency room because he had accidentally shot and killed another turkey hunter. He was tearful and agitated, wringing his hands and crying as he spoke. Although he was very remorseful about shooting the other man, he was most upset about the possibility that if his wife heard the information on the local police scanner, she would have a heart attack.

The local sheriff brought the client's wife to the waiting room of the mental health clinic, and sure enough, on the way to the clinic his wife overheard details of the accident on the police radio. True to the client's fears, upon arriving at the mental center waiting room, his wife went into cardiac arrest. The paramedics arrived, performed emergency medical procedures on her on the spot, and whisked her away in an ambulance along with her husband (my client). For me, this sequence of events, which transpired over about an hour and a half, was *extremely* upsetting. It took several days of processing with my supervisor and a coworker for me to resolve my own feelings of being unhelpful to the client, as well as also completely emotionally overwhelmed.

Earlier in the chapter I mentioned the book *Help for the Helper*. Rothschild (2006) goes into detail about how empathic responding is not only an internal emotional event in which we have particular feelings; it also triggers measurable reactions in our autonomic and central nervous systems. Therefore, becoming aware of these levels of responses can help us to consciously and mindfully take steps to undo or reverse the residual effect of sharing the suffering of our clients.

Compassion Fatigue   Figley (2002) stated, "The very act of being compassionate and empathic extracts a cost under most circumstances. In our effort to view the world from the perspective of the suffering we suffer. The meaning of compassion is to bear suffering. Compassion fatigue, like any other kind of fatigue, reduces our capacity or our interest in bearing the suffering of others" (p. 1434).

Compassion fatigue is a significant occupational hazard for individuals who deal frequently and extensively with crisis work (Corey-Souza, 2007). According to Figley (2002), compassion fatigue only happens for those individuals who are capable of empathy, and empathic ability is a minimum threshold skill for people in training to become counselors. Indeed, empathy is one of the main tools of the helping professions (Rothschild, 2006). The pertinent components that define compassion fatigue are:

- Exposure to a client, in which the counselor experiences the suffering of the client through direct exposure
- Empathic response, in which the counselor attempts to reduce the suffering of the client through empathic understanding
- Compassion stress, which is the residual emotional energy after an empathic response has been offered
- Degree of self-perceived achievement, which is the therapist's self-evaluation of his or her ability to either alleviate the client's suffering or otherwise solve the problem

Prolonged compassion stress, combined with these other factors, can result in compassion fatigue. The symptoms of compassion fatigue can include a chronic state of tension, anxiety, and stress that occurs in response to a counselor working with cumulative trauma reactions of victims. Other symptoms can include exhaustion, irritability, sleep disturbances, angry outbursts, and disengagement from painful events (Udipi, 2007).

Compassion fatigue might be particularly likely when there has been a large-scale crisis that has affected many people; these include natural and human-made disasters that require teams of crisis responders. In such cases, where there are many people who have a need for counseling, a therapist can become completely overwhelmed by the magnitude of suffering, both in terms of the number of people affected and also in the extent of loss associated with the trauma. Recent events such as the World Trade Center attacks and Hurricane Katrina are examples of crises in which some crisis workers themselves became overwhelmed by the task of helping victims. This type of reaction among crisis workers is also referred to in the professional literature as *secondary trauma.*

PERSONAL REFLECTION

Which types of clients, either those listed above or some other particular population such as court-ordered, would be extremely stressful or upsetting for you? What is it about that group that would make it so challenging?

SELF-INDUCED STRESS   Some people have personality characteristics in general that prompt them to choose helping professions. Furthermore, there may be specific aspects of your own life history that led you to this field. Generally speaking, people who enter the helping professions are those who feel a need to nurture, help, serve, protect, or contribute to others in some meaningful way. Our empathy, and the fact that we care about other people, in and of itself elevates the likelihood that we may be inclined to carry the suffering of others in our day-to-day lives. On top of that, we are working with people in need, some of whom grow and recover, and some of whom do not.

It is not unusual to feel responsible when clients do not improve. Perfectionism on our part, doubting our ability, and a reluctance to acknowledge our own emotional needs can all contribute to development of excessive stress.

Beyond those dynamics listed above, many of us carry residual emotional baggage from life experiences. Many of us come from homes where there were unhealthy communication patterns or relationships. In fact, family of origin experiences may have contributed to our own career choice. While this is certainly an asset from the perspective of having empathy and insight in our counseling sessions, it can also be a liability in that certain client situations may trigger reactions or push emotional buttons that can take a toll on the available emotional and cognitive reserves we have for competent work performance.

Countertransference   *Countertransference,* a concept that arises from psychodynamic theory, refers to the therapist relating to a specific client or client situation in a certain way because the client represents a key figure from the therapist's past. For example, a therapist might be working with an elderly client who reminds the therapist of his own grandmother, who was cold and rejecting. If the therapist were experiencing countertransference, he might experience the client's statements and behavior as similarly rejecting or judgmental despite the fact that others observing the client's behavior would not call the behavior rejecting. In other words, the therapist, because of his own life history, is relating to the client in a mode that is basically a reenactment of an earlier, influential relationship with a key figure.

Note that because the construct of countertransference arises from a theoretical model, some therapists may disagree that this phenomenon exists at all. Opponents of the countertransference construct might instead perceive and define the therapist's reaction to the client as a conditioned response (as defined from a behavioral perspective), for example, or an attempt to complete some unfinished business that requires closure (as defined in a Gestalt framework).

Regardless of the theoretical frame, though, the countertransference process is one that would be highly situation specific, meaning that the distressing or otherwise noteworthy internal experience of the therapist would be confined only to that particular client situation.

Symptoms of countertransference are as varied as individuals are. That is to say, the counselor's internal experience of countertransference may be a source of distress for the counselor. However, sometimes our countertransference reactions to a client are not completely in our conscious emotional and cognitive awareness. Despite our lack of awareness, however, our countertransference can have a significantly deleterious impact on our ability to effectively treat or work with the client in question.

Developing and Implementing a Self-Care Plan

Let's turn our attention in a hopeful direction now: generating a specific plan for managing your stress level and discussing what to do if you develop compassion fatigue. Each of us has our own unique vulnerabilities, and also our own unique combinations of plans for how to prevent or minimize the emotional toll that can be taken upon our psyches in this line of work. Beyond trying to mitigate the negative impact of stress, it is important to be mindful of nurturing ourselves for the simple sake of maximizing our enjoyment of life and our ability to contribute what gifts we have to offer others.

We will first talk in general about strategies various people use, and then progress to developing a personalized plan for handling work stress and challenges. Regardless of which stress-related categories seem to bear the most relevance to your situation, a good plan for self-care can never hurt. The following information would be pertinent no matter what your occupation. As an added benefit, these self-care strategies may be useful to teach to your clients. A good plan is one that considers and provides for the following: sleep, nutrition, spirituality, relaxation, and exercise.

SLEEP It is important to get enough sleep that you can go to work feeling energized and prepared to handle what comes your way. Keeping late hours, or "pulling all nighters" to get something done, may be necessary occasionally, but doing it continually will begin to quickly deplete your energy reserves.

NUTRITION Eating whole food that is high in nutritional value is likely to give your body more raw material to work with than the heavily processed, chemical-laden items one typically finds in a vending machine. It is also important that you not skip meals, even if it seems as if you don't have enough time in your day to eat. Giving yourself the chance for sustenance and setting aside time in your schedule is necessary to keep your body going without beginning to compromise your physical system. Poor nutrition can reduce your immunity to illness or otherwise stress your organ systems.

SPIRITUALITY Just as we need to feed our bodies to sustain output, we also need to nourish our souls. Religion and spirituality may be closely intertwined for some of you, while for others, spirituality happens outside the context of organized, structured religious practices. Regardless of where your own preferences lie in this domain, if the spiritual aspect of your life is a source of grounding and emotional strength, you absolutely need to consider how to integrate it in your ongoing self-care practice.

RELAXATION   It is of tremendous importance that you have some things you do for fun or that bring you pleasure, outside of work. Some people have hobbies that involve solitary activity; solitude, for those who enjoy it, is one way to recharge one's battery. For others who are highly social, spending time with friends is the key. Perhaps you've never really had time to pursue some interests because you were too busy with school or just never made it a priority. If that is the case, then the time that you enter the world of being a helping professional is a wonderful time to do it.

If you are drawing a blank as to what you might like to have as a hobby, think back to your childhood and recall the activities or places that brought you the most joy. As you think about them, try to pinpoint exactly what it was about the activity or location that accentuated your enjoyment. Is there anything like that in your current lifestyle? If not, what ideas do you have for how you might integrate some of those components?

One author, Mihaly Csikszentmihalyi, has devoted his professional career to studying and learning about peak or optimal experiences that people report. He has conducted extensive international research on this topic and has constructed a model for understanding optimal experience. This model, like the Hofstede model, transcends culture; while the content of people's experiences understandably varies substantially across regions of the world, the characteristics of peak experiences do not.

According to Csikszentmihalyi (1990), optimal experiences have the eight following characteristics:

1. The experience occurs when we confront tasks we have a reasonable chance of completing.
2. We must be able to concentrate on what we are doing.
3. The task has clear goals.
4. There is immediate feedback as to how we are progressing toward our goals.
5. There is a deep but effortless involvement that removes the everyday worries and frustrations from our lives.
6. While doing this activity, we have a sense of control over our actions.
7. Concerns for ourselves fade away, but our sense of self is actually more acute after the activity.
8. The sense of time passing is somehow altered; time either slows way down or speeds up.

PERSONAL REFLECTION

Do you have some activity that, when you engage in it, completely takes your attention and focus away from the mundane, day-to-day concerns and issues that are usually on your mind? How many of the above listed characteristics of an optimal experience fit with your *own* engagement in your favorite activity? How often do you have a chance to engage in this activity?

There are many different times and ways that people can incorporate optimal experiences in their lives. Some people are fortunate to have optimal experiences every day in their work. This is probably more an exception than the rule, though. Most of us have a reasonable degree of job satisfaction but seek our optimal experiences in places other than our place of employment.

PHYSICAL ACTIVITY AND EXERCISE   The word *exercise* may induce particular feelings for you; excitement and pleasant anticipation, guilt, or aversion. Your degree of physical exertion obviously needs to be well within the limits of your physical capabilities; if you have never been particularly physically active, it is clearly not advisable or realistic to expect yourself to begin a vigorous exercise regimen.

Intense physical exertion produces endorphins in our brains, and endorphins have been found to be a natural antidote for depression. Additionally, when people become heavily involved in some exercise, such as Tae Kwon Do, skiing, paddling, or jogging, they find their attention drawn to aspects of their present moment activity. This creates some of the requisite characteristics for one to experience "flow."

SOCIAL SUPPORT   We look carefully at the support systems of our clients; of course it makes sense to also consider the breadth and quality of our own support systems. Having friends and family who are supportive or can help out if we need it are of vital importance to maintaining emotional health. As you become increasingly aware of your own mental health and self-care, your sense of which people are and are not conducive to positive support may begin to shift.

One way to integrate a good self-care plan into your lifestyle is to find activities that meet needs in more than one category at a time.

AUTHOR'S REFLECTION

Although I have always been physically active, gym membership fees have usually been a waste of money because I'd only go for a month or two. I finally found a vigorous exercise activity I could do year-round when I began Tae Kwon Do. My children attend with me, so we have family time not only during class but on the way to and from the training hall. There is a community of people in class that are encouraging, supportive, and helpful. Kicking and yelling are frequent activities in class, and by the end of class any residual stress I carried in is diminished.

For example, sometimes school faculty or agency staff have organized intramural sports activities such as volleyball, basketball, or softball. Intramural activities with coworkers are a wonderful opportunity to connect socially and solidify work relationships, as well as getting the added benefit of both exercise and subsequent stress reduction.

Up to this point, the discussion has centered around developing a self-care plan in general. When someone develops compassion fatigue, the typical everyday stresses become more accentuated, and it becomes a pressing matter to attend to the symptoms. We will take a look at some of the recent findings about treating compassion fatigue.

RECENT RESEARCH ON COMPASSION FATIGUE   Samoray (2006) studied professionals, all of whom self-identified as suffering compassion fatigue, in a variety of helping professions that included law, education, medicine, mental health, and pastoral care. Several themes emerged: Creative expression can be healing, or a means of escape; it provided the participants with somatic relief; it enriched personal spirituality; and it enabled them to have a renewed sense of purpose, in general moving them from a place of fatigue to energized healing.

Other authors, as well, have articulated the value of therapists finding and engaging in creative expression as avenues for personal renewal and reenergizing (MacCluskie & Bauer, 2005). One study (Eastwood, 2007) found three self-care practices in particular that significantly lowered risk level: having a hobby that brings enjoyment, reading for pleasure, and taking pleasure trips or vacations.

Another author (Simpson, 2006) found presence of spirituality to have an inverse relationship to compassion fatigue; in other words, among her participants who worked in a variety of mental health settings (mental health centers, residential treatment centers, school counselors, and practitioners in private practice), higher scores on a measure of spiritual involvement and beliefs were associated with lower scores on the compassion fatigue instrument. She also found that higher numbers of clients with trauma history, coupled with low spirituality scores, were predictive of compassion fatigue symptoms.

One author (Kanter, 2007) sees a different pathway of causation in comparison to Figley (2002), and he also advocates a different avenue for treatment of compassion fatigue. His view identifies inadequate professional training, unrealistic expectations, and an array of countertransference responses as the source. Kanter (2007) advocates assessing and treating the root cause of the compassion fatigue; in his view, rest and relaxation are merely palliative care for overt symptoms and will not result in permanent benefit.

Regardless of whether we are talking about countertransference or a working through of a particular current trauma, it seems clear that a number of researchers have found that therapists themselves getting counseling can be very helpful in mitigating compassion fatigue. Especially if you have survived significant trauma or crises in your childhood, you will be at higher risk for developing it. You also will be at somewhat higher risk for developing it if you have not worked through or become clear about your own spiritual beliefs and practices.

This ties back in with the chapter on reflection of meaning, in which we talked about people needing to feel that there is some purpose in life. Many in the helping professions believe that there is a purpose being served by our work, which is separate from accumulating material wealth. Through processing with a therapist or with coworkers or a supervisor, we can verbalize and work through our own feelings, reactions, and experiences in our work with traumatized clients.

TEMPLATE FOR DEVELOPING A SELF-CARE PLAN BASELINE AND ONGOING SELF-ASSESSMENT   On a regular basis, make an honest assessment of the stressors in each of the categories mentioned by Kottler (1992). Following are suggestions for some questions you may ask yourself to gauge your stress level.

Work environment stress

- Is your job description reasonable?
- Have there been any recent changes that have affected your workload, and if so, have the changes been positive or detrimental to your overall well-being?

Client stress

- To what extent is the stress associated with your clients the result of your general caseload versus specific individual clients?

Event stress

- What ongoing stressors are you currently dealing with in your own life (parenting, relationships, illness, or other stressors)?
- How frequently are you exposed to stressful events in your personal life?
- On a scale of 1–10, how severe would you rate the intensity of each stressor alone? In combination of all of them, what rating would you give your overall stress level?

TABLE 16.1   Self-Assessment of Stressors

Source of Stress	Stress Load Rating (1–10; 10 = Heavy Stress)	What Factors Need to Change to Reduce the Stress Load?
Work environment		
Event-related stress		
Client-related stress		
Self-induced stress		

Self-induced stress

- How reasonable are your expectations of yourself and your performance at work and in your personal life?
- What are your currently unresolved concerns?
- What are the biggest fears that haunt you?
- On a 1–10 scale, to what extent to you believe the answers to the above three questions affect your ability to work with your clients?

After you have generated answers to those questions, use the information to complete the grids in Table 16.1.

Having completed the first table, turn your attention now to Table 16.2. As you are completing that table, ask yourself the following questions:

- What parts of a balanced lifestyle are missing or insufficient for me?
- What are some self-nurturing things I've yearned to do for myself but haven't given myself permission to do?
- What has prevented me from making those activities or practices part of my life now?
- How can I work around those impediments to actualize those things now?

Having completed those two exercises, you now should have a fairly good sense of the strengths and liabilities in your lifestyle, as well as some ideas about how to improve on what's working and reduce the impact of the parts that are not. Hopefully, working on these tables can assist you in the process of attaining or maintaining balance and health. It will serve you well to spend time considering these aspects of your life, not only now, but periodically

TABLE 16.2   Self-Assessment of Resources and Self-Care

Source of Strength/Nurturance	Quality Rating (1–10; 10 = Completely Ideal)	What Needs to Change to Improve the Quality Rating?
Sleep		
Nutrition		
Spirituality		
Exercise		
Relaxation		
Social support		

throughout your career, in order to help you maintain your well-being and therefore enhance what you are able to offer others.

Chapter Summary

This chapter has focused exclusively on your self-awareness and management of your own professionalism and stress level throughout your career. Undoubtedly there will be ups and downs, both professionally and in your personal life as well. Your work as a counselor may bring satisfaction, a sense of purpose and contribution. There will also be aspects of it that are sources of stress and difficulty. We covered a variety of reasons and sources of that difficulty. Working with people who are in distress makes it especially important that you be mindful of your own health, physically, emotionally, and spiritually, if spirituality is an important aspect of your life.

It is this author's hope that the self-assessment templates can help you create and maintain a balanced lifestyle that enables you to keep the stressors in check. You will go on from here to have other training experiences that will further facilitate your learning about how to balance the various skills and self-awareness components we have covered in the text.

Questions for Class Discussion

1. What do you see as costs or disadvantages of being conscientiously self-aware?
2. Among people you have observed to be burned out or fatigued, what were some of the factors that kept them stuck?
3. What barriers, if any, do you anticipate in your own life that make you worry about how well you will be able to implement a self-care plan?
4. What are some ways a person might be able to look at him-or herself and differentiate between countertransference and compassion fatigue?

Culminating Activity

At the conclusion of Chapter 1, I suggested you make a baseline tape of your helping someone, trying to be as helpful as possible. Now, with the reading and practicing behind you, listen to or watch your baseline tape.

- What parts of your helping style remain the same now as they were at the beginning?
- What are you doing differently?
- What are your goals for additional skill refinement?

ACA Code of Ethics

As approved by the ACA Governing Council, 2005
American Counseling Association
www.counseling.org

Mission

The mission of the American Counseling Association is to enhance the quality of life in society by promoting the development of professional counselors, advancing the counseling profession, and using the profession and practice of counseling to promote respect for human dignity and diversity.

Contents

ACA Code of Ethics Preamble — 295
ACA Code of Ethics Purpose — 295

Section A
The Counseling Relationship — 296

Section B
Confidentiality, Privileged Communication, and Privacy — 299

Section C
Professional Responsibility — 301

Section D
Relationships With Other Professionals — 303

Section E
Evaluation, Assessment, and Interpretation — 303

Section F
Supervision, Training, and Teaching — 305

Section G
Research and Publication — 308

Section H
Resolving Ethical Issues — 310

Glossary of Terms — 312

ACA Code of Ethics Preamble

The American Counseling Association is an educational, scientific, and professional organization whose members work in a variety of settings and serve in multiple capacities. ACA members are dedicated to the enhancement of human development throughout the life span. Association members recognize diversity and embrace a cross- cultural approach in support of the worth, dignity, potential, and uniqueness of people within their social and cultural contexts.

Professional values are an important way of living out an ethical commitment. Values inform principles. Inherently held values that guide our behaviors or exceed prescribed behaviors are deeply ingrained in the counselor and developed out of personal dedication, rather than the mandatory requirement of an external organization.

ACA Code of Ethics Purpose

The *ACA Code of Ethics* serves five main purposes:

1. The *Code* enables the association to clarify to current and future members, and to those served by members, the nature of the ethical responsibilities held in common by its members.
2. The *Code* helps support the mission of the association.
3. The *Code* establishes principles that define ethical behavior and best practices of association members.
4. The *Code* serves as an ethical guide designed to assist members in constructing a professional course of action that best serves those utilizing counseling services and best promotes the values of the counseling profession.
5. The *Code* serves as the basis for processing of ethical complaints and inquiries initiated against members of the association.

The *ACA Code of Ethics* contains eight main sections that address the following areas:

Section A: The Counseling Relationship
Section B: Confidentiality, Privileged Communication, and Privacy
Section C: Professional Responsibility
Section D: Relationships With Other Professionals
Section E: Evaluation, Assessment, and Interpretation
Section F: Supervision, Training, and Teaching
Section G: Research and Publication
Section H: Resolving Ethical Issues

Each section of the *ACA Code of Ethics* begins with an Introduction. The introductions to each section discuss what counselors should aspire to with regard to ethical behavior and responsibility. The Introduction helps set the tone for that particular section and provides a starting point that invites reflection on the ethical mandates contained in each part of the *ACA Code of Ethics*.

When counselors are faced with ethical dilemmas that are difficult to resolve, they are expected to engage in a carefully considered ethical decision-making process. Reasonable differences of opinion can and do exist among counselors with respect to the ways in which values, ethical principles, and ethical standards would be applied when they conflict. While there is no specific ethical decision-making model that is most effective, counselors are expected to be familiar with a credible model of decision making that can bear public scrutiny and its application.

Through a chosen ethical decision-making process and evaluation of the context of the situation, counselors are empowered to make decisions that help expand the capacity of people to grow and develop.

A brief glossary is given to provide readers with a concise description of some of the terms used in the *ACA Code of Ethics*.

Section A

The Counseling Relationship

Introduction

Counselors encourage client growth and development in ways that foster the interest and welfare of clients and promote formation of healthy relationships. Counselors actively attempt to understand the diverse cultural backgrounds of the clients they serve. Counselors also explore their own cultural identities and how these affect their values and beliefs about the counseling process.

Counselors are encouraged to contribute to society by devoting a portion of their professional activity to services for which there is little or no financial return (pro bono publico).

A.1. Welfare of Those Served by Counselors

A.1.a. Primary Responsibility

The primary responsibility of counselors is to respect the dignity and to promote the welfare of clients.

A.1.b. Records

Counselors maintain records necessary for rendering professional services to their clients and as required by laws, regulations, or agency or institution procedures. Counselors include sufficient and timely documentation in their client records to facilitate the delivery and continuity of needed services. Counselors take reasonable steps to ensure that documentation in records accurately reflects client progress and services provided. If errors are made in client records, counselors take steps to properly note the correction of such errors according to agency or institutional policies. *(See A.12.g.7., B.6., B.6.g., G.2.j.)*

A.1.c. Counseling Plans

Counselors and their clients work jointly in devising integrated counseling plans that offer reasonable promise of success and are consistent with abilities and circumstances of clients. Counselors and clients regularly review counseling plans to assess their continued viability and effectiveness, respecting the freedom of choice of clients. *(See A.2.a., A.2.d., A.12.g.)*

A.1.d. Support Network Involvement

Counselors recognize that support networks hold various meanings in the lives of clients and consider enlisting the support, understanding, and involvement of others (e.g., religious/spiritual/community leaders, family members, friends) as positive resources, when appropriate, with client consent.

A.1.e. Employment Needs

Counselors work with their clients considering employment in jobs that are consistent with the overall abilities, vocational limitations, physical restrictions, general temperament, interest and aptitude patterns, social skills, education, general qualifications, and other relevant characteristics and needs of clients. When appropriate, counselors appropriately trained in career development will assist in the placement of clients in positions that are consistent with the interest, culture, and the welfare of clients, employers, and/or the public.

A.2. Informed Consent in the Counseling Relationship

(See A.12.g., B.5., B.6.b., E.3., E.13.b., F.1.c., G.2.a.)

A.2.a. Informed Consent

Clients have the freedom to choose whether to enter into or remain in a counseling relationship and need adequate information about the counseling process and the counselor. Counselors have an obligation to review in writing and verbally with clients the rights and responsibilities of both the counselor and the client. Informed consent is an ongoing part of the counseling process, and counselors appropriately document discussions of informed consent throughout the counseling relationship.

A.2.b. Types of Information Needed

Counselors explicitly explain to clients the nature of all services provided. They inform clients about issues such as, but not limited to, the following: the purposes, goals, techniques, procedures, limitations, potential risks, and benefits of services; the counselor's qualifications, credentials, and relevant experience; continuation of services upon the incapacitation or death of a counselor; and other pertinent information. Counselors take steps to ensure that clients understand the implications of diagnosis, the intended use of tests and reports, fees, and billing arrangements.

Clients have the right to confidentiality and to be provided with an explanation of its limitations (including how supervisors and/or treatment team professionals are involved); to obtain clear information about their records; to participate in the ongoing counseling plans; and to refuse any services or modality change and to be advised of the consequences of such refusal.

A.2.c. Developmental and Cultural Sensitivity

Counselors communicate information in ways that are both developmentally and culturally appropriate. Counselors use clear and understandable language when discussing issues related to informed consent. When clients have difficulty understanding the language used by counselors, they provide necessary services (e.g., arranging for a qualified interpreter or translator) to ensure comprehension by clients. In collaboration with clients, counselors consider cultural implications of informed consent procedures and, where possible, counselors adjust their practices accordingly.

A.2.d. Inability to Give Consent

When counseling minors or persons unable to give voluntary consent, counselors seek the assent of clients to services, and include them in decision making as appropriate. Counselors recognize the need to balance the ethical rights of clients to make choices, their capacity to give consent or assent to receive services, and parental or familial legal rights and responsibilities to protect these clients and make decisions on their behalf.

A.3. Clients Served by Others

When counselors learn that their clients are in a professional relationship with another mental health professional, they request release from clients to inform the other professionals and strive to establish positive and collaborative professional relationships.

A.4. Avoiding Harm and Imposing Values

A.4.a. Avoiding Harm

Counselors act to avoid harming their clients, trainees, and research participants and to minimize or to remedy unavoidable or unanticipated harm.

A.4.b. Personal Values

Counselors are aware of their own values, attitudes, beliefs, and behaviors and avoid imposing values that are inconsistent with counseling goals. Counselors respect the diversity of clients, trainees, and research participants.

A.5. Roles and Relationships With Clients
(See F.3., F.10., G.3.)

A.5.a. Current Clients
Sexual or romantic counselor–client interactions or relationships with current clients, their romantic partners, or their family members are prohibited.

A.5.b. Former Clients
Sexual or romantic counselor–client interactions or relationships with former clients, their romantic partners, or their family members are prohibited for a period of 5 years following the last professional contact. Counselors, before engaging in sexual or romantic interactions or relationships with clients, their romantic partners, or client family members after 5 years following the last professional contact, demonstrate forethought and document (in written form) whether the interactions or relationship can be viewed as exploitive in some way and/or whether there is still potential to harm the former client; in cases of potential exploitation and/or harm, the counselor avoids entering such an interaction or relationship.

A.5.c. Nonprofessional Interactions or Relationships (Other Than Sexual or Romantic Interactions or Relationships)
Counselor–client nonprofessional relationships with clients, former clients, their romantic partners, or their family members should be avoided, except when the interaction is potentially beneficial to the client. *(See A.5.d.)*

A.5.d. Potentially Beneficial Interactions
When a counselor–client nonprofessional interaction with a client or former client may be potentially beneficial to the client or former client, the counselor must document in case records, prior to the interaction (when feasible), the rationale for such an interaction, the potential benefit, and anticipated consequences for the client or former client and other individuals significantly involved with the client or former client. Such interactions should be initiated with appropriate client consent. Where

unintentional harm occurs to the client or former client, or to an individual significantly involved with the client or former client, due to the nonprofessional interaction, the counselor must show evidence of an attempt to remedy such harm. Examples of potentially beneficial interactions include, but are not limited to, attending a formal ceremony (e.g., a wedding/commitment ceremony or graduation); purchasing a service or product provided by a client or former client (except-ing unrestricted bartering); hospital visits to an ill family member; mutual membership in a professional association, organization, or community. *(See A.5.c.)*

A.5.e. Role Changes in the Professional Relationship
When a counselor changes a role from the original or most recent contracted relationship, he or she obtains informed consent from the client and explains the right of the client to refuse services related to the change. Examples of role changes include

1. changing from individual to relationship or family counseling, or vice versa;
2. changing from a nonforensic evaluative role to a therapeutic role, or vice versa;
3. changing from a counselor to a researcher role (i.e., enlisting clients as research participants), or vice versa; and
4. changing from a counselor to a mediator role, or vice versa.

Clients must be fully informed of any anticipated consequences (e.g., financial, legal, personal, or therapeutic) of counselor role changes.

A.6. Roles and Relationships at Individual, Group, Institutional, and Societal Levels

A.6.a. Advocacy
When appropriate, counselors advocate at individual, group, institutional, and societal levels to examine potential barriers and obstacles that inhibit access and/or the growth and development of clients.

A.6.b. Confidentiality and Advocacy
Counselors obtain client consent prior to engaging in advocacy efforts on behalf of an identifiable client to

improve the provision of services and to work toward removal of systemic barriers or obstacles that inhibit client access, growth, and development.

A.7. Multiple Clients
When a counselor agrees to provide counseling services to two or more persons who have a relationship, the counselor clarifies at the outset which person or persons are clients and the nature of the relationships the counselor will have with each involved person. If it becomes apparent that the counselor may be called upon to perform potentially conflicting roles, the counselor will clarify, adjust, or withdraw from roles appropriately. *(See A.8.a., B.4.)*

A.8. Group Work
(See B.4.a.)

A.8.a. Screening
Counselors screen prospective group counseling/therapy participants. To the extent possible, counselors select members whose needs and goals are compatible with goals of the group, who will not impede the group process, and whose well-being will not be jeopardized by the group experience.

A.8.b. Protecting Clients
In a group setting, counselors take reasonable precautions to protect clients from physical, emotional, or psychological trauma.

A.9. End-of-Life Care for Terminally Ill Clients

A.9.a. Quality of Care
Counselors strive to take measures that enable clients

1. to obtain high quality end-of-life care for their physical, emotional, social, and spiritual needs;
2. to exercise the highest degree of self-determination possible;
3. to be given every opportunity possible to engage in informed decision making regarding their end-of-life care; and
4. to receive complete and adequate assessment regarding their ability to make competent, rational decisions on their own behalf from a mental health professional who is experienced in end-of-life care practice.

A.9.b. Counselor Competence, Choice, and Referral
Recognizing the personal, moral, and competence issues related to

end-of-life decisions, counselors may choose to work or not work with terminally ill clients who wish to explore their end-of-life options. Counselors provide appropriate referral information to ensure that clients receive the necessary help.

A.9.c. Confidentiality

Counselors who provide services to terminally ill individuals who are considering hastening their own deaths have the option of breaking or not breaking confidentiality, depending on applicable laws and the specific circumstances of the situation and after seeking consultation or supervision from appropriate professional and legal parties. *(See B.5.c., B.7.c.)*

A.10. Fees and Bartering

A.10.a. Accepting Fees From Agency Clients

Counselors refuse a private fee or other remuneration for rendering services to persons who are entitled to such services through the counselor's employing agency or institution. The policies of a particular agency may make explicit provisions for agency clients to receive counseling services from members of its staff in private practice. In such instances, the clients must be informed of other options open to them should they seek private counseling services.

A.10.b. Establishing Fees

In establishing fees for professional counseling services, counselors consider the financial status of clients and locality. In the event that the established fee structure is inappropriate for a client, counselors assist clients in attempting to find comparable services of acceptable cost.

A.10.c. Nonpayment of Fees

If counselors intend to use collection agencies or take legal measures to collect fees from clients who do not pay for services as agreed upon, they first inform clients of intended actions and offer clients the opportunity to make payment.

A.10.d. Bartering

Counselors may barter only if the relationship is not exploitive or harmful and does not place the counselor in an unfair advantage, if the client requests it, and if such arrangements are an accepted practice among professionals in the community. Counselors consider the cultural implications of bartering and discuss relevant concerns with clients and document such agreements in a clear written contract.

A.10.e. Receiving Gifts

Counselors understand the challenges of accepting gifts from clients and recognize that in some cultures, small gifts are a token of respect and showing gratitude. When determining whether or not to accept a gift from clients, counselors take into account the therapeutic relationship, the monetary value of the gift, a client's motivation for giving the gift, and the counselor's motivation for wanting or declining the gift.

A.11. Termination and Referral

A.11.a. Abandonment Prohibited

Counselors do not abandon or neglect clients in counseling. Counselors assist in making appropriate arrangements for the continuation of treatment, when necessary, during interruptions such as vacations, illness, and following termination.

A.11.b. Inability to Assist Clients

If counselors determine an inability to be of professional assistance to clients, they avoid entering or continuing counseling relationships. Counselors are knowledgeable about culturally and clinically appropriate referral resources and suggest these alternatives. If clients decline the suggested referrals, counselors should discontinue the relationship.

A.11.c. Appropriate Termination

Counselors terminate a counseling relationship when it becomes reasonably apparent that the client no longer needs assistance, is not likely to benefit, or is being harmed by continued counseling. Counselors may terminate counseling when in jeopardy of harm by the client, or another person with whom the client has a relationship, or when clients do not pay fees as agreed upon. Counselors provide pretermination counseling and recommend other service providers when necessary.

A.11.d. Appropriate Transfer of Services

When counselors transfer or refer clients to other practitioners, they ensure that appropriate clinical and administrative processes are completed and open communication is maintained with both clients and practitioners.

A.12. Technology Applications

A.12.a. Benefits and Limitations

Counselors inform clients of the benefits and limitations of using information technology applications in the counseling process and in business/billing procedures. Such technologies include but are not limited to computer hardware and software, telephones, the World Wide Web, the Internet, online assessment instruments and other communication devices.

A.12.b. Technology-Assisted Services

When providing technology-assisted distance counseling services, counselors determine that clients are intellectually, emotionally, and physically capable of using the application and that the application is appropriate for the needs of clients.

A.12.c. Inappropriate Services

When technology-assisted distance counseling services are deemed inappropriate by the counselor or client, counselors consider delivering services face to face.

A.12.d. Access

Counselors provide reasonable access to computer applications when providing technology-assisted distance counseling services.

A.12.e. Laws and Statutes

Counselors ensure that the use of technology does not violate the laws of any local, state, national, or international entity and observe all relevant statutes.

A.12.f. Assistance

Counselors seek business, legal, and technical assistance when using technology applications, particularly when the use of such applications crosses state or national boundaries.

A.12.g. Technology and Informed Consent

As part of the process of establishing informed consent, counselors do the following:

1. Address issues related to the difficulty of maintaining the confidentiality of electronically transmitted communications.
2. Inform clients of all colleagues, supervisors, and employees, such as Informational Technology (IT) administrators, who might have authorized or unauthorized access to electronic transmissions.
3. Urge clients to be aware of all authorized or unauthorized users

including family members and fellow employees who have access to any technology clients may use in the counseling process.

4. Inform clients of pertinent legal rights and limitations governing the practice of a profession over state lines or international boundaries.

5. Use encrypted Web sites and e-mail communications to help ensure confidentiality when possible.

6. When the use of encryption is not possible, counselors notify clients of this fact and limit electronic transmissions to general communications that are not client specific.

7. Inform clients if and for how long archival storage of transaction records are maintained.

8. Discuss the possibility of technology failure and alternate methods of service delivery.

9. Inform clients of emergency procedures, such as calling 911 or a local crisis hotline, when the counselor is not available.

10. Discuss time zone differences, local customs, and cultural or language differences that might impact service delivery.

11. Inform clients when technology-assisted distance counseling services are not covered by insurance. *(See A.2.)*

A.12.h. Sites on the World Wide Web

Counselors maintaining sites on the World Wide Web (the Internet) do the following:

1. Regularly check that electronic links are working and professionally appropriate.

2. Establish ways clients can contact the counselor in case of technology failure.

3. Provide electronic links to relevant state licensure and professional certification boards to protect consumer rights and facilitate addressing ethical concerns.

4. Establish a method for verifying client identity.

5. Obtain the written consent of the legal guardian or other authorized legal representative prior to rendering services in the event the client is a minor child, an adult who is legally incompetent, or an adult incapable of giving informed consent.

6. Strive to provide a site that is accessible to persons with disabilities.

7. Strive to provide translation capabilities for clients who have a different primary language while also addressing the imperfect nature of such translations.

8. Assist clients in determining the validity and reliability of information found on the World Wide Web and other technology applications.

Section B

Confidentiality, Privileged Communication, and Privacy

Introduction

Counselors recognize that trust is a cornerstone of the counseling relationship. Counselors aspire to earn the trust of clients by creating an ongoing partnership, establishing and upholding appropriate boundaries, and maintaining confidentiality. Counselors communicate the parameters of confidentiality in a culturally competent manner.

B.1. Respecting Client Rights

B.1.a. Multicultural/Diversity Considerations

Counselors maintain awareness and sensitivity regarding cultural meanings of confidentiality and privacy. Counselors respect differing views toward disclosure of information. Counselors hold ongoing discussions with clients as to how, when, and with whom information is to be shared.

B.1.b. Respect for Privacy

Counselors respect client rights to privacy. Counselors solicit private information from clients only when it is beneficial to the counseling process.

B.1.c. Respect for Confidentiality

Counselors do not share confidential information without client consent or without sound legal or ethical justification.

B.1.d. Explanation of Limitations

At initiation and throughout the counseling process, counselors inform clients of the limitations of confidentiality and seek to identify foreseeable situations in which confidentiality must be breached. *(See A.2.b.)*

B.2. Exceptions

B.2.a. Danger and Legal Requirements

The general requirement that counselors keep information confidential does not apply when disclosure is required to protect clients or identified others from serious and foreseeable harm or when legal requirements demand that confidential information must be revealed. Counselors consult with other professionals when in doubt as to the validity of an exception. Additional considerations apply when addressing end-of-life issues. *(See A.9.c.)*

B.2.b. Contagious, Life-Threatening Diseases

When clients disclose that they have a disease commonly known to be both communicable and life threatening, counselors may be justified in disclosing information to identifiable third parties, if they are known to be at demonstrable and high risk of contracting the disease. Prior to making a disclosure, counselors confirm that there is such a diagnosis and assess the intent of clients to inform the third parties about their disease or to engage in any behaviors that may be harmful to an identifiable third party.

B.2.c. Court-Ordered Disclosure

When subpoenaed to release confidential or privileged information without a client's permission, counselors obtain written, informed consent from the client or take steps to prohibit the disclosure or have it limited as narrowly as possible due to potential harm to the client or counseling relationship.

B.2.d. Minimal Disclosure

To the extent possible, clients are informed before confidential information is disclosed and are involved in the disclosure decision-making process. When circumstances require the disclosure of confidential information, only essential information is revealed.

B.3. Information Shared With Others

B.3.a. Subordinates

Counselors make every effort to ensure that privacy and confidentiality of clients are maintained by subordinates, including employees, supervisees, students, clerical assistants, and volunteers. *(See F.1.c.)*

B.3.b. Treatment Teams
When client treatment involves a continued review or participation by a treatment team, the client will be informed of the team's existence and composition, information being shared, and the purposes of sharing such information.

B.3.c. Confidential Settings
Counselors discuss confidential information only in settings in which they can reasonably ensure client privacy.

B.3.d. Third-Party Payers
Counselors disclose information to third-party payers only when clients have authorized such disclosure.

B.3.e. Transmitting Confidential Information
Counselors take precautions to ensure the confidentiality of information transmitted through the use of computers, electronic mail, facsimile machines, telephones, voicemail, answering machines, and other electronic or computer technology. *(See A.12.g.)*

B.3.f. Deceased Clients
Counselors protect the confidentiality of deceased clients, consistent with legal requirements and agency or setting policies.

B.4. Groups and Families

B.4.a. Group Work
In group work, counselors clearly explain the importance and parameters of confidentiality for the specific group being entered.

B.4.b. Couples and Family Counseling
In couples and family counseling, counselors clearly define who is considered "the client" and discuss expectations and limitations of confidentiality. Counselors seek agreement and document in writing such agreement among all involved parties having capacity to give consent concerning each individual's right to confidentiality and any obligation to preserve the confidentiality of information known.

B.5. Clients Lacking Capacity to Give Informed Consent

B.5.a. Responsibility to Clients
When counseling minor clients or adult clients who lack the capacity to give voluntary, informed consent, counselors protect the confidentiality of information received in the counseling relationship as specified by federal and state laws, written policies, and applicable ethical standards.

B.5.b. Responsibility to Parents and Legal Guardians
Counselors inform parents and legal guardians about the role of counselors and the confidential nature of the counseling relationship. Counselors are sensitive to the cultural diversity of families and respect the inherent rights and responsibilities of parents/guardians over the welfare of their children/charges according to law. Counselors work to establish, as appropriate, collaborative relationships with parents/guardians to best serve clients.

B.5.c. Release of Confidential Information
When counseling minor clients or adult clients who lack the capacity to give voluntary consent to release confidential information, counselors seek permission from an appropriate third party to disclose information. In such instances, counselors inform clients consistent with their level of understanding and take culturally appropriate measures to safeguard client confidentiality.

B.6. Records

B.6.a. Confidentiality of Records
Counselors ensure that records are kept in a secure location and that only authorized persons have access to records.

B.6.b. Permission to Record
Counselors obtain permission from clients prior to recording sessions through electronic or other means.

B.6.c. Permission to Observe
Counselors obtain permission from clients prior to observing counseling sessions, reviewing session transcripts, or viewing recordings of sessions with supervisors, faculty, peers, or others within the training environment.

B.6.d. Client Access
Counselors provide reasonable access to records and copies of records when requested by competent clients. Counselors limit the access of clients to their records, or portions of their records, only when there is compelling evidence that such access would cause harm to the client. Counselors document the request of clients and the rationale for withholding some or all of the record in the files of clients. In situations involving multiple clients, counselors provide individual clients with only those parts of records that related

directly to them and do not include confidential information related to any other client.

B.6.e. Assistance With Records
When clients request access to their records, counselors provide assistance and consultation in interpreting counseling records.

B.6.f. Disclosure or Transfer
Unless exceptions to confidentiality exist, counselors obtain written permission from clients to disclose or transfer records to legitimate third parties. Steps are taken to ensure that receivers of counseling records are sensitive to their confidential nature. *(See A.3., E.4.)*

B.6.g. Storage and Disposal After Termination
Counselors store records following termination of services to ensure reasonable future access, maintain records in accordance with state and federal statutes governing records, and dispose of client records and other sensitive materials in a manner that protects client confidentiality. When records are of an artistic nature, counselors obtain client (or guardian) consent with regards to handling of such records or documents. *(See A.1.b.)*

B.6.h. Reasonable Precautions
Counselors take reasonable precautions to protect client confidentiality in the event of the counselor's termination of practice, incapacity, or death. *(See C.2.h.)*

B.7. Research and Training

B.7.a. Institutional Approval
When institutional approval is required, counselors provide accurate information about their research proposals and obtain approval prior to conducting their research. They conduct research in accordance with the approved research protocol.

B.7.b. Adherence to Guidelines
Counselors are responsible for understanding and adhering to state, federal, agency, or institutional policies or applicable guidelines regarding confidentiality in their research practices.

B.7.c. Confidentiality of Information Obtained in Research
Violations of participant privacy and confidentiality are risks of participation in research involving human participants. Investigators maintain all research records in a secure manner.

They explain to participants the risks of violations of privacy and confidentiality and disclose to participants any limits of confidentiality that reasonably can be expected. Regardless of the degree to which confidentiality will be maintained, investigators must disclose to participants any limits of confidentiality that reasonably can be expected. *(See G.2.e.)*

B.7.d. Disclosure of Research Information

Counselors do not disclose confidential information that reasonably could lead to the identification of a research participant unless they have obtained the prior consent of the person. Use of data derived from counseling relationships for purposes of training, research, or publication is confined to content that is disguised to ensure the anonymity of the individuals involved. *(See G.2.a., G.2.d.)*

B.7.e. Agreement for Identification

Identification of clients, students, or supervisees in a presentation or publication is permissible only when they have reviewed the material and agreed to its presentation or publication. *(See G.4.d.)*

B.8. Consultation

B.8.a. Agreements

When acting as consultants, counselors seek agreements among all parties involved concerning each individual's rights to confidentiality, the obligation of each individual to preserve confidential information, and the limits of confidentiality of information shared by others.

B.8.b. Respect for Privacy

Information obtained in a consulting relationship is discussed for professional purposes only with persons directly involved with the case. Written and oral reports present only data germane to the purposes of the consultation, and every effort is made to protect client identity and to avoid undue invasion of privacy.

B.8.c. Disclosure of Confidential Information

When consulting with colleagues, counselors do not disclose confidential information that reasonably could lead to the identification of a client or other person or organization with whom they have a confidential relationship unless they have obtained the prior consent of the person or organization or the disclosure cannot be avoided. They disclose information only to the extent necessary to achieve the purposes of the consultation. *(See D.2.d.)*

Section C
Professional Responsibility

Introduction

Counselors aspire to open, honest, and accurate communication in dealing with the public and other professionals. They practice in a nondiscriminatory manner within the boundaries of professional and personal competence and have a responsibility to abide by the *ACA Code of Ethics*. Counselors actively participate in local, state, and national associations that foster the development and improvement of counseling. Counselors advocate to promote change at the individual, group, institutional, and societal levels that improve the quality of life for individuals and groups and remove potential barriers to the provision or access of appropriate services being offered. Counselors have a responsibility to the public to engage in counseling practices that are based on rigorous research methodologies. In addition, counselors engage in self-care activities to maintain and promote their emotional, physical, mental, and spiritual well-being to best meet their professional responsibilities.

C.1. Knowledge of Standards

Counselors have a responsibility to read, understand, and follow the *ACA Code of Ethics* and adhere to applicable laws and regulations.

C.2. Professional Competence

C.2.a. Boundaries of Competence

Counselors practice only within the boundaries of their competence, based on their education, training, supervised experience, state and national professional credentials, and appropriate professional experience. Counselors gain knowledge, personal awareness, sensitivity, and skills pertinent to working with a diverse client population. *(See A.9.b., C.4.e., E.2., F.2., F.11.b.)*

C.2.b. New Specialty Areas of Practice

Counselors practice in specialty areas new to them only after appropriate education, training, and supervised experience. While developing skills in new specialty areas, counselors take steps to ensure the competence of their work and to protect others from possible harm. *(See F.6.f.)*

C.2.c. Qualified for Employment

Counselors accept employment only for positions for which they are qualified by education, training, supervised experience, state and national professional credentials, and appropriate professional experience. Counselors hire for professional counseling positions only individuals who are qualified and competent for those positions.

C.2.d. Monitor Effectiveness

Counselors continually monitor their effectiveness as professionals and take steps to improve when necessary. Counselors in private practice take reasonable steps to seek peer supervision as needed to evaluate their efficacy as counselors.

C.2.e. Consultation on Ethical Obligations

Counselors take reasonable steps to consult with other counselors or related professionals when they have questions regarding their ethical obligations or professional practice.

C.2.f. Continuing Education

Counselors recognize the need for continuing education to acquire and maintain a reasonable level of awareness of current scientific and professional information in their fields of activity. They take steps to maintain competence in the skills they use, are open to new procedures, and keep current with the diverse populations and specific populations with whom they work.

C.2.g. Impairment

Counselors are alert to the signs of impairment from their own physical, mental, or emotional problems and refrain from offering or providing professional services when such impairment is likely to harm a client or others. They seek assistance for problems that reach the level of professional impairment, and, if necessary, they limit, suspend, or terminate their professional responsibilities until such time it is determined that they may safely resume their work. Counselors assist colleagues or supervisors in recognizing their own professional impairment and provide consultation and assistance when warranted with colleagues or supervisors showing signs of impairment and intervene as appropriate to prevent imminent harm to clients. *(See A.11.b., F.8.b.)*

C.2.h. Counselor Incapacitation or Termination of Practice

When counselors leave a practice, they follow a prepared plan for transfer of clients and files. Counselors prepare and disseminate to an identified colleague or "records custodian" a plan for the transfer of clients and files in the case of their incapacitation, death, or termination of practice.

C.3. Advertising and Soliciting Clients

C.3.a. Accurate Advertising

When advertising or otherwise representing their services to the public, counselors identify their credentials in an accurate manner that is not false, misleading, deceptive, or fraudulent.

C.3.b. Testimonials

Counselors who use testimonials do not solicit them from current clients nor former clients nor any other persons who may be vulnerable to undue influence.

C.3.c. Statements by Others

Counselors make reasonable efforts to ensure that statements made by others about them or the profession of counseling are accurate.

C.3.d. Recruiting Through Employment

Counselors do not use their places of employment or institutional affiliation to recruit or gain clients, supervisees, or consultees for their private practices.

C.3.e. Products and Training Advertisements

Counselors who develop products related to their profession or conduct workshops or training events ensure that the advertisements concerning these products or events are accurate and disclose adequate information for consumers to make informed choices. *(See C.6.d.)*

C.3.f. Promoting to Those Served

Counselors do not use counseling, teaching, training, or supervisory relationships to promote their products or training events in a manner that is deceptive or would exert undue influence on individuals who may be vulnerable. However, coun-

selor educators may adopt textbooks they have authored for instructional purposes.

C.4. Professional Qualifications

C.4.a. Accurate Representation

Counselors claim or imply only professional qualifications actually completed and correct any known misrepresentations of their qualifications by others. Counselors truthfully represent the qualifications of their professional colleagues. Counselors clearly distinguish between paid and volunteer work experience and accurately describe their continuing education and specialized training. *(See C.2.a.)*

C.4.b. Credentials

Counselors claim only licenses or certifications that are current and in good standing.

C.4.c. Educational Degrees

Counselors clearly differentiate between earned and honorary degrees.

C.4.d. Implying Doctoral-Level Competence

Counselors clearly state their highest earned degree in counseling or closely related field. Counselors do not imply doctoral-level competence when only possessing a master's degree in counseling or a related field by referring to themselves as "Dr." in a counseling context when their doctorate is not in counseling or related field.

C.4.e. Program Accreditation Status

Counselors clearly state the accreditation status of their degree programs at the time the degree was earned.

C.4.f. Professional Membership

Counselors clearly differentiate between current, active memberships and former memberships in associations. Members of the American Counseling Association must clearly differentiate between professional membership, which implies the possession of at least a master's degree in counseling, and regular membership, which is open to individuals whose interests and activities are consistent with those of ACA but are not qualified for professional membership.

C.5. Nondiscrimination

Counselors do not condone or engage in discrimination based on age, culture, disability, ethnicity, race, religion/spirituality, gender, gender identity, sexual orientation, marital status/partnership, language preference,

socioeconomic status, or any basis proscribed by law. Counselors do not discriminate against clients, students, employees, supervisees, or research participants in a manner that has a negative impact on these persons.

C.6. Public Responsibility

C.6.a. Sexual Harassment

Counselors do not engage in or condone sexual harassment. Sexual harassment is defined as sexual solicitation, physical advances, or verbal or nonverbal conduct that is sexual in nature, that occurs in connection with professional activities or roles, and that either

1. is unwelcome, is offensive, or creates a hostile workplace or learning environment, and counselors know or are told this; or
2. is sufficiently severe or intense to be perceived as harassment to a reasonable person in the context in which the behavior occurred.

Sexual harassment can consist of a single intense or severe act or multiple persistent or pervasive acts.

C.6.b. Reports to Third Parties

Counselors are accurate, honest, and objective in reporting their professional activities and judgments to appropriate third parties, including courts, health insurance companies, those who are the recipients of evaluation reports, and others. *(See B.3., E.4.)*

C.6.c. Media Presentations

When counselors provide advice or comment by means of public lectures, demonstrations, radio or television programs, prerecorded tapes, technology-based applications, printed articles, mailed material, or other media, they take reasonable precautions to ensure that

1. the statements are based on appropriate professional counseling literature and practice,
2. the statements are otherwise consistent with the *ACA Code of Ethics*, and
3. the recipients of the information are not encouraged to infer that a professional counseling relationship has been established.

C.6.d. Exploitation of Others

Counselors do not exploit others in their professional relationships. *(See C.3.e.)*

C.6.e. Scientific Bases for Treatment Modalities

Counselors use techniques/procedures/modalities that are grounded in theory and/or have an empirical or scientific foundation. Counselors who do not must define the techniques/procedures as "unproven" or "developing" and explain the potential risks and ethical considerations of using such techniques/procedures and take steps to protect clients from possible harm. *(See A.4.a., E.5.c., E.5.d.)*

C.7. Responsibility to Other Professionals

C.7.a. Personal Public Statements
When making personal statements in a public context, counselors clarify that they are speaking from their personal perspectives and that they are not speaking on behalf of all counselors or the profession.

Section D
Relationships With Other Professionals

Introduction
Professional counselors recognize that the quality of their interactions with colleagues can influence the quality of services provided to clients. They work to become knowledgeable about colleagues within and outside the field of counseling. Counselors develop positive working relationships and systems of communication with colleagues to enhance services to clients.

D.1. Relationships With Colleagues, Employers, and Employees

D.1.a. Different Approaches
Counselors are respectful of approaches to counseling services that differ from their own. Counselors are respectful of traditions and practices of other professional groups with which they work.

D.1.b. Forming Relationships
Counselors work to develop and strengthen interdisciplinary relations with colleagues from other disciplines to best serve clients.

D.1.c. Interdisciplinary Teamwork
Counselors who are members of interdisciplinary teams delivering multifaceted services to clients, keep the focus on how to best serve the clients.

They participate in and contribute to decisions that affect the well-being of clients by drawing on the perspectives, values, and experiences of the counseling profession and those of colleagues from other disciplines. *(See A.1.a.)*

D.1.d. Confidentiality
When counselors are required by law, institutional policy, or extraordinary circumstances to serve in more than one role in judicial or administrative proceedings, they clarify role expectations and the parameters of confidentiality with their colleagues. *(See B.1.c., B.1.d., B.2.c., B.2.d., B.3.b.)*

D.1.e. Establishing Professional and Ethical Obligations
Counselors who are members of interdisciplinary teams clarify professional and ethical obligations of the team as a whole and of its individual members. When a team decision raises ethical concerns, counselors first attempt to resolve the concern within the team. If they cannot reach resolution among team members, counselors pursue other avenues to address their concerns consistent with client well-being.

D.1.f. Personnel Selection and Assignment
Counselors select competent staff and assign responsibilities compatible with their skills and experiences.

D.1.g. Employer Policies
The acceptance of employment in an agency or institution implies that counselors are in agreement with its general policies and principles. Counselors strive to reach agreement with employers as to acceptable standards of conduct that allow for changes in institutional policy conducive to the growth and development of clients.

D.1.h. Negative Conditions
Counselors alert their employers of inappropriate policies and practices. They attempt to effect changes in such policies or procedures through constructive action within the organization. When such policies are potentially disruptive or damaging to clients or may limit the effectiveness of services provided and change cannot be effected, counselors take appropriate further action. Such action may include referral to appropriate certification, accreditation, or state licensure organizations, or voluntary termination of employment.

D.1.i. Protection From Punitive Action
Counselors take care not to harass or dismiss an employee who has acted in a responsible and ethical manner

to expose inappropriate employer policies or practices.

D.2. Consultation

D.2.a. Consultant Competency
Counselors take reasonable steps to ensure that they have the appropriate resources and competencies when providing consultation services. Counselors provide appropriate referral resources when requested or needed. *(See C.2.a.)*

D.2.b. Understanding Consultees
When providing consultation, counselors attempt to develop with their consultees a clear understanding of problem definition, goals for change, and predicted consequences of interventions selected.

D.2.c. Consultant Goals
The consulting relationship is one in which consultee adaptability and growth toward self-direction are consistently encouraged and cultivated.

D.2.d. Informed Consent in Consultation
When providing consultation, counselors have an obligation to review, in writing and verbally, the rights and responsibilities of both counselors and consultees. Counselors use clear and understandable language to inform all parties involved about the purpose of the services to be provided, relevant costs, potential risks and benefits, and the limits of confidentiality. Working in conjunction with the consultee, counselors attempt to develop a clear definition of the problem, goals for change, and predicted consequences of interventions that are culturally responsive and appropriate to the needs of consultees. *(See A.2.a., A.2.b.)*

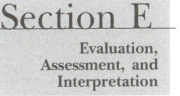

Section E
Evaluation, Assessment, and Interpretation

Introduction
Counselors use assessment instruments as one component of the counseling process, taking into account the client personal and cultural context. Counselors promote the well-being of individual clients or groups of clients by developing and using appropriate educational, psychological, and career assessment instruments.

E.1. General

E.1.a. Assessment

The primary purpose of educational, psychological, and career assessment is to provide measurements that are valid and reliable in either comparative or absolute terms. These include, but are not limited to, measurements of ability, personality, interest, intelligence, achievement, and performance. Counselors recognize the need to interpret the statements in this section as applying to both quantitative and qualitative assessments.

E.1.b. Client Welfare

Counselors do not misuse assessment results and interpretations, and they take reasonable steps to prevent others from misusing the information these techniques provide. They respect the client's right to know the results, the interpretations made, and the bases for counselors' conclusions and recommendations.

E.2. Competence to Use and Interpret Assessment Instruments

E.2.a. Limits of Competence

Counselors utilize only those testing and assessment services for which they have been trained and are competent. Counselors using technology assisted test interpretations are trained in the construct being measured and the specific instrument being used prior to using its technology based application. Counselors take reasonable measures to ensure the proper use of psychological and career assessment techniques by persons under their supervision. (See A.12.)

E.2.b. Appropriate Use

Counselors are responsible for the appropriate application, scoring, interpretation, and use of assessment instruments relevant to the needs of the client, whether they score and interpret such assessments themselves or use technology or other services.

E.2.c. Decisions Based on Results

Counselors responsible for decisions involving individuals or policies that are based on assessment results have a thorough understanding of educational, psychological, and career measurement, including validation criteria, assessment research, and guidelines for assessment development and use.

E.3. Informed Consent in Assessment

E.3.a. Explanation to Clients

Prior to assessment, counselors explain the nature and purposes of assessment and the specific use of results by potential recipients. The explanation will be given in the language of the client (or other legally authorized person on behalf of the client), unless an explicit exception has been agreed upon in advance. Counselors consider the client's personal or cultural context, the level of the client's understanding of the results, and the impact of the results on the client. (See A.2., A.12.g., F.1.c.)

E.3.b. Recipients of Results

Counselors consider the examinee's welfare, explicit understandings, and prior agreements in determining who receives the assessment results. Counselors include accurate and appropriate interpretations with any release of individual or group assessment results. (See B.2.c., B.5.)

E.4. Release of Data to Qualified Professionals

Counselors release assessment data in which the client is identified only with the consent of the client or the client's legal representative. Such data are released only to persons recognized by counselors as qualified to interpret the data. (See B.1., B.3., B.6.b.)

E.5. Diagnosis of Mental Disorders

E.5.a. Proper Diagnosis

Counselors take special care to provide proper diagnosis of mental disorders. Assessment techniques (including personal interview) used to determine client care (e.g., locus of treatment, type of treatment, or recommended follow-up) are carefully selected and appropriately used.

E.5.b. Cultural Sensitivity

Counselors recognize that culture affects the manner in which clients' problems are defined. Clients' socioeconomic and cultural experiences are considered when diagnosing mental disorders. (See A.2.c.)

E.5.c. Historical and Social Prejudices in the Diagnosis of Pathology

Counselors recognize historical and social prejudices in the misdiagnosis and pathologizing of certain individuals and groups and the role of mental health professionals in perpetuating these prejudices through diagnosis and treatment.

E.5.d. Refraining From Diagnosis

Counselors may refrain from making and/or reporting a diagnosis if they believe it would cause harm to the client or others.

E.6. Instrument Selection

E.6.a. Appropriateness of Instruments

Counselors carefully consider the validity, reliability, psychometric limitations, and appropriateness of instruments when selecting assessments.

E.6.b. Referral Information

If a client is referred to a third party for assessment, the counselor provides specific referral questions and sufficient objective data about the client to ensure that appropriate assessment instruments are utilized. (See A.9.b., B.3.)

E.6.c. Culturally Diverse Populations

Counselors are cautious when selecting assessments for culturally diverse populations to avoid the use of instruments that lack appropriate psychometric properties for the client population. (See A.2.c., E.5.b.)

E.7. Conditions of Assessment Administration

(See A.12.b., A.12.d.)

E.7.a. Administration Conditions

Counselors administer assessments under the same conditions that were established in their standardization. When assessments are not administered under standard conditions, as may be necessary to accommodate clients with disabilities, or when unusual behavior or irregularities occur during the administration, those conditions are noted in interpretation, and the results may be designated as invalid or of questionable validity.

E.7.b. Technological Administration

Counselors ensure that administration programs function properly and provide clients with accurate results when technological or other electronic methods are used for assessment administration.

E.7.c. Unsupervised Assessments

Unless the assessment instrument is designed, intended, and validated for self-administration and/or scoring, counselors do not permit inadequately supervised use.

E.7.d. Disclosure of Favorable Conditions

Prior to administration of assessments, conditions that produce most favorable assessment results are made known to the examinee.

E.8. Multicultural Issues/ Diversity in Assessment

Counselors use with caution assessment techniques that were normed on populations other than that of the client. Counselors recognize the effects of age, color, culture, disability, ethnic group, gender, race, language preference, religion, spirituality, sexual orientation, and socioeconomic status on test administration and interpretation, and place test results in proper perspective with other relevant factors. *(See A.2.c., E.5.b.)*

E.9. Scoring and Interpretation of Assessments

E.9.a. Reporting

In reporting assessment results, counselors indicate reservations that exist regarding validity or reliability due to circumstances of the assessment or the inappropriateness of the norms for the person tested.

E.9.b. Research Instruments

Counselors exercise caution when interpreting the results of research instruments not having sufficient technical data to support respondent results. The specific purposes for the use of such instruments are stated explicitly to the examinee.

E.9.c. Assessment Services

Counselors who provide assessment scoring and interpretation services to support the assessment process confirm the validity of such interpretations. They accurately describe the purpose, norms, validity, reliability, and applications of the procedures and any special qualifications applicable to their use. The public offering of an automated test interpretations service is considered a professional-to-professional consultation. The formal responsibility of the consultant is to the consultee, but the ultimate and overriding responsibility is to the client. *(See D.2.)*

E.10. Assessment Security

Counselors maintain the integrity and security of tests and other assessment techniques consistent with legal and contractual obligations. Counselors do not appropriate, reproduce, or modify published assessments or parts thereof without acknowledgment and permission from the publisher.

E.11. Obsolete Assessments and Outdated Results

Counselors do not use data or results from assessments that are obsolete or outdated for the current purpose. Counselors make every effort to prevent the misuse of obsolete measures and assessment data by others.

E.12. Assessment Construction

Counselors use established scientific procedures, relevant standards, and current professional knowledge for assessment design in the development, publication, and utilization of educational and psychological assessment techniques.

E.13. Forensic Evaluation: Evaluation for Legal Proceedings

E.13.a. Primary Obligations

When providing forensic evaluations, the primary obligation of counselors is to produce objective findings that can be substantiated based on information and techniques appropriate to the evaluation, which may include examination of the individual and/or review of records. Counselors are entitled to form professional opinions based on their professional knowledge and expertise that can be supported by the data gathered in evaluations. Counselors will define the limits of their reports or testimony, especially when an examination of the individual has not been conducted.

E.13.b. Consent for Evaluation

Individuals being evaluated are informed in writing that the relationship is for the purposes of an evaluation and is not counseling in nature, and entities or individuals who will receive the evaluation report are identified. Written consent to be evaluated is obtained from those being evaluated unless a court orders evaluations to be conducted without the written consent of individuals being evaluated. When children or vulnerable adults are being evaluated, informed written consent is obtained from a parent or guardian.

E.13.c. Client Evaluation Prohibited

Counselors do not evaluate individuals for forensic purposes they currently counsel or individuals they have counseled in the past. Counselors do not accept as counseling clients individuals they are evaluating or individuals they have evaluated in the past for forensic purposes.

E.13.d. Avoid Potentially Harmful Relationships

Counselors who provide forensic evaluations avoid potentially harmful professional or personal relationships with family members, romantic partners, and close friends of individuals they are evaluating or have evaluated in the past.

Section F

Supervision, Training, and Teaching

Introduction

Counselors aspire to foster meaningful and respectful professional relationships and to maintain appropriate boundaries with supervisees and students. Counselors have theoretical and pedagogical foundations for their work and aim to be fair, accurate, and honest in their assessments of counselors-in-training.

F.1. Counselor Supervision and Client Welfare

F.1.a. Client Welfare

A primary obligation of counseling supervisors is to monitor the services provided by other counselors or counselors-in-training. Counseling supervisors monitor client welfare and supervisee clinical performance and professional development. To fulfill these obligations, supervisors meet regularly with supervisees to review case notes, samples of clinical work, or live observations. Supervisees have a responsibility to understand and follow the *ACA Code of Ethics*.

F.1.b. Counselor Credentials

Counseling supervisors work to ensure that clients are aware of the qualifications of the supervisees who render services to the clients. *(See A.2.b.)*

F.1.c. Informed Consent and Client Rights

Supervisors make supervisees aware of client rights including the protection of client privacy and confidentiality in the counseling relationship. Supervisees provide clients with professional disclosure information and inform them of how the supervision process influences the limits of confidentiality. Supervisees make clients aware of who will have access to records of the counseling relationship and how these records will be used. *(See A.2.b., B.1.d.)*

F.2. Counselor Supervision Competence

F.2.a. Supervisor Preparation

Prior to offering clinical supervision services, counselors are trained in supervision methods and techniques. Counselors who offer clinical supervision services regularly pursue continuing education activities including both counseling and supervision topics and skills. *(See C.2.a., C.2.f.)*

F.2.b. Multicultural Issues/Diversity in Supervision

Counseling supervisors are aware of and address the role of multiculturalism/diversity in the supervisory relationship.

F.3. Supervisory Relationships

F.3.a. Relationship Boundaries With Supervisees

Counseling supervisors clearly define and maintain ethical professional, personal, and social relationships with their supervisees. Counseling supervisors avoid nonprofessional relationships with current supervisees. If supervisors must assume other professional roles (e.g., clinical and administrative supervisor, instructor) with supervisees, they work to minimize potential conflicts and explain to supervisees the expectations and responsibilities associated with each role. They do not engage in any form of nonprofessional interaction that may compromise the supervisory relationship.

F.3.b. Sexual Relationships

Sexual or romantic interactions or relationships with current supervisees are prohibited.

F.3.c. Sexual Harassment

Counseling supervisors do not condone or subject supervisees to sexual harassment. *(See C.6.a.)*

F.3.d. Close Relatives and Friends

Counseling supervisors avoid accepting close relatives, romantic partners, or friends as supervisees.

F.3.e. Potentially Beneficial Relationships

Counseling supervisors are aware of the power differential in their relationships with supervisees. If they believe nonprofessional relationships with a supervisee may be potentially beneficial to the supervisee, they take precautions similar to those taken by counselors when working with clients. Examples of potentially beneficial interactions or relationships include attending a formal ceremony; hospital visits; providing support during a stressful event; or mutual membership in a professional association, organization, or community. Counseling supervisors engage in open discussions with supervisees when they consider entering into relationships with them outside of their roles as clinical and/or administrative supervisors. Before engaging in nonprofessional relationships, supervisors discuss with supervisees and document the rationale for such interactions, potential benefits or drawbacks, and anticipated consequences for the supervisee. Supervisors clarify the specific nature and limitations of the additional role(s) they will have with the supervisee.

F.4. Supervisor Responsibilities

F.4.a. Informed Consent for Supervision

Supervisors are responsible for incorporating into their supervision the principles of informed consent and participation. Supervisors inform supervisees of the policies and procedures to which they are to adhere and the mechanisms for due process appeal of individual supervisory actions.

F.4.b. Emergencies and Absences

Supervisors establish and communicate to supervisees procedures for contacting them or, in their absence, alternative on-call supervisors to assist in handling crises.

F.4.c. Standards for Supervisees

Supervisors make their supervisees aware of professional and ethical standards and legal responsibilities. Supervisors of postdegree counselors encourage these counselors to adhere to professional standards of practice. *(See C.1.)*

F.4.d. Termination of the Supervisory Relationship

Supervisors or supervisees have the right to terminate the supervisory relationship with adequate notice. Reasons for withdrawal are provided to the other party. When cultural, clinical, or professional issues are crucial to the viability of the supervisory relationship, both parties make efforts to resolve differences. When termination is warranted, supervisors make appropriate referrals to possible alternative supervisors.

F.5. Counseling Supervision Evaluation, Remediation, and Endorsement

F.5.a. Evaluation

Supervisors document and provide supervisees with ongoing performance appraisal and evaluation feedback and schedule periodic formal evaluative sessions throughout the supervisory relationship.

F.5.b. Limitations

Through ongoing evaluation and appraisal, supervisors are aware of the limitations of supervisees that might impede performance. Supervisors assist supervisees in securing remedial assistance when needed. They recommend dismissal from training programs, applied counseling settings, or state or voluntary professional credentialing processes when those supervisees are unable to provide competent professional services. Supervisors seek consultation and document their decisions to dismiss or refer supervisees for assistance. They ensure that supervisees are aware of options available to them to address such decisions. *(See C.2.g.)*

F.5.c. Counseling for Supervisees

If supervisees request counseling, supervisors provide them with acceptable referrals. Counselors do not provide counseling services to supervisees. Supervisors address interpersonal competencies in terms of the impact of these issues on clients, the supervisory relationship, and professional functioning. *(See F.3.a.)*

F.5.d. Endorsement

Supervisors endorse supervisees for certification, licensure, employment, or completion of an academic or training program only when they believe supervisees are qualified for the endorsement. Regardless of qualifications, supervisors do not endorse supervisees whom they believe to be impaired in any way that would interfere with the performance of the duties associated with the endorsement.

F.6. Responsibilities of Counselor Educators

F.6.a. Counselor Educators

Counselor educators who are responsible for developing, implementing, and supervising educational programs are skilled as teachers and practitioners. They are knowledgeable regarding the ethical, legal, and regulatory aspects of the profession, are skilled in applying that knowledge, and make students and supervisees aware of their responsibilities. Counselor educators conduct counselor education and training programs in an ethical manner and serve as role models for professional behavior. *(See C.1., C.2.a., C.2.c.)*

F.6.b. Infusing Multicultural Issues/ Diversity

Counselor educators infuse material related to multicultluralism/diversity into all courses and workshops for the development of professional counselors.

F.6.c. Integration of Study and Practice

Counselor educators establish education and training programs that integrate academic study and supervised practice.

F.6.d. Teaching Ethics

Counselor educators make students and supervisees aware of the ethical responsibilities and standards of the profession and the ethical responsibilities of students to the profession. Counselor educators infuse ethical considerations throughout the curriculum. *(See C.1.)*

F.6.e. Peer Relationships

Counselor educators make every effort to ensure that the rights of peers are not compromised when students or supervisees lead counseling groups or provide clinical supervision. Counselor educators take steps to ensure that students and supervisees understand they have the same ethical obligations as counselor educators, trainers, and supervisors.

F.6.f. Innovative Theories and Techniques

When counselor educators teach counseling techniques/procedures that are innovative, without an empirical foundation, or without a well-grounded theoretical foundation, they define the counseling techniques/procedures as "unproven" or "developing" and explain to students the potential risks and ethical considerations of using such techniques/procedures.

F.6.g. Field Placements

Counselor educators develop clear policies within their training programs regarding field placement and other clinical experiences. Counselor educators provide clearly stated roles and responsibilities for the student or supervisee, the site supervisor, and the program supervisor. They confirm that site supervisors are qualified to provide supervision and inform site supervisors of their professional and ethical responsibilities in this role.

F.6.h. Professional Disclosure

Before initiating counseling services, counselors-in-training disclose their status as students and explain how this status affects the limits of confidentiality. Counselor educators ensure that the clients at field placements are aware of the services rendered and the qualifications of the students and supervisees rendering those services. Students and supervisees obtain client permission before they use any information concerning the counseling relationship in the training process. *(See A.2.b.)*

F.7. Student Welfare

F.7.a. Orientation

Counselor educators recognize that orientation is a developmental process that continues throughout the educational and clinical training of students. Counseling faculty provide prospective students with information about the counselor education program's expectations:

1. the type and level of skill and knowledge acquisition required for successful completion of the training;
2. program training goals, objectives, and mission, and subject matter to be covered;
3. bases for evaluation;
4. training components that encourage self-growth or self-disclosure as part of the training process;
5. the type of supervision settings and requirements of the sites for required clinical field experiences;
6. student and supervisee evaluation and dismissal policies and procedures; and
7. up-to-date employment prospects for graduates.

F.7.b. Self-Growth Experiences

Counselor education programs delineate requirements for self-disclosure or self-growth experiences in their admission and program materials. Counselor educators use professional judgment when designing training experiences they conduct that require student and supervisee self-growth or self-disclosure. Students and supervisees are made aware of the ramifications their self-disclosure may have when counselors whose primary role is as teacher, trainer, or supervisor requires acting on ethical obligations to the profession. Evaluative components of experiential training experiences explicitly delineate predetermined academic standards that are separate and do not depend on the student's level of self-disclosure. Counselor educators may require trainees to seek professional help to address any personal concerns that may be affecting their competency.

F.8. Student Responsibilities

F.8.a. Standards for Students

Counselors-in-training have a responsibility to understand and follow the *ACA Code of Ethics* and adhere to applicable laws, regulatory policies, and rules and policies governing professional staff behavior at the agency or placement setting. Students have the same obligation to clients as those required of professional counselors. *(See C.1., H.1.)*

F.8.b. Impairment

Counselors-in-training refrain from offering or providing counseling services when their physical, mental, or emotional problems are likely to harm a client or others. They are alert to the signs of impairment, seek assistance for problems, and notify their program supervisors when they are aware that they are unable to effectively provide services. In addition, they seek appropriate professional services for themselves to remediate the problems that are interfering with their ability to provide services to others. *(See A.1., C.2.d., C.2.g.)*

F.9. Evaluation and Remediation of Students

F.9.a. Evaluation

Counselors clearly state to students, prior to and throughout the training program, the levels of competency expected, appraisal methods, and timing of evaluations for both didactic and clinical competencies. Counselor educators provide students with ongoing performance appraisal and evaluation feedback throughout the training program.

F.9.b. Limitations

Counselor educators, throughout ongoing evaluation and appraisal, are aware of and address the inability of some students to achieve counseling competencies that might impede performance. Counselor educators

1. assist students in securing remedial assistance when needed,
2. seek professional consultation and document their decision to dismiss or refer students for assistance, and
3. ensure that students have recourse in a timely manner to address decisions to require them to seek assistance or to dismiss them and provide students with due process according to institutional policies and procedures. *(See C.2.g.)*

F.9.c. Counseling for Students

If students request counseling or if counseling services are required as part of a remediation process, counselor educators provide acceptable referrals.

F. 10. Roles and Relationships Between Counselor Educators and Students

F.10.a. Sexual or Romantic Relationships

Sexual or romantic interactions or relationships with current students are prohibited.

F.10.b. Sexual Harassment

Counselor educators do not condone or subject students to sexual harassment. *(See C.6.a.)*

F.10.c. Relationships With Former Students

Counselor educators are aware of the power differential in the relationship between faculty and students. Faculty members foster open discussions with former students when considering engaging in a social, sexual, or other intimate relationship. Faculty members discuss with the former student how their former relationship may affect the change in relationship.

F.10.d. Nonprofessional Relationships

Counselor educators avoid nonprofessional or ongoing professional relationships with students in which

there is a risk of potential harm to the student or that may compromise the training experience or grades assigned. In addition, counselor educators do not accept any form of professional services, fees, commissions, reimbursement, or remuneration from a site for student or supervisee placement.

F.10.e. Counseling Services

Counselor educators do not serve as counselors to current students unless this is a brief role associated with a training experience.

F.10.f. Potentially Beneficial Relationships

Counselor educators are aware of the power differential in the relationship between faculty and students. If they believe a nonprofessional relationship with a student may be potentially beneficial to the student, they take precautions similar to those taken by counselors when working with clients. Examples of potentially beneficial interactions or relationships include, but are not limited to, attending a formal ceremony; hospital visits; providing support during a stressful event; or mutual membership in a professional association, organization, or community. Counselor educators engage in open discussions with students when they consider entering into relationships with students outside of their roles as teachers and supervisors. They discuss with students the rationale for such interactions, the potential benefits and drawbacks, and the anticipated consequences for the student. Educators clarify the specific nature and limitations of the additional role(s) they will have with the student prior to engaging in a nonprofessional relationship. Nonprofessional relationships with students should be time-limited and initiated with student consent.

F.11. Multicultural/Diversity Competence in Counselor Education and Training Programs

F.11.a. Faculty Diversity

Counselor educators are committed to recruiting and retaining a diverse faculty.

F.11.b. Student Diversity

Counselor educators actively attempt to recruit and retain a diverse student body. Counselor educators

demonstrate commitment to multicultural/diversity competence by recognizing and valuing diverse cultures and types of abilities students bring to the training experience. Counselor educators provide appropriate accommodations that enhance and support diverse student well-being and academic performance.

F.11.c. Multicultural/Diversity Competence

Counselor educators actively infuse multicultural/diversity competency in their training and supervision practices. They actively train students to gain awareness, knowledge, and skills in the competencies of multicultural practice. Counselor educators include case examples, role-plays, discussion questions, and other classroom activities that promote and represent various cultural perspectives.

Section G
Research and Publication

Introduction

Counselors who conduct research are encouraged to contribute to the knowledge base of the profession and promote a clearer understanding of the conditions that lead to a healthy and more just society. Counselors support efforts of researchers by participating fully and willingly whenever possible. Counselors minimize bias and respect diversity in designing and implementing research programs.

G.1. Research Responsibilities

G.1.a. Use of Human Research Participants

Counselors plan, design, conduct, and report research in a manner that is consistent with pertinent ethical principles, federal and state laws, host institutional regulations, and scientific standards governing research with human research participants.

G.1.b. Deviation From Standard Practice

Counselors seek consultation and observe stringent safeguards to protect the rights of research participants when a research problem suggests a deviation from standard or acceptable practices.

G.1.c. Independent Researchers
When independent researchers do not have access to an Institutional Review Board (IRB), they should consult with researchers who are familiar with IRB procedures to provide appropriate safeguards.

G.1.d. Precautions to Avoid Injury
Counselors who conduct research with human participants are responsible for the welfare of participants throughout the research process and should take reasonable precautions to avoid causing injurious psychological, emotional, physical, or social effects to participants.

G.1.e. Principal Researcher Responsibility
The ultimate responsibility for ethical research practice lies with the principal researcher. All others involved in the research activities share ethical obligations and responsibility for their own actions.

G.1.f. Minimal Interference
Counselors take reasonable precautions to avoid causing disruptions in the lives of research participants that could be caused by their involvement in research.

G.1.g. Multicultural/Diversity Considerations in Research
When appropriate to research goals, counselors are sensitive to incorporating research procedures that take into account cultural considerations. They seek consultation when appropriate.

G.2. Rights of Research Participants
(See A.2, A.7.)

G.2.a. Informed Consent in Research
Individuals have the right to consent to become research participants. In seeking consent, counselors use language that

1. accurately explains the purpose and procedures to be followed,
2. identifies any procedures that are experimental or relatively untried,
3. describes any attendant discomforts and risks,
4. describes any benefits or changes in individuals or organizations that might be reasonably expected,
5. discloses appropriate alternative procedures that would be advantageous for participants,
6. offers to answer any inquiries concerning the procedures,
7. describes any limitations on confidentiality,
8. describes the format and potential target audiences for the dissemination of research findings, and
9. instructs participants that they are free to withdraw their consent and to discontinue participation in the project at any time without penalty.

G.2.b. Deception
Counselors do not conduct research involving deception unless alternative procedures are not feasible and the prospective value of the research justifies the deception. If such deception has the potential to cause physical or emotional harm to research participants, the research is not conducted, regardless of prospective value. When the methodological requirements of a study necessitate concealment or deception, the investigator explains the reasons for this action as soon as possible during the debriefing.

G.2.c. Student/Supervisee Participation
Researchers who involve students or supervisees in research make clear to them that the decision regarding whether or not to participate in research activities does not affect one's academic standing or supervisory relationship. Students or supervisees who choose not to participate in educational research are provided with an appropriate alternative to fulfill their academic or clinical requirements.

G.2.d. Client Participation
Counselors conducting research involving clients make clear in the informed consent process that clients are free to choose whether or not to participate in research activities. Counselors take necessary precautions to protect clients from adverse consequences of declining or withdrawing from participation.

G.2.e. Confidentiality of Information
Information obtained about research participants during the course of an investigation is confidential. When the possibility exists that others may obtain access to such information, ethical research practice requires that the possibility, together with the plans for protecting confidentiality, be explained to participants as a part of the procedure for obtaining informed consent.

G.2.f. Persons Not Capable of Giving Informed Consent
When a person is not capable of giving informed consent, counselors provide an appropriate explanation to, obtain agreement for participation from, and obtain the appropriate consent of a legally authorized person.

G.2.g. Commitments to Participants
Counselors take reasonable measures to honor all commitments to research participants. *(See A.2.c.)*

G.2.h. Explanations After Data Collection
After data are collected, counselors provide participants with full clarification of the nature of the study to remove any misconceptions participants might have regarding the research. Where scientific or human values justify delaying or withholding information, counselors take reasonable measures to avoid causing harm.

G.2.i. Informing Sponsors
Counselors inform sponsors, institutions, and publication channels regarding research procedures and outcomes. Counselors ensure that appropriate bodies and authorities are given pertinent information and acknowledgement.

G.2.j. Disposal of Research Documents and Records
Within a reasonable period of time following the completion of a research project or study, counselors take steps to destroy records or documents (audio, video, digital, and written) containing confidential data or information that identifies research participants. When records are of an artistic nature, researchers obtain participant consent with regard to handling of such records or documents. *(See B.4.a, B.4.g.)*

G.3. Relationships With Research Participants (When Research Involves Intensive or Extended Interactions)

G.3.a. Nonprofessional Relationships
Nonprofessional relationships with research participants should be avoided.

G.3.b. Relationships With Research Participants
Sexual or romantic counselor–research participant interactions or relationships with current research participants are prohibited.

G.3.c. Sexual Harassment and Research Participants
Researchers do not condone or subject research participants to sexual harassment.

G.3.d. Potentially Beneficial Interactions

When a nonprofessional interaction between the researcher and the research participant may be potentially beneficial, the researcher must document, prior to the interaction (when feasible), the rationale for such an interaction, the potential benefit, and anticipated consequences for the research participant. Such interactions should be initiated with appropriate consent of the research participant. Where unintentional harm occurs to the research participant due to the nonprofessional interaction, the researcher must show evidence of an attempt to remedy such harm.

G.4. Reporting Results

G.4.a. Accurate Results

Counselors plan, conduct, and report research accurately. They provide thorough discussions of the limitations of their data and alternative hypotheses. Counselors do not engage in misleading or fraudulent research, distort data, misrepresent data, or deliberately bias their results. They explicitly mention all variables and conditions known to the investigator that may have affected the outcome of a study or the interpretation of data. They describe the extent to which results are applicable for diverse populations.

G.4.b. Obligation to Report Unfavorable Results

Counselors report the results of any research of professional value. Results that reflect unfavorably on institutions, programs, services, prevailing opinions, or vested interests are not withheld.

G.4.c. Reporting Errors

If counselors discover significant errors in their published research, they take reasonable steps to correct such errors in a correction erratum, or through other appropriate publication means.

G.4.d. Identity of Participants

Counselors who supply data, aid in the research of another person, report research results, or make original data available take due care to disguise the identity of respective participants in the absence of specific authorization from the participants to do otherwise. In situations where participants self-identify their involvement in research studies, researchers take active steps to ensure that data is adapted/changed to protect the identity and welfare of all parties and that discussion of results does not cause harm to participants.

G.4.e. Replication Studies

Counselors are obligated to make available sufficient original research data to qualified professionals who may wish to replicate the study.

G.5. Publication

G.5.a. Recognizing Contributions

When conducting and reporting research, counselors are familiar with and give recognition to previous work on the topic, observe copyright laws, and give full credit to those to whom credit is due.

G.5.b. Plagiarism

Counselors do not plagiarize, that is, they do not present another person's work as their own work.

G.5.c. Review/Republication of Data or Ideas

Counselors fully acknowledge and make editorial reviewers aware of prior publication of ideas or data where such ideas or data are submitted for review or publication.

G.5.d. Contributors

Counselors give credit through joint authorship, acknowledgment, footnote statements, or other appropriate means to those who have contributed significantly to research or concept development in accordance with such contributions. The principal contributor is listed first and minor technical or professional contributions are acknowledged in notes or introductory statements.

G.5.e. Agreement of Contributors

Counselors who conduct joint research with colleagues or students/supervisees establish agreements in advance regarding allocation of tasks, publication credit, and types of acknowledgement that will be received.

G.5.f. Student Research

For articles that are substantially based on students course papers, projects, dissertations or theses, and on which students have been the primary contributors, they are listed as principal authors.

G.5.g. Duplicate Submission

Counselors submit manuscripts for consideration to only one journal at a time. Manuscripts that are published in whole or in substantial part in another journal or published work are not submitted for publication without acknowledgment and permission from the previous publication.

G.5.h. Professional Review

Counselors who review material submitted for publication, research, or other scholarly purposes respect the confidentiality and proprietary rights of those who submitted it. Counselors use care to make publication decisions based on valid and defensible standards. Counselors review article submissions in a timely manner and based on their scope and competency in research methodologies. Counselors who serve as reviewers at the request of editors or publishers make every effort to only review materials that are within their scope of competency and use care to avoid personal biases.

Section H
Resolving Ethical Issues

Introduction

Counselors behave in a legal, ethical, and moral manner in the conduct of their professional work. They are aware that client protection and trust in the profession depend on a high level of professional conduct. They hold other counselors to the same standards and are willing to take appropriate action to ensure that these standards are upheld.

Counselors strive to resolve ethical dilemmas with direct and open communication among all parties involved and seek consultation with colleagues and supervisors when necessary. Counselors incorporate ethical practice into their daily professional work. They engage in ongoing professional development regarding current topics in ethical and legal issues in counseling.

H.1. Standards and the Law
(See F.9.a.)

H.1.a. Knowledge

Counselors understand the *ACA Code of Ethics* and other applicable ethics codes from other professional organizations or from certification and licensure bodies of which they are members. Lack of knowledge or misunderstanding of an ethical responsibility is not a defense against a charge of unethical conduct.

H.1.b. Conflicts Between Ethics and Laws

If ethical responsibilities conflict with law, regulations, or other governing legal authority, counselors make known their commitment to the *ACA Code of Ethics* and take steps to resolve the conflict. If the conflict cannot be resolved by such means, counselors may adhere to the requirements of law, regulations, or other governing legal authority.

H.2. Suspected Violations

H.2.a. Ethical Behavior Expected

Counselors expect colleagues to adhere to the *ACA Code of Ethics*. When counselors possess knowledge that raises doubts as to whether another counselor is acting in an ethical manner, they take appropriate action. *(See H.2.b., H.2.c.)*

H.2.b. Informal Resolution

When counselors have reason to believe that another counselor is violating or has violated an ethical standard, they attempt first to resolve the issue informally with the other counselor if feasible, provided such action does not violate confidentiality rights that may be involved.

H.2.c. Reporting Ethical Violations

If an apparent violation has substantially harmed, or is likely to substantially harm a person or organization and is not appropriate for informal resolution or is not resolved properly, counselors take further action appropriate to the situation. Such action might include referral to state or national committees on professional ethics, voluntary national certification bodies, state licensing boards, or to the appropriate institutional authorities. This standard does not apply when an intervention would violate confidentiality rights or when counselors have been retained to review the work of another counselor whose professional conduct is in question.

H.2.d. Consultation

When uncertain as to whether a particular situation or course of action may be in violation of the *ACA Code of Ethics*, counselors consult with other counselors who are knowledgeable about ethics and the *ACA Code of Ethics*, with colleagues, or with appropriate authorities.

H.2.e. Organizational Conflicts

If the demands of an organization with which counselors are affiliated pose a conflict with the *ACA Code of Ethics*, counselors specify the nature of such conflicts and express to their supervisors or other responsible officials their commitment to the *ACA Code of Ethics*. When possible, counselors work toward change within the organization to allow full adherence to the *ACA Code of Ethics*. In doing so, they address any confidentiality issues.

H.2.f. Unwarranted Complaints

Counselors do not initiate, participate in, or encourage the filing of ethics complaints that are made with reckless disregard or willful ignorance of facts that would disprove the allegation.

H.2.g. Unfair Discrimination Against Complainants and Respondents

Counselors do not deny persons employment, advancement, admission to academic or other programs, tenure, or promotion based solely upon their having made or their being the subject of an ethics complaint. This does not preclude taking action based upon the outcome of such proceedings or considering other appropriate information.

H.3. Cooperation With Ethics Committees

Counselors assist in the process of enforcing the *ACA Code of Ethics*. Counselors cooperate with investigations, proceedings, and requirements of the ACA Ethics Committee or ethics committees of other duly constituted associations or boards having jurisdiction over those charged with a violation. Counselors are familiar with the *ACA Policy and Procedures for Processing Complains of Ethical Violations* and use it as a reference for assisting in the enforcement of the *ACA Code of Ethics*.

Glossary of Terms

Advocacy – promotion of the well-being of individuals and groups, and the counseling profession within systems and organizations. Advocacy seeks to remove barriers and obstacles that inhibit access, growth, and development.

Assent – to demonstrate agreement, when a person is otherwise not capable or competent to give formal consent (e.g., informed consent) to a counseling service or plan.

Client – an individual seeking or referred to the professional services of a counselor for help with problem resolution or decision making.

Counselor – a professional (or a student who is a counselor-in-training) engaged in a counseling practice or other counseling-related services. Counselors fulfill many roles and responsibilities such as counselor educators, researchers, supervisors, practitioners, and consultants.

Counselor Educator – a professional counselor engaged primarily in developing, implementing, and supervising the educational preparation of counselors-in-training.

Counselor Supervisor – a professional counselor who engages in a formal relationship with a practicing counselor or counselor-in-training for the purpose of overseeing that individual's counseling work or clinical skill development.

Culture – membership in a socially constructed way of living, which incorporates collective values, beliefs, norms, boundaries, and lifestyles that are cocreated with others who share similar worldviews comprising biological, psychosocial, historical, psychological, and other factors.

Diversity – the similarities and differences that occur within and across cultures, and the intersection of cultural and social identities.

Documents – any written, digital, audio, visual, or artistic recording of the work within the counseling relationship between counselor and client.

Examinee – a recipient of any professional counseling service that includes educational, psychological, and career appraisal utilizing qualitative or quantitative techniques.

Forensic Evaluation – any formal assessment conducted for court or other legal proceedings.

Multicultural/Diversity Competence – a capacity whereby counselors possess cultural and diversity awareness and knowledge about self and others, and how this awareness and knowledge is applied effectively in practice with clients and client groups.

Multicultural/Diversity Counseling – counseling that recognizes diversity and embraces approaches that support the worth, dignity, potential, and uniqueness of individuals within their historical, cultural, economic, political, and psychosocial contexts.

Student – an individual engaged in formal educational preparation as a counselor-in-training.

Supervisee – a professional counselor or counselor-in-training whose counseling work or clinical skill development is being overseen in a formal supervisory relationship by a qualified trained professional.

Supervisor – counselors who are trained to oversee the professional clinical work of counselors and counselors-in-training.

Teaching – all activities engaged in as part of a formal educational program designed to lead to a graduate degree in counseling.

Training – the instruction and practice of skills related to the counseling profession. Training contributes to the ongoing proficiency of students and professional counselors.

REFERENCE LIST

Aaronson, C. J., Bender, D. S., Skodol, A. E., & Gunderson, J. G. (2006). Comparison of attachment styles in borderline personality disorder and obsessive-compulsive personality disorder. *Psychiatric Quarterly, 77*, 69–80.

Aiken, L. R., & Groth-Marnat, G. (2006). *Psychological testing and assessment* (12th ed.). Boston: Allyn & Bacon.

American Counseling Association. (2005). ACA Code of Ethics. Washington, DC: Author.

American Psychiatric Association. (2000). *Diagnostic and statistical manual of mental disorders* (4th ed., text rev.). Washington, DC: APA.

Anderson, J. D. (2005). Client perception of counselor characteristics. University of Utah. *Dissertation Abstracts International,* AAI3166030, 66(2-A), 284.

Archer, J., Jr. & McCarthy, C. J. (2007). *Theories of counseling and psychotherapy.* Upper Saddle River, NJ: Prentice Hall.

Arrendondo, P., Rosen, D., Rice, T., Perez, P., & Tovar-Gamero, Z. G. (2005). Multicultural counseling: A 10-year content analysis of the *Journal of Counseling and Development* (Research). *Journal of Counseling and Development, 83*, 155–161.

Atkinson, D. R., Morten, G., & Sue, D.W. (1989). *Counseling American minorities: A cross-cultural perspective* (3rd ed.). Dubuque, IA: Brown.

Averill, J. R. (1994). Emotions unbecoming and becoming. In P. Ekman & R. J. Davidson (Eds.), *The nature of emotions: Fundamental questions* (pp. 265–269). Oxford, NY: Oxford University Press.

Baker, S. B., & Daniels, T. G. (1989). Integrating research on the Microcounseling Program: A meta-analysis. *Journal of Counseling Psychology, 36*, 213–222.

Baker, S. B., Daniels, T. G., & Greely, A. T. (1990). Systematic training of graduate-level counselors: Narrative and meta-analytic reviews of three major programs. *The Counseling Psychologist, 18*, 355–421.

Bargh, J. A. (1992). The ecology of automaticity: Toward establishing the conditions needed to produce automatic processing effects. *American Journal of Psychology, 105*, 181–199.

Bashan, F. (2005). Therapist self-disclosure of their sexual orientation: From a client's perspective. *Dissertation Abstracts International,* AAI3156916, 65(12-B), 6640.

Beatty, M. J. (1980). Social facilitation and listening comprehension. *Perceptual and Motor Skills, 51*(3, Pt. 2), 1222.

Beck, A. T., & Weishar, M. E. (2005). Cognitive therapy. In R. J. Corsini & D. Wedding (Eds.), *Current psychotherapies* (7th ed., pp. 263–295). Pacific Grove, CA: Thomson Brooks Cole.

Bergin, A. E., & Garfield, S. L. (Eds.). (1994). *Handbook of psychotherapy and behavior change* (4th ed.). New York: Wiley.

Bernal, G., & Scharron-del-Rio, M. R. (2001). Are empirically supported treatments valid for ethnic minorities? Toward an alternative approach for treatment research. *Cultural Diversity and Ethnic Minority Psychology, 7*, 328–342.

Berry, J. W. (2003). Origins of cross-cultural similarities and differences in human behavior: An ecocultural perspective. In A. Toomela (Ed.), *Cultural guidance in the development of the human mind* (pp. 97–109). Westport, CT: Ablex.

Beutler, L. E. (2000). David and Goliath: When empirical and clinical standards of practice meet. *American Psychologist, 55*, 997–1007.

Beutler, L. E. (2004). The empirically supported treatments movement: A scientist-practitioner's response. *Clinical Psychology: Science and Practice, 11*, 225–229.

Beutler, L. E., & Clarkin, J. F. (1990). *Systematic treatment selection: Toward targeted therapeutic interventions.* Philadelphia, PA: Brunner/ Mazel.

Beutler, L. E., Clarkin, J. F., & Bongar, B. (2000). *Guidelines for the systematic treatment of the depressed patient.* Oxford, NY: Oxford University Press.

Beutler, L. E., & Johannsen, B. E. (2006). Principles of change. In J. C. Norcross, L. E. Beutler, & R. E. Levant (Eds.), *Evidence-based practices in mental health: Debate and dialogue on the fundamental questions* (pp. 226–234). Washington, DC: American Psychological Association.

Bodenhausen, G.V., & Lichtenstein, M. (1987). Social stereotypes and information-processing strategies: The impact of task complexity. *Journal of Personality and Social Psychology, 52,* 871–880.

Boer, D. P., Hart, S. D., Kropp, P. R., & Webster, C. D. (1997). *Manual for the Sexual Violence Risk-20: Professional guidelines for assessing risk of sexual violence.* Vancouver: British Columbia, Canada: British Columbia Institute on Family Violence.

Bratter, T. E. (2003). Confrontation group psychotherapy with gifted, dually diagnosed, and self-destructive adolescents in a residential setting. *Group, 27,* 131–146.

Bretherton, I. (1992). The origins of attachment theory: John Bowlby and Mary Ainsworth. *Developmental Psychology, 28,* 759–775.

Bronfenbrenner, U. (1979). *The ecology of human development.* Cambridge, MA: Harvard University Press.

Brooks, C. I., Church, M. A., & Fraser, L. (1986). Effects of duration of eye contact on judgments of personality characteristics. *Journal of Social Psychology, 126,* 71–78.

Brown, L. S. (2006). The neglect of lesbian, gay, bisexual, and transgendered clients. In J. C. Norcross, L. E. Beutler, & R. E. Levant (Eds.), *Evidence-based practices in mental health: Debate and dialogue on the fundamental questions* (pp. 346–352). Washington, DC: American Psychological Association.

Brown, T. L. (1989). Automaticity in skill acquisition: Mechanisms for reducing interference in concurrent performance. *Journal of Experimental Psychology: Human Perception and Performance, 15,* 686–700.

Buchheim, A., George, C., Kachele, H., Erk, S., & Walter, H. (2006). Measuring adult attachment representation in an fMRI environment: Concepts and assessment. *Psychopathology, 39*(3), 136–143.

Burgoon, J. K., Buller, D. B., & Woodall, W. G. (1996). *Nonverbal communication: The unspoken dialogue.* New York: McGraw-Hill.

Canter, J. (2007). Compassion fatigue and secondary traumatization: A second look. *Clinical Social Work Journal, 35,* 289–293.

Capuzzi, D., & Gross, D. R. (Eds.). (2007). *Counseling and psychotherapy: Theories and interventions* (4th ed.). Upper Saddle River, NJ: Prentice Hall.

Carkhuff, R. R. (1969). Critical variables in effective counselor training. *Journal of Counseling Psychology, 16,* 238–245.

Carkhuff, R. R. (1987). *The art of helping* (6th ed.) Amherst, MA: Human Resource Development Press.

Carter, J. D., Hall, A., Carney, D. R., & Rosip, J. C. (2006). Individual differences in the acceptance of stereotyping. *Journal of Research in Personality, 40,* 1103–1118.

Cashwell, C. S., Shcherbakova, J., & Cashwell, T. H. (2003). Effect of client and counselor ethnicity on preference for counselor disclosure. *Journal of Counseling and Development, 81,* 196–201.

Castonguay, L. G. (2007). Toward the integration of technical interventions, relationship factors, and participants' variables. In S. G. Hofmann & J. Weinberger (Eds.), *The art and science of psychotherapy* (pp. 131–153). New York: Routledge.

Cattell, R. B. (1943). The description of personality: Basic traits resolved into clusters. *Journal of Abnormal and Social Psychology, 38,* 476–506.

Cattell, R. B. (1990). Advances in Cattellian personality theory. In L. A. Pervin (Ed.), *Handbook of personality: Theory and research* (pp. 101–110). New York: Guilford Press.

Cavanaugh, M. E. (1982). *The counseling experience: A theoretical and practical approach.* Prospect Heights, IL: Waveland Press.

Christopher, J. C. (2006). Hermeneutics and the moral dimension of psychotherapy. In L. T. Hoshmand (Ed.), *Culture, psychotherapy, and counseling* (pp. 179–203). Thousand Oaks, CA: Sage.

Ciarrochi, J., Heaven, P. C., & Davies, F. (2007). The impact of hope, self-esteem, and attributional style on adolescents' school grades and emotional well-being: A longitudinal study. *Journal of Research in Personality, 41,* 1161–1178.

Clinton, D., Gierlach, E., Zack, S. E., Beutler, L. E., & Castonguay, L. G. (2007). Toward the integration of technical interventions, relationship factors, and participants' variables. In S. G.

Hofmann & J. Weinberger (Eds.), *The art and science of psychotherapy* (pp. 131–153). New York: Routledge/Taylor & Francis.

Congress of the United States Congressional Budget Office. (February, 2006). Immigration Policy in the United States.

Constantine, M. G., & Kwan, K. K. (2003). Cross-cultural considerations of therapist self-disclosure. *Journal of Clinical Psychology, 59,* 581–588.

Cook-Greuter, S. R., & Soulen, J. (2007). The developmental perspective in integral counseling. *Counseling and Values, 51,* 180–192.

Corey, G. (2005). *Theory and practice of counseling and psychotherapy* (7th ed.). Pacific Grove, CA: Thomson Brooks Cole.

Corey-Souza, P. A. (2007). Compassion fatigue in members of the Florida Crisis Response Team: A consequence of caring. *Dissertation Abstracts International, AAI3264295, 68*(4-B), 2695.

Corsini, R. J., & Wedding, D. (2005). *Current psychotherapies* (7th ed.). Pacific Grove, CA: Thomson Brooks Cole.

Costa, P. T., Jr., & McCrae, R. (1995). Domains and facets: Hierarchical personality assessment using the revised NEO Personality Inventory. *Journal of Personality Assessment, 64,* 21–50.

Csíkszentmihályi, M. (1990). *Flow: The psychology of optimal experience.* New York: Harper and Row.

Cukrowicz, K. C., White, B. A., Reitzel, L. R., Burns, A. B., Driscoll, K. A., Kemper, T. S., et al. (2005). Improved treatment outcome associated with the shift to empirically supported treatments in a graduate training clinic. *Professional Psychology: Research and Practice, 36,* 330–337.

Darby, B. W., & Judson, N. (1987). Students' perceptions of faculty's office arrangements. *Perceptual and Motor Skills, 65,* 507–514.

Dastoor, B. (1993). Speaking their language. *Training and Development, 47*(6), 14–18.

Deighton, R. M., Gurris, N., & Traue, H. (2007). Factors affecting burnout and compassion fatigue in psychotherapists treating torture survivors: Is the therapist's attitude to working through trauma relevant? *Journal of Traumatic Stress, 20,* 63–75.

de Roten, Y., Darwish, J., Stern, D. J., Fivaz-Depeursinge, E., & Corboz-Warnery, A. (1999). Nonverbal communication and alliance in therapy: The body formation coding system. *Journal of Clinical Psychology, 55,* 425–438.

Diversity. (n.d.). *The American Heritage® Dictionary of the English Language, Fourth Edition.* Retrieved January 13, 2007, from Answers.com Web site: http://www.answers.com/topic/diversity.

Division 12 Task Force. (1995). Training in and dissemination of empirically supported psychological treatments: Reports and recommendations. Washington, DC: American Psychological Association.

Dohrenwend, B. S., Askenasy, A. R., Krasnoff, L., & Dohrenwend, B. P. (1978). Exemplification of a method for scaling life events: The PERI Life Events Scale. *Journal of Health and Social Behavior, 19,* 205–229.

Douglas, K. S., & Kropp, P. R. (2002). A prevention-based paradigm for violence risk assessment: Clinical and research applications. *Criminal Justice and Behavior, 29,* 617–658.

Draguns, J. G. (2002). Universal and cultural aspects of counseling and psychotherapy. In P. B. Pedersen, J. G. Draguns, W. J. Lonner, & J. E. Trimble (Eds.), *Counseling across cultures* (5th ed., pp. 29–50). Thousand Oaks, CA: Sage.

Droney, J. M., & Brooks, C. I. (1993). Attributions of self-esteem as a function of duration of eye contact. *Journal of Social Psychology, 133,* 715–722.

Dumont, F., & Lecomte, C. (1987). Inferential processes in clinical work: Inquiry into logical errors that affect diagnostic judgments. *Professional Psychology: Research and Practice, 18,* 435–438.

Duncan, B. L. (2002). The founder of common factors: A conversation with Saul Rosenzweig. *Journal of Psychotherapy Integration, 12,* 10–31.

Duran, E., & Duran, B. (1995). *Native American postcolonial psychology.* Albany: State University of New York Press.

Dutton, D. (2003). Theoretical approaches to the treatment of intimate violence. *Journal of Aggression, Maltreatment & Trauma, 7*(1–2), 7–23.

Dyer, W. W. (1995). *Your erroneous zones.* New York: Harper & Row.

Eastwood, C. D. (2007). Compassion fatigue risk and self-care practices among residential treatment center childcare workers. *Dissertation Abstracts International, AAI3264340, 68* (4-B), 2645.

Elfenbein, H. A., & Ambady, N. (2003). Universals and cultural differences in recognizing emotions. *Current Directions in Psychological Science, 12*(5), 159–164.

Ellis, A. (2005). Rational emotive behavior therapy. In R. J. Corsini and D. Wedding (Eds.), *Current psychotherapies* (7th ed., pp. 166–201). Belmont, CA: Thomson Brooks/Cole.

Ekman, P., & Friesen, W. V. (1971). Constants across cultures in the face and emotion. *Journal of Personality and Social Psychology, 17,* 124–129.

Ekman, P., Sorenson, E. R., & Friesen, W. V. (1969). Pan-cultural elements in facial displays of emotion. *Science, 164*(3875), 86–88.

Erikson, E. H. (1980). *Identity and the life cycle.* New York: W.W. Norton.

Fast, J. (1970). *Body language.* New York: M. Evans.

Feldman, D. B., & Snyder, C. R. (2005). Hope and the meaningful life: Theoretical and empirical associations between goal-directed thinking and life meaning. *Journal of Social and Clinical Psychology, 24,* 401–421.

Figley, C. R. (2002). Compassion fatigue: Psychotherapists' chronic lack of self care. *JCLP/In Session: Psychotherapy in Practice, 58,* 1433–1441.

Flores, P. J. (2004). Addiction as an attachment disorder: Implications for group psychotherapy. In B. Reading & M. Weegmann (Eds.), *Group psychotherapy and addiction* (pp. 1–18). Philadelphia, PA: Whurr.

Foley, J. M. (2004). Empirically supported treatment endeavor: A successful future or inevitable debacle? *Clinical Psychologist, 8,* 29–38.

Ford, J. G., & Maloney, M. (1982). Further considerations of the phenomenology of proxemics. *Psychological Reports, 50,* 943–952.

Frank, J. D., & Frank, J. B. (1991). Persuasion and healing: A comparative study of psychotherapy (3rd ed.). Baltimore: Johns Hopkins.

Frankl, V. (1997). *Man's search for ultimate meaning.* New York: Plenum Press.

Frankl, V. (2004). *On the theory and therapy of mental disorders: An introduction to logotherapy and existential analysis.* New York: Brunner-Routledge.

Fretz, B. R., Corn, R., Tuemmler, J. M., and Bellet, W. (1979). Counselor nonverbal behaviors and client evaluations. *Journal of Counseling Psychology, 26,* 304–311.

Gellerman, D. M., & Suddath, R. (2005). Violent fantasy, dangerousness, and the duty to warn and protect. *Journal of the American Academy of Psychiatry and the Law, 33,* 484–495.

Ginter, E. J. (1988). Stagnation in eclecticism: The need to recommit to a journey. *Journal of Mental Health Counseling, 10,* 3–8.

Glickman, G., Byrne, B., Pineda, C., Hauck, W. W., & Brainard, G. C. (2006). Light therapy for seasonal affective disorder with blue narrowband light-emitting diodes (LEDS). *Biological Psychiatry, 59*(6), 502–507.

Goldstein, E. G. (1994). Self-disclosure in treatment: What therapists do and don't talk about. *Clinical Social Work Journal, 22,* 417–433.

Haase, R. F., & DiMattia, D. J. (1970). Proxemic behavior: Counselor, administrator, and client preference for seating arrangement in dyadic interaction. *Journal of Counseling Psychology, 17,* 319–325.

Hackney, H. (1992). *Differentiating between counseling theory and process.* ERIC Digest, ED347485. Retrieved March 29, 2008, from http://ericdigests.org/1992-3/theory.htm.

Haggard-Grann, U. (2007). Assessing violence risk: A review and clinical recommendations. *Journal of Counseling and Development, 85,* 294–301.

Haidt, J., & Keltner, D. (1999). Culture and facial expression: Open-ended methods find more expressions and a gradient of recognition. *Cognition and Emotion, 13,* 225–266.

Haley, M. (2007). Gestalt theory. In D. Capuzzi & D. R. Gross (Eds.), *Counseling and psychotherapy: Theories and interventions* (4th ed., pp. 216–242). Upper Saddle River, NJ: Prentice Hall.

Hall, E. T. (1966). *The hidden dimension.* London: Bodley Head.

Hanson, R. K., & Thornton, D. (1999). Static 99: Improving actuarial risk assessments for sex offenders (User Report No. 1999-02). Ottawa, Ontario: Canada: Department of the Solicitor General of Canada.

Harrigan, J. A. (2005). Proxemics, kinesics, and gaze. In J. Harrigan, R. Rosenthal, & K. R.

Scherer (Eds.), *The new handbook of methods in nonverbal behavior research* (pp. 137–198). Oxford, NY: Oxford University Press.

Harris, G. T., Rice, M. E., & Quinsey, V. L. (1993). Violent recidivism of mentally disordered offenders: The development of a statistical prediction instrument. *Criminal Justice and Behavior, 20,* 315–355.

Harris, R. (2008). Racial microaggression? How do you know? *American Psychologist, 63,* 275.

Hazler, R. J. (2007). Person-centered theory. In D. Capuzzi & D. R. Gross (Eds.), *Counseling and psychotherapy: Theories and interventions* (4th ed., pp. 189–215). Upper Saddle River, NJ: Prentice Hall.

Hill, C. E., & O'Brien, K. M. (1999). *Helping skills: Facilitating exploration, insight, and action.* Washington, DC: American Psychological Association.

Hill, C. E., Stahl, J., & Roffman, M. (2007). Training novice psychotherapists: Helping skills and beyond. *Psychotherapy: Theory, Research, Practice, Training, 44,* 364–370.

Hill, C. E., Thompson, B. J., Cogar, M. C., & Denman, D. W. (2001). Beneath the surface of long-term therapy: Therapist and client report of their own and each other's covert processes. In C. E. Hill (Ed.), *Helping skills: The empirical foundation* (pp. 147–167). Washington, DC: American Psychological Association.

Hill, C. L., & Ridley, C. R. (2001). Diagnostic decision making: Do counselors delay final judgments? *Journal of Counseling and Development, 79,* 98–104.

Hinkle, J. S. (1999). A voice from the trenches: A reaction to Ivey and Ivey (1998). *Journal of Counseling and Development, 77,* 474–483.

Hofstede, G. (2001). *Culture's consequences* (2nd ed.). Thousand Oaks, CA: Sage.

Hofstede, G. (2007). *Geert Hofstede: About himself.* Retrieved January 24, 2007, from http://feweb.uvt.nl/center/hofstede/index.htm. Retrieved 1-24-07.

Holcomb-McCoy, C. C., & Myers, J. E. (1999). Multicultural competence and counselor training: A national survey. *Journal of Counseling and Development, 77,* 294–302.

Hollon, S. D. (2006). Randomized clinical trials. In J. C. Norcross, L. E. Beutler, & R. E. Levant (Eds.), *Evidence-based practices in mental health: Debate and dialogue on the fundamental questions* (pp. 96–105). Washington, DC: American Psychological Association.

Holmes, T. H., & Rahe, R. H. (1967). The social readjustment rating scale. *Journal of Psychosomatic Research, 11,* 213–218.

Hoshmand, L. T. (2006). *Culture, psychotherapy, and counseling.* Thousand Oaks, CA: Sage.

Hubble, M. A., Duncan, B. L., & Miller, S. D. (Eds.). (1999). *The Heart & Soul of Change: What Works in Therapy.* Washington DC: American Psychological Association.

Hughes, D. A. (2003). Psychological interventions for the spectrum of attachment disorders and intrafamilial trauma. *Attachment & Human Development, 5,* 271–277.

Ivey, A. E., & Collins, N. M. (2003). Social justice: A long-term challenge for counseling psychology. *The Counseling Psychologist, 31,* 290–298.

Ivey, A. E., & Ivey, M. B. (1999). Toward a developmental diagnostic and statistical manual: The vitality of a contextual framework. *Journal of Counseling and Development, 77,* 484–490.

Ivey, A. E., & Ivey, M. B. (2007). *Intentional interviewing and counseling: Facilitating client development in a multicultural society* (6th ed.). Belmont, CA: Thomson Higher Education.

Jakobsons, L. J., Brown, J. S., Gordon, K. H., & Joiner, T. E. (2007). When are clients ready to terminate? *Cognitive and Behavioral Practice, 14,* 218–230.

Kalodner, C. R. (2007). Cognitive-behavior theories. In D. Capuzzi & D. R. Gross (Eds.), *Counseling and psychotherapy: Theories and interventions* (4th ed., pp. 243–265). Upper Saddle River, NJ: Prentice Hall.

Kanter, J. (2007). Compassion fatigue and secondary traumatization: A second look. *Clinical Social Work Journal 35,* 289–293.

Kear-Colwell, J., & Boer, D. P. (2000). The treatment of pedophiles: Clinical experience and the implications of recent research. *International Journal of Offender Therapy and Comparative Criminology, 44,* 593–605.

Keltner, D., Ekman, P., Gonzaga, G. G., & Beer, J. (2001). Facial expression of emotion. In R. J. Davidson, K. R. Scherer, & H. H. Goldsmith (Eds.), *Handbook of affective sciences* (pp. 415–432). Oxford, NY: Oxford University Press.

Kendon, A. (1967). Some functions of gaze direction in social interaction. *Acta Psychologica, 26,* 22–63.

Kendon, A., & Ferber, A. (1971). A description of some human greetings. In R. P. Michael & J. H. Crook (Eds.), *Comparative ecology and behaviour of primates: Proceedings of a conference held at the Zoological Society.* Oxford, United Kingdom: Academic Press.

Kiracofe, N. M., & Wells, L. (2007). Mandated disciplinary counseling on campus: Problems and possibilities. *Journal of Counseling and Development, 85,* 259–268.

Kleinke, C. L. (1986). Gaze and eye contact: A research review. *Psychological Bulletin, 100,* 78–100.

Knackstedt, G., & Kleinke, C. L. (1991). Eye contact, gender and personality judgments. *Journal of Social Psychology, 131,* 303–304.

Knapp, S. (1994). *Anxiety disorders: A scientific approach for selecting the most effective treatment.* Sarasota, FL: Professional Resource Press.

Knox, S., & Hill, C. E. (2003). Therapist self-disclosure: Research-based suggestions for practitioners. *Journal of Clinical Psychology, 59,* 529–539.

Kottler, J. A. (1992). *Compassionate therapy: Working with difficult clients.* San Francisco: Jossey-Bass.

Kottler, J. A., & Schofield, M. (2001). When therapists face stress and crisis. In E. R. Welfel and R. E. Ingersoll (Eds.), *The mental health desk reference* (pp. 426–432). New York: Wiley.

Kronner, H. W. (2005). The importance of therapist self-disclosure in the therapeutic relationship as perceived by gay male patients in treatment with gay male therapists: A mixed methods approach. Loyola University of Chicago. *Dissertation Abstracts International, AAI3174247, 66*(5-A), 1959.

Kubler-Ross, E. (1969). *On death and dying.* New York: Simon & Schuster/Touchstone.

LaFrance, M., & Mayo, C. (1976). Racial differences in gaze behavior during conversation: Two systematic observational studies. *Journal of Personality and Social Personality, 33,* 547–552.

Lawson, B. (2001). *The language of space.* Oxford, United Kingdom: Architectural Press.

Ledoux, J. E. (2004). The degree of emotional control depends on the kind of personal system involved. In P. Ekman & R. J. Davidson (Eds.), *The nature of emotions: Fundamental questions* (pp. 270–272). Oxford, NY: Oxford University Press.

Lepore, S. J., & Revenson, T. A. (2006). Relationships between posttraumatic growth and resilience: Recovery, resistance, and reconfiguration. In L. G. Calhoun & R. G. Tedeschi (Eds.), *Handbook of posttraumatic growth: Research and practice* (pp. 24–46). Mahwah, NJ: Erlbaum.

Leong, F. T., & Ponterotto, J. G. (2003). A proposal for internationalizing counseling psychology in the United States: Rationale, recommendations, and challenges. *The Counseling Psychologist, 31,* 381–395.

Levant, R. L. (2004). The empirically validated treatments movement: A practitioner/educator perspective. *Clinical Psychology: Science and Practice, 11,* 219–224.

Lett, J. (2006) Emic/etic distinctions. Retrieved January 24, 2007, from http://faculty.ircc.edu/faculty/jlett/Article%20on%20Emics%20and%20Etics.htm. Retrieved 1-24-07.

Levenson, R. W. (1994). Emotional control: Variations and consequences. In P. Ekman & R. J. Davidson (Eds.), *The nature of emotions: Fundamental questions* (pp. 273–279), Oxford, NY: Oxford University Press.

Lister, S. (2006). *Meaning-making in bereaved parents: Process and outcome.* Unpublished dissertation, Concordia University, Canada. Dissertation Abstracts record AAINR09980.

Loevinger, J. (1976). *Ego development: Conceptions and theories.* San Francisco: Jossey Bass.

Lonner, W. J., & Ibrahim, F. A. (2002). Appraisal and assessment in cross-cultural counseling. In P. B. Pedersen, J. G. Draguns, W. J. Lonner, & J. E. Trimble (Eds.), *Counseling across cultures* (pp. 355–378). Thousand Oaks, CA: Sage.

MacCluskie, K. C., & Bauer, A. L. (2005). *Cultivating creativity.* Paper presented at the Association for Counselor Education and Supervision National Conference, October, 2005.

MacCluskie, K. C., & Ingersoll, R. E. (2001). *Becoming a 21st century agency counselor.* Pacific Grove, CA: Brooks/ Cole.

Mandal, M. K., Bryden, M. P., & Bulman-Fleming, M. B. (1996). Similarities and variations in facial expressing emotions: Cross-cultural evidence. *International Journal of Psychology, 31*, 49–58.

Maier, S. F., Seligman, M. E., & Solomon, R. L. (1969). Pavlovian fear conditioning and learned helplessness. In Campbell, B. A., & Church, R. M. (Eds.), *Punishment* (pp. 299–343). New York: Appleton-Century-Crofts.

Marcia, J. E. (1980). Identity in adolescence. In J. Adelson (Ed.), *Handbook of adolescent psychology.* New York: Wiley.

Marotta, S. A., & Watts, R. E. (2007). An introduction to the best practices section in the Journal of Counseling and Development. *Journal of Counseling and Development, 85,* 491–503.

Martiny, K., Lunde, M., Unden, M., Dam, H., & Bech, P. (2006). The lack of sustained effect of bright light, after discontinuation, in non-seasonal major depression. *Psychological Medicine, 36*(9), 1247–1252.

Matsumoto, D. (2004). Paul Ekman and the legacy of universals. *Journal of Research in Personality, 38*, 45–51.

Maurer, R. E., & Tindall, J. H. (1983). Effect of postural congruence on client's perception of counselor empathy. *Journal of Counseling Psychology, 30,* 158–163.

Maxwell, G. M., & Cook, M. W. (1985). Postural congruence and judgements of liking and perceived similarity. *New Zealand Journal of Psychology, 14,* 20–26.

McCarthy, A. S. (2005). Eye gaze displays are social signals of mental processing. *Dissertation Abstracts International, AAINQ99946, 66*(2-B), 1199.

McHenry, B., & McHenry, J. (2007). *What therapists say and why they say it: Effective therapeutic responses and techniques.* Boston: Allyn & Bacon.

Meadors, P., & Lamson, A. (2008). Compassion fatigue and secondary traumatization: Provider self-care on intensive care units for children. *Journal of Pediatric Health Care, 22,* 24–34.

Meyer, B., Ajchenbrenner, M., & Bowles, D. P. (2005). Sensory sensitivity, attachment experiences, and rejection responses among adults with borderline and avoidant features. *Journal of Personality Disorders, 19,* 641–658.

Michener, H. A., DeLamater, J. D., & Schwartz, S. H. (1990). *Social psychology* (2nd ed.). San Diego, CA: Harcourt Brace Jovanovich.

Miller, S. D., Hubble, M. A., & Duncan, B. L. (1996). *Psychotherapy is dead, long live psychotherapy.* Workshop presented at the 19th Annual Family Therapy Network Symposium, Washington, DC.

Miraglia, E., Law, R., & Collins, P. (2006). *A baseline definition of culture.* Retrieved on September 6, 2007, from http://www.wsu.edu/gened/learn-modules/top_culture/culture-definition.html

Mollen, D., Ridley, C. R., & Hill, C. L. (2003). Models of multicultural counseling competence. In D. B. Pope-Davis, H. L. Coleman, W. M. Liu, & R. L. Toporek (Eds.), *Handbook of multicultural competencies in counseling and psychology* (pp. 21–37). Thousand Oaks, CA: Sage.

Mosak, H. H., & Maniacci, M. (2005). Adlerian psychotherapy. In R. J. Corsini & D. Wedding (Eds.), *Current psychotherapies* (7th ed., pp. 63–106). Pacific Grove, CA: Thomson Brooks Cole.

Mulder, M. (1973). The power distance reduction hypothesis on a level of reality. *Journal of Experimental Social Psychology, 9,* 87–96.

Mulder, M. (1977). *International series on the quality of working life: VI. The daily power game.* Oxford, United Kingdom: Martinus Nijhoff.

Meyer, B., Ajchenbrenner, M., & Bowles, D. (2005). Sensory sensitivity, attachment experiences, and rejection responses among adults with borderline and avoidant features. *Journal of Personality Disorders, 19,* 641–658.

Myer, B., & Pilkonis, P. A. (2006). Developing treatments that bridge personality and psychopathology. In R. F. Krueger & J. L. Tackett (Eds.), *Personality and psychopathology* (pp. 262–291). New York: Guilford Press.

Myers, D., & Hayes, J. A. (2006). Effects of therapist general self-disclosure and countertransference disclosure on ratings of the therapist and session. *Psychotherapy: Theory, Research, Practice, Training, 43,* 173–185.

Nakayama, E. Y. (2003). Client perceptions of counselor confrontations in substance abuse counseling. *Dissertation Abstracts International, AAI3070547, 63*(11-B), 5530.

Nathan, P. E. (2007). Efficacy, effectiveness, and the clinical utility of psychotherapy research. In S. G. Hofman & J. Weinberger (Eds.), *The art and science of psychotherapy* (pp. 69–83). New York: Routledge.

National Institute of Mental Health (2008). *Schizophrenia*. Retrieved on February 18, 2008, from http://www.nimh.nih.gov/health/topics/schizophrenia/index.shtml.

Newman, J. L., & Fuqua, D. R. (1990). Stability of preferences for microskills across two videotaped clients. *Psychological Reports, 67,* 1379–1388.

Nichols, M. P. (1995). *The lost art of listening.* New York: The Guilford Press.

Nystul, M. S. (2006). *Introduction to counseling: An art and science perspective.* Boston: Pearson Allyn & Bacon.

Odeh, M. S., Zeiss, R. A., & Huss, M. T. (2006). Cues they use: Clinicians' endorsement of risk cues in predictions of dangerousness. *Behavior Sciences and the Law, 24,* 147–156.

Okun, B. F., & Kantrowitz, R. E. (2008). *Effective helping: Interviewing and counseling techniques* (7th ed.). Belmont, CA: Thomson Higher Learning.

Pabian, Y., Welfel, E. R., & Beebe, R. S. (2007, August). *Psychologists' knowledge and application of state laws in Tarasoff-type situations.* Poster presented at the annual meeting of the American Psychological Association, San Francisco.

Park, C. L., & Ai, A. L. (2006). Meaning making and growth: New directions for research on survivors of trauma. *Journal of Loss and Trauma, 11,* 389–407.

Patterson, L. E., Rak, C. F., Chermonte, J., & Roper, W. (1992). Automaticity as a factor in counseling skills acquisition. *Canadian Journal of Counselling, 26,* 189–200.

Patterson, L. E., & Welfel, E. R. (2005). *The counseling process: A multitheoretical integrative approach.* Pacific Grove, CA: Brooks/Cole.

Pedersen, P. B., Draguns, J. G., Lonner, W. J., & Trimble, J. E. (2002). *Counseling across cultures* (5th ed.). Thousand Oaks, CA: Sage.

Peterson, Z. D. (2002). More than a mirror: The ethics of therapist self-disclosure. *Psychotherapy: Theory, Research, Practice, Training, 39,* 21–31.

Phillips, J. G., & Hughes, B. G. (1988). Internal consistency of the concept of automaticity. In A. M. Colley & J. R. Beech (Eds.), *Cognition and action in skilled behavior* (pp. 317–331). Oxford, United Kingdom: North-Holland.

Pollack, J., Levy, S., & Breitholz, T. (1999). Screening for medical and neurodevelopmental disorders for the professional counselor. *Journal of Counseling & Development, 77,* 350–358.

Ponterotto, J. G., & Casas, J. M. (1987). In search of multicultural competence within counselor education programs. *Journal of Counseling and Development, 65,* 430–434.

Poorman, P. B. (2003). *Microskills and theoretical foundations for professional helpers.* Boston: Allyn & Bacon.

Pope-Davis, D. B., & Dings, J. G. (1995). The assessment of multicultural counseling competencies. In J. G. Ponterotto, J. M. Casas, L. A. Suzuki, & C. M. Alexander (Eds.), *Handbook of multicultural counseling* (pp. 287–311). Thousand Oaks, CA: Sage.

Prochaska, J. O. (1999). How do people change, and how can we change to help many more people? In M. A. Hubble, B. L. Duncan, & S. D. Miller (Eds.), *The heart and soul of change: What works in therapy* (pp. 227–255). Washington, DC: American Psychological Association.

Prochaska, J. O., Norcross, J. C., & DiClemente, C. C. (1994). *Changing for good.* New York: Quill.

Prochaska,, J. O., Velicer, W. F., DiClemente, C. C., & Fava, J. (1988). Measuring processes of change: Applications to the cessation of smoking. *Journal of Consulting and Clinical Psychology, 56,* 520–528.

Putilov, A. A., & Danilenko, V. (2005). Antidepressant effects of light therapy and "natural" treatments for winter depression. *Biological Rhythm Research, 36*(5), 423–437.

Rak, C. R., MacCluskie, K. C., Toman, S. M., Patterson, L. E., & Culotta, S. (2003). The process of development among counselor interns: Qualitative and quantitative perspectives. *Canadian Journal of Counselling. 37,* 135–150.

Raskin, J. D., & Lewandowski, A. M. (2000). The construction of disorder as human enterprise. In R. A. Neimeyer & J. D. Raskin (Eds.), *Constructions of disorder: Meaning-making frameworks for psychotherapy* (pp. 15–40).

Washington, DC: American Psychological Association.

Raskin, N. J., Rogers, C. R., & Witty, M. (2005). Client-centered therapy. In R. J. Corsini & D. Wedding (Eds.), *Current psychotherapies* (7th ed., pp. 141–186). Pacific Grove, CA: Thomson Brooks/Cole.

Reef Education Conference. Retrieved January 24, 2007, from http://www.reefed.edu.au

Ridley, C. R., & Kleiner, A. J. (2003). Multicultural counseling competence: History, themes, and issues. In D. B. Pope-Davis, H. L. Coleman, W. M. Liu, & R. L. Toporek (Eds.), *Handbook of multicultural competencies in counseling and psychology* (pp. 3–20). Thousand Oaks, CA: Sage.

Roberts, A. R., & Greene, G. J. (2002). *Social workers' desk reference*. Oxford, NY: Oxford University Press.

Rogers, C. R. (1961). *On becoming a person*. Boston: Houghton Mifflin.

Rogers, J. R. (2001). Suicide risk assessment. In E. R. Welfel & R. E. Ingersoll (Eds.), *The Mental Health Desk Reference* (pp. 259–264). New York: Wiley.

Rosenhan, D. L. (1973). On being sane in insane places. *Science, 179*(4070), 250–258.

Rothman, A. D., & Nowicki, S. (2004). A measure of the ability to identify emotion in children's tone of voice. *Journal of Nonverbal Behavior, 28,* 67–92.

Rothschild, B. (2006). *Help for the helper: The psychophysiology of compassion fatigue and vicarious trauma*. New York: W. W. Norton.

Samoray, J. M. (2006). The healing effects of creative expression experienced by people who identify themselves as having compassion fatigue: A phenomenological study. *Dissertation Abstracts International, AAI 3188544, 66* (9-B), 5103.

Satterly, B. A. (2004). The Intention and Reflection Model: Gay male therapist self-disclosure and identity management. *Journal of Gay and Lesbian Social Services: Issues in Practice, Policy & Research, 17,* 69–86.

Sax, J. G. (1816–1887). *The blind men and the elephant*. Retrieved from on March 17, 2008, from http://www.noogenesis.com/pineapple/blind_men_elephant.html

Schacht, T. E. (2008). A broader view of racial microaggression in psychotherapy. *American Psychologist, 63*, p. 273.

Scherer, K. R., Banse, R., & Wallbot, H. G. (2001). Emotion inferences from vocal expression correlate across languages and cultures. *Journal of Cross-Cultural Psychology, 32,* 76–92.

Schindler, A., Thomasius, R., Sack, P., Gemeinhardt, B., Kustner, U., & Eckert, J. (2005). Attachment and substance use disorders: A review of the literature and a study in drug dependent adolescents. *Attachment & Human Development, 7,* 207–228.

Schore, A. (2001). Effects of a secure attachment relationship on right brain development, affect regulation, and infant mental health. *Infant Mental Health Journal, 22,* 7–66.

Schuster, C. S., & Ashburn, S. S. (1980). *The process of human development: A holistic approach*. Boston: Little, Brown.

Schwartz, R. C., & Rogers, J. R. (2004). Suicide assessment and evaluation strategies: A primer for counseling psychologists. *Counselling Psychology Quarterly, 17,* 89–97.

Seligman, L. (2001). *Systems, strategies, and skills of counseling and psychotherapy*. Upper Saddle River, NJ: Merrill/Prentice Hall.

Seligman, L. (2004). *Technical and conceptual skills for mental health professionals*. Upper Saddle River, NJ: Merrill/Prentice Hall.

Seligman, M. E., Maier, S. F., and Geer, J. (1968). The alleviation of learned helplessness in dogs. *Journal of Abnormal Psychology, 73,* 256–262.

Selman, R. L., Jaquette, D., & Lavin, D. R. (1977). Interpersonal awareness in children: Toward an integration of developmental and clinical child psychology. *American Journal of Orthopsychiatry, 47,* 264–274.

Sexton, T. L., & Liddle, M. C. (2001). Practicing evidence-based mental health: Using research and measuring outcomes. In E. R. Welfel & R. E. Ingersoll (Eds.), *The mental health desk reference* (pp. 387–392). New York: Wiley.

Sharpley, C. F., & Sagris, A. (1995). Does eye contact increase counsellor-client rapport? *Counselling Psychology Quarterly, 8,* 145–156.

Sherman, M. (1999). Distress and professional impairment due to major life events and work factors among applied psychologists. *Dissertation Abstracts International, 59* (7-B), 3750.

Shorey, H. S., Little, T. D., Snyder, C. R., Kluck, B., & Robitschek, C. (2007). Hope and personal growth initiative: A comparison of positive, future-oriented constructs. *Personality and Individual Differences, 43,* 1917–1926.

Silvergleid, C. S., & Mankowski, E. S. (2006). How batterer intervention programs work: Participants and facilitator accounts of processes and change. *Journal of Interpersonal Violence, 21,* 139–159.

Simpson, L. R. (2006). Level of spirituality as a predictor of the occurrence of compassion fatigue among counseling professionals in Mississippi. *Dissertation Abstracts International, AAI3190581, 66*(9-A), 3223.

Smith, J. (2003). *Components of culture: Symbols, language, and values.* Fulbright-Hays research projects. Retrieved on September 7, 2006, from http://www.fulbright.org.nz/events/fulbrighthaysprojects/smithj.html

Snyder, C. R. (2002). Hope theory: Rainbows in the mind. *Psychological Inquiry, 13,* 249–275.

Snyder, C. R., Michael, S. T., & Cheavens, J. S. (1999). Hope as a psychotherapeutic foundation of common factors, placebos, and expectancies. In M. A. Hubble, B. L. Duncan, & S. D. Miller (Eds.), *The heart & soul of change* (pp. 179–200). Washington, DC: American Psychological Association.

Society for Psychotherapy Research. (2008). *Hans Strupp: A pioneer and giant in psychotherapy research.* Retrieved on August 16, 2008, from http://www.psychotherapyresearch.org/displaycommon.cfm?an=1&subarticlenbr=104.

Sodowsky, G. R., Taffe, R. C., Gutkin, T. B., & Wise, S. L. (1994). Development of the Multicultural Counseling Inventory: A self-report measure of multicultural competencies. *Journal of Counseling Psychology, 41,* 137–148.

Solley, R. F. (1988). *Posture mirroring and therapeutic alliance. Dissertation Abstracts International, 49*(5-B), 1957.

Spiro, R. J., & Jehng, J. (1990). Cognitive flexibility and hypertext: Theory and technology for the non-linear and multidimensional traversal of complex subject matter. In D. Nix & R. Spiro (Eds.), *Cognition, education, and multimedia* (pp. 163–205). Hillsdale, NJ: Erlbaum.

Stadler, H. A. (2001). Impairment in the mental health professions. In E. R. Welfel & R. E. Ingersoll (Eds.), *The mental health desk reference* (pp. 413–419). New York: Wiley.

Stafford, B. S., & Zeanah, C. H. (2006). Attachment disorders. In J. L. Luby (Ed.), *Handbook of preschool mental health* (pp. 231–251). New York: Guilford Press.

Strupp, H. H. (1973). *Psychotherapy: Clinical, research, and theoretical issues.* New York: Aronson.

Sue, D. W., Arrendondo, P., & McDavis R. J. (1992). Multicultural counseling competencies and standards: A call to the profession. *Journal of Counseling and Development, 70,* 477–486.

Sue, D. W., Bernier, J. E., Durran, A., Feinberg, L., Pedersen, P., Smith, E. J., et al. (1982). Position paper: Cross-cultural counseling competencies. *The Counseling Psychologist, 10,* 45–52.

Sue, D. W., Capodilupo, C. M., Torino, G. C., Bucceri, J. M., Holder, A. M., Nadal, K. L., et al. (2007). Racial microaggression in everyday life: Implications for clinical practice. *American Psychologist, 62,* 271–286.

Sue, D. W., & Sue, D. (2003). *Counseling the culturally diverse: Theory and practice* (4th ed.). New York: Wiley.

Sue, S., & Zane, N. (2006). Ethnic minority populations have been neglected by evidence-based practices. In J. C. Norcross, L. E. Beutler, & R. E. Levant (Eds.), *Evidence-based practices in mental health: Debate and dialogue on the fundamental questions* (pp. 329–337). Washington, DC: American Psychological Association.

Terry, M. (2005). *Through the eyes of the beholders: Stakeholder experiences with two adult literacy programs that include adult and youth-at-risk learners.* Unpublished doctoral dissertation, University of Regina, Regina.

Thomas, K. R. (2008). Macrononsense in multiculturalism. *American Psychologist, 63,* 274.

Thompson, B. J., & Hill, C. E. (1991). Therapist perceptions of client reactions. *Journal of Counseling and Development, 69,* 261–265.

Todd, D. M., Deane, F. P., & Bragdon, R. A. (2003). Client and therapist reasons for termination: A conceptualization and preliminary validation. *Journal of Clinical Psychology, 59,* 133–147.

Towberman, D. B. (1992). Client-counselor similarity and the client's perception of the treatment environment. *Journal of Offender Rehabilitation, 18,* 159–171.

Trimble, J. E., & Thurman, P. (2002). Ethnocultural considerations and strategies for providing counseling services for Native

American Indians. In P. Pedersen, J. Draguns, W. Lonner, & J. Trimble (Eds.), *Counseling across cultures* (5th ed., pp. 53–91). Thousand Oaks, CA: Sage.

Truscott, D., & Evans, J. (2001). Responding to dangerous clients. In E. R. Welfel and R. E. Ingersoll (Eds.), *The mental health desk reference* (pp. 271–276). New York: Wiley.

Truscott, D., Evans, J., & Marshall, S. (1995). Outpatient psychotherapy with dangerous clients: A model for clinical decision making. *Professional Psychology: Research and Practice, 26,* 484–490.

Udipi, S. (2007). An investigation of the personal and demographic predictors of compassion fatigue among genetic counselors. *Dissertation Abstracts International, AAI3252505,. 68*(2-B), 1323.

United Nations Educational, Scientific, and Cultural Organization. (2001). *UNESCO Universal Declaration on Cultural Diversity,* adopted by the 31st Session of the General Conference of UNESCO, Paris, 2 November 2001. Retrieved September 6, 2007, from http://portal.unesco.org/culture/en/ev.php-URL_ID=13066&URL_DO=DO_TOPIC&URL_SECTION=201.html.

Varenne, H. (2003). On internationalizing counseling psychology: A view from cultural anthropology. *The Counseling Psychologist, 31,* 404–411.

Vogel, D. L., Wester, S. R., & Larson, L. M. (2007). Avoidance of counseling: Psychological factors that inhibit seeking help. *Journal of Counseling and Development, 85,* 410–422.

Wampold, B. E. (2006). Not a scintilla of evidence to support empirically supported treatments as more effective than other treatments. In J. C. Norcross, L. E. Beutler, & R. E. Levant (Eds.), *Evidence-based practices in mental health: Debate and dialogue on the fundamental questions* (pp. 229–307). Washington, DC: American Psychological Association.

Ward, M. J., Lee, S. S., & Polan, H. J. (2006). Attachment and psychopathology in a community sample. *Attachment & Human Development, 8,* 327–340.

Webbink, P. G. (1986). *The power of the eyes.* New York: Springer.

Webster, C. D., Douglas, K. S., Eaves, D., & Hart, S. D. (1997). *The HCR-20 scheme: The assess-ment of dangerousness and risk (Version 2).* Burnaby, British Columbia, Canada: Simon Fraser University and Forensic Psychiatric Services Commission of British Columbia.

Weinberger, J., & Rasco, C. (2007). Empirically supported common factors. In S. G. Stefan & J. Weinberger (Eds.), *The art and science of psychotherapy* (pp. 103–129). New York: Routledge/Taylor Francis Group.

Weiner, M. (1978). *Therapist disclosure: The use of self in psychotherapy.* Baltimore: University Park Press.

Weinrach, S. G. (2006). Selecting a counseling theory while scratching your head: A rational-emotive therapist's personal journey. *Journal of Rational-Emotive and Cognitive Behavior Therapy, 24,* 155–167.

Welches, P., & Pica, M. (2005). Assessed danger-to-others as a reason for psychiatric hospitalization: An investigation of patients' perspective. *Journal of Phenomenological Psychology, 36*(1), 45–73.

Welfel, E. R. (1998). *Ethics in counseling and psychotherapy: Standards, research, and emerging issues.* Pacific Grove, CA: Brooks/Cole.

Wells, T. L. (1994). Therapist self-disclosure: Its effects on clients and the treatment relationship. *Smith College Studies in Social Work, 65,* 23–41.

Westen, D., & Bradley, R. (2005). Empirically supported complexity: Rethinking evidence-based practice in psychotherapy. *Current Directions in Psychological Science, 14,* 266–271.

Westen, D., Novotny, C. M., & Thompson-Brenner, H. (2004). The empirical status of empirically supported psychotherapies: Assumptions, findings, and reporting in controlled clinical trials, *Psychological Bulletin, 130,* 631–663.

What Is Culture? Retrieved September 17, 2006, from http://www.wsu.edu:8001/vcwsu/commons/topics/culture/culture-definition.html Retrieved 9/17/06.

White, M., & Epston, D. (1989). *Literate means to therapeutic ends.* Adelaide, Australia: Dulwich Center.

Wilber, K. (2001). *The eye of Spirit: An integral vision for a world gone slightly mad.* Boston: Shambala.

Wilson, G. T. (2005). Behavior therapy. In R. J. Corsini and D. Wedding (Eds.), *Current psychotherapies* (7th ed., pp. 223–262). Belmont, CA: Thomson Brooks/Cole.

Wood, J. A. (2006). NLP revisited: Nonverbal communications and signals of trustworthiness. *Journal of Personal Selling & Sales Management, 26,* 197–204.

Yalom, I. (1980). *Existential psychotherapy.* New York: Basic Books.

Yalom, I., & Leszcz, M. (2005). *The theory and practice of group psychotherapy* (5th ed.). New York: Basic Books.

Young, J. E., Klosko, J. S., & Weishar, M. E. (2003). *Schema therapy: A practitioner's guide.* New York: Guilford Press.

Young, M. E. (2005). *Learning the art of helping: Building blocks and techniques* (3rd ed.). Upper Saddle River, NJ: Prentice Hall.

Zachrisson, H. D., & Kulbotten, G. R. (2006). Attachment in anorexia nervosa: An exploration of associations with eating disorder pathology and psychiatric symptoms. *Eating and Weight Disorders, 11,* 163–170.

Zook, A., & Walton, J. M. (1989). Theoretical orientations and work settings of clinical and counseling psychologists: A current perspective. *Professional Psychology: Research and Practice, 20,* 23–31.

INDEX

Accountability, 45–46
Acculturation, 36
Action stage, 257, 259
Adler, Alfred, 185–186
Adlerian theory, 185–187
Aestheticism, 57
Affect, 118
Affiliation
  confrontation and, 176
  cultural differences and, 79
  feeling reflection and, 135
  paraphrasing and, 92
  questioning and, 112
  reflecting meaning and,
    149, 150
  silence and, 84
Ai, A. L., 146
Ainsworth, Mary, 188
Ambady, N., 128
American Counseling Association
  (ACA), 246, 294. See also Code of
  Ethics (American Counseling
  Association)
American Psychological Association,
  22, 246
APA Task Force report (1995), 255
Arrendondo, P., 26, 27
Assessment
  data for, 225
  explanation of, 225
  of impairment in daily functioning,
    231–232
  of inconsistent reporting, 229
  multicultural considerations
    in, 226
  of organic or medical conditions,
    226–229
  of personality style and typicality,
    229–230
  of precipitants that constitute
    crises, 230
  of precipitating events, 226
  of subjective distress, 230–231
  of suicide risk, 233–235
  of violence risk, 235–237
Attachment theory, 185, 188–189
Attending
  body posture and orientation
    and, 55–60
  from cognitive-behavioral
    perspective, 64–65

components of, 52
from developmental perspective,
  64, 65
eye contact and, 53–55
function of, 51
from humanistic perspective, 63, 65
multicultural aspects of, 62–63
verbal behavior and, 60–62
Automaticity, 43
Automatic thoughts, 198
Autonomy, 11–12
Availability heuristic, 241

Banse, R., 71
Beatty, M. J., 61
Beck, A. T., 198
Beck, Aaron, 64, 198
Beebe, R. S., 208
Behavior theory, 41, 64, 196–198
Beneficence, 12
Berry, J. W., 24–25
Beutler, Larry, 256
Body movement, 71
Bowlby, John, 188
Breitholtz, T., 226, 227
Bronfenbrenner, U., 25–26, 212
Brooks, C. I., 54
Brown, J. S., 213
Buller, D. B., 126
Burgoon, J. K., 126

Carkhuff, R. R., 42
Causal attribution of symptoms, 241
Chairs, 59
Change
  process of, 256
  readiness for, 167–168, 257–259
  resistance to, 8
Cheavens, J. S., 48
Classical conditioning, 197
Client-centered counseling, 190–192
Client observation
  congruence and, 75–76
  multicultural aspects of, 77–80
  nonverbal behavior and, 70–71
  overview of, 68–69
  paraverbal behavior and, 71–72
  role of, 69–70
  silence and, 76–77
  verbal behavior and, 72–75
Client Readiness Model, 211

Clients
  awareness of reactions of, 174
  development of hope in, 48
  discrepancies in thoughts of, 163
  emotional stability of, 165–166
  external resources of, 166–167
  inability to help, 14
  minors as, 214–216
  power differential between
    counselors and, 8
  questioning to clarify statements
    by, 107–108
  readiness for change in, 167–168,
    257–259
  relationship between counselors
    and, 47
  resistance to questions, 110–111
  responding to, 172, 173
Closed questions, 102
Code of Ethics (American Counseling
  Association)
  confidentiality, privileged
    communication, and privacy,
    299–301
  counseling relationship, 296–299
  evaluation, assessment, and
    interpretation, 303–305
  mission of American Counseling
    Association, 294
  overview of, 11–13
  Preamble, 295
  professional responsibility, 301–303
  purpose, 295
  relationships with other
    professionals, 303
  research and publication, 308–310
  resolving ethical issues, 310–311
  supervision, training, and teaching,
    305–308
Cognitive-behavioral models
  behavior theory, 197–198
  cognitive theory, 198–199
  common assumptions of, 196
  comparison of, 196
Cognitive-behavioral perspective
  on attending, 64–65
  on confrontation, 177
  on feeling reflection, 136
  on paraphrasing, 94
  on questioning, 113
  on reflecting meaning, 155–158

Cognitive-behavioral... *(contd.)*
  on silence, 85
  on summarizing, 97
Cognitive-behavioral theory, 196,
  199–201
Cognitive development
  reflection of meaning and, 143–144
  verbal behavior and, 74
Cognitive dissonance, 163
Cognitive flexibility, 37
Cognitive theory, 196, 198–199
Cognitive triad, 199
Collectivism, 33–34
Collins, P., 18
Common factors approach
  client extratherapeutic factors
    and, 252
  criticisms of, 255
  hope and placebo effect and,
    253–254
  relationship components and,
    252–253
  Rosenzweig on, 250–251
  strengths of, 254–255
  Strugg on, 251
  treatment techniques and, 254
Competence, multicultural, 17
Confidentiality, minor clients and, 215
Confirmatory bias, 69, 70
Confrontation
  case studies on, 178–180
  cognitive-behavioral perspective
    on, 177
  counselor use of, 163–164
  cultural considerations in, 175–176
  developmental perspective
    on, 177
  effectiveness of, 164–168
  explanation of, 162–163
  humanistic perspective on,
    176–177
  immediacy and, 172–175
  language use for, 168–171
  nonverbal and paraverbal
    behaviors during, 171–172
  timing of, 165
Congruence
  among nonverbal, paraverbal and
    verbal behavior, 75–76
  explanation of, 7, 75
  between verbal content and effect,
    74–75
Constructivism, 240
Contemplation state, 257, 258
Content, congruence between effect
  and verbal, 74–75

Council for Accreditation of Counseling
    and Related Educational Programs
    (CACREP), 22
Counseling
  balance of power in, 111
  counselors as participants
    in, 7–9
  crises, 217–219
  ethical standards in, 11–15
  mandatory, 216–217
  multiculturalism and, 10–11
  role of theory in, 9–10
  school, 216
  voluntary and involuntary, 216–217
  Western approach to, 16–17
Counseling outcomes
  categories of variables of, 252–254
  counseling process and, 206–207
  factors related to, 47
Counseling process
  counseling outcome and, 206–207
  homeostasis in, 212–213
  intake, assessment and relationship
    development in, 210–212
  situational factors that influence,
    214–219
  stages of, 207–210
Counseling profession
  Code of Ethics for, 11–13
  multiculturalism in, 22–24
Counseling sessions
  length and frequency of, 218–219
  questions at beginning of, 107
Counseling stages
  mismatching of technique with,
    259–260
  termination, 209–210, 213–214
  warm-up, 207–209
  working, 209
Counseling students, 36–38
Counseling theories
  case studies on, 204–205
  cognitive-behavioral, 196–201
  current trends in, 202–203
  developmental, 183–189
  humanistic, 190–195
  interplay of multicultural issues
    and, 201–202
  overview of, 181–182
  relationship between microskills
    and, 182–183
  role of, 9–10
  schools of, 183
Counselors
  clinical judgment errors of, 240–241
  as counseling participants, 7–9

cultural competence and, 211
  desire to be of service, 4
  metacognition in, 5
  microaggression exhibited by, 23
  personal growth in, 5
  power and responsibility of, 131
  power differential between clients
    and, 8
  recommendations for new, 260–261
  relationship between clients and, 47
  role of religion and spirituality in, 4
  self-awareness in, 2–3
  self-disclosure by, 219–222
  self-monitors in, 6
  strengths and liabilities of, 6
  use of confrontation by, 163–164
    (*See also* Confrontation)
Crises
  emergency counseling following,
    217–219
  precipitants that constitute, 230
Cultural diversity. *See also* Diversity;
    Multicultural considerations;
    Multiculturalism
  Hofstede's model of, 27–28
  immigration policy and, 21–22
  individualism and, 33–35
  long- and short-term orientation
    and, 36
  masculinity and femininity and, 35
  paraverbal behavior and, 71–72
  power distance and, 30–32
  uncertainty avoidance and, 32–33
Culture
  definitions of, 18–19
  microskills model and, 49

Darby, B. W., 59
Denial, clients in, 165
Depression, 48
Developmental perspective
  on attending, 64, 65
  on confrontation, 177
  on feeling reflection, 135–136
  on paraphrasing, 93
  on questioning, 112, 113
  on reflecting meaning, 153–155
  on silence, 85
  on summarizing, 97
Developmental stages, 74. *See also*
    Cognitive development
Developmental theories
  Adlerian theory, 185–187
  attachment theory, 188–189
  common assumptions of,
    183–185

comparison of, 185
Erikson's psychosocial
    development theory, 187–188
Diagnosis, 225, 237–238, 245
    DSM-IV-TR and, 238–239, 249
    judgment errors in, 240–241
    sociopolitical nature of, 239–240
Diagnostic and Statistical Manual,
    4th Ed. (DSM-IV-TR) (American
    Psychiatric Association), 238–240,
    249
DiMattia, D. J., 57
Disconnection and rejection schema,
    155
Diversity, 19–20. *See also* Cultural
    diversity; Multiculturalism
Division 12 Task Force Report, 251
Draguns, J. G., 32, 33
Droney, J. M., 54
Dumont, F., 241
Duncan, B. L., 47, 251, 252
Dutton, D., 216
Dyer, W. W., 299

Ecocultural Framework (Berry), 24–25
Ecological model of human
    development, 25–26, 212
Ego identity, 187
Ekman, P., 126
Elfenbein, H. A., 128
Ellis, Albert, 199
Emic approach, 240
Emotional maturity, 144
Emotional stability, 165–166
Emotions. *See also* Feeling reflection;
    Feelings
    Ekman's neurocultural theory of,
        127–128
    empathy and, 128–129
    explanation of, 118
    function of, 119
    physical well-being and, 119
    relativistic model of, 126–127
    research on, 126
    universalist model of, 126
    verbalizing, 130
Empathy
    development of, 37, 46
    integration of emotion theory and,
        128–129
Empirically supported techniques
    (ESTs)
    criticisms of, 248–250
    explanation of, 244–245
    historical background of, 245–247
    strengths of, 247–248

Empirically validated treatment
    (EVT), 202
Erikson, E. H., 187
Erikson's psychosocial model of
    development, 185, 187–188
Ethical standards
    beginner questions and concerns
        related to, 14–15
    in counseling profession, 11–14
    self-disclosure and, 220
Ethnocentrism, 20
Eustress, 230
Evans, J., 235–237
*Evidence-Based Practices in Mental
    Health: Debate and Dialogue
    on the Fundamental Questions*
    (Norcross, Beutler, & Levant),
    255
Existentialist perspective, 191,
    193–194
Exosystem level, 26
Expectations, perceptions and, 70
Eye contact
    multicultural aspects of, 54–55
    research on, 53–54

Facial expressions, 126
Families, pathogenic interactions in, 4
Fast, Julian, 55
Fear, of loss of control, 129–130
Feeling reflection. *See also* Emotions
    case studies on, 137–139
    cognitive-behavioral perspective
        on, 136
    counselor's role in, 131–134
    cultural considerations in, 134–135
    developmental perspective on,
        135–136
    emotional theory and, 126–129
    examples of, 121–123
    explanation of, 118–119
    humanistic perspective on, 135
    mechanical aspects of, 120–121
    steps in, 121
Feelings
    accurate identification of, 124–125
    ambivalent, 130
    awareness of one's own, 131
    explanation of, 118
    importance of, 129–130
    intensity of, 125
    processing, 125
    that are experienced when one's
        needs are satisfied, 122
    when needs are not
        satisfied, 123

Femininity. *See also* Gender roles
    characteristics of, 35
    confrontation and, 175–176
    eye contact and, 54
    reflecting meaning and, 147, 148
Fidelity, 13
Ford, J. G., 56
Frank, J. B., 253, 254
Frank, J. D., 253, 254
Frankl, Viktor, 4, 152, 193
Freud, Sigmund, 185
Fuqua, D. R., 45
Furniture arrangement, 57, 58

Gender roles. *See also* Femininity;
    Masculinity
    confrontation and, 175–176
    feeling reflection and, 134–135
    paraphrasing and, 92
    questioning and, 111–112
    silence and, 84
Generalization, 198
Gestalt theory, 191, 194–195
Ginter, E. J., 182
Global Assessment of Functioning
    axis, 239
Gordon, K. H., 213
Grounding objects, 57–58

Haase, R. F., 57
Hackney, H., 207
Haggard-Grann, U., 235
Hall, Edward T., 56
Harrigan, J. A., 53
HCR, 235
Health, emotions and, 119
The Heart and Soul of Change
    (Hubble, Duncan, & Miller), 251
The Hidden Dimension (Hall), 56
High ego strength, 165, 166
Hill, C. E., 163
Hill, C. L., 241
Hofstede, G., 28–29, 32
Hofstede's model of cultural
    differences
    development of, 28–30
    explanation of, 27–28, 31
    individualism and, 33–35
    long- and short-term orientation
        and, 36
    masculinity and femininity and, 35
    power distance and, 30–32
    theories and, 202, 203
    uncertainty avoidance and, 32–33
Holder of privilege, 215
Holmes, T. H., 230

Hope, 48, 253, 254
Hubble, M. A., 47, 48, 251, 252
Human development, ecological
    model of, 25–26
Humanistic perspective
    on attending, 63, 64
    on confrontation, 176–177
    on feeling reflection, 135
    on paraphrasing, 93
    on questioning, 112, 113
    on reflecting meaning, 152–153
    on silence, 84–85
    on summarizing, 97
Humanistic theories
    client-centered counseling, 190–192
    commonalities among, 190
    comparison of, 191
    existentialism, 193–194
    Gestalt, 194–195
Human Resource Development
    (HRD) model, 42
Humor, role of, 14

Ibrahim, F. A., 226
Immediacy, 172–175
Immigration policy, 21–22
Impaired autonomy and performance
    schema, 155
Impaired limits schema, 155
Impairment
    assessment of, 230–231
    in daily functioning, 231–232
Incongruence, 7, 8
Inconsistencies, 163
Individualism
    explanation of, 33
    function of, 33–35
    level of, 34
    reflecting meaning and, 150
Inferential judgment error, 241
Inflection, 62
Informed consent, 37–38
Ingersoll, R. E., 218, 232
Intake interviews
    information categories for,
        232–233
    overview of, 224–225
Integrated case conceptualization
    diagnostic impression and readiness
        for change and, 267, 273–274
    individual assessment/intake
        information and, 263–265,
        270–272
    overview of, 262–263
    spheres of influence in the
        ecological model and, 266–267

treatment plans and, 267–270,
    274–277
value preferences and, 265–266,
    272–273
Internal dialogue, 198
Internal dissonance, 7
Interpersonal Process Recall (IPR), 42
Interviews. *See* Intake interviews
Intimacy, of verbal content, 73–74
Involuntary counseling, 216–217
Irrational beliefs, 199
Ivey, A. E., 43, 49, 118
Ivey, M. B., 43, 118

Jakobsons, L. J., 213
Jehng, J., 37
Joiner, T. E., 213
*Journal of Counseling and
    Development*, 246, 260, 261
Judgment errors, diagnostic,
    240–241
Judson, N., 59
Justice, 13

Kagan, Norman, 42
Kendon, A., 53
Key word repetition, 87
Kinesics, 55
Kiracofe, N. M., 217
Klosko, J. S., 155
Kubler-Ross, E., 144

Language use, for confrontation,
    168–171
Larsen, L. M., 211
Law, R., 18
Lawson, B., 57
Leaning in, 56–57
Learned helplessness, 48
Lecomte, C., 241
Ledoux, J. E., 127
Lepore, S. J., 147
Leszcz, M., 4
Levy, S., 226, 227
Licensure, state, 11
Liddle, M. C., 260
Life experiences, 3–4
Lifespan development, 230
Lighting, 59–60
Lister, S., 144
Logotherapy, 193
Long-term orientation, 36
Lonner, W. J., 226
The Lost Art of Listening (Nichols),
    52, 213
Low ego strength, 166

MacCluskie, K. C., 218, 232
Macrosystem level, 26
Maintenance stage, 257, 259
Maloney, M., 56
Mandatory counseling, 216–217
Marotta, S. A., 260–261
Marshall, S., 235, 237
Masculinity. *See also* Gender roles
    characteristics of, 35
    confrontation and, 175–176
    cultural differences and, 78–79
    eye contact and, 54
    paraphrasing and, 92
    reflecting meaning and, 147, 149
    silence and, 84
May, Rollo, 4
McDavis, R. J., 26, 27
Meaning. *See* Reflection of meaning
Medical disorders
    assessment of, 226–229
    misdiagnosed as psychological
        disorders, 228
Mental health providers, 45–46
Mesosystem level, 26, 30
Metacognition, in counselors, 5
Michael, S. T., 48
Microaggression, racial, 22–24
Microassault, 23
Microinsult, 23
Microinvalidations, 23
Microskills. *See also specific microskills*
    in Adlerian context, 186–187
    advantages of, 44–46
    in attachment theory, 189
    in behavioral context, 198
    case studies on, 98–100
    in client-centered context, 192
    from cognitive-behavioral
        perspective, 201
    counseling process and outcome
        and, 47–48
    cultural and social forces and, 49
    in existential context, 194
    explanation of, 43–44
    in Gestalt context, 195
    historical background of, 41–42
    limitations of, 46–47
    overview of, 43–44
    relationship between theory and,
        182–183
    research on, 41
Microsystem level, 26, 30
Miller, S. D., 47, 251, 252
Minimal encouragers
    explanation of, 85–86
    intentional withholding of, 86–87

Minorities
  counselor awareness of
    discrimination and oppression of,
    222
  empirically supported techniques
    and, 250
  prescriptive approach to
    counseling, 28
Minors, as clients, 214–216
Miraglia, E., 18
Mirroring, 55
Mixed messages, 75
Mood, effect of lighting on, 60
Mulder, M., 30
Multicultural competence
  empathy and, 37
  explanation of, 17
  informed consent and, 37–38
  multiple dimensions of, 26–27
Multicultural considerations
  in assessment, 226
  of attending, 62–63
  of challenging, 175–176
  of client observation, 77–80
  of eye contact, 54–55
  of feeling reflection, 134–135
  function of, 17
  implications for students, 36–38
  interplay of theories and, 201–202
  of paraphrasing, 91–93
  of questioning, 111–112
  of reflecting meaning, 147–151
  in self-disclosure, 221–222
  of silence, 84
Multiculturalism. See also Cultural
    diversity; Diversity
  common cultural frames vs.
    stereotypes and, 10–11
  definitions of, 19, 20
  ecocultural models of human
    functioning and, 24–26
  Hofstede's model of cultural
    differences and, 27–36
  immigration policy and, 21–22
  personal views and, 10
  in professions of counseling and
    psychology, 22–24
  racial identity development and
    acculturation and, 36
  Sue and Sue's model of, 26–27

Narrative therapy, 60
Negative reinforcer, 197
NEO-PI-R, 57, 229
Neurocultural theory of emotion,
  127–128

Newman, J. L., 45
Nonmaleficence, 12
Nonverbal behavior
  body movement as, 71
  during confrontation, 171–172
  congruence among verbal,
    paraverbal and, 75–76
  eye contact as, 53–55
  facial expression as, 70–71
  posture and orientation as, 55–60
Note taking, 55–56
Novotny, C. M., 248–249
Nystul, M. S., 186

O'Brien, K. M., 163
Observation, 69. See also Client
    observation
Open questions, 102
Operant conditioning, 197
Organic conditions, 226–229
Other-directedness schema, 156
Outcomes. See Counseling outcomes
Overvigilance and inhibition schema,
  156

Pabian, Y., 208
Paralinguistics, 61–62, 71
Paraphrasing
  explanation of, 88
  multicultural aspects of, 91–93
  strategies for, 89–90
Paraverbal behavior
  during confrontation, 171–172
  congruence among verbal,
    nonverbal and, 75–76
  explanation of, 71–72
  importance of, 120
Parental consent, 215
Park, C. L., 146
Patterson, L. E., 206
Perceptions, 70
Perls, Fritz, 194
Personal appearance, 2
Personal characteristics, 2–3
Personal growth, 5
Personality, 229–230
Personal relationship, 2–3
Personal space, 56–57
Peterson, Z. D., 220
Pica, M., 236, 237
Pike, Kenneth, 19
Placebo, 253
Pollack, J., 226, 227
Positive reinforcer, 197
Post-Traumatic Stress Disorder
    (PTSD), 146

Postural congruence, 55
Posture, 55–56
Power differential, 8
Power distance
  confrontation and, 175
  cultural differences and, 78
  eye contact and, 54
  feeling reflection and, 134
  function of, 30–32
  paraphrasing and, 91
  questioning and, 111
  reflecting meaning and, 147, 148
Precipitating events, 226
Precontemplation stage, 257–259
Premorbid level of distress, 231
Prescriptive approach, to counseling
    minorities, 28
Processing feelings, 125
Prochaska, James, 256, 257
Psychology, role of multicultural in,
  22–24
Psychopathology
  from Adlerian perspective, 186
  from attachment perspective, 189
  from behavioral perspective, 197
  from client-centered
    perspective, 192
  from cognitive-behavioral
    perspective, 199
  from cognitive perspective,
    198–199
  from Eriksonian perspective, 188
  from Gestalt perspective, 194–195
Psychosocial development theory
    (Erikson), 185, 187–188
Psychosocial maturity, 144, 145

Questions
  achieving specific purposes
    through, 106–110
  case studies on, 114–117
  client resistance to, 110–111
  cognitive-behavioral perspective
    on, 113
  cultural considerations related to,
    111–112
  developmental perspective on,
    112, 113
  humanistic perspective on,
    112, 113
  imbalance of power and, 111
  implying problem solution, 111
  ineffective use of, 105–106
  mechanical aspects of, 103–104
  open and closed, 102–103
  overview of, 101–102

Racial identity development, 36
Racial microaggression
  controversy about, 23–24
  explanation of, 22–23
Racism, 22–23
Rahe, R. H., 230
Raison, Charles, 127
Randomized clinical trial (RCT), 247
Rational-Emotive Behavior Therapy,
  199
Readiness for Change Model,
  257–259
Reconfiguration, 147
Recovery, 147
Reflection of meaning
  case studies on, 159–161
  cognitive-behavioral perspective
    on, 155–158
  cognitive functioning level and,
    143–244
  cultural considerations in, 147–151
  developmental perspective on,
    153–155
  emotional and psychosocial
    maturity level and, 144, 145
  humanistic perspective on, 152–153
  overview of, 140–141
  personal nature of, 141
  resilience and, 147
  spirituality and, 142
  trauma and, 144, 146
Reinforcement, 197
Relapse prevention plan, 259
Relationships, 2–3
Relativistic model of emotion,
  126–127
Religious beliefs
  culture and, 19
  reflection of meaning and, 142
  role in counselors of, 5
Repetition, 87
Resilience, 147
Resistance
  to counseling, 211, 212
  explanation of, 147
Response latency, 77
Restatement, 87–88
Revenson, T. A., 147
Ridley, C. R., 241
Risky behavior, 167
Rogers, Carl, 1, 7, 37, 63, 190–192,
  253
Rogers, J. R., 234
Room arrangement, 57–60
Rosenhan, D. L., 240
Rozenzweig, Saul, 250–251

Sagris, A., 53–54
Satisfaction, 7
Saxe, J. G., 255
Schemas, 155
Scherer, K. R., 71
School counseling, 216
Self-awareness
  Gestalt theory and, 194
  humanistic perspective and, 152
  importance of, 2, 8, 16, 37
  life experiences and, 3–4
Self-disclosure
  counselor, 219–221
  elements of, 73–74
  multicultural considerations in,
    221–222
Self-fulfilling prophecy, 199
Self-monitors, 6
Self-report, client, 200
Self-talk, 198, 199
Seligman, L., 48, 124
Service to others, 4
Sexton, T. L., 260
Sexton, Thomas, 246
Sexual minorities, 222, 250
Sexual Violence Risk-20, 235
Sharpley, C. F., 53–54
Short-term orientation, 36
Significant movement toward
    growth, 164
Silence
  cognitive-behavioral perspective
    on, 85
  in counseling sessions, 76–77
  developmental perspective on, 85
  humanistic perspective on, 84–85
  intentional use of, 81–83
  multicultural aspects of, 84
  personality and use of, 85
  as therapy tool, 83
Situational appropriateness, 72–73
Skinner, B. F., 197, 245
Smith, J., 18
Snyder, C. R., 48, 253
Social context, 49
Space
  room arrangement and, 57–60
  use of personal, 56–57
Speech, rate of, 61–62
Spirituality
  culture and, 19
  reflection of meaning and, 142
  role in counselors of, 5
Spiro, R. J., 37
Static-99, 235
Stereotypes, 11

Storytelling, 60
Strugg, Hans, 251
Subjective distance, 56
Subjective distress, 230–321
Subjective unit of distress (SUD),
  198, 231
Sue, D. W., 26, 27
Sue and Sue's model of
    multiculturalism, 26–27
Suicide risk, 233–235
Summarizing
  beginning and ending sessions
    by, 96
  cognitive-behavioral perspective
    on, 97
  developmental perspective
    on, 97
  enumerating possible topics for,
    95–96
  example of, 94–95
  explanation of, 94
  humanistic perspective on, 97
  multicultural aspects of, 97
Supportive challenging, 162, 163
Systematic Treatment Selection,
  256–257

Termination, of counseling, 209–210,
  213–214
Terry, M., 26
Theories, 181. *See also* Counseling
    theories
Therapeutic resistance, 8
Therapeutic techniques, 48
Thompson-Brenner, H., 248–249
Timing
  of confrontation, 165
  of termination, 213–214
Transparency, in rooms
    arrangements, 58–59
Trauma, 144, 146
Treatment planning, 225, 242
Treatment strategies
  from Adlerian perspective, 186
  from attachment perspective, 189
  from behavioral perspective,
    197–198
  from client-centered pers-
    pective, 192
  from cognitive-behavioral
    perspective, 200–201
  from cognitive perspective, 199
  from Eriksonian perspective, 188
  from existential perspective, 193
  from Gestalt perspective, 195
Truscott, D., 235–237

Uncertainty avoidance
  confrontation and, 176
  cultural differences and, 79–80
  feeling reflection and, 135
  function of, 32–33
  paraphrasing and, 92–93
  questioning and, 112
  reflecting meaning and, 150, 151
  silence and, 84
Unconditional positive regard, 191
Unfinished business, 194
United States, immigration policy in,
  21–22
Universal Declaration of Cultural
  Diversity (United Nations
  Educational, Scientific and
  Cultural Organization), 18
Universalist model of emotion, 126
U.S. Immigration Service, 21

Vail Conference (American
  Psychological Association), 22
Verbal behavior
  congruence among nonverbal,
  paraverbal and, 75–76

congruence between content and
  affect and, 74–75
content and, 72
developmental appropriateness
  and, 74
effects of, 60–61
inflection and, 62
intimacy of content and, 73–74
judging situational appropriateness
  and, 72–73
paralinguistics and, 61
rate of speech and, 61–62
voice tone and, 62
voice volume and, 62
Verbal underlining, 71
Violence
  assessment of risk for, 235–237
  threshold for, 237
Violence Risk Appraisal
  Guide, 235
Vogel, D. L., 211
Voice cues, 61
Voice tone, 62
Voice volume, 62
Voluntary counseling, 216–217

Wallbot, H. G., 71
Warm-up stage, of counseling,
  207–209
Watson, John, 245
Watts, R. E., 260–261
Webbink, P. G., 53
Weinrach, S. G., 182
Weishar, M. E., 155
Welches, P., 236, 237
Welfel, E. R., 206, 208
Wells, L., 217
Wertheimer, Max, 194
Westen, D., 248–249
Wester, S. R., 211
"Why" questions, 106
Withholding, of minimal
  encouragers, 86–87
Wolpe, Joseph, 245
Woodall, W. G., 126
Working stage, of counseling,
  209

Yalom, I., 4, 152, 193
Young, J. E., 155

Rec. Feb. 10, 2014